THE DAILY PLEBISCITE

Federalism, Nationalism, and Canada

Essays by David R. Cameron
Edited by Robert C. Vipond

From the mid-1960s through the mid-1990s, Canada was in a state of ongoing political crisis. Within this thirty-year period, David R. Cameron was an active participant and observer of Canada's crisis of national unity. As a political scientist and former senior public servant, Cameron remains one of the most astute and respected analysts of Canadian federalism.

This volume assembles some of Cameron's best works on federalism, nationalism, and the constitution, including journal articles, book chapters, speeches, newspaper op-eds, and unpublished opinion pieces spanning nearly fifty years of engagement. In addition, *The Daily Plebiscite* includes a conversation between Cameron and Robert C. Vipond on the "long decade" of the 1980s in Canadian constitutional politics, a brief history of the mega-constitutional era, and concluding reflections on the broader lessons that other divided societies might take from the Canadian experience.

Providing rich fare for anyone interested in questions of federalism, nationalism, and constitutionalism, *The Daily Plebiscite* offers an informed, insider's perspective on the national unity question and considers the challenges faced by a federal, multinational, and multicultural country like Canada.

(Political Development: Comparative Perspectives)

DAVID R. CAMERON is Professor of Political Science and Special Advisor to the President and Provost at the University of Toronto.

ROBERT C. VIPOND is Professor of Political Science at the University of Toronto.

Political Development: Comparative Perspectives

Editors: JACK LUCAS (University of Calgary) and
ROBERT C. VIPOND (University of Toronto)

Political Development: Comparative Perspectives publishes books that explore political development with a comparative lens, with a particular focus on studies of Canadian, American, or British political development. Books in this series use historical data and narratives to explain long-term patterns of institutional change, public policy, social movement politics, elections and party systems, and other key aspects of political authority and state power. They employ cross-country comparison, within-country comparison, or single-case analysis to illuminate important debates in comparative political science and history.

Editorial Advisory Board

ESSAYS BY DAVID R. CAMERON
EDITED BY ROBERT C. VIPOND

THE
DAILY
PLEBISCITE

*Federalism, Nationalism,
and Canada*

UNIVERSITY OF TORONTO PRESS
Toronto Buffalo London

ISBN 978-1-4875-0626-1 (cloth)   ISBN 978-1-4875-3372-4 (EPUB)
ISBN 978-1-4875-2421-0 (paper)   ISBN 978-1-4875-3371-7 (PDF)

Political Development: Comparative Perspectives

Library and Archives Canada Cataloguing in Publication

Title: The daily plebiscite : federalism, nationalism, and Canada / essays by
    David R. Cameron ; edited by Robert C. Vipond.
Names: Cameron, David, 1941– author. | Vipond, Robert Charles, editor.
Description: Series statement: Political development : comparative perspectives |
    Includes bibliographical references.
Identifiers: Canadiana (print) 20210306521 | Canadiana (ebook) 20210306564 | ISBN
    9781487506261 (cloth) | ISBN 9781487524210 (paper) | ISBN 9781487533724
    (EPUB) | ISBN 9781487533717 (PDF)
Subjects: LCSH: Federal government – Canada. | LCSH: Nationalism – Canada. |
    LCSH: Constitutional history – Canada. | LCSH: Canada – Politics and
    government – 1980–
Classification: LCC JL27 .C28 2022 | DDC 320.971 – dc23

University of Toronto Press acknowledges the financial assistance to its publishing
program of the Canada Council for the Arts and the Ontario Arts Council, an agency
of the Government of Ontario.

Canada Council   **Conseil des Arts**
for the Arts   **du Canada**

ONTARIO ARTS COUNCIL
CONSEIL DES ARTS DE L'ONTARIO
an Ontario government agency
un organisme du gouvernement de l'Ontario

Funded by the   Financé par le
Government   gouvernement
of Canada   du Canada

We dedicate this volume to the memory of Richard Simeon and Ronald Watts, two towering figures in the study of federalism in Canada and around the world, engaged scholars who cared passionately about their country and about constitutional government. They were our dear friends and we miss them.

Contents

Acknowledgments

The idea for this collection came to me following a lecture I had delivered to an undergraduate class in Canadian politics at the University of Toronto. Part of the lecture included a brisk tour of the "mega-constitutional" era that had dominated Canadian politics from the 1960s to the 1990s. As I was packing up to leave, a student approached me to ask a question. She wore an expression of curious fascination on her face, as if she were approaching some sort of historical relic. Had I been personally involved in the debate over the Meech Lake Accord, she asked. I admitted, somewhat feebly, that my direct involvement in the Meech debate had been minimal at best and went on my way. But her question got me thinking and soon ripened into the idea that is the foundation for this collection, namely, to assemble essays by someone who had been directly involved in the national unity debate – and who could explain better than I why the constitutional politics of a multi-national state are neither simply of historical interest nor limited to Canada.

My first debt, therefore, is to David Cameron – colleague, friend, and scholar. Over the years, we have worked together, written together, and shared joys and sorrows together. His combination of principle and pragmatism is my model for what is the very best in Canadian public life.

The first person to whom I turned once the idea for a collection had crystallized was Andrew McDougall, my colleague in the Department of Political Science. At the time, Andrew was a PhD student, having first trained as a lawyer. He used his formidable research skills to track down David Cameron's corpus of scholarship (including one or two pieces that David had forgotten about!) and helped me select which articles and chapters packed the most punch. Andrew passed the baton to Charles Dumais, who provided superb assistance – both intellectual and technical – in seeing the project through to completion. His astute observations and eye for detail were invaluable. Several colleagues and friends generously read and critiqued the collection's introduction and the brief, potted history of the "thirty years of travail" that I wrote expressly for the collection. In this regard, I would be remiss if I did not thank Jack Lucas, Stephen Marcus, Andrew McDougall, Rob McLean, Kanta Murali, and David Rayside. I would also like to thank the three anonymous readers who did what good reviewers do: they provided the sort of helpful criticism that made the final product better. Thanks as well to Robin Studniberg and the other members of the production team at UTP; to Ruth Pincoe, who produced the index; and a special shout out to Daniel Quinlan, acquisitions editor par excellence, who guided the collection from start to finish with his usual care, adroitness, and intelligence.

Rob Vipond

My first debt of gratitude is to Rob Vipond. As you can see from what he says above, the idea of collecting some of my work on nationalism, secession, federalism, and constitutional reform was his, and I am honoured that he thought the enterprise worthwhile. Rob has been a treasured friend and fellow citizen at the University of Toronto for the more than three decades that I have spent there. Through his presence and his academic leadership, Rob has made my university life and that of my colleagues a far richer thing than it would otherwise have been.

I have had abiding preoccupations, but no game plan for my life. I am therefore immensely grateful for the abundant opportunities that have come my way, and I would like to express my respect and appreciation to the many colleagues and others in government, the university world and beyond with whom I have been associated over the years. Some I have worked with, and some – depending on their position on the national question – I have worked against, but all have taught me much, not least about how to remember the common humanity that lies behind even the most bitter divisions.

While it would not be true to say that my family shared my professional interests, they indulged me in them. I have been blessed beyond measure with the love and forbearance of my wife, Stevie, and my daughters, Tassie and Amy.

David Cameron

THE DAILY PLEBISCITE

ROBERT C. VIPOND

Introduction

For thirty years, from the mid-1960s through the mid-1990s, Canada was in a state of ongoing political crisis. From the Quiet Revolution to the election of the Parti Québécois; from the first sovereignty referendum to the promulgation of the Constitution Act, 1982; and from the Meech Lake and Charlottetown Accords to the second Quebec referendum in 1995 – this was an era in which the continued existence of Canada was in question. For the same thirty years, David R. Cameron was alternately a participant in, and an observer of, the social and political conflict that gripped the country. As a senior public servant, first in Ottawa and then at Queen's Park, Cameron was directly, deeply, and variously engaged in the mega-constitutional politics that defined the era. As a political scientist, first at Trent University and then at the University of Toronto, Cameron was (and remains) one of the most astute and respected observers of the challenging social and political terrain that Canada encountered in the late twentieth century – and that it continues to navigate. This collection of essays assembles some of Cameron's "greatest hits." They are dispatches, of a sort, from almost five decades of direct engagement, vigorous debate, and scholarly reflection on Canadian federalism, the relationship between Quebec and Canada, and the politics of the constitution.

David Cameron's work draws on, and draws out, the Canadian experience. It is not simply confined to Canada, however, and my hope in presenting these essays is that readers beyond Canada will find them of interest and use as well. One hint of this broader aspiration is contained in the collection's title – *The Daily Plebiscite* – which is taken from Ernest Renan's "What Is a Nation?," his famous 1882 lecture-turned-essay. Renan's lecture was delivered in the shadow of the Franco-Prussian War and the disputed status of Alsace-Lorraine. In it, he criticizes theories of nationalism that rely on fixed and exclusive characteristics (such as race, language, and religion) and proposes instead that a nation is best understood as a "large-scale solidarity" that combines "a rich legacy of memories" with "present-day consent." In this sense, he says, "a nation's existence is ... a daily plebiscite, just as an individual's existence is a perpetual affirmation of life."[1] As readers will see, the "daily plebiscite" is one of David Cameron's favourite metaphors that recurs throughout his writing. And for good reason. In the spirit of Renan, what Cameron brings to the study of federalism and nationalism is a keen sense of the contingency of national communities. They rise and fall – their legitimacy nurtured by trust, sustained by compromise, and "shaped by the myriad choices citizens make in their everyday lives."[2] These are lessons learned from experience with, and reflection on, Canada's history. But they speak, as Renan's reflections do, beyond this particular time and place.

I

The collection is divided into two parts and ends with a coda. The first part is largely historical and tracks some of the most important political developments that animated "the thirty years of travail"[3] in Canadian politics. For students who were born after 1995 (which means almost all current and recent undergraduates), the national unity era may seem like something of a black hole – a set of complicated and disconnected commissions, accords, and official reports, increasingly calcified and indistinct with the passage of time. The consequence, as I have found in my own teaching, is that it is often difficult for students to understand the underlying issues that brought the country to the brink of dissolution, much less to appreciate the nail-biting anxiety that suffused national politics for much of thirty years. And anxious years they were. More than a few political scientists in English Canada who came of age in the 1960s or 1970s chose that discipline either because they wanted to understand how we had managed to get ourselves into this existential predicament or to find a way to extricate ourselves from it. I count myself among them.[4] Few scholars, however, have contributed as much, for as long, in so many different ways, and on so many urgent, white-hot issues as has David Cameron. Even fewer bring his combination of insight and graceful prose to bear on these issues.

Cameron cut his teeth on the national unity file as a summer student working on the Bilingualism and Biculturalism Commission in the mid-1960s. While completing his doctorate at the London School of Economics on the social and political thought of Burke and Rousseau, he took up a position in the Department of Political Studies at Trent University, where he soon became chair of the department, then dean of the faculty. He returned to Ottawa in 1977 to serve as the director of research for the Task Force on Canadian Unity, where he co-authored the Pepin-Robarts report – one of the most important public documents on Canadian federalism of the era. From there he served in a number of capacities, first with the government of Canada and then with the government of Ontario, providing strategic direction at virtually every turn: on the first Quebec referendum in 1980 (as a member of the so-called Tellier group); on the negotiations that led to the passage of the Constitution Act, 1982 (as Assistant Secretary to Cabinet); on the Meech Lake Accord (1987–1990) when, following his relocation to the University of Toronto, he served as Ontario's deputy minister of Intergovernmental Affairs; and on the Charlottetown Accord (1992) and the second Quebec referendum in 1995 (as special constitutional advisor to the premier of Ontario). Whether scholar or participant, Cameron was driven by the same desire to see the country through the national unity debate, to understand the dynamics of Quebec politics, and to build bridges between Quebec and the rest of Canada.

These reflective interventions on the moving target of national unity form the core of Part I of this collection. The essays assembled here consist largely of previously published work that tracks the evolution of the national unity question, in real time as it were. (For those readers who are less familiar with the events of the period, I have provided a thumbnail history of the mega-constitutional era immediately following this introduction. In addition, each selection contains a headnote, written expressly for this collection, that contextualizes the piece in question.) Most of the selections originally appeared in conventional scholarly outlets, either as chapters in books or stand-alone articles. A few pieces, typically shorter and edgier, originally appeared (or were intended to appear) as op-eds in newspapers. The selection entitled "Current Reflections on the Past" is sui generis. Because he was working on the constitutional front lines for much of the 1980s, Cameron did not have an opportunity at the time to write systematically or thematically about the long decade that began with the creation of the Constitution Act, 1982 and ended with the Quebec referendum in 1995. To fill this gap, I asked him to reflect on the initiatives and dynamics of that decade. In an interlude that connects Parts I and II, he and I speak conversationally about the tumultuous decade of the 1980s.

The chapters are arranged in the order in which they were originally published, and it would be perfectly sensible for readers to engage with them in the order they appear here. This way they can connect the dots from initiative to initiative, episode to episode, and decade to decade. Alternatively, let me suggest that readers may equally find value in approaching the selections in what one might call developmental (rather than chronological) order so as to understand some of the deeper, historical-theoretical currents of the relationship between Quebec nationalism and the Canadian federal constitution. The Quiet Revolution of the 1960s and the sovereignty movement of the 1970s, after all, did not appear out of thin air. They were shaped by historical forces and intellectual commitments that pre-date the moment at which English Canada suddenly sat up and took notice of what was happening in Quebec. This being the case, readers may want to begin with chapter 3, Cameron's signature essay, "Lord Durham Then and Now," originally published in 1990.

"Lord Durham Then and Now" stands out because the example of Durham powerfully informs Cameron's own response to modern Quebec nationalism. As Cameron notes with wry understatement, "there have never been many fans of Lord Durham in French-speaking Canada, and it is not hard to see why."[5] Durham's condescending view of French culture ("They [French-Canadians] are a people with no history, and no literature."),[6] his English ethnocentrism ("It is to elevate them from that inferiority that I desire to give to the [French] Canadians our English character."),[7] and his quixotic project to bring Louisiana-style assimilation to Canada have been lightning rods for French-Canadian intellectuals and politicians ever since – and for good reason. "Like many another nineteenth-century liberal," Cameron says, "(Lord Durham) was insensitive to the power and durability of culture and nationality."[8]

What accounts for the "power and durability" of French-Canadian nationalism, and why did Durham misjudge it so badly? As Bernard Yack has argued in detail, the phenomenon of modern nationalism is distinctive because it combines "a sense of national loyalty and a commitment to the new understanding of popular sovereignty as a condition of political legitimacy" in a way that creates "an explosive mixture."[9] The rise of French-Canadian nationalism is a case in point. Durham seems to have believed that the cultural heritage with which French Canadians identified was old, tired, and not fit for the modern world. "The French Canadians," he maintained, "are but the remains of an ancient colonization, and are and ever must be isolated in the midst of an Anglo-Saxon world. Whatever may happen, whatever government shall be established over them, British or American, they can see no hope for their nationality."[10] What Durham misunderstood about French Canada (though, oddly, not about English Canada)[11] was the "explosive" and energizing potential of the marriage between the old idea of a cultural heritage community and the new idea of popular sovereignty; between an imagined community built on the foundation of language, religion, and the collective memory of conquest on the one hand and the powerful idea that the people are the only legitimate source, the fountain, of political power on the other. By this account, it is the members of the French-Canadian nation who inhabit that territory called Lower Canada or Quebec – not the British colonial authorities, not the Anglo business elite in Montreal, and not the majority of British or English Canadians beyond its borders – in whom constituent sovereignty is vested and who, therefore, alone have the rightful authority to shape their political life. Whether articulated in terms of *la survivance* or expressed as the goal to be *maîtres chez nous* or asserted as a right to self-determination, French-Canadian nationalism (like other modern nationalist claims) has typically been framed in a way that blends beliefs about political legitimacy with a collective memory, story, or imaginary about a particular territory. That is, it combines peoplehood with nationhood. In Cameron's formulation, "the point (demonstrated over the course of Canadian history) was not that a free society was impossible *without* assimilation, but that, in Canada at least, it was impossible *with* it."[12]

I linger on Durham's *Report* because Lord Durham and his legacy set the conceptual table for the essays in Part I. At one point in his essay on Durham, Cameron calls him "a sort of social geologist, exploring the great fault line of British North America and of Canada itself as it emerged."[13] Three diagnostic possibilities arise from this geological analogy. One might deepen and widen the fault line in a way that likely leads to some form of earthquake – more or less the position of those who advocate for Quebec sovereignty. One might make "futile efforts to erase the fault line"[14] – in the spirit of anti-nationalists like Pierre Trudeau. Or one might "learn to live with (the fault line), and to render the social and political institutions of the country, as far as possible, earthquake proof."[15] In this view – which is clearly and consistently Cameron's view – "the relationship between French and English in North America ... [is] an existential reality to be acknowledged and accommodated"[16] rather than denied or left to tectonic upheaval.

The essays in Part I develop these three inter-related themes – nationalism, anti-nationalism, and accommodation – in ways that illuminate the national unity crisis between 1965 and 1995. The selection that opens the collection (chapter 1) is drawn from Cameron's first major book on Canadian politics – *Nationalism, Self-Determination and the Quebec Question*,[17] published in 1974. The chapter places the national question front and centre and interrogates the intellectual coherence of the claim, central to the platform of the ascendant Parti Québécois, that Quebec has a right, even an absolute right, to self-determination. The intuitive appeal generated by framing Quebec's aspirations in this form reflects the extent to which the powerful combination of popular sovereignty and national identification that I sketched above has become an accepted part of liberal democratic discourse over the years. If the people are sovereign, surely they get to determine how the political institutions that govern their lives are configured. Yet as Cameron points out in his 1974 study, the intellectual foundations and political implications of a general and unilateral right to national self-determination are far from clear. How, after all, does one marry national loyalty to French Canada with the democratic and territorially defined polity of Quebec? Does French Canada include French-speaking persons outside of Quebec? By the same token, do the nationalized people of Quebec include those (like English speakers or immigrants) who lack some element of what it means to be a "real" Québécois (however that is defined)? And since Quebec is currently part of a larger political community called Canada, by what right are the people of Quebec permitted to decide unilaterally – with their voices alone – how their relationship with the people of Canada should be disentangled?

Cameron's questions, entered into the historical record well before the PQ won its first election in 1976, have proven to be remarkably prescient and accurate predictors of how the sovereignty debate would unfold over the next three or more decades. Indeed, the combination of scepticism about a unilateral right to self-determination and faith in "civilized values ... backed up by plain ordinary self-interest"[18] (on the part both of Canada and Quebec) is powerfully resonant. It both recalls Edmund Burke's attitude to American independence and anticipates the Supreme Court of Canada's argument, in 1998, when it was asked under what conditions a component part of the Canadian federation may secede.[19] The Court's position – unilateral secession, no; principle-driven and negotiated secession, yes (chapter 10) – is essentially the position adumbrated by David Cameron twenty-five years earlier.

The anti-nationalist position, however, is equally untenable in Cameron's view. For much of the period covered by these essays, of course, the anti-nationalist position was articulated most forcefully, uncompromisingly, and consequentially by Pierre Trudeau. In a certain sense, Trudeau can be seen as the modern version of Durham for, like Radical Jack, Trudeau wanted to cut the legs out from under Quebec nationalism once and for all. From Cameron's perspective, Trudeau was mistaken on two counts. The first is that Trudeau, no less than Durham, underestimated the sociological depth, historical resilience, and political appeal of French-Canadian (and specifically Québécois) nationalism. Durham believed that the material benefits of assimilation into British North America would persuade French Canadians to jettison their linguistic and cultural identities; Trudeau believed that re-imagining pan-Canadian citizenship in a way that is anchored to the protection of individual rights would produce thoroughly liberal, cosmopolitan anti-nationalists. Both were mistaken. French Canada did not disappear as Durham thought necessary and inevitable, but instead became one of the pillars of Confederation in 1867. As for Trudeau, having stated in May 1976 that the Parti Québécois had already conceded "the end of separatism,"[20] he spent much of his time as prime minister (and beyond) sparring with sovereignist governments and nationalist opinion in Quebec.

The second error, according to Cameron, is that Trudeau wanted to frame the most basic constitutional questions too rigidly – in a way that insisted above all on the uncompromising precedence of individual over collective rights. From Cameron's perspective – a view that boils over in his response to Trudeau's famous broadside against the Charlottetown Accord in 1992 (see Chapter 4) – protecting individual rights is an important part, but only one part, of the work that liberal democracies perform. A singular fixation on individual rights, therefore, misunderstands Canada's past, misreads its present, and threatens its future. Cameron the scholar concludes that "Trudeau's ideas don't add up";[21]

Cameron, the engaged public servant, finds that Trudeau's (and others') resistance to compromise on the questions of regionalism and dualism "exposed the country to greater risk than any other single issue in our national life."[22]

This leaves Cameron to define and defend a middle or third option – creative, equitable, and effective ways to accommodate Quebec's distinctiveness within a larger political community called Canada. As he puts it in "Lord Durham Then and Now": "(W)e have yet to achieve a settled and enduring answer to the issue Lord Durham raised 150 years ago – how can French-speaking Canadians exist on a footing of genuine equality with their fellow inhabitants of this vast continent and still remain true to themselves and their culture? Durham's flinty answer was that they cannot do both, and he was prepared, on their behalf, to have them give up culture for the sake of equality. Canadians rejected this prescription and have tried since that time to reconcile the two."[23] The essays that appear in Part I of this collection provide an account of several of the most important attempts over the course of thirty years to reconcile what Durham claimed could not be reconciled, namely Quebec's (national) distinctiveness within a larger Canadian political community. From his Burkean support of constitutional gradualism in the early 1970s, through the expansive proposals contained in Pepin-Roberts in the late 1970s (chapters 2, 5, 6), to his defence of the proposed constitutional reforms in Meech in the 1980s and Charlottetown in the 1990s – this idea of accommodation runs like a red thread through David Cameron's engaged scholarship over these "thirty years of travail." It is equally the idea that runs through and unifies Part I of this collection of essays.

II

Oliver Wendell Holmes Jr. once remarked that "hard cases make bad law."[24] Might one say, by the same token, that constitutional crises make for bad federalism? To what extent and in what ways has the bruising experience of the mega-constitutional era informed Canadian federalism since the 1995 referendum? What is the new "normal" of Canadian federalism and intergovernmental relations? And are there broader lessons – about democracy, legitimacy, and sovereignty, for example – to be gleaned from the Canadian experience that might helpfully illuminate the politics of other divided, multi-national, multi-cultural societies? These are the questions that guide Part II of this collection.

Although the enthusiasm for mega-constitutional politics has subsided since the 1995 referendum, scholarly interest in Canadian federalism has not. In fact, it is booming.[25] To be sure, the character of federalism scholarship in Canada has shifted to some extent. The over-heated era of mega-constitutional politics has given way to what Cameron calls the "normal politics" of electoral competition, policy-making, and intergovernmental relations, and with this change scholars have shifted their attention as well. Much of the most impressive recent federalism scholarship has favoured empirically rich studies in discrete policy areas or individual institutions – among them immigration,[26] agriculture,[27] education,[28] health care,[29] the environment,[30] indigeneity,[31] labour policy,[32] and the courts.[33] In some ways, much of the post-1995 federalism literature in Canada is reassuringly familiar in the sense that it often deals with the dynamics of centralization and decentralization and the politics of shared policy-making – a framework to which Canadian political scientists are well accustomed. To be sure, the complexity of the modern welfare state combined with the forces of globalization complicate the description of intergovernmental dynamics in virtually every policy field. Indeed, this complexity may well be one reason that recent federalism scholarship in Canada has become as specialized as it has. Still, as François Rocher and Miriam Smith argue, "the concepts of centralization/decentralization are essential to the analysis"[34] of Canadian federalism now as they were before the mega-constitutional era. Indeed, the reference points of centralization and decentralization are precisely part of what makes the politics of federalism in Canada seem "normal" again – even if the definition of the central terms remains somewhat difficult to pin down with precision and even if the binary terms seem overwhelmed by the complicated federal world they are meant to describe.[35]

Yet what is striking about the "normalized" politics of contemporary Canadian federalism is that it is accompanied and informed by a heightened and explicit sensitivity to the lens (or lenses) through which scholars and practitioners see, understand, and evaluate the politics of federalism. If Canadians learned nothing else from the national unity imbroglio they surely learned that different political and constitutional lenses provide strikingly different visions of the landscape in front of them. My hunch (and that is all it is) is that in coming to terms with these competing visions political scientists and other scholars were forced to pay more attention to, and to tease out the implications of, the larger theoretical assumptions that animate the study and practice of Canadian federalism. Besides, after thirty years of intense political and constitutional engagement scholars (David Cameron among them) had more intellectual space in which to consider – or consider again – whether and how the dynamics of Canadian federalism fit with "the changing theoretical and methodological concerns of the discipline as a whole."[36] Whatever the reason, the fact is that recent federalism scholarship has been alert – self-consciously so – to the ways in which larger theoretical commitments inform the study of federalism and, conversely, to the ways in which substantive studies help to build theory.

What are these theoretical approaches? At the inevitable risk of oversimplification, I want to identify three major (and often overlapping) streams of scholarship about Canadian federalism that have both earned a prominent place in recent political science literature and that help to situate David Cameron's distinctive approach to the subject. I call them functional, causal, and normative approaches.

I label the first stream *functionalist* to emphasize the commitment of those scholars who think of the institutions of Canadian federalism as an interconnected political system in much the same way that the human body is an interconnected physiological system. The challenge for the body politic, as for the body physical, is to ensure the overall smooth functioning of the system as a whole – in short, to ensure things work well. For Talcott Parsons, the intellectual father of functionalism, "workability" meant finding ways to attain the goals that the system had set for itself, adapt to changing circumstances, and avoid debilitating conflict – all the while adhering to the basic values and principles on which the system was built.[37] Even with such a telegraphic summary, one can easily see why scholars of Canadian federalism would be attracted to a functionalist approach to describe, explain, and evaluate the performance and effectiveness of the Canadian federal system.[38] It provides a useful vantage point from which to view the systemic world of intergovernmental relations.

Several of the selections in this volume are cast in a broadly functionalist mould. Of these, the essay entitled "Intergovernmental Relations in Canada: The Emergence of Collaborative Federalism," (chapter 13) is an especially vivid example. Co-authored in 2002 with Richard Simeon, the essay traces the development of intergovernmental relations in post-war Canada – from the Ottawa-led system of cooperative federalism that was instrumental in the creation of the welfare state in the 1950s and early 1960s, to the more competitive and oppositional intergovernmental system that was fueled both by the forces of the Quiet Revolution in Quebec and opposition to the National Energy Policy in the West, and finally to what the authors suggest is a new, post-1995 system of collaborative federalism characterized by the co-determination of broad national policies. As they put it, "the evolution of the Canadian federation over the last four decades has been substantially defined by two powerful forces: nation-building in Quebec and province-building elsewhere."[39] What Cameron and Simeon show in detail is how intergovernmental institutions in Canada have attempted to re-invent themselves over time so as to adapt to underlying change; to make federalism work as well as it can and to perform as effectively as it can in light of the structural constraints with which it must deal. Inchoate and fragile as the framework of collaborative federalism was (and is), Cameron and Simeon nevertheless provide the first major attempt to understand – and evaluate – the post-1995 system of intergovernmental relations in Canada as a functioning system.

This sort of functional analysis – certainly in its Parsonian form – builds on the premise that political institutions and systems (like federalism) are created and change in response to their social foundations and environment. Canada became a federation rather than a unitary state because granting a measure of sub-national autonomy was the only practicable and appropriate way "to unite a linguistically and regionally diverse citizen body within the confines of a single nation-state."[40] The imperative to build a national economy drove the federal government at various times to develop an intergovernmental system in which it was *primus inter pares*. Co-operative federalism gave way to competitive federalism in response to the evolution of Quebec nationalism and the growing salience of western grievance. A distinctive form of collaborative federalism developed post-1995 to respond more effectively to the pressures applied by the double phenomenon of national building and province building. And so on. To put it a tad too crudely: Deep and enduring social, cultural, and economic forces or structures emit powerful signals; political institutions respond and adapt – sometimes well, sometimes awkwardly. That is how functional analysis generally works.

Put slightly differently, structural functionalism implicitly assumes that the causal arrows generally point from society to state; that the social foundations of a polity largely explain why institutions are designed as they are and why they change as they do. But what if this assumption about the social foundations of federalism is mistaken – or at least over-stated? What if, as Alan Cairns argued provocatively in 1977,[41] the causal arrow points the other way? What if governments are themselves largely responsible for, and help to cultivate, the very diversity and conflict that functionalist theory would have them respond to? In retrospect, one can see that Cairns's intervention anticipated a broader move to "bring the state back in" to the study of comparative politics, a move associated with the landmark scholarship of Theda Skocpol and other scholars.[42] Soon enough the tri-focal lenses of state formation, state capacity, and state autonomy established their place in Canadian federalism scholarship.

The ongoing debate between society-centred and state-centred analyses of federalism (and politics more generally) has generated a significant corpus of scholarship over the years. It has also invited (or perhaps forced) many political scientists to be more attentive to patterns of *causal linkage* and to be more sensitive to claims of *causal inference*. As Richard Simeon suggests in his magisterial account of political science approaches to Canadian federalism over seven decades (2002), the stakes – both scholarly and practical – are high: "Is the federal system better seen as a consequence of the underlying regionalism or territorialism of Canada's social and economic organization; or is territorialism itself a consequence of the political structure of federalism?"[43] Simeon goes on to point out that "Canadian students of federalism have rarely been self-conscious or explicit about the theoretical models and assumptions, or about carefully delineating dependent and independent variables and the causal links between them. The analysis has tended to be descriptive, declaratory, and prescriptive rather than question-posing, puzzle-solving, and hypothesis-testing."[44] Yet this is where the trail leads when there are competing explanations for the patterns of federalism politics, and it is a trail that has become increasingly well-travelled and well-marked since Simeon wrote those words at the turn of the millennium. Mainstream political science in North America is characterized by its commitment to the task of understanding causal inference; this commitment informs the study of Canadian federalism as it does other branches and sub-fields within the discipline.[45]

One particularly pointed and important causal question arises in light of the national unity crisis in general and the near-miss referendum of 1995 in particular: Does federalism foster secession or hinder it? This is the question that Cameron addresses in "The Paradox of Federalism: Some Practical Reflections" (chapter 16), the theme of a special issue of the journal *Federal and Regional Studies*. As the editors note in their introduction to the assembled essays, the study of federalism has made something of a comeback in political science of late, in part because federalism is often touted "as a way to accommodate territorially based ethnic, cultural and linguistic differences in divided societies, while maintaining the territorial integrity of existing states."[46] But what if this intuition is wrong? What if "recognition perpetuates and strengthens the differences between groups and provides minority nationalists with the institutional tools for eventual secession?"[47] Then, paradoxically, the institutional measures adopted to reduce conflict may actually broaden and deepen the very conflict they were designed to mitigate. Federalism may be intuitively appealing, but does the empirical evidence demonstrate its usefulness as an instrument of conflict resolution in deeply divided societies? That is one of the questions – one of the *causal* questions – to which the example of Canadian federalism is meant to speak.

Cameron's response to the paradox outlined by the editors is equivocal. His first reaction is playful: "Does federalism foster or inhibit secession? As with so many good questions in social science, the answer seems to be yes."[48] His serious answer is that federalism in most cases is instrumental. Federal institutions may help in certain circumstances to deter secession, but "the likelihood of there being a secession movement in a given polity turns more on how people are treated than on whether or not they are federally governed."[49] In this sense, "(f)ederalism is unlikely to hold an unjust regime together; but, equally, it is unlikely to pull a just regime apart. Justice – rather than a glorified governing instrument – is surely closer to the heart of the matter than federalism."[50]

It is here that Cameron turns the key that unlocks the third major approach to federalism studies: to analyse the institutions and practices of federalism in light of *normative* principles and fundamental questions of political theory. Some scholars have suggested that this marriage between federal studies and normative political theory marks a new (and welcome) turn in federalism studies.[51] In David Cameron's case no turn was necessary. Over the course of his career he has consistently wanted to bring federalism studies back to, or point them towards, basic, enduring normative questions: What is the relation between federalism and democracy? Is the sort of executive-driven intergovernmental relations that suffuses Canadian federalism compatible with democratic goods like transparency, accountability, and participation? How does one define and deliver justice in a multi-racial, highly pluralistic, and deeply federal state?

Yet taking these normative questions seriously leads to quite a different approach from the one that gives priority to the search for causal inference. Where many scholars of Canadian federalism want principally to understand the causal relationship between state and society, scholars like David Cameron are more interested in understanding the principles and values that guide state and society, especially the reciprocal or reflexive interplay on the ground between federalism and democracy. This is key. Democratic principles like legitimacy, transparency, accountability, and responsiveness are not simply ideas that can be defined and expounded in the abstract. They are ideas that are embedded in practice, in which both state institutions and social actors – and the interplay between them – deserve and require close attention. The essays in Part II of this collection, then, represent one scholar's best efforts to look "under the hood" of Canadian federalism to examine critically how well intergovernmental and constitutional mechanisms perform as transmission belts between state and society and between multiple governments and their citizens. Cameron's overall project here is to examine the real world of federalism as a "daily plebiscite" on life in a complex, democratic and federal political community. Part institutional diagnostician, part democratic theorist, Cameron's goal is to elucidate the fundamental principles that animate democratic politics in a federation *and* to map these normative commitments onto institutional arrangements that work.

Take, for instance, the essay entitled "Intergovernmental Relations and Democracy: An Oxymoron If There Ever Was One?" (chapter 12). At first blush, this essay looks a lot like the essay on collaborative federalism noted above. The two essays were written at about the same time, had the same co-author (Simeon), and tracked some of the same developments in the practice of intergovernmental relations in Canada, notably the Social Union Framework Agreement (SUFA). In fact, however, the two essays are quite different. "Collaborative Federalism" provides a granular review and assessment of recent developments recorded largely in a functionalist register. "Intergovernmental Relations and Democracy," for its part, explores some of the new initiatives in intergovernmental relations that seek to overcome the view that the institutions of Canadian federalism are "a closed shop,"[52] and to establish democratic criteria against which these initiatives can be measured and evaluated.

What does democracy mean in this context? Potentially many different things. As Cameron and Simeon point out, there is no "one size fits all" definition of democracy that captures the range of behaviours and activities associated with intergovernmental relations. One can evaluate the democratic-ness of intergovernmental relations in the terms articulated by the authors of SUFA themselves – that is, transparency, accountability, and participation. Yet as Cameron and Simeon note, these three criteria are far from crystalline in their meaning or their application to the world of intergovernmental relations. Take participation. Does that mean that citizens should be directly involved in framing and ratifying important intergovernmental initiatives – the former through some version of citizen assembly, the latter through some form of referendum? Does it mean that citizens should be brought into the deliberative process at which initiatives are discussed and their relative merits judged? (On this point, readers are invited to refer to chapter 14, "Inter-Legislative Federalism.") Does it mean that citizens should have the opportunity to have their views registered at dedicated hearings? Or does it simply mean that citizens should have adequate information with which to form their judgments and render their government(s) accountable, especially through elections? All are plausible ways of thinking about the relationship between federalism and democracy; none is adequate on its own or in the abstract.

These reflections on intergovernmental relations speak to one aspect of the relationship between federalism and democracy. But there is a larger, overarching question here, and that is the question of legitimacy. As Cameron suggests in "Canada's Constitutional Legitimacy Deficit: Learning to Live with It" (chapter 18), the Damoclean sword hanging over the Canadian constitution is its "legitimacy deficit" in Quebec. "It is difficult to understand," he argues, "how a constitutional settlement that is rejected and opposed by one of the communities (in a binational or bicommunal polity) can be regarded as legitimate."[53] This is precisely what happened when, in 1982, Quebec's National Assembly not only refused to ratify but expressly rejected what is now known as the Constitution Act, 1982 – "a breach in the Canadian constitutional order that has not been repaired to this day."[54]

And yet Canada still stands. Why? Cameron sketches several possibilities in these final essays. One possibility is that, following the bruising referendum of 1995 Canadians, both in Quebec and the rest of Canada, sought shelter in the "abeyances" of the Constitution – those deep crevices in the relationship that are best left untouched and unexplored in order to maintain the health of the relationship. It is also possible that by spelling out the constitutional rules that would guide the next attempt at secession – in effect, to acknowledge the contingency of Canada as it exists – has "blunted the force of secession. In fact, the apparent willingness to accommodate the actual secession of Quebec, should that be necessary, appears to have been part of the context in which the power of the secessionist movement in Canada has, at least for the time being, waned."[55] In his 1974 book, Cameron was wary of the argument that "the extension to Quebec of the absolute right to self-determination might be the very thing which would ensure that it will never be exercised."[56] On the value of this strategy he has had second thoughts.

But there is clearly more to the curious erosion of the sovereignty movement than this. What Cameron wants to suggest in these final essays is that we need to think more creatively and differently about the various ways in which legitimacy is understood and registered in a complex, multi-national polity like Canada. Consent is the *sine qua non* of legitimacy in a democracy to be sure. We are, as Cameron says, "children of the Enlightenment" and "many of us have some version of the social contract model in our heads, in which a political order is constituted by the will of the people, ostensibly at a particular historical moment, namely, at the founding of the regime, in the form of an agreement on a constitution."[57] But consent is not a once-in-a-regime's-lifetime moment that crystallizes a founding or, alternatively, ratifies an abrupt and fundamental about-face in the way political life is practised. Consent is often more "quotidian," metered by a "practical, day-to-day form of acquiescence to the civil order."[58] In the absence of consent to a basic set of rules that governs the way in which power is exercised – call it a constitution – legitimacy can still be conferred through the many small acts that cement our status as citizens of a certain political community. This is not consent writ large, but it is consent nonetheless. It is, to quote one of Cameron's favourite aphorisms and the title of this collection – *un plébiscite de tous les jours* – a daily plebiscite.[59] It is in thinking through these forms of quotidian consent, poking and prodding to find ways to broaden and deepen this everyday consent, that David Cameron makes what is arguably his most important contribution to the study of Canadian politics.

All of which leads to a final question and to this collection's coda: Are there lessons to be gleaned from the Canadian experience that might be exported to, and applied by, other deeply divided societies? Does it provide clear guidance about how to configure institutions federally in a way that can accommodate territorially concentrated minority populations? Here again, David Cameron speaks with a combination of experience, insight, and eloquence. One vehicle for those qualities has been the Forum of Federations, an international network of federal countries, created in 1999, to facilitate the exchange of knowledge among practitioners and scholars about federalism and multi-level governance. The Forum's mandate includes a commitment to provide advice to new, emerging, and fragile democracies with the knowledge and tools "to learn and apply federal principles and practices to specific internal governance challenges."[60] It is in this context that Cameron has had an opportunity to study, visit, and provide advice to deeply divided states such as Sri Lanka and Iraq.

Chapter 16, "The Paradox of Federalism: Some Practical Reflections," represents one effort to assess the challenges facing fragile (Sri Lanka) or emerging (Iraq) states in light of the experience of one enduringly federal state (Canada). Do not expect either pie-in-the-sky idealism or local boosterism. Cameron is neither naïve about the challenges facing those countries nor self-congratulatory about the Canadian experience. With respect to the former (Sri Lanka and Iraq), Cameron argues (as noted above) that federalism is, in most cases, at best an instrumental good. For fragile and emerging democracies to survive and thrive, there are other, more important challenges (like cultivating social and political trust) that precede the institutionalization of federalism. With respect to Canada, Cameron argues that federalism is not just instrumental, it is – and always has been – contingent. The Canadian federal constitution has existed for more than 150 years, a record of endurance that makes it an outlier among constitutions in the modern world. Yet for all that "(i)t has not been possible during these years to assume that the country in which Canadians live is effectively eternal, that it will always be there for its citizens. Canadians have had to recognize that it may not."[61] Canada's history "reminds Canadians that the state itself is a human artefact, reared up to serve the interests and needs of the people for whom it is responsible, not an entity endowed with intrinsic moral or spiritual value."[62] If the thirty years of travail taught Canadians anything, it taught them that they cannot take the continued existence of their country for granted, that they need to approach the ongoing, even relentless, challenges with openness and flexibility, and that "the constitution and the values underlying the constitutional order"[63] do still provide a rudder with which to guide citizens through rough waters. "Canada, for its part, will exist as long as Canadians will it. As Ernest Renan said, a nation is a *plébiscite de tous les jours*." There are, Cameron concludes, "worse foundations on which to construct a community."[64]

NOTES

1 Ernest Renan, "What Is a Nation?," in *Nation and Narration*, ed. Homi K. Bhabha (London and New York: Routledge, 1990), 19.
2 In this volume, 299.
3 David R. Cameron, "Quebec and the Canadian Federation," in *Canadian Federalism: Performance, Effectiveness and Legitimacy*, (4th ed.), ed. Herman Bakvis and Grace Skogstad (Toronto: University of Toronto Press, 2020), 73.
4 In my case this led to a PhD dissertation, then a book, that explored the intellectual origins of the idea of provincial rights in English Canada. Like so many other books of the era, one can tell from the subtitle that it emphasized the negative (probably more than it should have). See *Liberty and Community: Canadian Federalism and the Failure of the Constitution* (Albany, NY: SUNY Press, 1991).
5 In this volume, 66.
6 Gerald M. Craig, ed., *Lord Durham's Report* (Toronto: McClelland and Stewart, 1969), 150.
7 Craig, *Lord Durham's Report*, 149.
8 In this volume, 71.

9 Bernard Yack, *Nationalism and the Moral Psychology of Community* (Chicago: University of Chicago Press, 2012), 153, 138.

10 Craig, *Lord Durham's Report*, 148.

11 Craig, *Lord Durham's Report*, 143. "They (British colonists in Canada) value the institutions of their country, not merely from a sense of the practical advantages which they confer, but from the sentiments of national pride; and they uphold them the more, because they are accustomed to view them as marks of nationality, which distinguish them from their Republican neighbours.... The British people of the North American colonies are a people on whom we may rely, and to whom we must not grudge power."

12 In this volume, 71.

13 In this volume, 70.

14 In this volume, 70.

15 In this volume, 70.

16 In this volume, 70.

17 David Cameron, *Nationalism, Self-Determination and the Quebec Question* (Toronto: Macmillan, 1974).

18 In this volume, 51.

19 *Reference re Secession of Quebec* (1998) 2 SCR 217.

20 "Quebec separatism dead, says Trudeau," *Montreal Gazette*, 11 May 1976, 1.

21 In this volume, 86.

22 In this volume, 102.

23 In this volume, 75.

24 The quip comes from Holmes's dissent in *Northern Securities Co. v. United States* 193 US 197 (1904), at 400.

25 See Jack Lucas and Robert Vipond, "Back to the Future: Historical Political Science and the Promise of Canadian Political Development," *Canadian Journal of Political Science* 50:1 (March 2017), 219–241, especially 227–228.

26 See, for instance, Mireille Paquet, *Province-Building and the Federalization of Immigration in Canada* (Toronto: University of Toronto Press, 2019); Jane Jenson and Mireille Paquet, "Canada's Changing Citizenship Regime Through the Lens of Immigration and Integration," in Elizabeth Goodyear-Grant et al., *Federalism and the Welfare State in a Multicultural World* (Montreal and Kingston: McGill-Queen's University Press, 2018), 175–200; and Edward Anthony Koning, "Three Hypotheses on the Relevance of Federalism for the Politics of Immigration and Welfare," in Goodyear-Grant et al., *Federalism and the Welfare State*, 201–222.

27 Grace Skogstad, *Internationalization and Canadian Agriculture: Policy and Governing Paradigms* (Toronto: University of Toronto Press, 2008).

28 See Jennifer Wallner, *Learning to School: Federalism and Public Schooling in Canada* (Toronto: University of Toronto Press, 2014); and Linda A. White, *Constructing Policy Change: Early Childhood Education and Care in Liberal Welfare States* (Toronto: University of Toronto Press, 2017).

29 See Gerard Boychuk, *National Health Insurance in the United States and Canada: Race, Territory, and the Roots of Difference* (Washington, D.C.: Georgetown University Press, 2008); Carolyn Hughes Tuohy, *Remaking Policy: Scale, Pace, and Political Strategy in Health Care Reform* (Toronto: University of Toronto Press, 2018).

30 Patrick Fafard and Kathryn Harrison, eds., *Managing the Environmental Union: Intergovernmental Relations and Environmental Policy in Canada* (Kingston: School of Policy Studies, 2000); Thomas J. Courchene and John R. Allan, eds., *Canada: The State of the Federation 2009: Carbon Pricing and Environmental Federalism* (Kingston: Institute of Intergovernmental Relations, 2010); and Mark Winfield and Douglas Macdonald, "Federalism and Canadian Climate Change Policy," in *Canadian Federalism: Performance, Effectiveness, Legitimacy*, (4th ed.), ed. Bakvis and Skogstad (Toronto: University of Toronto Press, 2020), 363–392.

31 Kiera Ladner, "Treaty Federalism: An Indigenous Vision of Canadian Federalisms," in Rocher and Smith, *New Trends in Canadian Federalism*, 2nd ed. (Toronto: University of Toronto Press, 2003) 167–194; Thomas Courchene, *Indigenous Nationals, Canadian Citizens: From First Contact to Canada 150 and Beyond* (Kingston: Queen's School of Policy Studies, 2018).

32 See Rodney Haddow, *Partisanship, Globalization, and Canadian Labour Market Policy: Four Provinces in Comparative Perspective* (Toronto: University of Toronto Press, 2006); and Rodney Haddow, *Comparing Quebec and Ontario: Political Economy and Public Policy at the Turn of the Millennium* (Toronto: University of Toronto Press, 2015).

33 See Gerald Baier, *Courts and Federalism: Judicial Doctrine in the United States, Australia, and Canada* (Vancouver: UBC Press, 2006); and Robert Schertzer, *The Judicial Role in a Diverse Federation: Lessons from the Supreme Court of Canada* (Toronto: University of Toronto Press, 2016).

34 François Rocher and Miriam Smith, eds., *New Trends in Canadian Federalism*, 2nd ed. (Peterborough: Broadview, 2003), 9.

35 Rocher and Smith, *New Trends in Canadian Federalism*, 9–10.

36 Richard Simeon, *Political Science and Federalism: Seven Decades of Scholarly Engagement* (Kingston: Institute of Intergovernmental Relations, Queen's University, 2002), 1.

37 Talcott Parsons, *The Structure of Social Action* (New York: Free Press, 1968). In the context of Canadian federalism, the "workability thesis" was most closely associated with J. Stefan Dupré. See "Reflections on the Workability of Executive Federalism," in *Intergovernmental Relations*, ed. Richard Simeon (Toronto: University of Toronto Press, 1985), 1.

38 A good example of a functionalist perspective well applied to Canada is Bakvis and Skogstad, *Canadian Federalism* (note 3 above), in which Canadian federalism is evaluated explicitly against the standards of performance and effectiveness. Theirs is not a purely functional analysis, however. Bakvis and Skogstad also build in a normative element into the volume organized around the theme of legitimacy. See also Richard Simeon's discussion of functionalist approaches to Canadian

federalism in *Political Science and Federalism*, 6–13. I tend to interpret functionalism (and its applicability to Canada) more broadly than Simeon did.

39 In this volume, 193.

40 This is the first sentence – and heralds the *leitmotif* – of the excellent collection of essays on Canadian federalism assembled by Herman Bakvis and Grace Skogstad. See Bakvis and Skogstad, *Canadian Federalism*, 3.

41 Alan C. Cairns, "The Governments and Societies of Canadian Federalism," *Canadian Journal of Political Science* 10:4 (December 1977): 695–725.

42 See Theda Skocpol, "Bringing the State Back In: Strategies of Analysis in Current Research," in *Bringing the State Back In*, ed. Peter Evans, Dietrich Rueschemeyer, and Theda Skocpol (Cambridge UK: Cambridge University Press, 1985), 3–38.

43 Simeon, *Political Science and Federalism*, 4.

44 Simeon, *Political Science and Federalism*, 31.

45 The most important text in this regard is surely Gary King, Robert Keohane, and Sidney Verba, *Designing Social Inquiry: Scientific Inference in Qualitative Research* (Princeton N.J.: Princeton University Press, 1994).

46 Jan Erk and Lawrence Anderson, "The Paradox of Federalism: Does Self-Rule Accommodate or Exacerbate Ethnic Divisions," *Regional and Federal Studies* 19:2 (May 2009): 191–202 at 191.

47 Ibid., 192.

48 In this volume, 253.

49 In this volume, 254.

50 In this volume, 253–4.

51 See Simeon, *Political Science and Federalism*, 44.

52 In this volume, 173.

53 In this volume, 272.

54 Ibid.

55 In this volume, 253.

56 In this volume, 42.

57 In this volume, 282.

58 In this volume, 283. It should be noted that this quotidian legitimacy is just one of several forms of legitimacy that Cameron identifies in the essay. He also speaks of legitimacy that has its sources in a social contract, tradition, and performance. He returns to these themes in the conclusion to this volume.

59 See Renan, *What Is a Nation?*, 19.

60 Extracted from the website of the Forum of Federations – www.forumfed.org. Accessed 10 December 2019.

61 In this volume, 252.

62 In this volume, 253.

63 Ibid.

64 Ibid.

ROBERT C. VIPOND

A Brief History of the Mega-Constitutional Era in Canada

The essays in Part I of this collection focus on what Peter Russell calls the era of "mega-constitutional" politics in Canada, roughly from the mid-1960s to the mid-1990s.[1] To say that the period was characterized by *constitutional* politics means that the issues and debates that normally animate the politics of industrialized democracies – how to generate and re-distribute wealth, ensure the population's health, and educate the country's youth, for instance – were often eclipsed or refracted by *regime* questions: What are the rules that govern the access to, and exercise of, power? Who gets to make those rules? How is citizenship and membership in a national community (or communities) defined? What is the relationship between nation and state? To say that constitutional politics took on a "mega" form means that the constitutional agenda in Canada over these three decades was both expansive in scope and prolonged in length. Like a thousand-piece jigsaw puzzle spread out on the coffee table, debate over these issues was engaged, then paused, then re-engaged. In short, this was a thirty-year period in which just about everything in the Canadian polity seemed to be up for grabs – including the country's continued existence.

The goal of Part I is to understand this part of the Canadian experience, guided and interpreted by David Cameron and in light of some of the large, often normative, questions that dominated political discussion: sovereignty, nationalism, federalism, and democratic legitimacy chief among them. To fully appreciate these interventions a brief political history of the period may be helpful. What follows is such a thumbnail history, organized by decades.

1960s

Most accounts of Canada's mega-constitutional era begin with the Quiet Revolution, heralded by the 1960 Quebec provincial election in which Jean Lesage led his Liberal party to decisive victory. Lesage's election launched a decade of political, economic, social, and cultural change that "effected a significant rupture with the traditional past"[2] – a historical moment both of rejection and construction. Three political developments stand out. The first is that, during the 1960s, Quebec committed itself to building a modern, secular, social welfare state. Functions that had previously been performed in large measure by the Church, like education, healthcare, and social assistance, were expanded and placed under state control. Public utilities, none more important than electric power generation, were nationalized with the creation of Hydro Quebec in 1962. Beyond this, the government created economic and financial institutions, like the *Caisse de dépôt et placement* (1965), to spur and guide economic investment. The upshot is that state capacity grew dramatically. Indeed, by the mid-1980s the number of provincial civil servants per capita in Quebec was triple the number it had been in 1960.[3]

Quebec's ambitions to create a welfare state depended both on having the policy space to deliver "made in Quebec" social programs and the ability to pay for them. The need for policy autonomy and fiscal capacity brought Quebec into negotiation – and often conflict – with the federal government. This is the second major development associated with the Quiet Revolution. Rallying around the slogan *maîtres chez nous* (masters in our own house), Quebec's essential goal across a number of social policy domains was to secure access to the funds generated by federal taxation while opting out of some or most elements of the federal government's programmatic template. In so doing, the province issued a fundamental challenge to what many in the rest of Canada regarded as the basic norms of Canadian federalism.

Third, and more broadly, the core definition and meaning of Quebec nationalism began to change. As Geneviève Zubrzycki puts it, "national history (in Quebec) began to follow a new narrative arc, shifting the framework of identification and affiliation from a pan-North American, ethnic French-Canadian identity based on language and religion to one circumscribed by the territory of Québec and a civic and secular identity centered on language."[4] The political consequences of this re-imagined national identity were profound. On the one hand, it gave the politics of language unrivalled status at the top of the political agenda, where it remained throughout the mega-constitutional era. On the other, the transformation of French-Canadian into Quebec nationalism helped establish the logic of sovereign independence. If the territory of Quebec marked the linguistic and cultural boundaries of the nation, did it not follow that it should be left to the people of Quebec (and to them alone) to define the nature of their political community, up to and including the creation of an independent, sovereign state? This was a controversial and contested claim, as Cameron's exploration in chapter 1 demonstrates. Yet more and more Quebecers came to embrace the logic of self-determination. As early as 1961 groups began to form with the explicit purpose of achieving Quebec's independence, and the creation in 1968 of the Parti Québécois (PQ), led by René Lévesque, gave the nationalist cause an almost immediate and serious presence in electoral politics in Quebec.

Lévesque, who ultimately served as Quebec's premier between 1976 and 1985, liked to quip that the Quiet Revolution was not, as he recalled, particularly quiet. Certainly, it reverberated loudly and clearly in Ottawa, and Lester Pearson's Liberal government responded to it as Canadian governments often do when faced with difficult issues: It struck a royal commission to study the question. The Bilingualism and Biculturalism Commission (or B and B) produced a preliminary report in 1965 that outlined the gravity of the threat posed by Quebec nationalism. Canada, it said, "without being fully conscious of the fact, is passing through the greatest crisis in its history,"[5] and it went on to sketch a view of the Canadian political community that could and would serve as a counterpoise to the new nationalism in Quebec. In this dualistic view, the Canadian political community is best understood as an equal partnership of the country's "two founding peoples" in which both francophones and anglophones feel at home anywhere in the country. Concurrently, the federal Liberals recruited a significant number of talented political figures from Quebec. Of these the most important was Pierre Trudeau, who joined the Pearson government in 1965, became minister of justice in 1967 and, as the new leader of the Liberal party, won a majority government in the general election of June 1968. Profiting from the tailwinds created both by the B and B Commission and a majority Liberal government, Parliament, in 1969, passed the Official Languages Act. The Act made English and French official languages for all matters concerning the Parliament and government of Canada. It also mandated the provision of services to citizens in either official language, a requirement that justified federal support for second-language education in the provinces.

1970s

Already by the end of the 1960s, then, "two starkly contrasting visions of the relationship between anglophones and francophones"[6] had crystallized, represented by competitive, office-seeking political parties and articulated by charismatic leaders. It is hardly surprising that, as the 1960s gave way to the 1970s, "the constitutional debate became increasingly polarized between these antithetical views, and personalized in the leadership of Prime Minister Trudeau and Premier Lévesque."[7] Yet while Quebec nationalists used the decade of the

1970s to build support and momentum for the sovereignty project, the federal government spent most of the decade on its political back foot as it mishandled issues (the White Paper relating to Indigenous issues), headed down constitutional cul-de-sacs (the Victoria Charter), reacted to exogenous shocks (the 1973 oil crisis), and encountered significant differences of approach to national unity within federalist ranks (the Task Force on Canadian Unity).

Consider this contrast. In Quebec, a political party founded in 1968 and dedicated to fundamental regime change had, already by 1972, established a secure electoral toehold in provincial politics, and in 1976 decisively won a general election. By 1978 it had used its majority in the Quebec National Assembly to pass ground-breaking legislation – Bill 101, the Charter of the French Language – to ensure that French would be the normal language of everyday life in Quebec. And by 1980 the PQ in government was ready to redeem its promise to hold a referendum which, if successful, would provide the government of Quebec with a mandate to negotiate the province's withdrawal from Canada. The PQ's project could easily have derailed along the way, especially had it come to be associated with, and tainted by, the actions of the revolutionary, paramilitary Front de Libération du Québec (FLQ). The FLQ supported the use of violence as a means to achieve sovereignty. Its abduction of two political figures (and the subsequent assassination of one of them) led directly to the October Crisis of 1970 and the imposition of draconian measures under the federal War Measures Act (WMA). Yet far from undermining support for sovereignty, Lévesque's pointed critique of the use of the WMA together with his steadfast commitment to achieving sovereignty through democratic and constitutional means almost surely helped to solidify the legitimacy of the PQ's project and to consolidate his standing as leader.

For the federal government on the other hand, the 1970s brought one intractable problem after another – and, more importantly for our purposes, constitutionalized one issue after another. The first serious misstep occurred with respect to Canada's Indigenous peoples. In 1969 the federal government introduced its so-called White Paper, or formally the "Statement of the Government of Canada on Indian Policy," that proposed repealing the Indian Act, doing away with reservations, and excising references to "Indians" in the British North America Act, 1867 (Canada's principal constitutional document at the time). Reform was necessary, in the words of the White Paper, to realize "the fundamental right of Indian people to full and equal participation in the cultural, social, economic and political life of Canada." Not to accept this fundamental right, the brief maintained, was "to argue *for* discrimination, isolation and separation."[8] The federal government completely misjudged its audience, however. In the event, the idea that all citizens are free and equal rights-bearing individuals collided massively with growing Indigenous national self-identification. The policy was widely criticized as a thinly veiled, tone-deaf attempt to assimilate Indigenous people to white Canadian society; others went further, arguing that this amounted to a form of cultural genocide. The White Paper was ultimately withdrawn, but a significant number of Indigenous leaders drew an important strategic lesson from this and other similar episodes: The place of Canada's Indigenous people, their treaty and land rights, were too important to be left to the ordinary political process alone.

Second, on its own major constitutional proposal, the Victoria Charter, the federal government encountered a serious roadblock. Even before he became prime minister, Pierre Trudeau had floated the idea of a charter of rights that would guarantee basic political and civil liberties to all Canadians. Canada already had a Bill of Rights, championed by former Prime Minister John Diefenbaker and enacted by Parliament in 1960. But that instrument was both limited in scope (it didn't apply to provinces for instance) and, as an ordinary act of Parliament, left the impression that individual and minority rights were created *by* legislatures when in fact a core idea of modern liberalism was to defend rights *from* the acts of legislatures and governments. Trudeau was determined to remedy these defects, to which end he introduced a draft constitutional charter of rights at a meeting of first ministers in 1971. Known as the Victoria Charter, Trudeau's constitutional package foregrounded the fundamental importance of political rights (like freedom of thought and assembly), defined constitutionally protected language rights, outlined changes to the criteria and process by which justices are appointed to the Supreme Court, proposed modest re-balancing of the division of legislative powers between federal and provincial governments, and ended with a cluster of procedures for amending the constitution.

The inclusion of an amending formula is an especially important theme in the unfolding constitutional story. The British North America Act, 1867 (BNA) contained no provisions for changing the terms of the constitution itself. In one respect, this omission was understandable. Since the BNA Act was an act of the Imperial Parliament, the Canadian Fathers of Confederation may have presumed that any changes to the Act would begin and end in London. As Canada became increasingly responsible for its own affairs, as provincial governments grew in constitutional importance, and as Canadian governments struggled to align twentieth-century responsibilities with nineteenth-century legal categories, the absence of a mechanism to effect constitutional change became impossible to ignore. In 1949, the BNA Act was amended to give Parliament authority to rearrange most of the constitutional furniture in its own house, that is matters over which the federal Parliament had exclusive legislative jurisdiction. But about changes that affected others – provincial governments or the linguistic rights of citizens, for instance – there were still no clear rules. Absent such rules, amendments that affected the federation as a whole were usually deemed as a matter of practice to require unanimity among federal and provincial governments.

This patchwork practice was clearly not ideal, so among its provisions the Victoria Charter included an explicit constitutional amending formula that would codify the process of, and rules governing, constitutional change. In fact, the Victoria Charter came tantalizingly close to being accepted. An apparent agreement dissolved at the last moment when Quebec's Premier Robert Bourassa found he lacked support upon presenting the Charter to his cabinet and officials. In particular, the proposals did not go far enough to decentralize control over social policy, a key and consistent Quebec goal. Most observers at the time, including federal officials, agreed that without Quebec's consent the Victoria Charter could not go forward. When Quebec concluded it could not support the plan, therefore, it died. The failure at Victoria did not end Ottawa's quest for comprehensive constitutional reform, however. Rather, it set the tone for the rest of the decade. On the one hand, the federal government continued to engage in "federal-provincial diplomacy"[9] to negotiate constitutional change that was acceptable to all the provinces. On the other, it began to explore the possibility of acting unilaterally as a way "to escape the paralyzing consequences of the unanimity requirement."[10] Neither approach bore immediate fruit.

The oil crisis of 1973 further roiled Canadian politics, bringing to the surface deeply felt regional grievances, especially in western Canada. In the aftermath of the Arab-Israeli War in 1973, the Organization of Petroleum Exporting Countries (OPEC) had drastically cut its production of oil, thus sharply increasing the cost of oil and gas in Europe and North America. In Canada, the hubs of oil production (the West) and the largest centres of consumption (central Canada) had starkly different interests. When the federal government took steps to mitigate soaring energy costs by controlling the price and exportation of domestically produced oil, many in the West felt aggrieved, building on a century of resentment at trade policies widely seen as damaging the West to fuel central Canadian manufacturing.[11] The reaction to the federal government's National Energy Program in the 1980s, pungently conveyed by the bumper sticker "Let the Eastern Bastards Freeze in the Dark," speaks eloquently enough to a later incarnation of protest. But what makes the 1970s significant is that the control of natural resources found its way onto an increasingly crowded constitutional agenda. In the words of Roy Romanow, Saskatchewan's Attorney General throughout much of this period: "The major new element in constitutional reform after 1973, therefore, was the economic fight waged between the western region and the centre. The fight soon turned into competition over jurisdiction to control resources and collect economic rents; it became intensely bound up with the constitutional struggle and remained a driving force to the process that continued into 1981."[12] The specifics of energy policy aside, the oil crisis thus revealed another basic truth about Canadian politics in the 1970s: Regionalism and province-building, no less than French-English dualism, was capable of producing combustible social and political tension that demanded solutions at a fundamental, that is constitutional, level. "New centrifugal forces now tugged at the fabric of Canada's unity."[13]

Finally, even among those members of the political elite who considered national unity to be of urgent importance, significant differences in approach began to appear. The example of the Task Force on Canadian Unity, created a few months after the PQ's victory in 1976, stands out. The task force was established by Prime Minister Trudeau "to allow the public to air its views on national unity and the government to buy some time."[14] Chaired by Jean-Luc Pepin (a former member of Trudeau's cabinet) and John Robarts (former premier of Ontario), the original remit of the Task Force was relatively modest. It was meant to be "a national exercise in public consultation reporting on public opinion but offering little or nothing in the way of policy proposals."[15] The Task Force itself had other ideas. Ultimately, it developed its own approach to national unity, articulated here by David Cameron (see chapters 2, 5, and 6) who served as the commission's director of research. That approach carved out a third option between Quebec's sovereignty-association and Trudeau's "anti-nationalist individualism," one that "recognized, accepted and sought to accommodate the very forces in Canadian life and politics that Trudeau was combatting."[16] As one might expect, the Pepin-Robarts report was received "with thin-lipped reserve by the Trudeau government,"[17] and as long as Trudeau was in charge the third option remained very much in the shadows. Still, the Task Force demonstrated that there was more than one way to think about and address the unity question, various versions of which took centre stage in subsequent constitutional performances.

In May 1979, the Trudeau Liberals were defeated in a general election by the Progressive Conservatives (PC), led by Joe Clark. The Clark interregnum lasted only nine months, but the election results revealed troublingly deep regional divisions among the electorate: Clark's Conservatives captured a minority government, but won only two seats in Quebec. The Trudeau Liberals lost in large part because they returned only three seats west of the Manitoba border. Thus ended the 1970s – with Quebec nationalism on the rise, Indigenous people energized to take their place as full constitutional actors, regional tensions rising, and national leadership searching for the rudder with which to steer the ship of state.[18]

1980s

"We are entering a very dangerous decade," Pierre Trudeau told Parliament in April 1980, "and many lethal currents are swirling about our shores.... These are great dangers, but in a sense the greatest enemy is the enemy within, not the enemy without...."[19] Trudeau spoke as prime minister, having led his Liberal party to victory over Joe Clark and the Conservatives in an unexpected election held in February (although one that still left his government with virtually no representation from the West). The "enemy within" presumably referred to the Quebec government, which had scheduled its promised referendum on sovereignty for May 20, 1980. What the people of Quebec were asked to vote on was not a direct up or down on sovereignty. It was, rather, a referendum on something called "sovereignty-association" – political and juridical sovereignty combined with economic association with Canada. Nor would a positive result in the referendum immediately trigger a unilateral declaration of independence. Rather, the referendum simply sought a mandate for the government of Quebec to negotiate independence from and association with Canada. The more attenuated and hesitant language was designed to reassure those Quebecers who thought that a claim for outright and direct sovereignty was too risky. Whatever the calculation, the referendum failed by a margin of 60–40, with francophone Quebecers about evenly split between "Oui" and "Non."

David Cameron and I discuss the upshot of the 1980 Quebec referendum (and other signal events in the 1980s) in greater detail in "Current Reflections," the interlude that connects Part I and Part II of the collection. To get a basic sense of the decade's political dynamics, however, it is perhaps enough at this point simply to flag the different reactions to the referendum. For his part, René Lévesque interpreted the defeat less as a rebuke than as an invitation to continue building the independence movement in Quebec – which is exactly what happened. On the other side, Pierre Trudeau interpreted the results of the referendum as an opportunity to realize the sort of fundamental and lasting constitutional change that had eluded him and his government since the collapse of the Victoria Charter a decade earlier. To that project he and his rejuvenated federal team turned almost immediately.

Two years of often intense intergovernmental negotiations culminated in the passage of the Constitution Act, 1982, reflecting the federal government's attempts to sharpen, refine, and narrow the substantive focus of its constitutional strategy. The Trudeau government made its priorities clear. It wanted to patriate the constitution, enshrine a charter of rights, provide more secure protection for linguistic minorities, and codify an amending formula. Where Quebec and the western provinces talked largely about re-balancing the division of powers between federal and provincial governments, Trudeau and his government talked about re-imagining the relationship between citizens and governments. Trudeau called his proposals "the people's package" of constitutional reform, theirs "the governments' package" and, as he famously put it, he was not about to trade "rights for fish."[20] The appeal of Trudeau's vision of a rights-based liberal polity came to dominate much of the discussion about constitutional renewal over the next two years, picking up a head of steam as it went. The Special Joint Committee of the Senate and the House of Commons on the Constitution, which held multiple public hearings on the Charter between November 1980 and February 1981, was an especially important forum because it provided a public stage on which Trudeau's people's package earned prime time exposure. As Adam Dodek argues, "the joint committee process ignited and mobilized widespread public support for the Charter, which significantly strengthened the federal government's bargaining position vis-à-vis the provinces."[21] Reflecting on their participation in the negotiations surrounding the Constitution Act, three prominent members of the Saskatchewan team – no great fans of Trudeau's project – put it this way: "The idea of a liberal state clashed with western regionalism and Quebec nationalism and, from our present perspective, liberalism appears to have won."[22]

But how, having failed so badly to advance its constitutional positions in the 1970s, did Trudeau's government succeed in realizing fundamental constitutional change in the early 1980s? One part of the answer is that the federal government refused to be bound by the principle or practice of unanimity (outlined above) that had underpinned most earlier attempts at constitutional renewal. After long, rancorous, and largely unsuccessful intergovernmental negotiations over the summer of 1980, Ottawa, supported by Ontario and New Brunswick, announced that it would proceed unilaterally to extract formal authority over the British North America Act from Britain and thereby begin the creation of a Canadian fundamental law. Over the next year, opposition parties attempted to derail the package in Parliament, and delegations from Indigenous organizations travelled to Britain to persuade the House of Lords to intervene on their behalf. ("The empire strikes back," Trudeau retorted.) The most effective opposition, however, came from the remaining provincial governments – the "Gang of Eight" as they were called – who mounted a series of legal challenges to a federal initiative taken without the consent of the provinces. Conflicting judgments in three provincial courts on the still hypothetical question of unilateral patriation led to an appeal to the Supreme Court of Canada.

The Supreme Court's judgment, broadcast live on television in late September 1981, was a remarkable piece of judicial statesmanship that gave something to both sides.[23] On the one hand, the Court argued that, as a matter of law, the federal Parliament did have the right to proceed with patriation unilaterally. On the other, it argued that a constitutional convention or norm exists that requires agreement from a "substantial majority" of provincial governments for amendments to be legitimate. The decision thus simultaneously enabled and constrained both federal and provincial positions, which produced powerful incentives for all the governments to return to the bargaining table. In early November 1981 provincial and federal delegations met yet again to find a consensual way forward. Following a week of high-wire, give-and-take negotiations, a deal was reached – but one, crucially, that did not include Quebec. Whether defended as a realistic assessment of Quebec's intransigent opposition to any compromise or condemned as an act of betrayal, the decision not to engage Quebec in the final negotiations meant that when the Constitution Act became the law of the land in April 1982, it applied to Quebec even though the province's government and National Assembly repudiated it.[24]

Under other circumstances, the successful patriation of the constitution and the creation of a new constitutional blueprint might have ended the constitutional saga that had begun with the Quiet Revolution. But given Quebec's constitutional isolation[25] – many would say exclusion[26] – it was clear that there was still unfinished constitutional business. The conditions for closing the constitutional circle soon enough turned more propitious. For one thing, both Trudeau (1984) and Lévesque (1985) – "the two old gladiators"[27] – retired from politics. For another, elections in both Canada and Quebec subsequently brought new leadership and attitudes to the question. The newly elected prime minister, Brian Mulroney, enjoyed strong country-wide support for his Conservative government, including in Quebec, where his greater sympathy for nationalist objectives played well. In Quebec, the federalist Liberal party, led by Robert Bourassa, decisively swept the PQ from office. Moreover, the rules of the game were now much clearer. The Constitution Act, 1982, after all, included an amending formula; its very existence, one might think, would remove one of the sources of intergovernmental contention that had plagued earlier rounds of negotiation.

Thus began "the Quebec round" of constitutional negotiations that led, in 1987, to the intergovernmental agreement called the Meech Lake Accord. Mulroney explained that his objective as prime minister was to bring Quebec into the "constitutional family" with "honour and enthusiasm," something Trudeau had been unable or unwilling to achieve. For his part, Bourassa wanted to demonstrate that it was possible to be both a nationalist who could protect and enhance Quebec's political autonomy and a federalist who could imagine Quebec situated comfortably within the larger political community of Canada. To this end, his government set out a series of conditions that would guide Quebec's constitutional re-engagement. The most novel and controversial of these conditions turned out to be a broad statement of constitutional principle that Quebec forms a "distinct society" within Canada. The other conditions largely re-visited familiar demands to consolidate Quebec's leverage over discrete policy domains (immigration and shared cost programs), institutions (the Supreme Court), and that old chestnut, the amending formula. These conditions morphed into a set of proposals that, while still centred on Quebec, were framed broadly enough to attract interest and support from other provincial governments. After two years of quiet but intense shuttle diplomacy among governments, the First Ministers signed off on the Meech Lake Accord in June 1987 and committed themselves to bring the proposals forward "as soon as possible" to their respective legislatures for ratification as a package of constitutional amendments.

The process of moving from intergovernmental accord to constitutional amendment entailed two challenges. The first is that, by the new constitutional rules outlined in the Constitution Act, 1982, all amendments require legislative approval. The second is that the Meech amendments were presented as a package that had to meet the most demanding constitutional standard – unanimous agreement. In fact, the process began promisingly enough. Quebec's National Assembly was the first to ratify the amendments, and by the fall of 1988 all of the provinces save Manitoba and New Brunswick had assented to them. But soon thereafter the wheels came off the constitutional bus. Provincial elections in several provinces brought in governments less sympathetic to Meech than their predecessors, and public opinion was shifting. Despite frantic last-minute attempts to save the Accord, Manitoba ultimately did not ratify the agreement before the constitutionally imposed deadline of June 1990, and Newfoundland (ready to rescind its original ratification) followed suit. With that, having failed to win unanimous legislative support, the Meech Lake Accord died.[28]

David Cameron and I discuss the reasons for Meech's demise in our extended conversation on the 1980s. For the purposes of reconstructing the basic story of the mega-constitutional era, however, three things stand out. First, while dubbed the "Quebec round" of constitutional reform, the failure of Meech underscored the rising importance of Indigenous people as constitutional actors and their concerns as constitutionally important. In this case, the actor in the limelight was Elijah Harper, the only Indigenous member of Manitoba's legislative assembly, who refused to go along with the Meech initiative, but the point is broader. Second, the Meech failure revealed the powerful potential of the Charter and its rhetorical appeal to equality. Newfoundland's Premier Clyde Wells, whose opposition to Meech made him something of a national celebrity, argued that the Accord violated the principle of equality from top to bottom. Just as "every province in any true federation is in its status as a province … equal to any other," so "every citizen is, in his or her status and rights as a citizen, equal to every other. And just as citizens have equal rights, so "the two founding linguistic cultures" are equal.[29] Third, the reaction to Meech served as a rebuke to the processes of "executive federalism," the process of high-level intergovernmental bargaining that dominated the mega-constitutional era. As Peter Russell puts it: "Many citizens did not take kindly to a bundle of constitutional amendments cobbled together by eleven men behind closed doors and put to the legislature on the basis that not a word could be changed. It was the undemocratic process that created the Meech Lake Accord, as much as its contents, that led to its final demise."[30]

1990s

Quebec and the rest of Canada drew quite different conclusions from Meech's collapse.[31] In Quebec, a sense of national rejection was both widespread and deeply felt.[32] The Accord's failure was particularly bitter because this was the first time in the mega-constitutional era that the government of Quebec had accepted the risk of agreeing to a multilateral and comprehensive package of constitutional reforms with English Canada, and its rejection stung. In the immediate aftermath of Meech, support for Quebec sovereignty grew to unprecedented heights – 60–65 per cent in some public opinion polls, and Premier Bourassa vowed to boycott any further constitutional negotiations. The reaction in English Canada was more varied. Some prominent public figures began to wonder aloud whether keeping Canada together was still worth the effort. Others – and this resonated especially strongly among citizens – were simply tired of their governments' preoccupation with constitutional questions; the body politic, according to this diagnosis, was suffering from "constitutional fatigue." The intergovernmental class in English Canada – officials both elected and appointed who were responsible for the national unity file – responded quite differently. However reluctantly, federal and provincial governments concluded that the national unity question was ever more urgent, that sentiment in Quebec favouring separation had grown to dangerous new heights, and that it was therefore crucial to overcome Quebec's constitutional isolation before time ran out on the federalist cause.

This time, however, the approach would be different. One popular interpretation of the Meech debacle was that the Accord failed less for what it included than for what it excluded, from which it followed that any future initiative should broaden the focus of debate beyond the Quebec question. As Richard Johnston has observed, the basic idea was to create a constitutional logroll, in which the rest of Canada would get something it wanted from constitutional reform in return for accommodating Quebec.[33] With that premise and strategy in place, the Quebec round of constitutional negotiations gave way to the Canada round.

There was no shortage of candidates for inclusion. Elijah Harper's dramatic intervention in the Meech debate put (or kept) Indigenous issues high on the list of constitutional priorities. Several provincial governments, especially in western Canada, had argued for some time that the Senate should be reformed and strengthened to provide most robust regional representation in Parliament; equal, elected, and effective was the Triple-E Senate they imagined. Everyone understood that Quebec's distinctive identity had to be recognized in some meaningful way, but there were also powerful voices demanding recognition of equality between the provinces. There were calls for decentralization and counter calls for more vigorous national standards. And then there was the process. Meech, the argument ran, had failed because it had been produced by and for governments, not citizens. Determined to correct the error, virtually all of the governments engaged in constitutional discussions created a more open and consultative process that was meant to forestall the sort of populist and democratic criticism that had derailed Meech. The result was that, between mid-1990 and mid-1992, one roving federal commission, two peripatetic parliamentary committees, six mini-constitutional conferences, and ten provincial commissions all engaged in taking the constitutional pulse of the nation.

By July 1992, intensive multilateral negotiations produced yet another blueprint for constitutional reform at which point Quebec was persuaded to join the discussions. By late August an accord was in place – this one named after the site of the first Confederation conference in 1864. The Charlottetown Accord was a complex, sprawling agreement that incorporated several divergent constitutional claims. If there was one basic idea that ran through its sprawling body, though, it was the idea of inclusion. In response to claims from the West (especially Alberta) that the single member plurality electoral system too often left it with little or no representation in the government, Charlottetown proposed Senate reform that moved closer to the Triple-E ideal. In response to Quebec's festering constitutional exclusion, the Accord once again contained a distinct society clause, and added fixed representation for Quebec in the House of Commons (25 per cent of all seats) as a hedge against demographic decline. The Accord recognized (but did not precisely define) an "inherent right of self-government" for Indigenous peoples. And it was decided, again in the spirit of inclusivity, to submit the Accord to a national referendum.

The Accord would have been a tough sell in Quebec under the best of circumstances. At least one-third of Quebecers consistently self-identified as sovereignist at the time and more were sympathetic to the aims of Quebec nationalism. Sovereignists could hardly be expected to embrace an agreement "specifically designed to foreclose their preferred option,"[34] and even among those nationalists who were in principle open to a constitutional rapprochement there were reasons to be sceptical of the Accord. True, it included a statement of Quebec's distinctiveness, but this seemed to many a diluted version of what had appeared in Meech. A redesigned Senate in which all provinces would have equal representation was a non-starter for many, and the Accord's inclusion of a statement of the country's commitment to social programs – a Social Charter – was viewed by some as a Trojan horse that would legitimate federal interference in Quebec's social policy domains. Still others worried that the inherent right of self-government for Indigenous people might trump Quebec's initiatives in the area of economic development.

In the rest of Canada, the "Yes" side at first enjoyed stronger support. When a referendum was called (with a vote scheduled for late October 1992), polling showed a comfortable 60/40 lead in English Canada. Opinion shifted dramatically, however, after an intervention by Pierre Trudeau – the ghost of charisma past as one wag put it at the time. In a widely circulated speech on October 1, Trudeau unleashed a furious attack on the Charlottetown Accord, in which he denounced it as a provincialist "power grab," a betrayal of individual rights, and a repudiation of the principle of equality. Though some were unimpressed with Trudeau's critique (see Chapter 4 for David Cameron's reaction), it clearly resonated with the English-Canadian public. Within a week, public opinion flipped from 60/40 in favour of the Accord to 60/40 against. On October 26, the referendum was defeated when only 46 per cent of Canadians voted to approve it, failing to secure majority support in six of ten provinces – including

Quebec and all four of the western provinces. As Johnston puts it: "Negotiators hoped that by 1992 they had finally found an equilibrium, a logroll sufficiently inclusive to survive referral to the people. Instead they seem to have gotten the logic of the logroll upside down: they may have overestimated both how much each group wanted what it got and how intensely some groups opposed key concessions to others."[35]

In the aftermath of the Charlottetown defeat, the results of two separate elections shaped subsequent steps. The first was the federal election of 1993, held almost exactly a year after the referendum, in which the Progressive Conservatives (now led by Kim Campbell) suffered a devastating defeat. The Liberals under Jean Chrétien won a majority government, but the big story – and one reason the election came to be known as the 1993 earthquake – was that two regional parties, the nationalist Bloc Québécois (led by Lucien Bouchard) and the conservative, western-based Reform party (led by Preston Manning), each won a significant number of seats. Indeed, the Bloc – a party pledged to Quebec's departure from Canada – became the official Opposition in Canada's Parliament. No less important was the 1994 victory in Quebec of the Parti Québécois, now led by Jacques Parizeau, over the incumbent Liberals. With this configuration, "the table was set for a second Quebec referendum."[36]

In the course of the election campaign Parizeau had promised to hold a referendum on sovereignty if elected, which he then called for late October 1995. Parizeau had wanted the referendum to centre on a direct question about Quebec sovereignty. The final version was somewhat more complicated than he had originally wanted, but it was still more straightforward than the 1980 question on sovereignty-association. After a frenzied and often desperate campaign in which momentum swung back and forth between the two sides, an extraordinary 94 per cent of Quebecers cast ballots, voting "No" to sovereignty by the slimmest of margins – 50.6 per cent to 49.4 per cent. It was that close.

If the near-death experience of 1995 did nothing else, it jolted English Canadians from their complacency about the depth and tenacity of Quebec nationalism and forced them to think more clearly about what would happen the next time round. At first, the federal government seemed unsure about how to respond, but with the appointment of Stéphane Dion as minister of intergovernmental affairs Ottawa's strategy crystallized. The first step was to ask the Supreme Court to clarify the rules that govern secession – that is, whether and by what process a province like Quebec may leave the federation. Like its decision in 1981 with respect to patriation, the Supreme Court managed to thread the constitutional needle in the *Secession Reference* with what many regard as great skill. (See chapter 10.) Following this, Ottawa crafted its own legislative roadmap – known as the Clarity Act (2000) – intended to establish clear procedural rules for secession. And though the Act's provisions have received decidedly mixed reviews, it remains the law of the land.[37]

At a deeper level, however, the 1995 referendum marked the end of the mega-constitutional era. Unlike in 1980, most sovereignists in Quebec did not take the 1995 defeat as a sign to re-double their efforts to achieve regime change through a decisive act of popular sovereignty – even though the "Yes" side came ever so close to winning the referendum. And in English Canada, thirty years of trying to achieve national unity in every which constitutional way led most members of the political elite, both nationally and provincially, to think twice before they put regime questions on the table once again. David Cameron was among the first to glimpse a "paradigm shift" in Canadian politics. As he puts it in chapter 11 (from 1998): "If you think of the Quiet Revolution as opening a bracket at the beginning of a period in which deep, existential questions of identity, community and national purpose have been in play, both within Quebec and within Canada as a whole, then the paradigm shift of which I speak can be thought of as closing the bracket at the end of that turbulent historical period, and heralding the commencement of a new and discernibly different era in our evolving political experience."[38] What such a paradigm shift entailed, how it was metered, and how it was managed is the subject of Part II of this collection. But that is to get ahead of ourselves.

NOTES

1 Peter H. Russell, *Constitutional Odyssey: Can Canadians Become a Sovereign People?*, 2nd ed. (Toronto: University of Toronto Press, 1993).

2 Geneviève Zubrzycki, *Beheading the Saint: Nationalism, Religion, and Secularism in Quebec* (Chicago: University of Chicago Press, 2016), 5.

3 John Dickinson and Brian Young, *A Short History of Quebec*, 3rd ed. (Montreal and Kingston: McGill-Queen's University Press, 2003), 313.

4 Zubrzycki, *Beheading the Saint*, 7.

5 Canada, *Royal Commission on Bilingualism and Biculturalism, Preliminary Report* (Ottawa: Queen's Printer, 1965), 13.

6 Keith Banting and Richard Simeon, eds., *And No One Cheered: Federalism, Democracy, and the Constitution Act* (Toronto: Methuen, 1983), 11.

7 Ibid., 12.

8 "Statement of the Government of Canada on Indian Policy, 1969," in *This Is Not a Peace Pipe: Towards a Critical Indigenous Philosophy*, Dale A. Turner (Toronto: University of Toronto Press, 2006), 130. Emphasis in original. The full Statement is reproduced as an appendix to Turner's book.

9 The term was coined by Ricard Simeon. See Simeon, *Federal-Provincial Diplomacy: The Making of Recent Policy in Canada*, rev. ed. (Toronto: University of Toronto Press, 2006).

10 Alan C. Cairns, "The Politics of Constitutional Conservatism," in *And No One Cheered*, ed. Banting and Simeon, 37.

11 See Mary Janigan, *Let the Eastern Bastards Freeze in the Dark: The West Versus the Rest Since Confederation* (Toronto: Knopf, 2012). For a classic treatment of the question, see Seymour Martin Lipset, *Agrarian Socialism: The Cooperative Commonwealth Federation in Saskatchewan: A Study in Political Sociology* (Berkeley: University of California Press, 1950).

12 Roy Romanow, John Whyte, and Howard Leeson, eds., *Canada Notwithstanding: The Making of the Constitution 1976–1982* (Toronto: Carswell/Methuen, 1984), xix.

13 Ibid., 1.

14 In this volume, 90.

15 In this volume, 91.

16 In this volume, 101. For a sympathetic account of Pepin-Robarts (and a withering critique of Trudeau's philosophy) from a leading Quebec intellectual, see Guy Laforest, *Trudeau and the End of a Canadian Dream* (Montreal and Kingston: McGill-Queen's University Press, 1995).

17 In this volume, 106.

18 In addition to the discrete policy challenges noted above, it is important to understand the way in which changing patterns of immigration affected the structure of Canadian society in the 1970s. In Quebec one of the drivers of language policy was the need to ensure that newly arrived immigrants whose first language was not French were educated and worked in French. The policy largely worked. In 1971–2 (that is, before Bill 101), 15% of school-aged children whose mother tongue was neither French nor English were educated in French in Quebec. In 1987–8, fully two-thirds of "allophones" were schooled in French. (See Dickinson and Young, *Short History,* 326). In English Canada, more relaxed rules governing immigration "sharply increased the racial, cultural, linguistic, and religious diversity of Canada's immigrants and contributed to the reconceptualization of Canada from a British North American community with a large French minority to a multicultural society composed of two language groups." As Cameron argues, "(s)ome of the stress on the federation arose, then, out of the effort to accommodate and reconcile these two overlapping but distinctive processes of change." (See David Cameron, "Quebec and the Canadian Federation," in *Canadian Federalism: Performance, Effectiveness, and Legitimacy,* (4th ed.), ed. Herman Bakvis and Grace Skogstad (Toronto: University of Toronto Press, 2020), 78.

19 Romanow, Whyte, and Leeson, *Canada Notwithstanding,* xv.

20 See Banting and Simeon, *And No One Cheered,* 5.

21 Adam Dodek, *The Charter Debates: The Special Joint Committee on the Constitution, 1980–81, and the Making of the Canadian Charter of Rights and Freedoms* (Toronto: University of Toronto Press, 2018), 5.

22 Romanow, Whyte, and Leeson, *Canada Notwithstanding,* xvii.

23 See Peter H. Russell, 'Bold Statecraft, Questionable Jurisprudence," in Banting and Simeon, *And No One Cheered,* 210–238.

24 At the same time, it should be noted that 74 of the 75 Members of Parliament from Quebec represented the Liberal Party and supported the Constitution Act, 1982 –

a fact to which Prime Minister Trudeau frequently drew attention. In Cameron's view, this does not fundamentally alter the feeling of exclusion or sense of betrayal in Quebec itself.

25 Gérard Bergeron, "Quebec in Isolation," in Banting and Simeon, *And No One Cheered*, 59–73.

26 Daniel Latouche, "The Constitutional Misfire of 1982," in Banting and Simeon, 96–118.

27 Peter H. Russell, *Canada's Odyssey* (Toronto: University of Toronto Press, 2017), 395.

28 For one participant's acute analysis of the demise of the Meech Lake Accord, see Patrick J. Monahan, *Meech Lake: The Inside Story* (Toronto: University of Toronto Press, 1991).

29 Robert C. Vipond, "From Provincial Autonomy to Provincial Equality (Or, Clyde Wells and the Distinct Society)," in *Is Quebec Nationalism Just? Perspectives from Anglophone Canada,* ed. Joseph H. Carens (Montreal and Kingston: McGill-Queen's University Press, 1995), 109.

30 Russell, *Canada's Odyssey*, 398.

31 The next several paragraphs are adapted from Robert C. Vipond, "Seeing Canada through the Referendum: Still a House Divided," *Publius: The Journal of Federalism* 23 (Summer 1993), 39–55.

32 See, for instance, Guy Laforest, *Trudeau and the End of a Canadian Dream* (above, note 16) and Pierre Fournier, *A Meech Lake Post-Mortem* (Montreal and Kingston: McGill-Queen's University Press, 1991).

33 Richard Johnston, "An Inverted Logroll: The Charlottetown Accord and the Referendum," *PS: Political Science and Politics,* vol. 26:1 (March 1993), 43–48.

34 Johnston, *"Inverted Logroll,"* 46.

35 Ibid., 43.

36 Russell, *Canada's Odyssey,* 419. For a helpful analysis of the options after the defeat of the Charlottetown Accord, see Alain-G. Gagnon and Guy Laforest, "The Future of Federalism: Lessons from Canada," *International Journal* 48, no. 3 (1993): 470–491.

37 See François Rocher and Nadia Verrelli, "Questioning Constitutional Democracy in Canada: From the Canadian Supreme Court Reference on Quebec Secession to the *Clarity Act,*" in *The Conditions of Diversity in Multinational Societies,* ed. Alain-G. Gagnon, Montserrat Guibenau, and François Rocher (Ottawa: Institute for Research on Public Policy, 2003), 207–237; and Patrick J. Monahan, "Doing the Rules: An Assessment of the Federal *Clarity Act* in Light of the Quebec Secession Reference," *Commentary* (Toronto: C.D. Howe Institute, 2000), 3–39.

38 In this volume, 124.

PART I   National Unity and the Thirty Years of Travail

1 Quebec and the Right to National Self-Determination

Nationalism, Self-Determination, and the Quebec Question   1974

This is a chapter drawn from a volume entitled Nationalism, Self-Determination, *and the Quebec Question, which was published in 1974. As one can see from the chapter's contents, the question of whether or not Quebec possessed a right – or an absolute right – to national self-determination was exercising the minds of many Canadians at the time. The book arose out of a comment a friend and then colleague at Trent University made to me; in the course of a conversation about Quebec, W.F.W. Neville said casually: "Well, of course Quebec has a right to national self-determination." I contested that, without very much in the way of thought or evidence, but the exchange stuck in my mind. This book sprang from that modest seed.*

The issue of Quebec's right to self-determination is quite frequently raised, but less often discussed. In political debate Canadians are inclined to assert as self-evident the existence or non-existence of such a right, but a good deal less inclined to subject the matter to careful analysis and assessment and to uncover the implications of the various opinions. Supporting argument, whichever case is being advanced, tends to be assumed, rather than expressed.

Whatever one's ultimate conclusion about the right of self-determination might be, the fact that there has at no time been any sustained consideration of it may be regarded as unfortunate by all who believe that there is a clear and continuing possibility of the country breaking up. This is so because a discussion of the right of self-determination inevitably focuses attention upon the respective interests and attitudes of French and English Canada as distinct communities and upon the posture each might legitimately assume with re-spect to the other in the event of a declared intention of secession.

There have been a few occasions when the question of self-determination emerged in public discussion, although they have been infrequent. We men-tioned in the previous chapter the case of the truncated debate within the New Democratic Party in 1971 in which the Waffle group and the Quebec provincial branch of the party called upon the NDP (and ultimately the Canadian people as a whole) to recognize Quebec's absolute right to self-determination.

Abraham Rotstein picked up the theme in the March 1971 issue of *Canadian Forum*[1] and argued that the critical feature of this position might be the fact that English Canada formally recognized Quebec's right to determine its own future, for this would provide a symbolic separation and fresh start for the two communities and would perhaps exorcise at last the ghost of 1759. Thus the ex-tension to Quebec of the absolute right to self-determination might be the very thing which would ensure that it will never be exercised. This is a peculiar and peculiarly Canadian argument, as Rotstein himself realized. Most independ-ence movements, for example, assert the right, not as a means of wresting sym-bolic concessions from the other side, but as a device to smooth the pathway to sovereignty and to accelerate the pace of change. In the context of Quebec society as a whole, it is conceivable that a symbolic gesture of this sort might be of some marginal significance, although the reality for which the symbol presumably stands is surely what will count in the crunch. If we have the sym-bol without the corresponding open-mindedness and willingness to consider fundamental political change, we shall not have improved our situation; and if we have the latter, I suspect we can get along very well without the former.

As we mentioned earlier, the special Joint Committee of the Senate and the House of Commons on the constitution, which produced its *Final Report* in 1972, included a chapter dealing with the question of self-determination. There is some useful supporting argument in the chapter, but the position of the com-mittee is summarized in the two relevant recommendations:

6. The preamble of the Constitution should recognize that the Canadian federa-tion is based on the liberty of the person and the protection of basic human rights as a fundamental and essential purpose of the State. Consequently, the preamble should also recognize that the existence of Canadian society rests on the free con-sent of its citizens and their collective will to live together, and that any differences among them should be settled by peaceful means.

7. If the citizens of a part of Canada at some time democratically declared them-selves in favour of political arrangements which were contrary to the continuation of our present political structures, the disagreement should be resolved by political negotiation, not by the use of military or other coercive force.[2]

What the committee was seeking to do, as it made clear in its explanation of the recommendations, was to map out a position which will permit the rejection of the logic and rhetoric of nationalism, and yet make possible a peaceful resolution of a secessionist crisis, should such a crisis at some point arise. It did this by lodging the right of self-determination in the individual rather than in the nation or the state, and by starting from the firm assumption that the liberty of the person and the protection of human rights is "a fundamental and essential purpose of the State" (*the* fundamental purpose, in the French-language version). From this the committee argued that the employment of force by the state to keep a section of the country within Confederation when it had democratically declared its will to go was illegitimate and unacceptable, and that the conflict should be resolved by negotiation.

This seems to me to be perfectly sensible so far as it goes, and as a brief and general statement of a highly complex issue it covers the ground as well as could be expected. I would, however, enter two caveats. First, the compatibility of the rights of the individual and the rights of the collectivity is asserted, rather than explained and, since the case rests on the interconnection between these two notions, fuller explication would seem to be called for. One of the continuing problems of democratic theory is the reconciliation of democracy as a form of government with the rights of minorities and individuals. Secondly, the case for including clauses relating to the possible disintegration of the country within the revised constitution has not perhaps been satisfactorily established. While the committee's formulation of the approach to a secessionist crisis has much to recommend it, inclusion of statements such as those quoted above as clauses within the constitution may impose rigidities on the situation and create difficulties which could have been avoided if the conflict were left more open to the workings of the political process. It should be remembered, however, that the committee was suffering from considerable internal stress, and this may account in part for the particular form which the recommendations took and, indeed, for their inclusion in the *Report*.

The publication of the *Final Report* occasioned dissenting statements from a number of the committee members, the most important of which was that of two Quebec MPs, Pierre de Bané (Liberal) and Martial Asselin (Progressive Conservative). Their statement objected to the *Final Report* on the grounds that it did not deal in any adequate way with the central issue in constitutional reform: the position of Quebec in the Canadian federal system.[3] The two authors argued forcefully that Quebec's difficulties were "the result of basic contradictions between Canada's political and sociological reality and her legal and institutional system," and asserted the view that much more drastic measures than those which were contained in the *Report* must be implemented if the growing tension in Canadian political affairs were to be resolved. De Bané and Asselin made three specific constitutional recommendations: first, that the preamble of the constitution should include explicit recognition of the existence and aspirations of Quebec society; second, that within the body of the constitution itself Quebec society, and hence Quebec, be accorded a basic right to self-determination; and third, that the central government be shorn of its residual powers and that it have jurisdiction only over those areas which are expressly assigned to it.

We are of course particularly interested in the second recommendation, and the authors advanced two arguments in support of it. First, it is possible that Quebec may opt for independence at some point in the future, and the inclusion of a right to self-determination in the constitution is likely to encourage a rational and orderly resolution of the problem. Second, because the dissatisfaction in Quebec is due in part to certain psychological causes, it could be (à la Rotstein) that "if Quebec did have the right to self-determination, it might not make use of it for the very reason that it knew this option existed."[4] However, it seems to me that these arguments are drastically weakened by the fact that the enunciation of such an extraordinary right in a constitution must inevitably be done in abstract and general terms, whereas circumstances and detail count for everything in its application. Also, as in the case of the Rotstein argument, the assertion of the principle is likely to be of little benefit, and may even be harmful, unless the meaning and implications of the principle are well understood by Canadians and there is a general willingness to permit it to be applied in a concrete situation. There is very little evidence to suggest that English Canada at the moment is prepared to see a radical change in the position of Quebec *within* Confederation, and I therefore fail to see how one can expect there to be much readiness to accept a province's right to *leave* Confederation. The question of theoretical adequacy aside, what is the point of asserting a right if the conditions which are essential to its exercise do not exist?

What do people mean when they speak of Quebec possessing a right of self-determination? In one sense, they are suggesting that with respect to the most fundamental decisions a community is likely to make, Quebec should be regarded as if it were *already* independent and possessed of sovereign power. Quebec is conceptually set apart and distinguished from the country as a whole, and it is argued that so far as the principles of its internal organization and its relationship to the rest of the country are concerned, it ought to be the sole judge and final arbiter of what this organization and these relationships shall be. Quebec may decide to continue its membership in Confederation or it may not, but that is something for the Québécois themselves to decide, as and when they see fit. Federalism is rather like a voluntary association in which one can take out or turn in one's membership.

When the right of self-determination is analysed in this way, it can be seen that it has already departed a fair distance from reality, for it makes no sense to suggest that Quebec will negotiate with the federal government (as it does) about Medicare and taxation and family allowances, and that it will abide by authoritative rulings of a single Supreme Court, but that when it comes to the question of secession it may justifiably exercise a right unilaterally to make its own, independent decision. And yet what else can be meant by the assertion of the right, especially in the case of those (such as the NDP Quebec, the Waffle and Abraham Rotstein) who speak of Quebec's *absolute* right to self-determination? Why absolute? And, anyway, what *is* an absolute right?

One might perhaps prefer at this point to scale down the claim considerably, and point out that there is a danger of treating the passion-filled terms of politics as if they were philosophical statements. Thus the practical message in such a claim, it may be said, is tolerably clear; in plain language what most people really mean when they employ this high-flown talk of absolute rights is that if Quebec decides it wants to get out, then the rest of Canada shouldn't fight to keep it in. Assuming that it is possible to specify satisfactorily what would constitute a "decision" by Quebec to depart and what would compose a fair separation settlement, this seems to me to be eminently sensible and will, I hope, prove to be the ultimate view of those Canadians who think about such matters.

However, this simple and reasonable position is unnecessarily puffed up by the appeal to an absolute right of self-determination, and this at the price of considerable intellectual confusion and the gratuitous creation of opposition in circles where there need be little or none. There is as well a more practical danger; to approach the issue on the assumption that it involves the *rights* rather than or more than the *interests* of the two communities is very likely to produce a set of attitudes on each side which will exacerbate rather than help to resolve the conflict, and when the issue touches people's lives in the way that secession does, this is no small matter. Interests may legitimately be the subject of bargaining and adjustment, whereas rights are expressed or asserted or claimed – no one except Faust bargains with his rights.

One need not look far to find the reason for such rhetorical inflation. Since the eighteenth century there has been an ever-increasing reluctance to speak of expedience, however broadly and humanely defined, and in consequence an elaborate vocabulary has arisen to assist people in the task of disguising their thoughts from themselves. The British philosopher J.D. Mabbott gives a graphic indication of the modern tendency to employ the doctrine of natural rights at every opportunity: "Six months' scrutiny of a correspondence column revealed a natural right to a living wage, a right to work, a right to trial by jury, a right to buy cigarettes after 8 p.m., a right to camp in a caravan by the roadside, and a right to walk on the grouse moors of Scotland during the close season."[5]

At the international level, the sudden rise and the great strength of nationalism and the widespread appeal of the politics of national liberation has been one of the major factors introducing the language of moral absolutes into the mundane affairs of state. In many circumstances the concept of the rights of nations supplanted that of *raison d'état*, and was able to get a powerful purchase on men's minds and awaken a sympathy in their hearts. We have seen in an earlier chapter the animus of Wilsonian liberal nationalism against the tawdry demands of national self-interest, but we have had occasion to note as well the difficulties into which Wilson's brand of international morality led him and many of those with whom he came in contact. Canadians, it may be pointed out, who have disengaged themselves from one sphere of influence only to find they have unwittingly backed into another, are veritable specialists in avoiding unpleasant talk of national interest; indeed, Canada's fate has always been viewed within the context of a larger political and economic system. French Canadians, because their situation has been more sharply defined, have customarily evinced a more lively collective sense of the interests of their community than have their fellow citizens. This disparity continues today and presents an alarming prospect for English Canadians who see French Canada defining itself more and more autonomously, without a strong reciprocating movement emerging in the rest of the country directed towards defining or redefining the character and purpose of English Canada.

I can think of three, and perhaps four, ways in which an attempt might be made to establish the existence of Quebec's right to self-determination, and on balance none of them is satisfactory. The first, which we can dispose of quickly, is the argument that there is some provision in the positive law of the Canadian state which recognizes the right of component parts of the federation to secede. This, it is widely recognized, is simply not true. Canada, like many countries, recognizes the right of individuals to resign membership and to emigrate with their possessions, but there is nothing to be found in the British North America Act or related legislation which provides for a single province's unilateral decision to secede from the federation. Indeed, there are no explicit, stipulated procedures allowing for a collective decision by the eleven constituent governments together to terminate the federal experiment, although there are clearly ways in which this might in fact be done, perhaps via the existing arrangements for constitutional amendment.

It would appear that in terms of existing constitutional principles any legitimate secession on the part of one of the provinces would be effected by the normal procedures for constitutional amendment, which is to say, a Joint Address of the Canadian Parliament to the United Kingdom Parliament. The British Parliament would be involved in this process because the Canadian provinces and federal government have never been able to agree on a domestic amending procedure, and so the ultimate although admittedly pro forma constitutional authority would lie with Great Britain.

It is unlikely in the extreme that Britain would intervene directly in such a matter, and still more unlikely that it would be prepared to deal directly with the seceding province. Just because it is a pro forma authority, the obvious posture for Great Britain to adopt would be one of non-interference, and it could best accomplish this by maintaining its traditional role in Canadian constitutional affairs. Thus, in matters affecting the constitution it is to be expected that Britain would listen to the federal government and be deaf to the provinces.

There are a variety of precedents relating to secession, some of them conflicting, which have arisen out of Great Britain's relations with its colonial or ex-colonial territories.[6] The one which almost certainly would be taken to apply here is the case of the state of Western Australia in the 1930s. As a result of growing dissatisfaction within that state about its membership in the Australian federation, a referendum was held at which secession was approved. The state government then sent a petition directly to the British Parliament requesting that it pass legislation dissolving Western Australia's ties to Australia as a whole. The British Parliament refused to receive the petition on the grounds that it did not have the support of the federal government. A generally similar position was taken up with respect to Penang in Malaya in 1951 and Western Nigeria in 1954.

Although there are conflicting precedents, it is reasonable to argue that these do not apply to Canada. An instance of quite different behaviour on the part of the British government may be found in the break-up of the West Indies Federation; there Britain permitted Jamaica to secede without prior consultation with the federal government. But apart from the fact that Jamaica was by far the most influential member of the federation, with the largest territory, more than half the federal population and almost half the revenue, the West Indies Federation was a new political organization. In fact, it was formed in 1958 and dissolved in 1962. One will find that the conflicting cases are almost invariably those in which the participants have had only a brief and often turbulent experience with federal government. Consider, for example, not just the West Indies Federation, but the partition of India in 1947, the post-referendum separation of the Southern Cameroons in 1961, and the granting of separate independence to Zambia and Malawi in 1962 – all of which Britain accepted.

If the argument from positive law, from the constitution of the country, is of no use in establishing a right to self-determination, one might fall back on the second alternative, which is to ground Quebec's right in principles which are taken to be superior to the positive law of any particular state, to appeal, for example, to natural law. The idea of a law of nature has had a long and colourful tradition, but there are limits beyond which even this most pliant and serviceable of principles cannot be made to stretch. It has traditionally served as a transcendent, non-political criterion for assessing the actions of rulers and subjects. In Roman and medieval times it was indeed often related to another concept, the *jus gentium* or "law of nations," which was employed to assist in the regulation of relations between communities with distinct cultures and backgrounds. But this latter was mainly a conservative principle which was used to smooth out relations between human groups, not to justify political secession. That sort of thing never went down well in the Roman Empire. In the modern period the concept of natural law has been utilized to explain the proper relationship between the individual and the state and between the individual and his fellow man. In this way of thinking, as we have suggested above, the basic unit of analysis and the natural entity which political activity benefits is the individual person, not an aggregate of persons such as the state, the nation, or a social class. Unless one were to suppose that a universal, natural duty obliging states to recognize the right of component parts to dissolve the bonds tying them to the larger structure is part of a system of natural law, it is difficult to imagine how the concept of a law of nature can be of much service in establishing Quebec's right unilaterally to determine its own future.

A third alternative, and no doubt the one that most advocates have in mind, is to rest Quebec's case squarely on the right of nations to lead an independent existence if they so choose. Although this apparently straightforward nationalist argument has been prevalent for more than a century, we have seen in earlier chapters that it nevertheless contains a nest of difficulties. To recap briefly, in order to speak of a group of people possessing a collective right, it is first necessary to invest that collectivity with some corporate identity. The members of an audience at a pop festival or the fans at a hockey game do not as a body possess rights, whereas the members of a trade union or service club do; the important difference between these groups lies in this corporate dimension. There is no difficulty in appreciating how such juridically defined units as states and business corporations may be understood to have rights and duties, but such associations are the product of human decision and identifiable acts of recognition. A nation, however, does not derive its identity from recognition, for it is deemed to be a natural unit. The point of the nationalist argument is that a nation is not the creation of a political order (as is a business corporation, for example), but is itself the creator of a political order; where a nation exists, so should a state. A nation is prior to the state in the same sense that individuals are, and it enjoys the right to form a state for itself. Where does this right come from? A nationalist will invest rights in the nation by following a process which is rather similar to that of an individualist when he or she lodges rights and duties in the human individual. One views the individual, the other the nation, as the political ultimate.

However, unlike the individualist, the nationalist faces a thorny problem of definition, for nationhood is a much more elusive identity than human personality. No one could declare that they are unable to "see" individuals without awakening suspicions about their sanity, but it is perfectly possible for someone to say that they cannot perceive nations in the sense that the nationalist intends without being thought soft in the head. To provide straight nationalist grounds for Quebec's right to self-determination noticeably alters the basis of the whole argument, for whatever realistic set of indicators might be used for identifying the "Quebec nation" the result would certainly not be simply to identify the nation with the existing population and territory of the province of Quebec. The French-Canadian nation would obviously exclude some of the people living in Quebec and include some of the people (and some of the territory?) beyond its borders. If there were to be a referendum on secession, within the terms of the nationalist argument why shouldn't the French-Canadian communities in the Ontario counties bordering Quebec be included, as well as the Acadian population of New Brunswick? Why, on the other hand, shouldn't the English-language communities on the Quebec side of the Ottawa River be given the separate opportunity to declare with which group they choose to associate? For obvious reasons, people choose not to put this sort of argument forward directly, preferring to detect a happy but fictional coincidence between the province of Quebec and the French-Canadian nation.

Given the problems of definition and implementation, then, a pure nationalist argument for the right to self-determination either will not work properly, or else it works too well. Either it has to be manhandled and quite seriously twisted out of shape in order to be made to fit the actual circumstances, or else it places in the hands of any substantial and coherent cultural minorities who care to wield it a potent weapon and a justification for minority self-determination which, on principle, it will be very difficult for the newly independent nation to resist. Such an argument seems to be neither theoretically satisfactory, nor practically tenable in Canadian circumstances.

Nevertheless, we have seen in an earlier chapter that the doctrine of self-determination has been asserted with great frequency in modern times and, although its status in international law and relations is still very unclear, it has in this century gained fairly wide acceptance. However, the important thing from our point of view is that, even if it could be conclusively established that the right to self-determination is a valid principle of international law, it would nevertheless have to be recognized that Quebec does not fall into the category of cases to which that right would then apply. And so an appeal to the principles of international law fails on two grounds: first, self-determination has not as yet been conclusively established as an international legal right; and second, the principle of self-determination, which has developed primarily in connection with European decolonization, does not at present apply to a case such as that of Quebec or French Canada.

Although an attempt might be made to extend that right by analogy to "national" groups wishing to secede from the political communities to which their members belong, it seems clear that this is not as yet an accepted construction of the right to self-determination. Given the vexing ambiguity of nationalist concepts, it is no wonder that international lawyers, who exercise a Burkean circumspection in these matters, have been reluctant to venture into that "great Serbonian bog, betwixt Damiata and Mount Casius old, where armies whole have sunk."[7]

This leaves us, then, with the fourth and final alternative which might be called the Hobbesian hypothesis, after the seventeenth-century political philosopher who presented this argument in its most convincing form. Viewing the maintenance of life and limb as the first and foremost goal of human beings, Hobbes argued that individuals have an absolute right to preserve themselves; that is to say, a person can justifiably do anything to save them self if their life is in danger. One can see that this reasoning might be readily transferred to a province or nation which believes its existence is threatened, and, indeed, Hobbes himself actually applied the same sort of analysis to the field of international relations, arguing that states have an absolute right to act in any way they deem necessary to preserve themselves.

Apart from the fact that Hobbes explicitly denied the exercise of this right to all subordinate entities in a state so long as there was a sovereign effectively maintaining the peace, this line of reasoning founders as soon as one appreciates the idiosyncratic way in which Hobbes uses the term "right." Neither the natural right of individuals nor the parallel right of sovereign states entails duties; that is to say, there is no duty laid upon any given individual or state to respect the natural right of others, nor is there any duty laid upon the others to respect the rights of the given individual or state. The right of each individual and of each state is not limited by the requirement of respecting the rights of others. *Absolute* natural rights are not logically speaking part and parcel of a moral order, but the symbol of the absence of a moral order. Therefore, if Quebec is considered to have this kind of right, it does not follow that the rest of Canada has a duty to respect it.

It should be apparent now that those Canadians who speak of Quebec's absolute right to self-determination, if their words are taken literally, have left the world of moral discourse behind them. For they are saying that Quebec, unilaterally and without regard to the rest of the country, must possess the freedom to organize its affairs as it sees fit, and that the rest of the country has an unlimited obligation to stand aside while Quebec does this. The logical weakness of this position, as we have seen, is that conditions are enunciated in which right is entirely on one side and duty entirely on the other, which means in fact that there is neither right nor duty. The practical difficulty is that one is not speaking of two communities which are already sovereign and distinct from one another, but of a single country which is to be broken apart, and it is absurd to think that the group which is proposing to secede should or could be permitted unilaterally to dictate the conditions of secession on the understanding that the other group would be committed willy-nilly to accept and respect them. *Real politik* is preferable to this kind of absolutist morality.

I would argue, then, that the claim that Quebec possesses a right to self-determination is either mistaken or else it is a misleading and unfortunate way of saying something worthwhile and important: namely, that the values of civility to which Canadians aspire, and which they sometimes achieve, preclude the application of force to stop a secessionist movement of the kind contemplated, and that civilized values are in this case backed up by plain ordinary self-interest, since the group in question is large enough to knock the whole political system off its foundations if its settled desires go unrecognized for too long.

Edmund Burke is no doubt *persona non grata* with some of the people who assert Quebec's absolute right to self-determination, but he nevertheless displayed a wonderful capacity to talk sense, and he was clearly on the "right" side in the American struggle for independence in the eighteenth century. He refused to discuss the issues involved in that controversy in terms of abstract rights. "It is not," he writes in his *Speech on Conciliation with America*, "what a lawyer tells me I *may* do; but what humanity, reason and justice tell me I ought to do. Is a politic act the worse for being a generous one? Is no concession proper, but that which is made from your want of right to keep what you grant? Or does it lessen the grace or dignity of relaxing in the exercise of an odious claim, because you have your evidence-room full of titles, and your magazines stuffed with arms to enforce them? What signify all those titles, and all those arms? Of what avail are they, when the reason of the thing tells me, that the assertion of my title is the loss of my suit; and that I could do nothing but wound myself by the use of my own weapons?"[8]

Burke's lesson is as timely today as when he wrote, and it is instructive to note that his argument was directed against the dogmatic assertion of right in Great Britain, not in America. The moral is applicable to both sides of the controversy. Where there is basic conflict between two segments of a political community, argument about absolute rights is of little help. It is misleading. It engenders needless opposition (and perhaps the wrong kind of support). And it encourages the development of hardened positions which are relatively impermeable to negotiation, rather than a spirit of toleration, or at least a willingness to recognize limits beyond which action will be mutually destructive. If either side construes the issue as one of "national honour," "absolute rights" and "the integrity of the state," then the outlook will be bleak indeed; if, on the other hand, it is viewed less dramatically as a conflict about the institutional arrangements appropriate to the two communities, there is at least the possibility that if we have to take the trip we shall all arrive at our destination (whatever it may be) uninjured, and – who knows? – perhaps even the better for our journey.

NOTES

1 Abraham Rotstein, "Symbolic Formula for Quebec," *The Canadian Forum*, March 1971, 410.
2 Canada, Parliament, *Special Joint Committee of the Senate and of the House of Commons on the Constitution of Canada, Final Report*, 28th Parl, 4th Sess., May 29, 1972.
3 Pierre de Bané and Martin Asselin, "Quebec's Right to Secede," *The Canadian Forum*, May 1972, 8–11.
4 Bané and Asselin, "Quebec's Right," 10.
5 J.D. Mabbott, *The State and the Citizen* (London: Arrow Books, 1958), p.58.
6 R.L. Watts's article "The Survival or Disintegration of Federations," in *One Country or Two?*, ed. R.M. Burns, (Montreal: McGill-Queen's University Press, 1971), 41–72 is useful here, and I am indebted to it.
7 John Milton, *Paradise Lost*, bk. II, lines 592–594.
8 *The Works of Edmund Burke*, vol. I, p.479

2 The Marketing of National Unity

In Donald N. Thompson et al., eds., *Macromarketing: A Canadian Perspective* 1980

A national business marketing association got in touch with the Privy Council Office, asking to have someone come to speak to them about how the government of Canada was marketing national unity to Canadians, and particularly to Quebecers. The government was investing heavily in this priority, and the association members were interested in understanding the strategy and its implementation. I was picked to go to the association to make the presentation on the topic. What I remember most vividly about the encounter was the severe criticism I received for the amateurishness of the federal government's strategy, at least as I had presented it to the group.

National Unity and Marketing

Someone recently asserted that the unity crisis constituted the biggest macro-marketing challenge of them all. In this paper I plan to look at the crisis in Confederation from this angle. I propose to begin by making some general remarks and by entering a caveat – or should I say a caveat emptor – and then to proceed to describe the activities of two bodies, the Canadian Unity Information Office and the Task Force on Canadian Unity.

First the caveat. I am adopting what I understand to be a marketing perspective for the purpose of discussion and to permit concentration on certain aspects of the "unity debate," as it is often called. I remain agnostic (at the very least) as to whether that is the most appropriate or comprehensive perspective for approaching the issues which are now troubling Canada. I do not believe that, taken on its own, a marketing perspective is at all an adequate framework within which to confront Quebec nationalism and the strong regional pressures of other parts of Canada.

A marketing perspective is not sufficient as the exclusive or *primary* approach to national unity if it is the case, as I think it is, that there are genuine inequities in the distribution of benefits and burdens among the people of Canada and genuine deficiencies in our political system and public policy processes. Our federal system, alas, is not the equivalent of a Maytag washing machine which (so they say) never needs repair; we have got problems, and they need to be resolved. It is therefore, I suspect, beyond the reach even of the arcane and powerful arts of the advertising world to persuade people that what is going wrong with their country is, in fact, going right. I believe that our traditional political concepts and vocabulary which refer to such things as the satisfying of grievances, the righting of injustices, and the achievement of reform are more serviceable in this respect than the notions of market research, product development, and sales promotion.

It is nevertheless my impression that the marketing approach may help in understanding a good deal about the issue of unity and may provide a line of action which bears directly on certain significant aspects of the problem. What the approach holds out for us is, first, a methodology for studying or analyzing the problem, and second, a strategy for solving the problem so analyzed.

As a methodology, marketing falls presumably within the general realm of social psychology and directs our attention to the springs of human behaviour – in this case, to the motivations of Canadians. What are the hopes and fears of the Québécois that animate and support the forces of nationalism in the province? What are the attitudes of Canadians in other parts of the country? How is the behaviour of one group interpreted by the other and how does that contribute to disunity? If the experience of the Task Force is any guide, such questions as these are fascinating, important, and extremely difficult to handle systematically.

As a strategy, the marketing approach, as we will see in a moment, presents a wide array of possible actions, all of them designed to communicate information and to structure opinion in ways that enhance the unity of the country. But what is Canadian unity? How does one establish what the factors are which contribute to disunity in a country? You would probably get more people in this country to agree that disunity is a problem than to agree on precisely what it entails or how important it is. Some would contend that it is at bottom a phony crisis, and is in reality the best trick yet devised by one part of the country to extract benefits from the rest. Some would identify the major threat to unity as being the intention of the government of Quebec to hold a referendum. Others would argue that the referendum is merely symptomatic of deeper structural forces that are transforming Quebec society and the rest of the country and their relations with one another. Still others would insist that it is a problem of attitudes.

Who is right? And, more to the point, how does one decide who is right? One suspects intuitively that each opinion expresses a fragment of the whole, but that no such single point of view captures the truth of the matter comprehensively. While it is necessary to make use of all the resources of social science – survey and interview data, historical scholarship, economic analysis, and so forth – one must go beyond this to arrive at even a rough appreciation of the thing itself. What we fall back on, *faute de mieux*, is our best judgment of people, circumstance, and opportunity, our general experience of life, common sense – in short, those non-quantifiable qualities which are an essential component of political wisdom.

There is another factor that bears on our discussion, and that is the difference between a practical definition of the problem and a theoretically satisfactory definition of the problem. While intellectually, one may appreciate the comprehensive nature of the issue and its manifold ramifications, in practice one will behave as if the issue was much narrower and more amenable to specific reform than it really is.

Most countries have had, at some point in their history, periods of acute difficulty in which the danger of fragmentation and even collapse has been great. Many have, in fact, collapsed. One has only to look at the forces of regional separation at work in such historic states as Britain, France, and Spain to realize how prevalent they are. The United States fought a civil war in the last century on the subject of national unity; Nigeria and Pakistan fought civil wars in this century for the same reason. It is not just empires that rise and fall, but countries as well. The causes of such occurrences are as varied as human personality and circumstances themselves.

A crisis of national unity, in Canada or elsewhere, is typically a crisis of disintegration in which certain centrifugal forces threaten to break the country apart. To speak more precisely of those centrifugal forces, I cannot do better than to quote the Task Force on Canadian Unity. In their final report, *A Future Together*, the Commissioners write:

> We believe that the heart of the present crisis is to be discovered in the intersecting conflicts created by two kinds of cleavages in Canadian society and by the political agencies which express and mediate them. The first and more pressing cleavage is that old Canadian division between "the French" and "the English." We will consider the present configuration of this historic problem of Canadian duality in a moment. The second cleavage is that which divides the various regions of Canada and their populations from one another. Regionalism, like duality, also has an extended lineage in Canadian social, economic, and political life, and we pursue this matter subsequently as well.
>
> Both duality and regionalism, then, are deeply rooted in our history and are major elements in the social and economic foundation of Canada. The shape of

these two structural forces of Canadian life has altered quite rapidly in the last quarter of a century as power has shifted within and between various groups and as their aspirations have changed.

In our judgment, the first and foremost challenge facing the country is to create an environment in which duality might flourish; the second is to provide a fresher and fuller expression of the forces of regionalism in Canada's constitutional system and power structure. We wish to emphasize that it is in the context of the *present* crisis that we assign priority to these two, and we do so for a very simple reason. Each, if ignored or left unsatisfied, has the power to break the country, and each must accept the other if a new period of harmony is to be achieved.[1]

For the Task Force, the present crisis of unity is shaped primarily by the existence of significant linguistic, cultural, and regional differentiation – in their vocabulary, by the forces of duality and regionalism. If one could pick and choose the kind of problems one would prefer to work on, these might not be the forces one would select, but they do seem to correspond fairly closely to the actual character and dynamic of the crisis as it has unfolded in Canada.

I have briefly explored the link between disunity and the threat of national disintegration. What of unity? Is it enough to say that national unity exists and the problems disappear when the forces of disintegration are stilled? Is unity the absence of disunity? Obviously, one could be forgiven for thinking that something was going right if the voices raised in regional and "dualist" complaint fell silent. But a certain kind of silence would make one uneasy. It is important to understand the causal factors that lie behind the expressions of grievance and the reason why they have ceased, in order to be able to appreciate the character of the problems the country faces and to assess whether they have been genuinely resolved. There is, for example, the calm before the storm, and the silence of fear or hopelessness. Neither of these is soil in which the seed of national unity can be readily sown.

Let us return for a moment to the words of the Task Force Report. It speaks of unity as follows:

> It is the sum of conditions upon which the various communities and governments of Canada agree to support and sustain the Canadian state. As such, it endows each of the parts with something it would not have if it stood alone. It is, then, a just union of constituent elements, or, as one dictionary puts it, a harmonious combination of parts.[2]

The significant element in this definition is the notion of consent or agreement, for it is that which supports and defines the character of national unity. Canadians seek a union which is grounded in the freely offered consent of the citizens of the country.

The French writer Ernest Renan offered the following definition of a nation: "Une nation, c'est un plébiscite de tous les jours."[3] The notion of a continuing, daily plebiscite directs our attention not only to the quite serious limitations attendant upon any *single* consultation with the people (such as Quebec referendum), but also to the heart of what constitutes the unity of a country, namely, the sustaining consensus expressed by individuals in everyday acts of loyalty and acceptance.

All this may seem to roam a long distance from the subject of marketing, but it indicates the nature and outer limits of activity in this field. It is my layman's belief that in normal marketing situations the object of the exercise is pretty clear. No matter how lovingly the market survey is carried out, or how sophisticated the sales pitch may be, the central and sustaining goal is to get the consumer to consume the product you are selling. And in most cases you know pretty clearly what it is you are selling. That is not the case with national unity; it is not always clear precisely what you are selling, and it is not always obvious when someone has bought it.

I would think this point of differentiation applies even in comparison to such diffuse macro-marketing projects as improving national fitness or educating the public to use energy more efficiently. In those cases, a range of appropriate consequential behaviour, given the goal of the marketing operation, would be fairly clear and fairly readily measurable. But what would be appropriate "unity behavior," and how would one measure the degree to which it had emerged? It would appear that in such a case as this, the challenge outreaches the methodology. It is here that a narrower definition of the problem renders the work at once more manageable and less comprehensive. If one approaches unity from the perspective of the referendum which is to be held in Quebec, it becomes quite easy to say what "unity behavior" is – namely, opposing the referendum. And yet we know perfectly well that that is only a part of the truth.

In addition, with the marketing of national unity the consumer is a citizen in a democratic society and the issue is his allegiance to the country of which he is a member. The goal of the marketing operation cannot be to instil unjustified fear or to peddle phony propaganda about the country and its prospects. It is one thing to advise that one fear what is fearful, quite another to encourage fear where such an emotion is without rational foundation. This will be something to watch out for on all sides as the debate heats up in the months prior to the referendum. Despite not infrequent charges of "psychological terrorism" and "fear campaigns," it seems to me that the national unity discussion so far has been remarkably free from such tendencies. The next few months or years are likely to provide a much stiffer test of the "procedural fairness" in all of us. It is obvious that the event which pushed the question of national unity to the forefront was the election of the Parti Québécois as the government of Quebec on November 15, 1976. It is the two and a half years since then that will be the period on which this article will focus, and it is the activity of two federally based agencies that will receive direct attention. One is the Canadian Unity Information Office, a unit within the government of Canada, and the other the Task Force on Canadian Unity, an independent commission of enquiry established by the government of Canada.

The Task Force on Canadian Unity

The Task Force on Canadian Unity was created during the summer of 1977 and received a mandate with three basic elements:

- to support, encourage and publicize the efforts of the general public, and particularly those of voluntary organizations, with regard to Canadian unity
- to contribute the initiatives and views of the commissioners concerning Canadian unity, and
- to advise the government of Canada on unity issues

It was created under the Inquiries Act and thus enjoyed the status and independence from government of a royal commission. The eight commissioners held hearings and attended meetings of all kinds across Canada from September 1977 to April 1978. In the summer and fall of 1978, the Task Force consulted with experts, worked with its staff and tested its ideas with many people in informal meetings as it prepared its final reports.

These reports were published in the first three months of 1979. The first, which appeared in January, was *A Future Together*, and contained the observations and recommendations of the Task Force. The second, *Coming to Terms*, appeared in February and provided what was, in effect, a primer for the unity debate – that is, extended definitions of the meaning of critical terms and a good deal of information about the Canadian political system and the main constitutional options in contention. The third, *A Time to Speak*, was released in March and provided an account of the Task Force's national tour (in which many of the volume's readers would have themselves participated).

I would suggest that the "promotional function" of the Task Force was much less important than its role as an animator and as a policy body in the widest sense. If simply to raise the profile of an issue or thing is to market it, then clearly the Task Force was heavily involved in marketing, but I think the main contributions of the Task Force lay elsewhere.

During the winter of 1977–8 when it was engaged in its national tour, it functioned very much as a citizen animator and as a conduit for the expression of public opinion on the unity issue. Its visit to each of fifteen cities across Canada served as a focal point for the activity of local unity groups and an opportunity for private citizens to speak their mind. The media provided extensive coverage, and thus helped to ensure that people in other parts of Canada heard what was on the minds of the people in a particular region.

Thus, the function of the tour and the active public discussion that it involved was to raise the consciousness of Canadians about the challenge to national unity and to permit Canadians to express their own views on their country and its prospects. It was not the function of the Task Force at that stage to promote a particular view of the country or of its constitutional system, but to permit the citizens of Canada to speak for themselves.

The second aspect of the Task Force's role was the provision of policy advice in the widest sense, that is to say, the sharing with the government of Canada and with Canadians in general of its ideas on the country, its problems and possible reforms. That was the job which preoccupied the Task Force from the summer of 1978 until the conclusion of its work. One might say that the Task Force was more involved with the creation of the product than with its sale and promotion. Indeed, the irony is that, consistent with the customary practice of royal commissions, it wound up its operations just as the promotional phase was needed. It has been left to others, or to the commissioners acting individually and privately, to sell the final report and its recommendations.

With these points in mind, consider the other organization under discussion, the Canadian Unity Information Office. It was created at about the same time as the Task Force, but its responsibilities were significantly different and fell much more directly into a broadly defined marketing perspective.

The Canadian Unity Information Office

The story of the Canadian Unity Information Office and its activities properly begins with the prior creation of another organization, the Coordination Group of the Federal-Provincial Relations Office. This unit, popularly known as the Tellier Group, was established three months after the election of the Parti Québécois. Headed by Paul Tellier, who is a deputy secretary to the Cabinet, and made up of a half-dozen senior officers, it was designed to provide a focus for the government of Canada's thinking on national unity, to prepare information and advice to assist the government in the decisions it was to make, and in general to develop and implement a Canadian unity strategy. After the PQ victory, the Canadian government found, not surprisingly, that it was not organized to deal in a coherent fashion with the challenge from the government of Quebec. The Coordination Group was the main organizational response to this lack within the federal public service.

To carry out its role, the Group has fulfilled the following functions:

- making periodic general evaluations of the Canadian unity situation
- anticipating the strategy and tactics of the Parti Québécois
- ensuring the coordination from a Canadian unity point of view of the activities of the main government departments and agencies

- assessing the criticism of federalism and the program and policies of the federal government expressed by the government of Quebec or the Parti Québécois and advising the government of Canada on possible reactions; and
- planning, developing, and supervising the implementation of an information program in the area of Canadian unity

This last function really carries over into the domain of the Canadian Unity Information Office. It soon became evident to members of the Coordination Group and others that one thing that was woefully lacking was a coherent, vigorous information program on the part of the federal government. A great country-wide surge of interest in Canadian unity followed in the wake of the election of the PQ and revealed that Canadians concerned about the future of their country had surprisingly little in the way of documentation and analysis, displays, systems for exchanges with people in other parts of the country, information kits for school children, and so forth, which would permit productive discussion and citizen participation in the issue. It also revealed that there was widespread ignorance of the federal system of government and how it operated in Canada, an ignorance to which government inactivity on this front was a contributing factor. It was in this atmosphere that both the CUIO and the Task Force on Canadian Unity were conceived and born.

The CUIO was established in August 1977 as the operational information arm of the Coordination Group with a mandate to carry out the following broad functions:

- to gather, develop and distribute information and documentation designed to acquaint Canadians with issues relating to Canadian unity
- to respond to requests for information from individuals and organizations on matters relating to Canadian unity
- to guide and advise groups seeking assistance with projects promoting Canadian unity; and
- to work in cooperation with federal departments to help coordinate those components of their information programs relating to Canadian unity

At the outset, the CUIO was established with a staff of fewer than two dozen people, limited financial resources and an enormous, but very unfocussed assignment. In the period following its establishment, the small nucleus of staff at CUIO sought to define its goals and organize its work, and to determine *who* should be reached with *what* message.

It is at this point that the question of a comprehensive as distinct from a narrow definition of the issue arose. If the election of the PQ and the prospect of an impending referendum occasioned the creation of the CUIO, it was a genuine question of whether and how these factors should define the work of the Office. Partly because of these factors and partly because of the limitation on resources, it was decided that the primary target audience initially would be the population of Quebec.

As for the message which was to be conveyed to Quebecers, it was decided that, during the indeterminate period which was to precede the referendum campaign proper, the referendum vote would not directly constitute the defining focus for the Canadian Unity Information Office's activities. During the first phase of operations a broader definition of the problem was accepted, relating to the strength of attachment of Quebecers to Canada and Confederation. The communications effort was devoted to painting a portrait of Canada and of what Quebecers derive from being Canadians, showing that they benefit from the wide range of federal government services and programs available to all citizens, and generally making them more aware of the positive effects of federal government activity. It is obvious that this general communications strategy is more suitable to the period prior to the referendum campaign, and that information and communications activities more directly related to the actual vote would be more appropriate during the campaign itself for any body that chooses to participate actively in that process.

There are three general activities in which the Canadian Unity Information Office is engaged. First, there is its role as a documentation centre, assembling kits on unity subjects (of which some 23,000 have been distributed), summarizing and analysing speeches and papers on Canadian unity (of which some 600 have been done), and filing and cross-referencing under 200 subject heads data from publications, press, radio and T.V. Second, there is the role of the CUIO as a research and analysis unit, preparing rebuttals to the major PQ criticisms of the Federal system, drafting material for speakers' kits, and so on.

The third role involves the unit in publishing, distribution, and public relations, and this is an activity which is perhaps worthy of some expansion here. The five broad categories of work are as follows.

Publications and Distribution

CUIO has prepared a wide variety of publications dealing with Canada in general, its political system, and federal programs and services. As of April 1979, 24-million copies of this material have been distributed via mailing lists, through members of Parliament, on display stands in federal buildings, in exhibitions, and in response to advertising. This material is targeted at a wide audience, although there is as well a series of more technical studies designed to provide a database for federalist spokesmen. Five papers in this latter series have been produced so far on trade realities and economic association, the concept of sovereignty-association, the textile industry, transportation, and Quebec's access to capital markets.

Exhibitions

There are three main types of exhibits to be noted here. First, the CUIO has pre-pared and administers two travelling exhibitions, shown in shopping centres across Canada, entitled "Notre chez nous – It's all ours," which feature Canada's beauty and natural characteristics as a country. Second, the Office has developed and administers five exhibitions entitled "Libre service – Self-service," which describe federal programs and contributions to five regions of Quebec (Bas-St-Laurent, Gaspésie, Mauricie-Bois-Francs, Saguenay-Lac-St-Jean, Montreal, and Quebec). These exhibitions are tailored to each region and are shown in motorized trailers. Third, there are several information kiosks and special exhibits during the summer months which distribute information on Canadian unity.

Advertising

The CUIO has initiated several advertising campaigns designed to inform Que-becers of the diversity of programs and services offered by the federal govern-ment, and to inform Quebecers of certain aspects of Canadian federalism. One specific example is "the Beavers" campaign, which publicizes the list of federal departments which are at the service of the people of Canada. Another exam-ple is the series of maps which appear in Quebec shopping centres and in the Montreal metro informing citizens of the locations of federal offices. A third example is the "notes on federalism" series of advertisements, which is being run in Quebec weekly newspapers.

The CUIO also plays a coordination role vis-à-vis the advertising of the fed-eral government, reviewing all major advertising programs of federal depart-ments from a Canadian unity point of view.

Audio-Visual

The CUIO in connection with the National Film Board is producing two 30-minute films, which will be ready for release in September. One is aimed at Canadians in general and is designed to show with humour the foibles and prejudices of Canadians, while the other is directed at Quebecers in particu-lar, and is designed to demonstrate that being a Quebecer and being a Cana-dian are perfectly compatible. The Office has also been developing a series of audio-visual presentations aimed at the Quebec market dealing with aspects and advantages of the federal system and Canada. The Office, also in conjunc-tion with the National Film Board, produced a film to accompany the music of the national anthem, and this film is used by many T.V. stations as their sign-off at the end of the day.

Liaison and Special Projects

Finally, the CUIO is working with 95 federal departments and agencies and with crown corporations to ensure that their information and publicity programs inform Canadians about Canada and the role of the government of Canada as well as about the specific services which the given department provides.

Concluding Remarks

One point that comes rapidly to mind in considering the work and experience of these two organizations is that there is a widespread and quite natural tendency among citizens and observers to regard government information and promotion programs with a certain scepticism. Both the Task Force and the Canadian Unity Information Office began their lives in the midst of criticism that they were little more than propaganda arms of the Liberal Government.

We have seen that the Task Force was structurally independent of the government and that its central role in any case was not directly to promote Canadian unity, but to stimulate public discussion of the subject, to study it, and to offer policy advice. The Task Force gradually extricated itself from the atmosphere of suspicion in which it was born, and I should think that the publication of the *Final Report* washed away the last vestiges of such sentiment.

With the CUIO the structural situation was and remains today quite different, for it is properly and explicitly an agency of the government of Canada. While one may choose to question the expenditure of public funds on such activities or the efficiency with which the funds have been spent, it must, at the same time, be recognized that it is inevitable that any institution involved in education, information or communications will have a point of view of some kind, and that the orientation of the CUIO is federal and Canadian. But surely one would not expect anything else from an agency of the government of Canada. When looking at the actual activities of the Canadian Unity Information Office, it is evident that the vast majority of the things which it does fall into two broad categories: in the first category, the Office informs Canadians about Canada, about their federal system of government and about the role of the government of Canada in their lives; in the second, it seeks ways of strengthening Canadian identity and the sense of patriotism of Canadians. The CUIO is thus in part trying to do what many Canadian educators have said for a long time needs desperately to be done. Canadians are notoriously ignorant of their country and lack a common attachment to national symbols; there seems little doubt that this renders the country more vulnerable to threats of disunity and fragmentation. The CUIO is attempting to repair some of the omissions of the past and to establish a more solid foundation of knowledge and sentiment for the future.

There is an irony in all of this. The Task Force and the CUIO would not have been created if the election of the PQ and the consequent threat to Canadian unity had not occurred. If the supporters of unity, as exemplified by such bodies as these, are successful in their efforts, we may end up with a country much stronger than before. If we do, who can deny that we will owe something to Mr. Lévesque and his supporters for that advance?

This is simply yet another example of the application of Dr. Johnson's hoary dictum that, when a man knows he is to be hanged in a fortnight, it concentrates his mind wonderfully. Dr. Johnson ought to know. If I remember correctly, he wrote *Rasselas* in 48 hours to pay for his mother's funeral.

NOTES

1 Canada, Task Force on Canadian Unity, *A Future Together: Observations and Recommendations* (Ottawa: Minister of Supply and Services Canada, 1979), 21.
2 Canada, Task Force on Canadian Unity, *A Future Together*, 6.
3 Ernest Renan, *Qu'est-qu'une nation?*, lecture delivered at a conference at the Sorbonne, Paris, 11 March 1882.

3 Lord Durham Then and Now

Journal of Canadian Studies **1990**

I was asked to give the Morton Lecture in May 1989 at Trent University, where I had formerly taught. At the time I was deputy minister of intergovernmental affairs in the government of Ontario, and it was with difficulty that I carved out the time required to prepare this address. Yet I found it very productive to be asked to reflect systematically on a number of the large forces and energy fields that were pulsating through Canadian life. The final three paragraphs on compromise and living together were added some time after I had completed the paper, but they are needed, I believe, to complete the thinking that supports the analysis.

Royal Observations on the Lord

Queen Beatrix of the Netherlands visited Canada a year ago. While she was here, Her Majesty gave an address before both Houses of Parliament in Ottawa. Figuring largely in her remarks, along with William of Orange, Mary Stuart, and the Glorious Revolution of 1688, was Lord Durham, of whom the Queen said:

> In Canada in 1839 Lord Durham laid the foundations for a democratic form of government in his *Report on the Affairs of British North America*. On the basis of the "responsible government" principle he entrusted the government of the colony to the colonists themselves. The policy of placing the responsibility for government with the people was thereby extended to Canada.[1]

It is not hard to understand the *frisson* of anxiety that started up in the breasts of those listening to the Queen's address, for she had touched a nerve in the

Canadian body politic by mentioning Durham at all on a ceremonial occasion of this kind, and – worse still – by mentioning him *favourably*.

It would, I presume, be *lèse majesté* to suggest that Queen Beatrix had been maladroit and undiplomatic in making this comment, so I will simply say that her advisers, Dutch and Canadian, failed her by not expunging the Durham reference, in order to ensure that the address was kept as anodyne as these addresses are meant to be.

Both the Queen's statement and the *frisson* which followed contain within them the seeds of much of what I have to say tonight. For the Queen may have been ill advised in what she said, but she was not wrong; the Durham *Report*[2] did stoutly affirm the principles of responsible government as the way to compose the ills common to all five of Britain's North American possessions, if not the disease specially afflicting Lower Canada. What Queen Beatrix did *not* mention about the Durham *Report* is the other thing Lord Durham said, the thing which made the Queen's Canadian listeners uneasy – namely, that the French in North America had to be obliterated as a nationality if peace, progress, and social equality were to prevail. The anxiety occasioned by the Queen's remarks is a good indication that the *Report*'s currency continues, that it is a document of contemporary significance, at the very least at the level of political folklore.

My purpose here is to begin with an assessment of Lord Durham's diagnosis and prescription, then to offer some thoughts about the evolution of English-French relations in Canada and about the increasingly important phenomenon of multiculturalism. That context will provide the occasion to reflect on some · of the conceptual and practical issues that attend the attempt to find a happy home for both liberal principles and cultural pluralism within the framework of a single political community.

The Canadas in Lordly Perspective

To put it mildly, there have never been many fans of Lord Durham in French-speaking Canada, and it is not hard to see why. Radical Jack Durham was an uncomfortable colleague even for many of his British aristocratic associates, not only because of his gritty and unbending commitment to advanced social and political views, but also because of his prickly, austere and, at times, arrogant demeanour. Indeed, for some of his British colleagues, one of the not inconsiderable advantages of Durham taking on his commission in British North America was that it would keep him out of Britain for a while. With his own political allies feeling this way about him, it is not, perhaps, surprising that he did not go down well with the French Canadians of Lower Canada either.

But, more to the point, Durham was an enthusiastic British imperialist who saw the hand of God and destiny in the ultimate domination of the entire North American continent by the English people, "the great race which must, in the lapse of no long period of time, be predominant over the whole North American Continent." The resources of British North America, Durham declared, "are the rightful patrimony of the English people, the ample appanage which God and Nature have set aside in the New World for those whose lot has assigned them but insufficient portions in the Old."[3] Hardly a reassuring point of view for the French community that had inhabited the banks of the St. Lawrence for more than a century by the time he visited British North America.

In addition, with a candour characteristic of an earlier age, Lord Durham launched a merciless and scathing attack on the French Canadians, who clung "to ancient prejudices, ancient customs and ancient laws, not from any strong sense of their beneficial effects, but with the unreasoning tenacity of an un-educated and unprogressive people." Retaining "their peculiar language and manners," they were a people with no history and no literature, "an old and stationary society in a new and progressive world."[4] These powerful, declarative statements have echoed down the years on both sides of the language divide, shaping prejudices and perceptions through the generations. Small wonder that French-speaking Canadians have customarily remembered Durham for his English ethnocentrism, not for his liberalism, and have regarded him warily as a kind of pit-bull terrier of the British imperial establishment.

Yet these two convictions, namely, his belief in the superiority and mission of the English race and his commitment to the progress of liberty in the world, co-existed without apparent difficulty in Lord Durham's mind and received synthetic expression in the pages of his *Report*.

Living, as we do, in a more relativistic and culturally sensitive age, we find Durham's comfortable reconciliation of liberalism, cultural superiority, and empire to be a good deal more problematic than he did, and his confident as-sertion that God Himself has had a hand in establishing the dominion of the English-speaking people in North America more a rationalization than an ar-gument. But anyone who consults the political literature of Victorian England will be aware that Lord Durham was far from unusual in holding this combina-tion of opinions. He is not the only Englishman of enlightened views to break his liberal lance on the tough hide of empire.

Durham's views place him squarely in the John Stuart Mill camp as far as the re-lationship between cultural pluralism and liberty is concerned. "Free institutions," Mill wrote, "are next to impossible in a country made up of different nationali-ties."[5] The diversity which Mill so avidly sought in his liberal philosophy was a diversity of belief and ideas, not a diversity of ethnic origin, language, or culture.

The contrary view was ably stated by another famous Victorian liberal, Lord Acton, who, in a celebrated essay, wrote: "The co-existence of several nations under the same State is a test, as well as the best security of its freedom. It is also one of the chief instruments of civilization ... and indicates a state of greater advancement than the national unity which is the ideal of modern liberalism."[6]

For Canadians, who have been living *à la* Lord Acton both in freedom and in two national communities for more than a century, the contention of Lord Durham and John Stuart Mill is empirically doubtful and conceptually flawed. It is easy, then, for us to say that Lord Durham got it wrong. In the years since Durham's *Report* appeared people have been saying just that – in the brutally frank characterization of the French-Canadian community which he found, or thought he found, on the shores of the St. Lawrence, and in his prescription for its assimilation into the English community, Lord Durham blotted an otherwise masterful report to his Sovereign on the affairs of British North America.

Indeed, I think it is fair to identify this as the conventional historical understanding of Lord Durham and his *Report*. But, if we are not to inflict Whig history on a prominent nineteenth-century liberal – something, I suspect, which Lord Durham himself would not have hesitated to do to his own intellectual ancestors – we would do well to consider carefully why Lord Durham adopted such – from our point of view – wrong-headed views. He was, after all, a cultured intellectual of advanced social opinions, an able politician if a discomfiting cabinet colleague, a man with international experience, and a militant and uncompromising liberal, in both thought and action. In addition, despite its signal flaw, his *Report* is acknowledged to be one of the great state papers in the English language.

Why, then, did he get the French-Canadian issue wrong? The question is worth asking, I think, not simply as a matter of antiquarian interest, but because the answer may illuminate vexing issues which we continue to wrestle with in our national life. Durham's line of reasoning, I would suggest, can be summarized in a series of propositions.

1 French Canadians, while currently more numerous in Lower Canada than their English-Canadian compatriots, were destined with the passing of the years to be submerged numerically by the growing population of British settlers.
2 French Canadians were an amiable but backward people, quite incapable, with the existing constitution of their society and culture, of competing with the socially advanced and commercially competitive English community.
3 The organization and assignment of power in British North America, especially in Lower Canada, had to be made with a view to ensuring that stable government was established, social and economic progress was made possible, and liberal political principles were advanced.
4 This meant that a limited form of representative government had to be introduced, specifically, that the domestic affairs of the colonies had to become the responsibility of the colonists themselves. Thus, the advisers of the Queen's representative in Canada had themselves to be responsible in these matters to the popularly elected assembly.

5 This meant further that in Lower Canada the legislative assembly to which
the executive had to be responsible had itself to be dominated by English-
speaking Canadians, not by the French – hence the proposal of legislative
union of Lower and Upper Canada which would give the English a clear
majority in the single assembly.

These are, I think, the key points of Lord Durham's argument. Taken together, they fulfil his commission in British North America "for the adjustment
of certain important questions depending in the Provinces of Lower and Upper
Canada, respecting the form and future Government of the said Provinces." His
recommendations set the stage, he thought, for achieving a critical long-term
objective – namely, the gradual assimilation of the French Canadians into the
English community and, with that done, the receipt by the French Canadians of
all the benefits of social and economic progress, English style.

The Fault Line in Canadian Life

At the beginning of his *Report,* Lord Durham wrote that he had expected to
find "a contest between a government and a people," of a sort familiar to the
English for many generations. Instead, he found in Lower Canada "a struggle,
not of principles, but of races,"[7] and recognized in consequence that a simple
legal or constitutional reform that left the elements of society unaltered would
fail of its purpose. It is for this reason that the union of the two Canadas was
so critical; while admittedly a constitutional change in form, its object was to
compose Lower Canadian society differently. Durham's proposal, in response
to the 1837 troubles in Lower Canada, was to offer resolution by dissolution; he
resolved the problem of two warring nations by dissolving one into the other.

This was undoubtedly a recommendation based on *real politik* and on Durham's assessment of how best to protect and advance British imperial interests
in North America. It was also clearly grounded in an effort to meet the needs
and aspirations of the British colonists in North America, even if it was not
warmly received by all of them. But it is a recommendation which is rooted in
yet another species of rationale and justification, less frequently observed and
remarked on, but conceptually more interesting. Lord Durham proposed the
assimilation of French Canada into British North American nationality in part
because he believed that, in the final analysis, this was the best route to follow
to secure the interests, well-being, and future prospects of the French Canadians themselves. It is my impression that this was a genuine consideration,
although by no means the dominant one, in the framing of his analysis and
recommendations.

Any other approach, in his view, was likely to consign the French in British
North America to a status of perpetual inferiority, constrained by increasingly

antiquated social, cultural, and religious institutions, forced either to remain in stagnant backwaters while the real life of North America went on all about them or, alternatively, to seek escape from the increasingly untenable conditions of rural life by entering the cities and commercial establishments dominated by the English, and doing so at the most inferior level.

Consider Lord Durham's comment on what he deemed to be a relevant parallel in the United States. He wrote favourably of the experience of the French in Louisiana who, gradually adjusting themselves to the reality of life in English North America, learned to compete effectively – but in English – in the wider field of commerce and politics presented by the American union. An implicit bargain was struck, according to Lord Durham, decidedly to the advantage of the Acadians of Louisiana. They agreed to give up, over time, most of the active features of their nationality; in return, they received the opportunity of full and equal participation in the life and affairs of the American union. A choice as fateful presented itself to the French Canadians of British North America, and the moral and prudential calculus led, in his opinion, to the same conclusion. What are we to make of all this?

The troubles which brought Lord Durham to Lower Canada were social and cultural in character and went to the core, not only of British North America's relatively brief history, but of whatever future it could construct for itself as well. That Durham saw the character and seriousness of the crisis is evident in his observation that a response which left the elements of society unaltered would fail. The relatively simple introduction of limited representative government in the other colonies would be sufficient to relieve the tensions there, but in Lower Canada that would not suffice. He saw the seriousness of the crisis clearly, but did not appreciate that it was in fact too serious – too structural – in its character to be successfully addressed by the means he suggested.

Without perhaps fully appreciating it, Durham was acting as a kind of social geologist, exploring the great fault line of British North America and of Canada itself as it emerged. The line dividing English and French was as primordial in the social geology of British North America in 1839 as it is in Canada today. If the society forming itself on the northern half of the continent were to crack, it would crack along that line. The point, then and now, is not to make futile efforts to erase the fault line, but to learn to live with it, and to render the social and political institutions of the country, as far as possible, earthquake proof. In the 1830s, the ancillary controversy over representative government was a problem that could, in principle, be solved; the relationship between French and English in North America was not. Indeed, it was not, in the same sense, a problem at all, but an existential reality to be acknowledged and accommodated, one which spawned a slew of problems, admittedly, but which was too intimately related to existence and identity to be considered a problem like the others.

It was this, I think, that Lord Durham failed to appreciate, probably because, like many another nineteenth-century liberal, he was insensitive to the power and durability of culture and nationality. By using the yardstick of progress to find French Canada grievously wanting and, therefore, of relatively little account, Durham allowed his analysis to lead him to a flawed conclusion – namely, that a society which he judged to be backward was, therefore, weak and without significant defense, and could be dismantled through peaceful and political means. He did not realize that that territory would not be won easily, if at all.

Indeed, it was the very effort to reconcile political liberty and cultural assimilation that was doomed to failure. A sufficient exercise of power may well keep the national sentiments of a subject people in check, at least for a time, although Mikhail Gorbachev, now struggling with the powerful expression of Georgian and other forms of nationalism in the Soviet Union, would no doubt have a rueful word to say about just how long that power has to be applied to ensure that the job of assimilation is done.

In the absence of that power, and in fact with the specific intent of establishing government based on consent, the notion that a numerically powerful minority could be assimilated through constitutional means – at least in the context of British North America – was doubtful in the extreme. The point was not that a free society was impossible *without* assimilation, but that, in Canada at least, it was impossible *with* it.

Not Mill and not Durham, but Lord Acton was the thinker who provided the intellectual foundation for the direction which British North America – despite Durham's *Report* – was already destined to take. The course British North America was set upon was not the suppression of one national community but the mutual accommodation of two, a development which was ultimately to play a key role in the fashioning of a federal system and the establishment of Canada.

It would be quite inaccurate to imply that the evolution of Canada in this way was the expression of some explicit collective preference. Certainly, on the part of the British in North America, it was more a matter of circumstance than volition. The capacity of the colonies scattered along the northern edge of the United States to do otherwise than they did was ultimately recognized to be fairly limited. The mutual accommodation of French and English, then, was a necessity, and, for many, a regrettable necessity. One might characterize a good deal of the history of French-English relations since that time, especially recent history, as an attempt to make a virtue of necessity. It is an enterprise that is still underway.

Making a Virtue of Necessity

If Lord Durham failed to appreciate the fact that British North America had, tacitly, settled on the path of cultural duality and accommodation between French and English, he was accurate beyond a shadow of a doubt in his sense of just how difficult that path, if taken, would be. As we have seen, one of his reasons for advocating assimilation was his belief that any other course would condemn French Canadians to perpetual inequality vis-à-vis their English-speaking compatriots. In this he was for a great many years substantially correct, for the effort to secure and maintain a settlement between French and English in Canada depended for more than a century on the existence of what might be called mutually compatible solitudes. On the French-Canadian side, this meant that the social and economic circumstances of French Canadians for generations appear not to have been materially different from those which Durham had predicted for them in the absence of integration into English-speaking North America.

By "mutually compatible solitudes," I mean to refer to the fact that the character and values of French-Canadian society were sufficiently different from those of English Canada that the scope for direct conflict and competition between the two was more restricted than it otherwise would have been. At the risk of oversimplification, one might point to an important dimension of the situation by saying that the English could get on with commerce and industry in the cities and the westward expansion of Canada if the French were prepared to satisfy themselves with a substantially agrarian lifestyle on the banks of the St. Lawrence. If a French Canadian during this period were to break out of the cycle of economic disadvantage, social inequality, and political weakness to which his community had been largely consigned, it could normally be done only with great difficulty and only if he were prepared to play the game *à l'anglais* and to leave his cultural baggage at the door before entering the trading halls of prosperity.

One would be hard pressed to describe this as an arrangement which was the product of free choice on the part of French Canadians. It was rather the situation as it emerged, but as such it constituted the terms of accommodation that were to govern French-English relations in Canada for more than a hundred years and that allowed two different communities (should I say "distinct societies"?) to live side by side within one country. Clearly, it was not ideology or culture, but circumstance and opportunity that tied French and English together.

The post-war period, and particularly the years since 1960, have seen French Canada's approach to ensuring its survival in North America evolve very rapidly. This has led both Quebec and the country as a whole to engage in fundamental reflection upon the destiny of Canada. Social and economic forces had been pushing Quebec towards the adoption of a new collective cultural strategy for generations, but the political and attitudinal transformation was substantial when it came, and it brought the two linguistic communities much more directly into contact and competition with each other. From a condition of mutually compatible solitudes, we moved to a condition in which the aspirations of the francophones of Quebec came directly into conflict with the English minority of the province and the assumptions of the rest of the country. With respect to a number of central public policy matters, such as the language regime in Quebec, it became a zero-sum game, for what the Québécois sought necessarily involved the denial of practices, assumptions and prerogatives that English Quebec had enjoyed for generations.

The irony is that it is at least in part the fact that French Quebec's values and aspirations have become more like those of English Canada, which has contributed to the conflict and tension that has marked much of our last thirty years. Quebecers have become the modem, secular, commercial, bustling society that Lord Durham thought they were incapable of becoming. But they have done it *en français* and collectively, not by assimilation.

Quebec's rapid evolution has been a major factor in the remarkable transformation of English-Canadian thinking about national identity. Several decades ago it would have been common ground for anglophones to think of Canada as an English-speaking country, a member of the family of British Commonwealth countries which happened to have a substantial French-speaking minority within its borders. It would have been understood that it was up to the minority to learn the language of the majority, even in the province of Quebec where the numbers told a different story. Today, the conventional English-Canadian understanding of Canada is that it is a country composed of two linguistic communities with two official languages. This is understood to imply that the country's common institutions will function in both official languages, will serve citizens in either language, and will offer career opportunities equally to members of both language communities. It has also produced a further, but far from complete, understanding of the duty to protect linguistic minorities. Bilingualism is now an acquirement of the professionally ambitious. The powerful and distinctively Canadian movement in favour of French-language immersion education is evidence of the degree to which these views have implanted themselves in the minds of many English-speaking Canadians. For many, historical necessity has become a contemporary virtue, and the French-English fact is celebrated as a defining characteristic of Canadian society.

While Québécois welcome both the institutional expression of Canadian official-language policy and its growing acceptance on the part of English Canadians, they would insist that this addresses but one dimension of the many-faceted reality they are confronting. In the final analysis, it is not the dimension most intimately related to the survival of French in North America.

The recognition of the equality of two official languages and the policy of institutional bilingualism in the organization and operations of the Canadian government is appropriate and necessary, given that the government serves two language communities. But that, for French-speaking Quebecers, does not imply that the institutions of Quebec society should equally reflect the two Canadian official languages.

During the past twenty-five years Québécois have aggressively used their control of the provincial government to establish a language regime which has significantly altered the face of Quebec. The object is to establish conditions in which French will survive and flourish as the dominant language in Quebec. The pursuit of linguistic dominance has involved confining the use of English and placing limits on the rights of the English-speaking minority in the province. The resurgence of linguistic conflict and an unfortunate increase in linguistic intolerance in Canada today suggests that the two language communities may be tragically "out of synch" with one another yet again, as they have been on several occasions in the past.

French-speaking Canadians discern at times a double standard and a generous dollop of hypocrisy in English Canada's outbursts about language. They could more readily accept the severe criticism of Quebec's Bill 178 and the use of the notwithstanding clause if it had been matched by equally severe criticism of Alberta and Saskatchewan. A few months before, both had acted to restrict the rights of the francophone minorities in their provinces which had just been confirmed by a decision of the Supreme Court.

Many English-speaking Canadians find Quebec's language policies incomprehensible and objectionable. Given the confidence and energy displayed by Quebec society today, English-speaking Canadians outside Quebec find it very difficult to appreciate how deeply seated Quebec's feelings of cultural insecurity continue to be. French is now an official language in Canada, English Canadians are fighting to get their children into immersion classes, francophones make up the vast majority of Quebec's population and the proportion is growing. English Canadians are inclined to ask, "How can they feel insecure about their language situation?"

The fact is that they do, and for a number of reasons. Their long struggle to endure in an indifferent or hostile environment, the galloping assimilation of most francophone minorities outside of Quebec, the dwindling population base in the Province, their tiny minority status in North America (about 2 per cent of the total continental population), the impact of American television and music on their young people, the English language's dominion over the computer and scientific worlds – all these factors play to Quebecers' sense of vulnerability and feed each successive language crisis as it arises.

I suspect we may not be far from the time when we will need, as a country, to establish a new basis of accommodation of our two national tongues. During the past twenty-five years, the English-Canadian sense of identity has increasingly encompassed the concept of cultural duality. In what direction have the Québécois been moving? A country whose two great language communities do not share a common sense of civic identity is unlikely, in the modern era, to remain tranquil and stable for long. What we have now is not simply differing language regimes animated by rather different values, but mutual incomprehension; Canadians, in many cases, honestly do not understand the reasons for what is happening linguistically in other parts of the country.

More generally, we have yet to achieve a settled and enduring answer to the issue Lord Durham raised 150 years ago: How can French-speaking Canadians exist on a footing of genuine equality with their fellow inhabitants of this vast continent and still remain true to themselves and their culture? Durham's flinty answer was that they cannot do both, and he was prepared, on their behalf, to have them give up culture for the sake of equality. Canadians rejected this prescription and have tried since that time to reconcile the two.

Immigration and Canadian Society

In his examination of the troublesome co-existence of two national communities within British North America, Lord Durham was tackling, as we have seen, large questions relating to the foundations of liberty and culture. Multiculturalism in Canada raises a parallel set of issues concerning the interplay between cultural pluralism and liberalism in modern societies, and it is to that matter I should like to turn. Cultural pluralism is now thoroughly entangled in our history, it is a rising force in our contemporary life, and it will most assuredly be central to our future destiny as a nation.

If one considers the non-native population of the country at the time of Confederation, it is a fair generalization to say that Canada was bicultural in its social composition. With the successive waves of immigration during the late nineteenth and twentieth centuries, Canada has become a multicultural society. In the 1986 Census, 40 per cent of Canadians reported that their culture or ancestry was other than totally French or British.[8]

Three points are germane to our story at this stage. First, immigration to Canada has benefited the English side of the French-English equation disproportionately. From Confederation until just after the Second World War, the high fertility rate of French-speaking Canadians counterbalanced the benefits that the English-speaking community derived from immigration and assimilation; at the same time it allowed the French to preserve their relative population position in the country at about 30 per cent. The situation has radically changed, to Quebec's disadvantage, since the 1960s. For the last twenty years, the fertility rate of Quebecers has been the lowest in the country, thus turning the "revenge of the cradles" argument on its head. Quebec's acute interest in immigration policy and its government's introduction in May 1988 of a $3,000 allowance for the third child in a family, now increased to $4,500, can be readily understood with these demographic facts in mind. They also explain, to an extent often not realized by Canadians living outside of Quebec, the Québécois preoccupation with language policy; from this perspective it is not so much the English minority in Quebec, but the immigrant population which is the crucial target of policies to give French clear predominance within the province.

The second point to underline is the shift in the parts of the world from which our immigrants have come. The regional origins of Canada's immigrants have altered substantially since Confederation, from Western Europe at the beginning, to Southern and Eastern Europe in the 1950s and 1960s, to Third World countries in the last two decades. With the introduction in 1967 of an immigration policy that eliminated preferences for particular national groups, there has been a dramatic change in the composition of Canadian immigration: 80 per cent of Canada's immigrants used to come from Europe or from countries of European heritage (like the US); now almost 75 per cent come from Asia, Africa, Latin America, and the Caribbean. Currently, Asian immigration accounts for about half the annual total. The size of the Canadian population born in Asia, Latin America and Africa increased by 340 per cent between 1971 and 1986.

The third point concerns the destination of immigrants arriving in Canada. Historically, a substantial proportion of Canada's immigrants came to make a better life for themselves in the rich and relatively undeveloped farmlands of the country. Today the situation is profoundly different. For one thing, post-war immigration has focused in particular on the provinces of Ontario and British Columbia to the disadvantage of Quebec and the Atlantic provinces. Less than 5 per cent of the population of the Atlantic provinces is foreign-born, and 8 per cent of Quebec's, as compared to 23 per cent of Ontario's and 22 per cent of BC's. If one looks exclusively at the size of Ontario's Canadian-born population, it is only 17 per cent larger than that of Quebec; if one adds in the foreign-born, Ontario is 30 per cent larger. For another thing, immigrants now come overwhelmingly to cities rather than to rural areas, and particularly to the larger metropolitan centres. Toronto, which for thirty years has received nearly twice its share of immigrants, has demonstrated the most rapid increase in ethnic diversity. Vancouver is the only other metropolitan area which consistently attracts more than its share of immigrants. Between 1976 and 1986, 90 per cent of Canada's immigration went to the country's eight largest metropolitan areas.

These, then, are some key facts about post-war Canadian immigration; it has benefited English Canada far more than Quebec; Canadian immigration now comes chiefly from Third World countries; and immigrants typically go to just a few Canadian provinces and almost exclusively to large metropolitan centres. In conjunction with this rapidly emerging demographic reality, there has been, over the past twenty-five years, a gradually expanding consciousness among Canadians of the importance of cultural pluralism. Along with that, both at the federal level and in the immigrant-receiving provinces, a chain of policy initiatives has attempted to recognize that growing reality and work it into our national life.

A concentration on ethnocultural traditions and folklore has been supplemented by a recognition of the necessity to establish conditions of equality and fair treatment in the workplace, in government and in the common institutions of society, whatever a person's cultural origin may be. Multiculturalism, which had historically been a relatively marginal feature of our cultural landscape, has, within the past twenty-five years, become a central force in Canadian life. A number of policy matters which will call for attention in the future are discernible in the forces at work at present.

With a low birth rate and an aging population in Canada, immigration becomes a strategic component of any national effort at population planning. Since its foundation, Canada has shaped its development and continually replenished its ranks by welcoming people from other lands, and, assuming the country is capable of absorbing newcomers adequately, immigration levels will likely need to be increased substantially in coming years if the country is to stave off population stagnation or decline. We have noted that immigration consistently favours the English-language community over the French-language community. That, combined with Quebec's extraordinarily low birth rate, is a rivetting reality for Quebec's francophones, but I would argue that it should be a matter of concern for English-speaking Canada as well.

Canadian society is constructed on the basis of the two great language communities. A serious weakening of one or the other should worry both. Who we are and what we stand for are in no small measure defined by the French-English fault line of which I spoke earlier, and by the ongoing accommodation of two language communities within a single state. If the French community in Quebec is seriously weakened over time by a low birth rate and only feeble replenishment of its population by immigration, it is likely that its self-perceived capacity to function effectively within Confederation will be called increasingly into question and more protective measures will be sought. All Canadians have an interest in the preservation within Confederation of a strong and confident Quebec. This being so, it seems clear to me that there is a concomitant interest in supporting Quebec's efforts to attract substantial numbers of immigrants who will integrate themselves into the francophone community.

For the Québécois there is some difficult terrain to traverse. Immigration has to be regarded not as a threat but as one of the keys to their cultural health and vitality. They face all the challenges any other part of the country faces with immigration – plus one, namely, language. Language not only acts as an impediment to increased levels of immigration, reducing the attractiveness of Quebec as a destination, but it is also an indispensable dimension of the integration process, if that process is to be accounted a success. The natural flow in the rest of the country, and, in the absence of government policy, even in Quebec, is towards English; no special effort is necessary to make sure that English will be the language of choice for immigrants in the rest of Canada. Not so in Quebec, which must fashion policies and arrangements to ensure that her immigrants adhere to the French community, if a potentially beneficial instrument is not to be turned back against the community as a destructive agent.

Another observation can be made on the basis of the aforementioned data. Without quite realizing it, Canadians are in the process of building a new country within the old one. The new country is composed of the large cities, especially the great metropolitan centres of Montreal, Toronto, and Vancouver. The old country is all the rest. Life in the former bears little resemblance to life in the latter, whether with regard to cultural expression, crime, the sense of neighbourhood, price and income levels, traffic, or the pace of life.

What has a small community like Peterborough, Ontario, got to do with Toronto, except for the fact that it too is finally being caught in the jet-stream of development radiating from the greater metropolitan area? I often think of the sentiments that must be aroused in the breast of an Ontarian who has lived his or her life in a small community and who visits Toronto periodically. There must be a sense of loss mixed with a feeling of wonderment – the loss of an urban centre you once knew and understood, and wonderment in the face of an urban landscape and mix of lifestyles that have become quite alien. It must be a bit like being a foreigner in your own country, with the underlying, disquieting realization that what you are visiting used to, in some greater sense, belong to you.

In Canada, one of the most significant agents of change is immigration, and its role in the transformation of our large cities is unlikely to abate. What this will probably mean is that Canada will increasingly be composed of a few, vast metropolitan centres which are riotously multicultural, surrounded by hinterlands where "old style" Canadians continue to live. And some parts of the country, such as most of Canada east of Montreal, will be virtually passed by in the process. The Canadian Human Rights Commissioner recently gave a speech on multiculturalism in which he spoke of federal employment equity legislation and the importance of achieving non-discriminatory employment practices and equitable representation of ethnocultural groups in the Canadian workplace. The speech was given in Montreal. Consider just how remote the message would have been had the speech been given in Chicoutimi, where well over nine out of ten residents are French in origin, or in St. John's, Newfoundland, which is 93 per cent British.

If, as seems likely, we continue to be a country with a low birth rate and high immigration levels, and we decline to engage in aggressive efforts to disperse newcomers to Canada over a wide geographical area, Canadians and their governments will need to prepare themselves to tackle the stresses and strains that are bound to arise more acutely in our large cities. We will also have to learn to cope with the increasing gulf between city and countryside and the fact that multicultural forces will likely become elements in the expression of Canadian regionalism in ways that they have never been before. The social and cultural character of Canada in the twenty-first century is likely to be determined as much by how we respond to immigration and cultural pluralism as by any other single factor.[9]

The Internationalization of Cultural Pluralism

It is often said that the world is small, and growing smaller. Another way of putting this, I think, is to say that more and more things, once thought to be purely domestic, are now caught in a web of international relationships and forces that significantly alter their flavour and character. We have to take account today of matters our forefathers never dreamed of. Certainly this is true of cultural pluralism. We have all recently witnessed the spectacle of an individual act of creation producing a paroxysm of cultural and religious anger on the other side of the globe, with subsequent reverberations felt right round the world.

Salman Rushdie, a distinguished English writer of Indian and Muslim origin, published *The Satanic Verses* in 1988. In February 1989 the Ayatollah Khomeini called for Rushdie's murder – or his execution, depending on your point of view – on the grounds that his novel was a blasphemy against the Muslim religion for which, according to the law of Islam, the sentence is death. Salman Rushdie has gone into hiding, in perfectly justified fear for his life, and a dozen countries, Asian and Western, have been wrestling with the controversy that this train of events has created.

The Satanic Verses, although innovative and, I suspect, mischievous in intent, is no joy to read. I know; I tried. I would hazard the guess that it is the least read and most discussed work of fiction in this century. But reading it, for those opposed to it, does not appear to be the point. The point is found in the book's very existence, for it manifestly performs a symbolic function of enormous importance. It has served as an instrument to demonstrate the purity and rigour of the more radical adherents of Islam. It is probably not unfair to say that it performed a more secular role as well, in assisting the Ayatollah in reawakening Iran's revolutionary fervour in the wake of the unhappy conclusion of the Iran-Iraq war.

For Westerners, the Rushdie affair starkly illuminates questions concerning multiculturalism and human rights that most of us have not had seriously to deal with as yet. The Rushdie affair has also exposed the extent to which most Western countries are now, at least to a degree, multicultural in their social composition. Canada, the United States, and Australia, for example, have known this about themselves for a long time. As immigrant societies their very identity has been shaped by the reality of people from many parts of the world building a new society in a new land.

But two observations are warranted. First, Canada, the US, and Australia are no longer new countries; they have been in existence far longer than most of the states that are members of the United Nations. Second, the old countries of Western Europe are increasingly multicultural in character. While obviously not similar in origin to the settler societies of the new world, they have, to a degree, converged with these societies, from the point of view of cultural pluralism, as a consequence of the winding up of empire, the increasing economic integration of post-war Europe, and the search for cheap labour.

With the new societies becoming old and the old societies of Europe, in this respect at least, becoming new, the movement of populations and the issues of immigration and multiculturalism are matters of concern to all.[10]

Strangers and Citizens: Cultural Distinctions and Common Values

Salman Rushdie's unhappy experience reveals, then, not only the contemporary internationalization of immigration and cultural pluralism but something else which is new, and it is to this relatively unexamined matter that I should like now to turn. Multiculturalism as a value emphasizes the mutually beneficial coexistence of different peoples within a single political community. The emphasis is typically placed on the existence of cultural diversity and the necessary framework which is required of the larger community if diversity is to be respected and to flourish. Less frequently recognized is the fact that, if the framework itself is to be sustained, there must be a common adherence, shared by all cultural groups, to certain fundamental values; in this sense "uniculturalism" must always underlie and sustain multiculturalism. More than that, it must at certain points limit and constrain the expression of multiculturalism.

This – the other half of the equation – has become a significant matter in recent years, and bids fair to become yet more important in the years to come. A nation must ultimately be grounded in a set of common values, shared customs and habits, and implicit understandings. These may change over the years, and will be leavened and influenced by people from other cultures associating themselves with the national community. But there must be an ongoing core of consensus and common belief if the country is not to fly apart.

The experience of Salman Rushdie draws our attention to that side of the equation, to the fact that multiculturalism inevitably implies a pre-existing, substratum of common culture. The pronouncement of a sentence of death, by a foreigner in a foreign land, on a British national constitutes a rejection of British and Western values and an outrage against the Western conception of the rule of law. To incite the Islamic population in Western countries to carry out the murder is to increase the affront.

This is not a legitimate expression of cultural pluralism, nor is it something about which Western societies can exercise forbearance and understanding. While the pronouncement is based on different motivations, it is no more acceptable than an attempted gang-land slaying. An example such as this, and the confusion and ambiguity with which it has been greeted in some quarters, suggest that a clearer and more self-conscious appreciation of the place of cultural pluralism in a nation is required by all concerned, Canadian and immigrants to Canada alike.

In retrospect, it is not perhaps surprising that the need to specify limits in the expression of multiculturalism should have arisen fairly recently. Until the last two decades, immigration to Canada has been principally European. In looking back from the vantage point of contemporary experience, one can see that during this period, beneath the differences in language, culture and religion, there lay a vein of common belief so strong that it hardly needed comment.

For the most part, when immigrants during this period came to Canada, they brought with them not just their distinctive cultural heritage, but also a set of fundamental beliefs and values that they shared with those in Canada whom they were joining. Both the integration into Canadian society and the celebration of cultural distinctiveness were made easier because of the existence of this common underlying cultural frame of reference. The balance between the common culture and multiculturalism could be fairly readily struck, very often without even an explicit acknowledgement that this was occurring.

Immigration from other parts of the world in the last two decades has been a different story. Not only has the phenomenon of visible minorities become much more significant, but the cultural, racial, religious, and linguistic distance between these new communities and the general Canadian population is greater by far than was the difference between the general Canadian population and the earlier migrations from various parts of Europe. Less is shared between the communities at the outset; therefore, there is much more ground to be covered by both sides to close the gap between them. There is also much greater scope for mutual suspicion, misunderstanding, and ethnic and racial tension.[11]

This has been one of the main reasons why, in recent years, the leading edge of policy development in this field has focused more and more intensively on ensuring equality of opportunity, regardless of ethnic origin, and guaranteeing respect for rights. Our success as a society in effectively addressing equality and rights issues will test the depth of our belief in multiculturalism and the honesty of our commitment to the full respect of human rights. We will have to make sure that what we mean by cultural pluralism is honestly reflected in our behaviour and attitudes, in our daily life, and in the concrete expression of Canadian citizenship.

However, it is also true that in the years to come we will increasingly be confronted with the necessity of saying what we do *not* mean by multiculturalism. What are the limits to the expression of cultural diversity in Canada? At what point does an act or a practice cease to be a legitimate manifestation of cultural diversity and become offensive to the basic values we hold as Canadians?

The case of Rushdie is clear. The punishment proposed for the author of *The Satanic Verses* can in no way be accepted as an instance of freedom of religious expression; it is not only offensive to Canadian values and beliefs, it is against the law of the land. But many cases are not as clear. Multiculturalism, if it is to flourish and enrich a nation, depends on a high degree of tolerance and enlightened views on the part of the majority population, but it does not imply anything other than intolerance for acts and practices which contravene the most fundamental values of the society, particularly as they are expressed in the law of the land.

The Canadian Charter of Rights and Freedoms, after all, does two things. It enunciates a system of rights to ensure the enjoyment of liberty for Canada's citizens and to provide legal remedy for those whose rights have been flouted. In a multicultural, federal country, composed of two great language communities, a formal system of rights enunciation and rights protection is a perfectly comprehensible device for ensuring maximum respect for freedom and equality of opportunity in a social environment of considerable diversity. In this sense, the Charter acknowledges differences, determines their relevance or irrelevance, and guarantees equitable treatment. But the Charter does something else. In its enumeration of fundamental freedoms, its declaration of democratic, legal, equality and mobility rights, its provisions relating to official languages and minority language educational rights, its references to Aboriginal rights and freedoms, the multicultural heritage of Canadians, and the equal status of men and women, the Canadian Charter formally expresses a number of fundamental values which stand as emblematic of Canadian society.

Thus, the Canadian Charter of Rights and Freedoms recognizes multiculturalism and at the same time places it in the context of a set of shared values, confirmed by law, which give structure and strength to the common culture underlying all Canadian life.

The interrelationship between cultural distinctions and common values can and should be placed on a broader foundation than simply the constitutional expression of a charter of rights, important as that undoubtedly is. Let me suggest what I mean with a reference to Toronto's experience. People are fond of noting how much post-war immigration has changed Toronto. That is true, but it is only part of the story. When the Italians and the Greeks and the Chinese and the Jamaicans and the East Indians flooded into the city after World War II, they did not find forests and empty fields; they found a flourishing Upper Canadian city, displaying many of the characteristics of civility and order and cleanliness for which Toronto is internationally recognized to this day. It was not immigration alone that transformed Toronto, but the fruitful interplay between newcomers and residents, between a longstanding, settled urban community and the unfamiliar ideas and different forms of cultural expression which the new arrivals brought with them. Both those who were already here and those who came were altered in the process, and contemporary Toronto is the quite marvellous cultural artifact that this interchange has created. The features of Toronto life which existed prior to the arrival of post-war immigration, and which the immigrants were, in part, seeking in coming here, suggest the more comprehensive, underlying cultural values and traditions that constitute the foundation of identity and shared purpose upon which a multicultural society is built.

Canadians are inclined to think of immigrants, correctly, as bringing something here from back there, but they forget that the immigrant experience is about leaving as well as arriving. Typically, immigrants come to Canada because of what they think is here, not because they want to bring what they left behind. They hope both to discard and to acquire. Part of what they acquire should be the Canadian cultural values and traditions which provide the substratum for everything else.

Conclusion

The issue Lord Durham was commissioned to address is still with us today: How can two national communities be accommodated within a single state? The route we have followed is not Durham's, but the enterprise of working out the relationship between French and English has become an inescapable part of Canada's identity. The conceptual questions which formed the backdrop to Durham's analysis are alive today as well. While we may criticize Lord Durham's approach to reconciling the demands of liberalism with the more intimate affiliations of nationality, it would be folly to think that we've got that all sorted out. Far from it.

French-English relations in Canada are, in significant degree, a continuing dialogue about the terms of this ongoing reconciliation. In addition, our recent experience of multiculturalism, which has emerged as an increasingly insistent overlay on the country's fundamental duality, suggests that there is much practical and conceptual work to be done before we can say that the legitimate requirements of liberalism and cultural pluralism have been adequately addressed.

A few years ago many people argued that, at least for a time, Canada's eternal verities of language and culture would recede in importance, to be replaced by a preoccupation with the economy and questions of international trade and industrial development. I suspect that this assertion would be made with more circumspection today. I have the growing conviction that we are entering a new and difficult period in the building of our country, a period in which questions of language and culture will play a central part.

I am fond of Ernest Renan's definition of a nation – "*un plébiscite de tous les jours*," a daily plebiscite. For me, it calls to mind the importance of time, and the importance of the affirmation and re-affirmation of a will to perpetuate a common existence. The act of living together one day after another, solving problems, making things work, is after all how most free societies hang together. And time, well used, is the best negotiator. With time we adapt, we enlarge our views, we accommodate ourselves to new situations; with time we domesticate what initially seemed to be alien and troublesome forces; with time we make friends.

One of the ingredients in using time well is the spirit of compromise. Unlike the Iron Lady and her supporters, I believe in compromise. Reaching a compromise between people who are free and equal and who hold strong opinions and well-developed views is difficult, not easy. And it has more of nobility about it than it has of a tawdry diminution of the human spirit. Successful compromise requires an effort to understand the other person's position and point of view, and it requires an honest search for a resolution or a common interest around which both can rally. It implies a relationship "*de tous les jours*," for it leaves each person with dignity and each in a position to approach the next round – for a next round there will certainly be – not in a spirit of revenge or conquest, but in a spirit of good faith and mutual respect.

Canadians, at critical moments in their history, have shown that they have learned this lesson well. We will, I think, have need of it again. Indeed, I think we need to remember it daily.

NOTES

1 House of Commons, *Debates,* 10 May 1988.

2 The edition of Lord Durham's *Report* to which I refer in the text is that edited by G.M. Craig, in *An Abridgement of the Report on the Affairs of British North America by Lord Durham* (Ottawa: Carleton University Press, 1982).

3 *Report*, 146, 20.

4 Ibid., 28, 150.

5 John Stuart Mill, *Considerations on Representative Government*, ed. Currin V. Shields (Indianapolis: Bobbs-Merrill, 1958), ch. 16.

6 Lord Acton. "Nationality," in his *Essays on Freedom and Power* (Cleveland: World Publishing, 1964).

7 *Report*, p.23.

8 The data on immigration and multiculturalism in Canada are drawn from *The Review of Demography and Its Implications for Economic and Social Policy*, Update Number 5, Health and Welfare Canada, Winter 1988.

9 Interestingly enough, most of the policy fields relevant to multiculturalism lie principally within the jurisdiction of provincial governments and their municipalities which are responsible for housing and municipal planning, immigrant settlement, education, social services, most workplace regulation, and so on. This raises nice questions about the role of the federal government. The government of Canada shares jurisdiction for immigration with the provinces, and traditionally it has played a leadership role in most of the nation-building projects and nation-threatening crises of our past. Unless we are witnessing a fundamental shift in the nature of Ottawa's responsibilities and its chosen role, it would be surprising if the federal government did not seek – or was not offered by some provinces – active

participation of some kind in these fields. The reverse may be true as well. Immigration is the source which feeds multiculturalism; as the size and the composition of the flow become more critical to the life of the receiving provinces, we may find that jurisdictions other than Quebec begin to express an active interest and a desire to participate in the country's immigration policy and programs.

10 I hope those responsible for immigration policy in Ottawa are actively assessing the implications for Canadian immigration of the liberalization of the Communist world which is changing the face of international relations so dramatically.

11 One should also note, however, that Norman Buchignani and Doreen Indra, in *Continuous Journey: A Social History of South Asians in Canada* (Toronto: McClelland & Stewart, 1985), have argued that recent immigrants from former colonies in the British Empire have brought with them to Canada close familiarity with the English language, parliamentary democracy and government, and professional and occupational identities quite similar to those of their counterparts in Canada. One might argue, then, the case for less difference from the general population than was the case when illiterate Ukrainian peasants left Czarist Russia for the Canadian prairies near the turn of the century. This may suggest, then, an additional factor to bear in mind; the destination of the immigrants – unsettled farmland or large city – no doubt powerfully shapes the character of intercultural relations.

4 Maison Egg Roll

Unpublished   3 October 1992

On 1 October 1992, Pierre Trudeau gave a speech at the eleventh Cité Libre *dinner which took place at a Chinese restaurant in Montreal.* Cité Libre *was a magazine of ideas founded in the 1950s by Pierre Trudeau and Gérard Pelletier. After an extended hiatus, it reappeared the year before this event. Trudeau's was a highly anticipated speech on the Charlottetown Accord and the accompanying referendum, presented to an audience of 400 at the restaurant and to half a million Quebecers listening on the radio. There was massive press coverage, with many Canadians elsewhere following Trudeau's remarks with close attention. Trudeau launched a savage, over-the-top attack on the draft constitutional agreement, aimed at destroying public support for it and excoriating the politicians who had put it together. While I was as aware as anyone of the flaws and problems of the Charlottetown Accord, Trudeau's slashing assault was so unbalanced and so poorly argued in places that I felt the need to reply. This piece was the result. I am not sure at this point whether it ever appeared in print; I have not been able to identify a published version.*

Yesterday's Man

Trudeau: "Pythagoras was a man of yesterday, but 2 and 2 still make 4."
Quite right. But the trouble is that Trudeau's ideas don't add up.

Inequality Means Dictatorship

Trudeau: "When the citizen is not equal to all other citizens in the state, one has a dictatorship ..."

Inequality in many of its forms is an evil which must be combatted, but Trudeau's line of reasoning is not worthy of a high school civics essay. If inequality means dictatorship, then Trudeau was a dictator during his many years as prime minister.

In his Maison Egg Roll speech Trudeau confuses "being different" with "being unequal," although he seemed to have had a clearer grasp of things when he was prime minister. Canada is founded on a recognition that certain social characteristics that differentiated French Canadians from their fellow citizens, such as the French language, civil law, and the Catholic religion, had to be given constitutional expression. Is this an entrenchment of inequality, creating a hierarchy of citizens? Is this a dictatorship? No. It's a perfectly justifiable acknowledgement that Canadians are not one undifferentiated mass, but people with distinguishing characteristics that call for recognition.

To his credit, Trudeau himself made the constitutional establishment of two official languages a central objective of his political career. Does the fact that French and English are Canada's official languages mean that Korean and Italian immigrants, whose mother tongue is neither, are relegated to inferior status and forced to live in a Canadian dictatorship? Hardly.

Trudeau played a distinguished role in establishing the 1982 Charter of Rights and Freedoms. That Charter recognizes both the equality rights of individuals before the law and the fact that unjustifiable inequality exists in Canada that should be rectified. Section 15 (2) of the Charter acknowledges the existence of groups and individuals who are disadvantaged because of race, national and ethnic origin, colour, religion, sex, age, mental and physical disability. Do these unjustifiable inequalities make Canada a dictatorship? Section 15 (2) also permits positive-action programs to combat these inequalities; this means singling out groups and individuals for special treatment not available to others. Is this illegitimate because the state is providing unequal treatment under the law and Constitution of Canada? No. Not in the real world in which Trudeau lived when he was prime minister. But apparently "yes" in the fanciful world of abstractions which he currently inhabits.

Collective and Individual Rights

Trudeau: "We must look at history.... When collective rights carry the day over individual rights, one sees in countries where the ideology forms the collectivity, one sees what can happen to people who intend to live freely in society."

This is an understandable concern, looking at the international world, but what on earth does that have to do with Canada? If Canada has a problem, it is not that it espouses a single, oppressive ideology that it is force-feeding down the throats of all its citizens, but that it has none – or too many! In the *Star* excerpts, Trudeau singles out the Canada Clause of the Charlottetown Accord for special criticism. If anywhere, this is where you would expect to find the single "ideology forming the collectivity." And what in fact do you find there? About a half-dozen ideologies or fundamental characteristics existing side by side – Aboriginal peoples, cultural diversity, minority-language communities, Quebec as a distinct society, the equality of the provinces, Canada as a parliamentary democracy. The idea that one of these constitutes a single dominant ideology that will oppress the freedom of Canadians is laughable. This is true neither in Canada as a whole nor in the province of Quebec. Premier Bourassa's government has agreed to this clause applying as fully to Quebec as it does to the rest of the country.

Trudeau: "It is not of secondary importance, the question of whether we are going to live in a society where personal, individual rights have more importance than collective rights."

Having made this declaration, Trudeau proceeds to demonstrate to his own satisfaction that collective rights take precedence over individual rights in the Charlottetown Accord by creating a "hierarchy of classes of citizens." Again he points to the Canada Clause as the culprit.

This, again, is dead wrong. Section 2 (1) of the Canada Clause, which establishes Trudeau's alleged hierarchy, is an interpretive provision. It is a guide to courts in future interpretation of the Constitution, including the Charter of Rights and Freedoms. What is fundamental are the substantive provisions of the constitution, including the 34 sections of the Charter of Rights. The Canada Clause alerts the judges to characteristics they should bear in mind in deciding Charter cases, but the cases must be decided on the basis of the formal clauses of the Charter. It is, therefore, literally preposterous to claim that collective rights, to the extent they are reflected in the Canada Clause "have more importance" than individual rights or that they take precedence over the rights and liberties of citizens. These provisions of the Canada Clause have the same status as Section 27 of Trudeau's Charter which makes multiculturalism an interpretive provision.

Trudeau, in his Eggroll speech, takes a dim view of collective rights. But what then is he to make of the "aboriginal and treaty rights of the aboriginal peoples of Canada" that he himself agreed to put into Section 35 (1) of his 1982 Constitution. Are these not collective rights? Do they not enjoy formal constitutional status?

Compromise: The Canadian Way (and Trudeau's Way When He Was Prime Minister)

Trudeau has rediscovered the intellectual liberty which he enjoyed as a writer for *Cité Libre* years ago, and is using his authority as a former prime minister to excoriate the politicians who have succeeded him.

However, when he was in power he had to deal with reality, and he compromised with the best of them. The best single example of this was his acceptance in the 1982 Constitution of the Notwithstanding Clause. He accepted this, not because he liked it, but because he had to if he wanted to achieve his objectives.

It appears that what he did in 1982 is not acceptable when others do it in 1992. There should be perfection, at least in the eyes of one beholder, or there should be nothing at all.

5 Not Spicer and Not the B & B: Reflections of an Insider on the Workings of the Pepin-Robarts Task Force on Canadian Unity

International Journal of Canadian Studies **1993**

Invited by the International Journal of Canadian Studies *to contribute some thoughts on the Pepin-Robarts Task Force on Canadian Unity, I took the opportunity – as its former director of research and one of the two principal authors of the volume,* A Future Together *– to offer a sketch of the internal biography of a royal commission, focusing not so much on what it did but on how it did it – how its internal workings and choices led to an outcome unwelcomed by the government which created it.*

A commission is chiefly remembered for its final report. The untold story, normally, is how the commission produced the thing for which it is remembered. My focus in these reflections is principally on the how, not the what – on the inner workings of the Task Force on Canadian Unity rather than the analysis and policy recommendations contained in the final report.

A New Kind of Commission? Relations Between the Government and the Task Force

The Task Force on Canadian Unity was established on 5 July 1977 in the wake of the November 1976 election of the Parti Québécois.

The commission was set by Prime Minister Trudeau to allow the public to air its views on national unity and the government to buy some time.[1] The government wanted to proceed cautiously in light of the PQ victory to reassure the Canadian public that it was not on the edge of a precipice and to give the impression that the national unity issue was being prudently managed. Although set up under the Inquiries Act, it was called a "task force," not a commission, presumably to indicate that it was a horse of a different colour from the run-of-the-mill commission. I remember John Robarts, who was keen on the expression, saying early on in the life of the commission that "task force" was a word used in World War II to designate a small number of ships given a limited, very specific mission. At the time of this remark, it was still perhaps possible to believe that the commissioners would restrict themselves to the mission the government had assigned them.

In the beginning, there was the belief that the Task Force would probably not make a final report in the conventional sense. The fact that it was initially given a one-year timetable within which to do its work reflected this view. It would hold hearings across Canada, allow Canadians to speak their minds and give an account of what it had heard. The medium would be the message. It would not do research, develop policy, or offer substantive proposals about the means by which the crisis of Confederation might be resolved. The prime minister had a clear view of the challenge coming from Quebec and of the national policies appropriate to addressing it; his government would not welcome the articulation of an alternative approach by a federally established commission. Indeed, the Trudeau government's own constitutional proposals – The Constitutional Amendment Bill (Bill C-60) – were released in June 1978 and must have been in preparation well before the Task Force completed its hearings in April of that year.

So the Pepin-Robarts Task Force – for those who gave it life – was supposed to be rather like what the Spicer Commission became more than a dozen years later: a national exercise in public consultation reporting on public opinion but offering little or nothing in the way of policy proposals.

This was not to be. Instead, the Task Force produced three publications at the end of its life, one of which was a substantial report with an analysis and a set of recommendations far from congenial to the Trudeau government. What happened?

I think one factor was the sheer force of tradition: a commission's work conventionally included a final report and recommendations. How could this one do otherwise? A second factor was the predisposition of the commissioners and some of the staff. It is difficult to imagine a Gérald Beaudoin, a Solange Chaput-Rolland or – after John Evans's early resignation – a Ron Watts on a commission and not expect a substantive report. Jean-Luc Pepin, as co-chair, was a man with vital intellectual and public policy interests who was unlikely to be satisfied with simply reporting, largely unmediated by analysis, what other people said. Most of the key Commission staff were recruited from the academic, public service, and professional world and assumed that the job of the Task Force was to produce a substantive report with recommendations. Lastly, the Task Force was held in low regard by the public at the beginning of its life and confronted a good deal of scepticism; committing itself to the production of a first-class report was one way of coping with these pressures.

There is another dimension here worthy of remark. While the government, as we shall see, found ways of making its views of the Task Force's approach quite clear, the prime minister and the government of Canada scrupulously respected the tradition of independence in which Canadian royal commissions have functioned. It established the commission, gave it its mandate, named the commissioners, and then stepped back and allowed the Task Force to operate freely as it saw fit. Indeed, Jean-Luc Pepin, the full-time co-chair and former Liberal cabinet minister, did not even talk to Prime Minister Trudeau during the life of the commission between 1977 and 1979, even to discuss his own future political career plans.

That the government got more than it bargained for from the Task Force is not surprising. When a government launches an enquiry into a large and ill-defined field such as national unity, the degree to which it can shape the commission's work by the definition of its mandate is small. Resourceful minds and strong wills can find ample room to manoeuvre within even the most cleverly constituted mandate.

In the mandate which the government assigned to the Task Force, no mention was made of a final report; the conventional phrase "to inquire into and report upon" was notably absent. However, the injunctions "to contribute ... the initiatives and views of the Commissioners" and to "be a source of advice to the government" were more than sufficient foundation to permit the commissioners to do as they wished. As with other commissions, so with Pepin-Robarts: the personalities of commissioners, the unfolding of events during the life of a commission and the impact on a commission of the data, people, and organizations with which it comes in contact, all proved to be potent forces in shaping what it would do and how it would do it.

As a kind of declaration of independence, the Task Force, at the end of its first full meeting, released a statement declaring that it saw its job as finding a third way, presumably between the status quo and sovereignty-association:

> It is our intention to assemble concepts and policies which could constitute some of the elements of a third option for Canada. The Members of the Task Force do not feel bound by existing legislation or practices nor are they committed to views of any federal or provincial political party ... [we are] aware that our autonomy is essential to our credibility and usefulness.[2]

This was controversial, both because it evinced an intention to move beyond public consultation and into substance and because "the policy direction and implicit strategy it blocked out, however tentatively – "a third option" – were antithetical to the direction in which the federal government appeared to wish to move.

There were clear indications that autumn that the Privy Council Office was increasingly worried about the Task Force getting out of control, and Prime Minister Trudeau rapped the commission's knuckles in a statement in the House of Commons on 19 October 1977 in which he said:

> ... I submit respectfully to everybody, including members of my own party and of the Pepin-Robarts Commission, that this third option business is a trap we should not fall into.

Given the choice between maintaining comfortable relations with the federal government and charting its own course, the Task Force chose the latter.

The Culture of a Commission

Commissions are temporary, project-driven organizations.[3]

By its very nature, a commission is set up to do a specific job – to fulfil its mandate, to tackle a project. This project is clearly finite, even if the duration of some commissions suggests otherwise. (The B & B Commission, for example, was brought to a halt, not having completed its work after seven years of existence.) Once the project is completed, the commission disappears; it "goes out of commission." The Task Force held its first full commission meeting on 31 August 1977 and released its final report less than 18 months later, on 25 January 1979. It formally went out of commission a couple of months later.

The temporary, project-focussed nature of commission work in large measure defines the unique culture of a commission. People come from somewhere else to do a temporary job. Some are involved in a particular aspect of the commission's work, such as the organization of hearings, and leave once that work is done; others – the commissioners, commission executives and support staff – have tasks that keep them there throughout. That their tenure at the commission is temporary is known from the very beginning. Everyone leaves when the commission winds up. As the life of the commission moves to its conclusion, commissioners and staff increasingly turn their attention to what they are going back to or where they are going – or hoping to go – next.

If the experience of the Pepin-Robarts Task Force is any indication, the intensity of the work is fierce: long hours, unpredictable schedules; uncertainties which vein almost every working day; searing conflicts about the largest issues and the smallest slights; moments of giddy exhilaration and matchless camaraderie. All of this occurs in a small but bubbling cauldron of experience, some of it very much in the public eye, but much of it confined within the walls of the commission itself. Few people who have given themselves up to this curious form of professional existence leave unaffected.[4]

Yet, if it is temporary, and if it is project driven, a commission is also an organization. It has a budget and a bureaucracy; it establishes positions; there are financial and personnel management problems; records must be kept, hearings organized, travel schedules and meetings arranged. Most, if not all, of these administrative and executive functions a commission holds in common with other organizations. The chief difference, however, is that a commission literally starts from scratch; all of it has to be established and most of it, it seems, simultaneously. High policy and mundane bureaucratic procedures both have to be determined at once, and there is a sense that everything enjoys the same priority; such matters as the recruitment of key staff, the establishment of a budget and a practical means of paying the bills and the organization of meetings get almost equal consideration as the mandate, the organization of a public hearings process, and the development of a research agenda.

Having watched the chaos flower at the Task Force and then subside as professional administrative staff were brought in to reduce the day-to-day life of the commission to routines and more or less normal management practices, I have to conclude that these difficulties must arise in every commission, that they are not in their nature politically charged or policy laden, and that the skills and experience necessary to address them are eminently transferrable.

Given that there are royal commissions in operation in Ottawa all the time, it seems to me a good case can be made for the establishment of a generic unit within the federal government which would provide the basic administrative and financial support necessary to allow the commission to get up and running faster and to do so with far less angst and roiling about in the early days than is currently the case. Federal officials from this unit could be seconded to a new commission to establish the necessary support functions and to recruit the staff with the skills required to carry the system on.

One might learn from the experience of Parliament which has developed staff with omnibus administrative skills charged with supporting the various legislative committees which are regularly being set up. It seems to me that the provision of neutral, professional infrastructure support would significantly improve the efficient conduct of national public inquiries, particularly in the start-up period, and could be arranged to do so without compromising the necessary independence of these enterprises.

The Hearings Process and the Research Function

Some commissions are identified almost as much by their research and research publications as by their final report and its recommendations. The Macdonald Commission and the B & B Commission seem to me to fall into that category. The B & B Report itself contained a substantial array of data and research findings, and the research studies provided a significant range of more specialized analyses. The experience of working at the B & B marked a whole generation of Anglophone and Francophone social scientists with consequences that were felt over the next 15 to 20 years. Likewise, the 1,900 pages of the Macdonald Report are packed with data, and the 72 research reports give an extraordinarily comprehensive picture of Canadian academic thinking about the issues that the commission was addressing.

It was quite otherwise with the Task Force on Canadian Unity. The Task Force, in many ways, *is* its final report. Indeed, while there was discussion within the commission about the possible release of some of the internal studies that had been carried out, that was never done.

The Task Force, in fact, released only three documents in reverse order from what one would expect:

A *Future Together: Observations and Recommendations,* published on 25 January 1979, the report proper, containing the commission's analysis of the plight the country found itself in and offering a comprehensive set of proposals for addressing it.

Coming To Terms: The Words of the Debate, published on 4 February 1979, a glossary of key political terms and concepts, produced as a labour of love by several of the commissioners and still used as a reference work in university classrooms.

A *Time to Speak: The Views of the Public,* published in March 1979, a report on what the people who appeared before the Task Force had to say about their country and the issues confronting it.

The fact that no working papers or studies were released does not mean that none was done. In fact, mountains of paper were produced over the short life of the Task Force, and the fate of some of this material was not decided until very near the end. In the event, its chief function was simply to support the commissioners in their work.

In this sense, research and the hearings processes performed parallel functions. Both provided input to the commissioners which was ultimately synthesized in the final report. The research function was not a matter of doing original work nor, for the most part, contracting specialized projects out to scholars and experts; it was rather to collect and display relevant information, synthesize and represent significant findings and expert opinion in key areas, arrange for direct consultation with key people and present coherent policy alternatives to the commissioners. Executing this mandate brought the research staff into fairly close contact with the hearings process.

Indeed, the hearings themselves regularly included appearances before the Task Force of people with real expertise and a substantial record of achievement in the matters being discussed. During the eight-month formal hearings period, from September 1977 to April 1978, the Task Force held full sessions in fifteen cities. The normal pattern called for public sessions in the evenings and consultations with groups and specialists during the day. In addition, there were numerous private sessions with political figures and experts along the way.

In addition, the commission engaged the services of "the three wise men" – Léon Dion of Laval, Edward McWhinney of Simon Fraser, and John Meisel of Queen's. They met with the Commissioners periodically to offer general counsel on the Task Force's work, to review draft material and to reassure the commissioners about the validity of the information and advice they were receiving from the research staff.

During the summer of 1978, after the public hearings were completed, there came what amounted to a private hearing process – an intensive round of consultations with a wide range of specialists designed to advance and enrich the thinking of the commission. The research staff was intimately involved in this process, which one of the academic commissioners described as "the best seminar on Canada" anywhere.

While it is true that the public hearings and the research enterprise were distinguishable streams of activity in the work of the commission, and depended on different sets of staff, there was a good deal of overlap at certain points, and it is undeniable that the former helped support the latter.

Fasten Your Seatbelts: The Preparation of the Final Report

Given the initial one-year mandate, combined with the commissioners' decision to prepare a conventional final report, discussion of the shape of the Task Force analysis and the nature of its recommendations became a recurrent issue during the winter months of 1977–8. Consideration was given to the possibility of producing an interim report, but it was fairly soon recognized that some extension of the mandate would be required and that the Task Force should concentrate its efforts on producing a good final report.

With the completion of the public hearings in the spring of 1978 and the wind-up of the specialist consultations that summer, the Task Force turned its attention in earnest to the production of its final report.

A great deal of effort was spent during the next four months, both attempting to settle on policy conclusions and recommendations and physically preparing a working draft of the final report. The territory to be covered was so vast and ill-defined, it was difficult to give it shape and focus.

For a number of the commissioners and staff, the moment of truth was approaching. A final decision on recommendations, for example, concerning national language policy and the constitutional status of Quebec in Confederation could not be avoided much longer, and it was clear that conflicting views would have to be worked out. Constitutional matters were the rock on which the B & B Commission had foundered a decade before, or at least were left unresolved by the Commission when it folded in 1970, to the evident satisfaction of the then recently arrived prime minister, Pierre Trudeau. Pepin-Robarts commissioners were acutely aware of what would and would not please Prime Minister Trudeau, now in office for ten years, but nevertheless were developing a diagnosis and approach materially different from his.

Although some progress was made in the autumn of 1978, both on the preparation of the report and the recommendations, it did not feel much like progress at the time. The research staff produced fat, black, three-ring binders filled with draft chapters of the report which seemed to the staff, and I am sure to the commissioners as well, ponderous and unwieldly.

An experienced editor, brought in from Toronto, expressed something close to horror at the unmanageable bulk of the chapter drafts. Another writer/editor, who had had extensive experience in shaping copy for *Reader's Digest,* was recruited and hacked manfully at the accumulation of words, much to the consternation of their writers. Nothing seemed to be working; neither the recommendations nor the text seemed to be coming into focus, and we were finding it hard to coherently express the integrating principles of regionalism, duality, and power sharing that the Task Force had fashioned for itself in the course of the previous twelve months. We were also finding it difficult to settle on a set of recommendations that adequately reflected those principles.

Our salvation came from outside.

In June 1978 the government of Canada released proposals for constitutional change in the form of draft legislation (Bill C-60). The existence of that document, and provincial reaction to it and to a federal schedule for 12 constitutional discussions, led the prime minister to convene a Constitutional Conference for 30 October to 1 November 1978. This was the beginning of another attempt at comprehensive constitutional reform seven years after the aborted Victoria Charter of 1971. Discussion at the October Conference appeared to disclose sufficient grounds to establish a ministerial Constitutional Committee to prepare specific proposals for a second First Ministers' Conference on the Constitution, to be held on 5 to 6 February 1979.

These events led members of the Task Force to believe that the February meeting was likely to be of critical importance to the country and to the resolution of the constitutional issue; there was a sense that the Task Force, if it did not speak prior to that event, might very well miss the boat and its work be made largely irrelevant.

In the event, this was far from true, as some of the Task Force members privately realized. While Prime Minister Trudeau appeared to be willing to consider proposals that were more generous to the provinces than had been the case in the past, political considerations on the part of the provincial participants, given the prospect of a federal election in a few weeks or months, meant that the chances of reaching an agreement were slim. In addition, the Parti Québécois government of Quebec was committed to sovereignty-association – a non-starter in English-speaking Canada – and the PQ had yet to test the acceptability of its ideas among its own electorate in a referendum.

Nevertheless, the notion that a significant constitutional agreement might be possible in February was an extraordinarily helpful "activating fiction" that galvanized commissioners and staff. At a meeting before Christmas, the commissioners committed themselves to the preparation and release of their final report including recommendations prior to the Vancouver constitutional meeting. For this reason, three volumes the Task Force produced came out in reverse order from what might have been expected.

Setting a real deadline, credible to themselves and authoritative so far as the staff were concerned, was probably the most critical single decision the commissioners made with respect to the final report. All other matters for resolution became consequential on that prior commitment. Recommendations *had* to be decided; a satisfactory draft of the final report, reflecting the philosophy of the commissioners, *had* to be produced. All of this – not to mention the editing, translation, printing, and distribution – had to be completed within a space of seven weeks.

The psychological impact on commissioners and staff alike was dramatic; as one researcher said:

> The commissioners have fastened their seat belts and returned their chairs to the upright position. They're getting ready to land.

At a stroke, the commission members began to focus on essentials, not details. Setting a deadline helped the Task Force unburden itself of the unwieldly drafts of the final report produced in autumn, and to use them simply as resource material to be drawn on as needed.

The responsibility for preparing a draft of an entirely new version of the report was entrusted to one commissioner and one member of the research staff; they agreed between themselves on the general areas each would be responsible for, and the commission broke for Christmas.

The first sentences of what was to become the final report were written on Boxing Day. *A Future Together: Observations and Recommendations,* the final report of the Task Force on Canadian Unity, was released in both official languages one month later. This must surely set a record for the rapid production of a royal commission report. Recently, one of my colleagues, currently laboring on another royal commission, observed wearily:

> Oh. Commissions…. Commissions are a lot like elephants. They're big and slow moving and they tend to sit down and squash things. The only difference is they don't have memories.

It is true that the pace set by many commissions has been painfully slow, but that certainly cannot be said of the final days of the Pepin-Robarts Task Force, nor, I think, of its existence in general, given that its active life was less than a year and a half in total.

The commission reconvened at the beginning of January to review and improve the draft, to finalize the recommendations and to oversee the translation. Fortunately, the draft that the authors had prepared was generally to the liking of the commissioners and, by then, the pressure of the looming deadline forced a consensus in even the most divisive areas in which they intended to make recommendations.

These areas were many: decentralization, the Senate, the Supreme Court, and other contentious issues. But by far the most difficult matter was federal language policy, and the commissioners – particularly an active core group from Ontario and Quebec – spent hours during the days and nights of early January in an ultimately successful struggle to reach agreement on a set of language-policy recommendations. These were among the most controversial when the report was publicly released.

The role of John Robarts was important here. He was neither troubled by nor terribly interested in the detailed recommendations with which several of the other commissioners were wrestling. However, he did care passionately about one thing: he thought his country was in very serious trouble, and it needed to get fixed, and quickly. Robarts used to say, when confronted with yet another set of arcane policy proposals, that dealing with these national unity issues was like "shovelling fog." He would also say that Canada needs to "reach finality" on these issues, that is to say, to settle the matter once and for all, get it over and done with, and stop talking about it. These views, I think, allowed him to accept quite "comfortably" (a favourite Robarts word) what must have been, for him, a fairly radical set of recommendations. They also explain his insistence during the final discussions that the report be unanimous; if the Task Force's recommendations were to be credible and authoritative there could be no minority report. And there was none.

The Impact of the Task Force

The Task Force's final report was given to the government a couple of days before its public release, and several of the commissioners went to Prime Minister Trudeau's office to discuss it with him and Marc Lalonde. Trudeau and Lalonde had had very little time to review the report. It came as no surprise to any of us that neither of them liked it much, but what I found interesting was the way that each, given the limited time available, approached the report.

Marc Lalonde had flipped to the back and read through the recommendations; he then proceeded to render his judgment of the document on that basis.

Trudeau, for his part, had started at the beginning of the report and read his way as far as he could into the substance of the argument; he then discussed with the commissioners their substantive approach and line of reasoning. While I thought it a pity – though not surprising – that the prime minister did not care for the report's analysis and intellectual framework, it pleased me as a citizen and an academic that the prime minister of my country had a cast of mind that drove him to tackle arguments, not just recommendations.

The government of Canada received the Task Force's report publicly with restraint and circumspection. When Prime Minister Trudeau tabled it in the House he stated carefully that the government of Canada "accepts the broad lines of the Task Force's analysis of the problem and endorses the basic principles which it believes should underlie the renewal of the Canadian federation." The opposition leaders, Joe Clark and Ed Broadbent, were more outspoken in their support. It was in the days which followed that the prime minister began to make it clear that the government had considerable reservations about the report. There was much in the report to which he took exception, not least its positive emphasis on duality and regionalism, its support for some decentralization of social and cultural policy (although combined with some centralization in the economic field) and, in particular, its position on federal language policy.

The report was made public just two weeks before the Vancouver Constitutional Conference. As such, it became a central topic of conversation in Vancouver, but its release so close to the meeting meant that it did not have a structural impact on the agenda or the substantive discussions that took place. Some interest was expressed in the approach of Pepin-Robarts by several provinces, and it appeared that the Parti Québécois government of Quebec was startled by the report's forthright recognition of Quebec's distinct character and its willingness to give that distinctiveness some significant constitutional expression. Claude Morin, then the Quebec minister responsible for intergovernmental affairs, was reported to have said, apropos of the Pepin-Robarts approach: "We're not in the same boat, but we're sailing down the same river."

Probably the most concrete example of the effect the Report had in some quarters is the *Beige Paper*, the constitutional document put together by the Quebec Liberal Party under the leadership of Claude Ryan. It drew heavily on the Task Force approach. However, the defeat of Ryan and the re-election of the PQ after the referendum meant that that stream of influence was effectively blocked off.

Despite some internal advice to the contrary, the Trudeau government dealt with the Pepin-Robarts report by ignoring it. This strategy was largely successful in reducing its immediate, practical impact, in part because no provincial government or governments took Pepin-Robarts up seriously as a *cause célèbre* and in part because the country was embarking on a tumultuous 18 months in its history which saw the defeat of the Liberals in June 1979, the nine-month reign of the Clark Conservative Government, the re-election of Trudeau and the Liberal Party in February 1980, and the Quebec referendum in May 1980.

The Clark government, during its brief term of office, showed some interest in the report, and the work that Arthur Tremblay, appointed to the Senate by Prime Minister Clark, had begun, made use of the Pepin-Robarts report as a significant policy resource.

The report of the Task Force on Canadian Unity came, then, at the beginning of a series of national events that followed fast on the heels of one another and which transformed the context in which Canadian unity and constitutional reform were addressed. With the utterly unexpected re-election of a majority Liberal Government under a rejuvenated Pierre Trudeau, followed by the defeat of the Quebec referendum on sovereignty-association, the philosophy and proposals espoused by the Task Force were definitively set aside. From 1980 to 1984, the Trudeau approach to national unity, constitutional reform, and the management of the federation held complete sway.

Eloquent evidence of this reality is to be found in the fate of Jean-Luc Pepin, co-chairman of the Task Force, who was re-elected as a Liberal in the 18 February 1980 federal election which brought Trudeau back to power. The prime minister made Pepin minister of transport, at that time an active and very heavy portfolio which was far removed from the referendum and constitutional action, and he was allowed to have no significant role in the federal government's conduct of these matters.

What of the Task Force's general influence – its "atmospheric" impact – in the fourteen years since it folded its tent? Any response to that question must be highly speculative. However, I have the impression that the Pepin-Robarts Task Force accomplished in substantial measure what it had announced it intended to do at the beginning of its work – namely, to present a third option for Canada. In the event, it offered an approach which was different from both the sovereignty-association proposal of the Parti Québécois government and the Trudeau view of national unity and federalism.

It constituted the most coherent, standing federalist alternative to the political ideas of Pierre Trudeau. His anti-nationalist individualism led him to foster the recognition of individually based language rights and to stoutly resist any expanded recognition of the community-based reality of the French fact in North America. While clearly a believer in federalism, his experience in government created in him a strong resistance to any strengthening of the provinces in Confederation.

The Pepin-Robarts report recognized, accepted, and sought to accommodate the very forces in Canadian life and politics that Trudeau was combatting. It accepted and celebrated diversity, and in its development of the concepts of duality and regionalism, the Task Force fashioned a view of Canada and

Confederation that comfortably acknowledged the communitarian foundation of much of what was most valuable and most strongly cherished in our national existence. What is more, the report frankly accepted the structural role of the Province of Quebec as the "foyer" of the Francophone community in North America and the role of the other provinces in expressing the regional loyalties of Canadians in other parts of the country.

It was, I think, the first public body to advance this conception of Canada with such clarity and vigour. The Task Force was explicit in acknowledging that, politically, regions were best understood as provinces and that, with respect to duality, the key issue was the status of Quebec in Confederation. There is no doubt that the Task Force was correct in designating these as the two central forces in the country which required mutual accommodation.

The failure to reconcile regionalism – transmuted into the principle of the equality of the provinces – and duality – understood as the need to recognize Quebec as a distinct society – has, in the 14 years since the Task Force published its report, exposed the country to greater risk than any other single issue in our national life.

Conclusion

The Task Force's conception of Canada; its frank acceptance of the central principles of duality and regionalism and the determination to knit them more creatively into the fabric of our national life, rather than to deny them; the recognition of Quebec as a distinct society; the willingness to tackle the assignment of power between the two orders of government and to accept a degree of decentralization – all of these bespeak an approach materially different from that which dominated our national life until 1984. The pressure to give them some degree of constitutional accommodation, however, appears not to have diminished with time, although we have not so far been successful in addressing this matter, nor have we succeeded in giving constitutional expression to the aspirations of Canada's aboriginal peoples.

Both Meech Lake and the Charlottetown Accord attempted to establish greater constitutional space for the communitarian realities of Canadian life; in this they were at one with the central direction of the Pepin-Robarts Report. With the establishment of the constitutional Charter of Rights and Freedoms in 1982, we have given powerful expression to the voice of individualism to which Pierre Trudeau was so strongly committed and which unquestionably forms part of the very foundation of Canadian life. This is not the place for a review of the unhappy fortunes of Meech and Charlottetown, but it does seem to me that there is another voice – as thoroughly Canadian as that to which the 1982 Constitution gives expression – which is still calling for recognition.

NOTES

I am indebted to Ralph Heintzman, Ken McRoberts, Jean-Luc Pepin, and Ron Watts who commented on an earlier draft of this paper.

1 See Jean-Luc Pepin's comments on this subject in his delightful appreciation of John Robarts, given as the closing address of York University's May 1984 inaugural ceremonies for the establishment of the Robarts Centre for Canadian Studies. Jean-Luc Pepin, "Closing Address," in *Se Connaître: Politics and Culture in Canada,"* ed. J. Lennox, (North York ON: Robarts Centre for Canadian Studies, 1985), 111–117.

2 The *Role of the Task Force,* September 1, 1977. Reproduced in the Task Force's final report, *A Future Together: Observations and Recommendations,* 139–43.

3 Alan Cairns has spoken of this commission culture in "Reflections on Commission Research," *Commissions of Inquiry,* ed. Paul Pross, et al. (Toronto: Carswell, 1990), 91–3.

4 Alan Cairns speaks of the atmosphere of the Macdonald Commission in "Reflections," 93.

6 A Passionate Canadian, Pepin Heard Voice of Communities within Federalism

The Gazette (Montreal)   13 September 1995

This article was an appreciation of the life and contribution of Jean-Luc Pepin, a dear friend, a remarkable Canadian, and co-chair of the Pepin-Robarts Task Force on Canadian Unity. Pepin led the Task Force in preparing a report that articulated "the most coherent, standing federalist alternative to the political ideas" of then Prime Minister Pierre Trudeau.

Jean-Luc Pepin – as loyal a servant of his country as ever lived – died almost a week ago. His funeral, held yesterday at the Catholic Cathedral in Ottawa, bore witness to the countless Canadians who remember Jean-Luc Pepin and his work.

When I learned of his death, I felt the sense of loss one normally experiences when a young person is taken prematurely. Why is that, I wonder? Jean-Luc Pepin was 70 years old, and by far the largest portion of his life's work was complete. Why this kind of sadness, as if for someone who was young and limber? The answer lies in his effervescent spirit. His body may have let him down, but the young and limber thing in him whose passing I lament is his unquenchable curiosity, his intellectual gusto, his determination to try to get it right.

His curiosity was not idle; it was intensely focused on the things that mattered most to him, and what mattered most to him, I think – apart from his family – was the health and functioning of his political community. If one were to say his passion was politics or government, that would mark out the circle of his concern too narrowly. No, his interests and affections were roomier, more capacious; they were those of a patriot and a lover of learning – not merely those of a specialist or politician.

His life reminds us of that long, distinguished tradition of French-speaking Canadians for whom there is no inconsistency in loving Canada and Quebec at the same time. And so strong was his love of teaching and learning that it never left him as a politician, powerfully shaping his view of the activity to which he was devoted throughout much of his life; for him, I think, politics had to be understood, not just as a great game or as a form of public therapy or as conflict resolution, but as education. If citizens could be helped to see things more clearly, understand more deeply, appreciate more comprehensively, the political community would be healthier and better governed.

Jean-Luc Pepin's patriotism and intellectual gusto were never more fully engaged than during his time as co-chairman of the Task Force on Canadian Unity. If his colleague, former Ontario Premier John Robarts, brought solidity, a taste for the bottom line, and an unexpected daring to his work at the commission, Pepin's contribution was different. The former federal transport minister brought intellectual vivacity, a profligate expenditure of personal energy, and an abiding sense of the task force's high calling. The ideas the task force was to bring forth were too important to the country not to get them right. Robarts understood the public virtues of a unanimous report; Pepin believed in the indispensability of the right report.

And getting it right was not an easy task for Pepin, as any of the commissioners would attest. This was partly because, en route to the final report, he found himself having to discard earlier categories of thought for new ones. The report was Pepin's hard-won declaration of intellectual independence from the Trudeau approach to federalism and national unity.

At the time of its publication in January 1979, the task force report was the most coherent, standing federalist alternative to the political ideas of Pierre Trudeau, who was then prime minister. Trudeau's anti-nationalist individualism led him to support the recognition of individually based language rights and to resist stoutly any expanded recognition of the community-based reality of the French fact in North America. While clearly a believer in federalism, his experience in government also led him to fight against any strengthening of the provinces of Confederation.

The Pepin-Robarts report recognized, accepted, and sought to accommodate the very forces in Canadian life and politics that Trudeau was combatting. In its development of the concepts of duality and regionalism the task force fashioned a view of Canada and Confederation that comfortably acknowledges the communitarian foundation of much of what was most valuable and most strongly cherished in our national existence. What is more, the report frankly accepted the structural role of the province of Quebec as the "*foyer principal*" of the francophone community in North America and the role of the other provinces in expressing the regional loyalties of Canadians in other parts of the country.

The task force was, I think, the first public body to advance this conception of Canada with such clarity and vigor. Not surprisingly, its report was greeted with thin-lipped reserve by the Trudeau government, and, when Pepin was re-elected as a Liberal in the February 1980 federal election that brought Trudeau back to power, he was made minister of transport, a punishing portfolio far removed from the referendum and constitutional action – which is exactly where Trudeau wanted him to be.

With the establishment of the constitutional Charter of Rights and Freedoms in 1982, the country has given powerful expression to the voice of individualism to which Trudeau was so strongly committed and that unquestionably forms part of the very foundation of Canadian life.

As our history before 1982 and since attests, however, there is another voice – as thoroughly Canadian as that to which the 1982 constitution gives expression – that is still calling for recognition. To Jean-Luc Pepin's credit, he had ears, and he heard that voice, and he spoke of what he heard.

Take care, Jean-Luc. We will miss you.

7 A Very Canadian Independence Movement. Quebec Separatists Avoid the Language of an Oppressed People: They Know It Would Be Silly

Ottawa Citizen **10 February 1995**

I was irritated with some of the inflated rhetoric and shoddy reasoning ped-dled by Jacques Parizeau and his separatist colleagues as he marched the people of Quebec towards a referendum on sovereignty they weren't actively asking for.

In a document tabled in the National Assembly on 6 December, Premier Jacques Parizeau said that Quebec's Declaration of Sovereignty would be modelled on the American Declaration of Independence.

Really?

The American document was adopted by the Continental Congress on 4 July 1776, in the early stages of a six-year war in which the American colonists fought for their liberty from Great Britain. The American colonists, acknowledging that prudence dictates "that Governments long established should not be changed for light and transient causes," assert that "when it becomes necessary for one people to dissolve the political bands which have connected them with another..., a decent respect to the opinions of man-kind requires that they should declare the causes which impel them to the separation."

What were these causes? More than two dozen specific evils and abuses are listed, all of them demonstrating to the satisfaction of the Continental Congress that "the history of the present King of Great Britain is a history of repeated injuries and usurpations, all having in direct object the establishment of an absolute Tyranny over these States." These are no peccadilloes; they are black political sins. A few examples:

- the repeated dissolution of legislatures and the refusal to hold elections;
- the obstruction of justice;
- the keeping of standing armies, in times of peace, without civil consent;
- cutting off trade with other parts of the world; imposing taxes on the people without their consent; the denial of trial by jury;
- the waging of war against the people. ("He has plundered our seas, ravaged our Coasts, burnt our towns, and destroyed the lives of our people.")

This is the model for the premier of Quebec's Declaration of Sovereignty?

What causes of separation are offered by the government of Quebec to satisfy "a decent respect to the opinions of mankind?" In all the documents placed before the National Assembly on 6 December at this solemn moment in the history of the people of Quebec, only one cause of separation was mentioned: "to settle definitely the constitutional problem that has been confronting Quebec for several generations." No allegations of tyranny, no abuse of power, no denial of democratic rights, no confiscation of property, no infringement on the liberties of the citizen. Just a "constitutional problem." Thomas Jefferson would have wept.

The American colonists were struggling to free themselves from despotism, from the tyrannical oppression of Great Britain.

Why do some people in Quebec want to secede from Canada? I would argue that for separatists in Quebec the issue is not freedom in any conventional sense. Most classical nationalist independence movements want to get out of the country they are in; they want to separate, set up their own shop, and get free of the old regime. Many are seeking to escape the oppression of a tyrannical majority that is bullying them; some seek to become a dominant majority in their own right. Some aspire to create a new society better and different than the one that they plan to escape from.

Freedom is a very important element in most independence movements. The difficulty for nationalists in Quebec is that they already are free.

As individuals they are unquestionably living in one of the freest countries on the face of the globe, protected by the rule of law, an independent judiciary and a constitutional charter of rights, benefitting from membership in a society that places a high value on respect for freedom and the rights of others, operating in a democratic political system muscular enough to allow a secessionist political party to form the official Opposition in the Parliament of Canada.

As members of a national community, the separatists are free again. The vast majority of francophones in Canada live within Quebec, where they make up more than 80 per cent of the population. Enjoying the benefits of what is arguably the most decentralized federal system on the globe, their government is free to fashion very much the kind of society that the majority wants – in health care, in education, in social policy, in the structure of the economy and, to a substantial degree, in immigration. Their government is able to borrow abroad, sell hydroelectric energy internationally, engage in quasi-diplomatic representation, set up an "embassy" in Paris larger than that of many sovereign states.

I believe that if you ask a nationalist in Quebec what it is that the national community of Quebec needs to do that it has been unable to do, there would be a long pause before you got an answer. The direct question, "Where are you blocked in your progress, in your actions, in what you require as a nationalist community?" is not an easy one for a nationalist in Quebec to answer. Quebec, in the space of three or four decades, has transformed itself from the allegedly backward, priest-ridden society of popular legend into a dynamic, pluralistic society with a modern economy substantially owned and operated by local, Québécois entrepreneurs.

Where Quebec has wanted to experiment with distinct social and economic arrangements, for example the co-operative movement or the *Caisse de dépôt*, it has been able to do so. Where it has felt insecure, linguistically, it has been able to pass legislation to protect the French language. Where it has perceived the need to have substantial control over the reception and integration of immigrants into Quebec, that has been arranged.

It has done all of this and more without a single change to the division of powers in the Constitution and all within the framework of Confederation. When the people of Quebec have pushed on the door, it has opened. This is tyranny?

Meanwhile – despite the regrettable fact that the country has been unable to recognize Quebec as a distinct society in the Constitution – Canada has nevertheless substantially redefined itself to take into account the French fact, which 35 years ago was barely acknowledged as being of national significance. This is oppression?

Separatists in Quebec implicitly recognize all this. They do not use the language of an oppressed people; that would be silly. Quebecers are already in charge. They don't argue that they need to separate so that the rights and freedoms of the people can be protected properly; they already are. They don't contend that it is their desire to build a new economic order, based on different principles; they wish to maintain the existing role of the private sector and they want in, not out of, the FTA and NAFTA and GATT and any other economic acronym going. Part company with the western military alliance? No way: they aim to be part of NATO and NORAD. They are not fed up with an alien British parliamentary system: in fact, they intend to keep it as is and plan to seek membership in the British Commonwealth.

So why do the separatists want out? Why do they want to be free? A cynic, or a tired federalist, might say that they want out so they can get back in. They want to be free of the rest of Canada so that they can economically associate with it. They want to separate from the country, but keep Canadian citizenship. They want to secede, but continue to use the Canadian dollar. They want open borders, free movement of people, closer economic ties with Ontario. And Jacques Parizeau is supposed to be far more committed to hard-line independence than René Lévesque was years ago. The next thing you know, they will be saying they want to keep Elizabeth as the Queen of Quebec.

This is a very Canadian national independence movement.

You can see why the rest of the world finds it a little difficult to take our perpetual wrangling too seriously. The idea of seceding from one of the wealthiest and freest democracies in the world makes about as much sense as it would for you to agree to your genial dentist's proposal that he pull all your teeth out so you won't have to worry about cavities.

John Adams and Thomas Jefferson and the other members of the Continental Congress are, I have no doubt, speechless in heaven.

8 Responsible Government: Quebec Would Serve Its People Better if It Were to Agree to Play by the Constitutional Rules Instead of a Unilateral Declaration of Independence

The Gazette (Montreal)   **13 September 1996**

Guy Bertrand, a lawyer and a private citizen, launched a court action seeking to have a potential unilateral declaration of independence by Quebec declared illegal. His actions began a process that led ultimately to the Supreme Court's Reference on Secession decision in 1998, and to the passage of the federal Clarity Act two years later. These initiatives were in response to the claim made by successive governments of Quebec that the province possessed a unilateral right to national self-determination and that its secession from Canada would not be governed by Canadian constitutional law. I contended that the specious arguments supporting this claim served the people of Quebec poorly.

Justice Robert Pidgeon has ruled that Guy Bertrand may proceed with his efforts to have a unilateral declaration of independence (UDI) after a yes vote in a sovereignty referendum declared illegal. Having failed to block the process in the most recent skirmish, the government of Quebec has decided to pick up its marbles and go home. It will boycott any further proceedings.

From a tactical and political point of view, this decision is not surprising. It must be as clear to the Parti Québécois as it is to everyone else that its contention that the existing constitution and the Canadian rule of law have no role to play in relation to Quebec's secession faces a mauling in the courts.

Even the five international-law experts retained by the National Assembly in 1992 concluded that international law does not apply to the case of Quebec.

If not domestic law, if not international law, what law? The "law" of public opinion? A government anxious to ensure that its people hold to the naive belief that secession will be a piece of cake, and that it is a matter for them and them alone to decide, will not wish to participate in a further judicial proceeding that demonstrates real life isn't this simple. Better to cast stones at the whole thing from the sidelines.

Yet from the point of view of its responsibility for the prudent stewardship of the welfare of the Quebec people, the government of Quebec would surely do well to think again. Because the sovereignists came so close to success in the Oct. 30 referendum, the people of Quebec – not to mention the people of Canada as a whole – are entitled to some honest talk about what might actually happen in the future.

Let us suppose that there is another referendum and that the Yes side wins. What then? Is it really believed that Quebec will simply step out of the Canadian constitutional and legal system the way you might step off a bus? Enormously powerful interests would be at grave risk during any attempt at secession, and passions would be running high.

Although it is awful to contemplate, it is not difficult, given the PQ's position, to imagine a period in which there would be profound instability, with two authorities battling for sovereign control over the same territory and the same people. The prospect of this version of the Hobbesian state of nature should terrify any law-abiding community.

Setting aside the simple logic of nationalism and the demands of political strategy, are there rational grounds for the government of Quebec's commitment to UDI? One is that a commitment to the alternative, a commitment to abide by Canadian constitutional law, is fraught with danger for the *indépendantiste* side; there is a serious risk that you give yourself over to the status quo and the not-so-tender ministrations of your federalist opponents. After all, the country cannot make the constitutional amending provisions work now: witness Meech and Charlottetown. Why should anyone think that we could make them work to provide for the departure of Quebec from confederation?

In addition, what assurances would sovereignists have that the other parties to a post-referendum secession discussion would not use the rule of law to block the process? Why should the PQ believe that the federal government or the rest of the country would decline to exploit its control over the amending formula in a vengeful, obstructive fashion? It is surely not unreasonable for the PQ to suppose that governments in the rest of Canada might very well use their leverage over the formula for constitutional amendment either vindictively or as a bargaining chip.

Thus, the sovereignists reject the relevance of Canadian constitutional law and due process and argue that the sovereignty of Quebec is a political matter, not a legal matter. But, in fact, it is both. The real question is: What is the role of politics and what is the role of law?

It has become clear during the last two decades of debate that the vast majority of Canadians would agree with the proposition that, if Quebecers make a definitive and democratic decision to secede, that decision should be respected and accepted by the rest of Canada. I see little serious indication of a willingness to try to block the settled democratic will of the people of Quebec on this matter. And, given the gravity of the issue, a credible way in which this preference can be expressed and confirmed is via referendums held in Quebec. Are you in favor of Quebec seceding from Canada? Do you agree with and accept the negotiated terms of secession? These are political questions that are properly addressed politically by the people of Quebec, at the beginning and at the end of the process. That is the position René Lévesque espoused at the time of the 1980 referendum.

But how do you give effect to the desire to secede? What legal and regulatory framework applies during the extraordinarily difficult negotiations that must follow any such expression of preference?

What writ prevails between the declaration of the desire to secede and its realization or its withdrawal? How do you attempt to resist entering the whirlpool of warring sovereignties in which the most vital interests of citizens will be put at risk? This, surely, is in part the province of law.

Canada has a constitution. It applies to Quebec as much as the rest of Canada. All participants in the national-unity drama have an interest in maintaining the constitutional order unless or until it is constitutionally changed.

A common commitment to the rule of law becomes even more important than normal as the political temperature rises.

The rule of law, plus a thorough respect for the democratic process, are arguably the two most critical supports that we – sovereignists and federalists alike – have to help us through what would be a daunting and dangerous process.

If the PQ is committed, not only to the sovereignty of Quebec, but to democracy and the rule of law as well, it will acknowledge the vital principle at stake in the Bertrand proceedings. For what Bertrand is defending at bottom is the principle of constitutional government. I think most Canadians – sovereignist or federalist, wherever they live – believe in that, too.

A UDI, a unilateral declaration of sovereignty, as envisaged by the PQ, is a flagrant violation of that principle. If it can be justified at all, it is only after all constitutional avenues of change have been exhausted or found wanting. It is only at the end of the process, after the PQ's worst fears have been fulfilled, not at the beginning, before the process has even begun, that an unconstitutional break might be justified.

Were the PQ to acknowledge the imperatives of constitutional government and address itself to the complexities entailed in any actual secession process, it would serve the needs and interests of the people it represents far better than it is doing now, and it would force the debate on to new and more solid ground. Surely, it is time to begin to talk seriously about what we may be getting ourselves into.

9 Does Ottawa Know It Is Part of the Problem?

In John Trent, Robert Young, and Guy Lachapelle, eds.,
Québec-Canada: What Is the Path Ahead? 1996

These remarks were given at a conference organized weeks after the 1995 Quebec referendum, which delivered a razor-thin rejection of secession. Its elevated emotional tone reflects the stresses of that period. The remarks were given, though, before the government of Canada had decided what to do. In the months that followed, the federal government appointed Stéphane Dion as minister of intergovernmental affairs, who took the fight to the souverainistes; it also passed the Clarity Act, building on the Supreme Court's opinion in the Secession Reference. The Clarity Act set out the principles which would guide the government of Canada's response to any future referendum on secession.

There has been growing concern among Canadians about the government of Canada's confused and uncertain response to the referendum results. We have been left pretty much in the dark about what the government thinks about all this. At no time since 30 October has Prime Minister Chrétien laid out his considered view of the meaning of the referendum vote, its consequences for Canada and Canadians, and the overall direction his government intends to pursue in its policies. His government's amending formula and distinct society initiatives have an air of improvisation about them, and the sudden assertion that the POGG (peace, order, and good government) power might be used to fend off a future referendum came as a surprise, not just to members of the public, but to members of his own government. Until the Cabinet shuffle at least, one was left with the impression that policy is being shaped less by a coherent analysis of the situation, and more by the strong desire that the issue will go away, and we can all get back to business as usual. Would that it would, and would that we could.

There is now evidence that many Canadians are unable or unwilling to coun-
tenance this approach. The growing ferment in the country suggests that the
extraordinary pre-referendum Montreal rally may have been more than a flash
in the pan. But the energy of increasing numbers of Canadians is currently
washing back and forth in the system without much focus and with little direction or guidance from the political leadership of the country. If Ottawa doesn't
act fast, Keith Spicer may inflict another Spicer Commission on the country,
whether we like it or not.

There are now signs that the prime minister and the government of Canada
are feeling this rising pressure and that they may be readying themselves to
respond. For example:

- The pamphlet outlining Ottawa's post-referendum initiatives, sent to every
  household in Quebec, is likely to be a harbinger of things to come. There
  seems to be a realization in Ottawa that the secessionists have controlled
  virtually unchallenged the making of myth and the definition of fact, and
  that an aggressive communications effort is required.
- Allan Rock, the minister of justice, speaking before a Senate Committee,
  alluded to the fact that contingency planning to deal with a possible future
  referendum is under way.
- The government's national unity cabinet committee has apparently been
  fine-tuning a unity strategy that will be presented to the federal Cabinet
  and caucus in the next few weeks.
- And – most significant of all – the recent Cabinet shuffle has clearly been
  undertaken with the intention of substantially strengthening the government of Canada's national unity capacity and its clout in Quebec – witness
  in particular the appointment of our colleague, Stéphane Dion, as minister
  of intergovernmental affairs. Perhaps the most striking thing about the
  Cabinet shuffle was the fact that this normally cautious and conservative
  (though Liberal) prime minister felt it necessary to invest his prestige in the
  appointment of two very able but politically inexperienced Quebecers, who
  do not as yet even have seats in the House of Commons.

But supposing Ottawa *is* ready to respond, what will it do? That's what I
would like to speak about in the balance of these remarks.

Obviously, what it decides to do will depend on its analysis of the situation.
To oversimplify madly, you could argue that there are two broad alternative
understandings of the situation. The first I will call political, and the second,
structural.

1. The political understanding of the plight we are in would claim that there is
nothing fundamentally wrong with the way the country is set up, but that we are going through a bad political patch. Secessionist sentiment in Quebec was more or less

dormant until the election of the PQ in September 1994, and they came into office, not because of their program but because they were *there,* the only possible alternative to an increasingly unpopular Quebec Liberal government. Luckily for federalists, at that time Jacques Parizeau was Premier of Quebec, which was a sure-fire way of keeping the sovereignty vote down. Midway in the referendum campaign, however, the game changed, when Lucien Bouchard was made de facto leader of the sovereignist forces; with his energy and charisma, he turned the campaign around, and was almost able to snatch victory from the jaws of defeat. So what you have here, it is argued, is a conjuncture of circumstances that produced a "Yes" vote substantially higher than anyone was predicting and higher than its "natural" level. All of this is the product of the fortunes of politics, not the result of deep problems in the nature and functioning of our country or profound alienation on the part of Francophone Quebecers. Canada is a good product, but it has been badly sold.

On this understanding, then, what the government of Canada will need to be engaged in over the next couple of years is the equivalent of an extended election campaign. Rhetoric and communications therefore lie at the heart of a proper federal strategy. The good story of Canada needs to be told, the falsehoods and distortions of the separatists need to be countered at every opportunity, and the rest of the country should say and do the right things and avoid saying and doing the wrong things. What is essentially required is for the government of Canada to go on a systematic and aggressive communications offensive. This would be the kind of strategy that would grow logically out of what I have called a political understanding of our recent referendum experience.

2. A structural understanding would look quite different and would lead to different strategic and policy consequences. A structural understanding would be more likely to pay attention to experience in Quebec and elsewhere in Canada during the last several decades as a guide to grasping the forces at work in the recent referendum. It would note the following: that Quebec has been engaged in a sustained enterprise of national affirmation for more than 35 years; that, despite recurrent and laudable efforts, Canada has never been able to achieve a stable equilibrium with the new Quebec; that, at the same time, English-speaking Canada has altered substantially in its socio-demographic composition; that many of the English-speaking provinces have been engaged in powerful processes of province-building; and finally that the resources of the government of Canada have declined and its pre-eminence in the federation has been reduced. As for the referendum campaign itself, this approach would take very seriously some of the early findings of Quebec social scientists that the growth in support for the Yes side began *before* Bouchard assumed the leadership of the sovereignist campaign.

If you're the government of Canada and this is your understanding of what is going on, your approach is likely to be quite different. The policies and strategies you fashion in consequence are likely to be broader and much deeper than if you have formed an essentially political understanding of the situation.

You are more likely to be persuaded of the following: that Canadians are facing something like the challenge of re-confederating; that the reasons for Canada need to be stated anew; that the roles and responsibilities of the two orders of government require to be thought through in principled terms; and that the policy and program consequences of this modernized understanding of the Canadian federation need to be pushed forward aggressively. Given this view, if Canada is a product, it needs to be re-designed so that it can be successfully marketed. The existence of Lucien Bouchard and the PQ is not an invitation to an extended election style campaign – or not only that but a trigger that should release basic reflection and reform.

Obviously, the situation is more complicated than this distinction between the political and structural would have us believe, and there may be other ways of characterizing the choices facing Canada and its national government. And pursuing one approach does not preclude pursuing the other as well. But this device does permit us to ask the question: Where are we and where should we be going?

For myself, I am inclined to believe that the structural analysis is nearer the mark, that the country is in need of significant renovation, and not just in the way it manages relations between Quebec and the rest of Canada. There is no question that the country is already changing quite rapidly, and not, by any means, always to our liking. The pressures of Quebec nationalism and public sector penury have probably had more to do with this than anything else. But it seems to me that Canadians and Canadian governments – more than we would like and more than is necessary – are the *creatures* and *sufferers*, rather than the *agents*, of change. It would be nice to get out in front of the wave.

If you asked me how I think the government of Canada understands our current situation and the manner in which it is likely to respond, I would say, regretfully, that the adoption of the political approach is more probable than the structural. This is for several reasons.

1. The political approach is easier, certainly in the short run, although if it is mistaken it is likely to heap up even greater problems in the medium to long term. All conventional, day-to-day political experience argues for the adoption of what I have called the political approach; it is what we do most of the time, and it is what governments and political parties presumably do best.

2. The federal government's performance to date reveals a pronounced preference for incremental measures and for preserving the existing regime at all costs. There seems to be little capacity in Ottawa to recognize that Ottawa itself is part of the problem. Take the example of the Canada Health and Social Transfer (the CHST). If ever there was a moment for a complete re-think of federal fiscal transfers and the way in which we manage our social programs, it was the last Martin budget. However, the notion that the jurisdiction which in theory is constitutionally responsible for the country's social services should be constitutionally responsible in fact was apparently too radical to contemplate. Thus, the federal spending power, which was without doubt a creative and

constructive force three or four decades ago, is now used as a crutch, partly to protect Canada's social safety net from the impact of Ottawa's own withdrawal of funds. Is this really the best we can do as a country?

3. There are extraordinarily powerful interests which would be directly challenged by the pursuit of a structural approach. People who have built their careers in national public service or in national political life will find much to oppose in a substantial overhaul of Confederation, and there are many individual Canadians and organizations across the country who have for years looked to Ottawa for the protection and advancement of the things they hold dear.

4. Finally, there is the matter of the prime minister. It is unthinkable that the Government of Canada could adopt and pursue a structural approach in the absence of the determined, sustained commitment of the prime minister. One must therefore ask the question: Is this his game? Jean Chrétien is an adroit and able politician who, I think, benefitted throughout much of his career from being consistently underrated. It is possible that in his first two years in office he has suffered from being overrated. We thought he made governing during those first two years look easy, but perhaps governing in those first two years *was* easy. He now faces the largest challenge of his political life, and getting it right matters greatly not just to him but to all of us. What will he think is "getting it right"? I believe that Lawrence Martin implicitly answered that question in a comment he made in the first volume of his fine biography of Chrétien, published before the Quebec referendum took place. Summing up Jean Chrétien's strengths and weaknesses at the moment when he was poised to take power, first as leader of the Liberal Party and then as prime minister of Canada, Martin identified as one of Chrétien's flaws the following: the fact that "he showed few signs of being able to understand, as perhaps the greatest of leaders must, the great currents of change, both the dismal and the grand, sweeping the world around him."[1]

By way of conclusion, let me say that I hope I am wrong in either one of two ways. Either that I am wrong in thinking that structural change is necessary, which would permit me to hope that the political approach likely to be pursued by Ottawa might carry the day. Or that I am wrong in thinking that Ottawa is not capable of pursuing much more than the political approach, and that it is in fact on the point of embarking on a process of structural change or re-Confederation. For, like it or not, Ottawa is key to the resolution of this country's difficulties. On its own, it cannot ensure success, but it has within its power the capacity to guarantee failure.

NOTE

1 Lawrence Martin, *Chrétien: The Will to Win*, vol. 1 (Toronto: Lester Publishing, 1995), 376.

10 The Court's Supreme Wisdom

Ottawa Citizen **25 August 1998**

This piece was written a few days after the Supreme Court released its decision. I argued here that the Court served the country well: first, by ensuring that the decision was unanimous; second, by declining to enter into hypotheticals and future details best left to politicians to handle; third, by forcefully enunciating a framework of constitutional principles which must guide any secession negotiations; and finally, by definitively dismissing any argument that Quebec possessed a unilateral right to self-determination under either domestic or international law. It was already becoming clear, even at that early moment, that – remarkably – virtually all the actors on all sides were finding something to celebrate in the decision.

Sage. Prudent. Wise.

These are the words that came to my mind as I read the Supreme Court opinion on the secession of Quebec.

First, the Court spoke with one voice.

Second, the judges made it perfectly clear that they knew what they should not speak about.

Third, what they chose to speak about they addressed with authority and confidence, forcing the national-unity debate onto a deeper, more principled plane, and making it harder for politicians and citizens to evade full responsibility for what they say and do.

Consider first the effect a split decision would have had. Think of the confusion and unproductive division a variety of minority positions would have created. The Patriation Reference of 1981, the next most important opinion the Supreme Court has rendered, split 7:2 and 6:3 on the two main questions it was asked. While that 1981 opinion forced the constitutional negotiators back to the bargaining table, it also set the stage for a settlement without Quebec that has remained controversial to this day. This time round there is complete agreement of the full bench on the reasoning and opinion in response to the questions posed by the government of Canada. By this achievement – and it is an achievement – the judges have guaranteed that the politics of secession may be the subject of intense public debate, but that the politics of the Court will not.

What of the opinion itself? The judges in their reasoning could have chosen to go forward; instead they have gone back. They could have gone forward by pushing their thinking into the realm of a hypothetical future: What is a clear referendum question on secession? What is a clear majority? Must there be a second referendum at the end of the secession negotiations? Can the Cree in northern Quebec stay in Canada if they choose? Do Quebec's minority communities have the right of self-determination, too?

Wisely, in my opinion, they declined to put their collective hand into this hornets' nest, arguing persuasively that these are inherently political issues that citizens and their leaders should sort out for themselves.

Instead, the Supreme Court went back – back to the guiding principles and values that have shaped Canada since its founding and that we live by still: federalism; democracy; constitutionalism and the rule of law; respect for minority rights. They argued that all are important; none is pre-eminent; each entails duties as well as rights. The judges insisted that all participants in the national unity debate – on both sides of the issue – have a duty to give these principles honest life and to employ them as authoritative guides in addressing the issue of the secession of Quebec. Negotiation in good faith; mutual respect; a conscientious effort to consider and accommodate the concerns of the other side – these, rather than ultimatums, trickery and threats, are the touchstones of proper conduct in this debate.

This means that what the Court calls "principled negotiations" should define the process by which the secession matter is addressed. The government of Quebec has no right to proceed unilaterally but is rather obliged conscientiously to pursue its objective of secession within the existing constitutional framework. The government of Canada and the other provincial governments, for their part, are denied the luxury of not responding to a clear Yes vote by a clear majority of the population of Quebec; they have the obligation to enter in good faith into negotiations to address the issues that the Yes vote raises. And all the government actors in the negotiations must attend to the aspirations and material interests of others, such as the Aboriginal and minority-language communities, whose situation must be accommodated in any final settlement.

So far, almost everyone – the federal government, the PQ government in Quebec City, the Bloc, Reform. the NDP, Jean Charest's Liberals, Gary Filmon, Roy Romanow, Matthew Coon Come, even Jacques Parizeau, for goodness' sake – are declaring victory, or are at least displaying grudging satisfaction with the opinion. One might think that an opinion with which everyone agrees must be an opinion without principle or substance. But in the case of this opinion, at least, that would be unfair.

I think the reason for this uncharacteristic display of universal happiness is that everyone is pointing to the element of the opinion with which he or she agrees, and forgetting the rest. Ironically, this is exactly what our Supreme Court Justices warn against; their whole argument is based on the proposition that Canadians adhere to a set of fundamental principles and share a number of key values, and that proper conduct must take into account all of these principles and values. You can't responsibly pick and choose the ones you want at any given moment and leave the rest.

Just as there are elements of the opinion which people like, so there are elements which will cause real discomfort to each of the major actors. This is because both the things which people like and the things which they do not are rooted in a deeper framework of principle. This framework, if accepted, will structure and discipline future discussion and conduct relating to Quebec's secession from Canada. If the Court's framework is accepted, participants will have to alter their positions in ways they don't much like. And if that happens, we will have reached a new level of political maturity and civility in our seemingly never-ending national-unity debate.

We all – sovereignists and federalists alike – owe our Supreme Court a vote of thanks. They have served the country well, no matter whether it ends up being one country or two.

11 National Unity and Paradigm Shifts

In Thomas A. McIntosh, ed., *Drift, Strategy, and Happenstance: Towards Political Reconciliation in Canada?* 1998

As you can see, this was a speculative piece, arguing that Quebec's long-running dispute with Canada was at a significant turning point. The paper was first presented at a seminar at Harvard, and I can remember Keith Banting, the distinguished social scientist from Queen's University who was spending a year's leave at Harvard, getting up at the session and saying that he had only been away from Canada for a few months, and he could hardly believe the situation was changing so quickly. In the event, the passage of more time made it abundantly clear that a major shift was indeed occurring.

My modest goal in this paper is to explore whether Canada and Quebec may be on the cusp of a paradigm shift in French-English relations. What I am asking is whether we are on the verge of something big in our history, a shift from one historical era to another.

Let me give you the short answer to that question first: I don't know.

Now for the long answer, which is necessarily speculative. It will proceed in the following stages.

- First, I will turn ignorance into a methodological virtue, using its existence to help us open our minds to the possibility that there are new worlds and shiny new paradigms out there, waiting to be discovered.
- Second, I will examine features of our present world for hints or intimations of potential change and possible transformation. The idea here is to see whether the seeds of a new era are embedded in the old.
- Third, assuming that there is the potential for transformation, I will consider how that potential might be actualized. Here it will be a question of

identifying actors or historical agents which might bring about the birth of this potential new era.

- Finally, I will reflect on the possibility that our earnest efforts to address our national-unity problem over the last three decades is in fact what has kept the problem in existence. If I am successful in making a case here, it will give the phrase "Just say no" new meaning.

Before I begin, I should sketch briefly what a new era or a new national-unity paradigm might look like.

I am not talking just about the possibility – with Jean Charest at the helm of the provincial Liberals – of defeating the PQ in the next provincial election, or of winning the next referendum if the PQ is not electorally defeated. I am not thinking about the kind of momentary lull in our national-unity storm that we have known from time to time in the last 30 years.

I am asking you to consider whether there might be grounds for believing that a radical reconstruction of political discourse in Quebec concerning the national question is imaginable, whether it may be possible for us to shift the focus away from our debilitating concentration on constitutional disunity, grievance politics, partition, the terms of secession, Plan B and French-English tension.

I am talking about reaching an enduring, stable accommodation between the French-speaking and English-speaking communities in this country, the kind of allegedly sunny pasture we always hoped was waiting for us around the next constitutional corner, but which we never found.

If you think of the Quiet Revolution as opening a bracket at the beginning of a period in which deep, existential questions of identity, community, and national purpose have been in play, both within Quebec and within Canada as a whole, then the paradigm shift of which I speak can be thought of as closing the bracket at the end of that turbulent historical period, and heralding the commencement of a new and discernibly different era in our evolving political experience.

Now you know what I mean by a new paradigm. Let's try to see whether we are on the cusp of it.

I'll begin now with the first stage of my argument – turning our ignorance into a virtue.

No One Can Read the Future: Therefore, It Is Hard to Learn from the Past

As I look back at all the twists and turns of the last four decades of Canadian history, and then try to peer into the murky future, what strikes me is this: the country's ultimate fate, quite simply, defies my understanding and is certainly beyond my predictive powers. It probably defies everyone's understanding. We all do our analysis, adopt our positions, launch our arguments, make our predictions, reconstruct the past to fit our present requirements – but the full picture consistently escapes us. We are repeatedly surprised by the next turn in the road of our national journey. Looking back:

- Who, in the 1960s – with the separatists nothing more than a disreputable fringe movement – thought that a sovereignist party would form the government of Quebec in 1976 and become an enduring force on the political scene?
- Who could have foreseen the rapid, though temporary, demobilization of the sovereignist movement following the patriation of the Constitution without Quebec's consent in 1982?
- Who, in 1987, could have anticipated the demise of the Meech Lake Accord in 1990?
- Who would have predicted that the Yes side would come within a hair's breadth of winning the 1995 referendum on sovereignty?
- Who could have forecast the impact that the unexpected resignation of Daniel Johnson as leader of the Liberal Party would have on the national-unity debate?

It is as if the country is a giant, complex organism, moving according to rhythms and cadences all its own. Each generation struggles to understand, aspires to direct or control, but the creature moves how and when and where it wants, observant of its own sovereign imperatives, and faithful to a life cycle it keeps to itself. Hence our sense of wonder as the next station in this unfathomable creature's procession through life is duly revealed to us.

At this first stage of the argument, then, my message is three-fold, and it is this:

- We have been surprised in the past.
- We will be surprised again.
- In the hazardous business of forecasting, there is no particular reason to privilege linear extensions of the unaltered present into the future. We should keep ourselves open to the possibility that we may encounter unexpected shifts, sudden *virages,* startling reconfigurations of historical forces, that will carry the country in directions we would never have expected.

Intimations of Change

Let me turn now to intimations of change, elements in our present situation that may be harbingers of new things to come.

Because the nationalist world view has dominated debate and structured thinking in Quebec for years – even among federalists – the rich potential for transformation has not been appreciated. We have not been paying enough attention to some of the facts and forces that have been at work in the last while. What are some of these facts and forces?

1 Most Quebecers do not want another referendum on sovereignty. 60 per cent plus are against, according to opinion polls, and this includes a lot of sovereignists – almost a third, according to some surveys. Mario Dumont, the leader of the ADQ, says there should be a ten-year moratorium on referendums in Quebec. The Québécois know better than most people how divisive and costly referendums like this are.

2 Younger Quebecers appear to approach sovereignty differently from their elders – even if they are favourable to Quebec independence, they treat it as something that is likely to occur at some point, rather than as a goal that they are passionately pursuing as their central political aspiration. Indeed, Quebec looks as if it is about to go through a generational shift in its politics; not only will the style of political leadership change as a new, younger generation begins to replace the old guard, but so too may the substance of Quebec's politics. Generation X and the decline of deference are alive and well in Quebec as they are elsewhere in the industrialized world.

3 Quebecers stubbornly continue to acknowledge an ongoing attachment to Canada. Polls regularly confirm this fact. One survey, a couple of months before the last referendum found that 80 per cent (including 61 per cent of YES supporters) were "proud to be both Quebecers and Canadians." When Quebecers were asked in May 1997 how they would vote, or be tempted to vote, in response to the following hypothetical referendum question: "Do you want Quebec to remain a province of Canada?", 67 per cent answered Yes. When they were asked the same question in April of this year, the number had risen to 77 per cent. The very durability of the partnership element of the sovereignty project may respond not just to calculated self-interest, but also to a genuine belief in the value of continued association with Canada.

4 Canadians, since 1982, have proven themselves to be incapable of achieving comprehensive constitutional reform. Bilateral practical amendments, yes; but complex, highly symbolic amendments, no. And there is no reason to believe that the prospects are any better today. Trying and failing to amend the constitution has proven to be almost as divisive and conflict ridden at the Canadian level as referendums have been in Quebec.

5 In many of the ways that matter, the country is working well. A good many Quebecers are prepared to say that Canada is the best country in the world to live in. Canadians love to grumble and complain, but most realize that we're doing all right – the economy is ticking along nicely, inflation is low, unemployment though high is coming down, Ottawa and most of the provinces are running surpluses, and the talk is now all about how the money

pouring into public coffers should be spent. Quebec, at the moment, is one of the fiscal laggards, but it is getting there. More serious than the fiscal lag, perhaps, is an apparent drag on economic development in Quebec. It is, for example, suffering from what has been called a deficit of investment intentions; with one-fourth of the population and output of Canada, Quebec is attracting only one-sixth of the investment intentions.

6 My sixth and final point. Quebec, since the Quiet Revolution, has been a remarkable success story. In the last four decades, Quebec has transformed its society, restructured its economy, and created a place of safety in North America for the French language. There has been no significant barrier to Quebec's concrete development as a modern, predominantly French-language community, to its project of constructing a distinct society. The justification for sovereignty, such as it is, has had everything to do with symbolic politics, little to do with the practical business of building what is, after all, an admirable and distinctive political community.

The potential for transformation, which I am arguing may be embedded in such facts and forces as these has not been evident because, until now, the usual suspects – the all too familiar political actors, located primarily in Ottawa and Quebec City – have been locked in sterile combat, with none able or willing to try a different way. Postreferendum, it has been the more extreme opinions on both sides that have been most heard, even though the capacious middle ground is where most Canadians – inside and outside Quebec – find themselves.

Actualizing the Potential

Well, let us suppose that there is in fact the potential for major change. That doesn't necessarily mean that it will be realized. Many of the factors I have identified have been in existence for some time, and that hasn't led to any astonishing *virage*. Why should we think it might happen now?

It is obviously true that what is potential is not actual. There needs to be a catalyst to secure the release of the potential. The dynamite needs an igniter. Someone needs to throw the switch on the power grid. The skids have to be pulled out from under the new ship for it to be launched. Maurice Duplessis had to die before the Quiet Revolution could commence.

What plausible catalytic agents are on the horizon in the situation I have described? As possible agents of transformation, I would offer you a person and a generation.

The person, of course, is Jean Charest. He assumes his role as a political leader in Quebec at an auspicious moment; he is presented with a wider range of policy choices than is customarily the case in politics, and a greater potential than normal to effect political change. Don't get me wrong: he is no miracle worker. A large-dimension opportunity is there, that is all; whether he will be willing and able to seize it is another matter.

He brings considerable personal assets to the task:

- his authentic Quebec roots
- his rhetorical skill and his talent for reaching people emotionally
- his youth
- his forthright commitment to Canada and to Quebec within Canada

Quebec has not had in living memory a prominent provincial politician prepared to make an unvarnished case in favour of Canada and Quebec's place within it. Jean Charest's willingness to do so opens up a new line of debate in the province, and holds the possibility of releasing sentiments and preferences long stopped up in that society.

Mr. Charest can present himself as a leader from the new political generation in Quebec which is prepared to offer Quebecers politics in a new style. He can underline the contrast between himself and the older generation of Mr. Bouchard and Mr. Chrétien, drawing a distinction between his egalitarian, post-modern way of doing politics and the stiffer, more formal, top-down, old-fashioned manner in which Mr. Bouchard conducts himself. He can remain relentlessly positive, confident and up-beat, demonstrating his refusal to play the negative politics of grievance, complaint, and humiliation that has fed so much of the sovereignty movement.

In policy terms, he can oppose Plan B, the holding of another referendum, and any discussion of the constitution. He can commit himself and his government, if elected, to active participation in the common life and intergovernmental affairs of the country. Much of this Jean Charest is already doing.

Until now, the politics of hope has been the politics of sovereignty. Jean Charest has an opportunity to wrestle hope from the grasp of the sovereignists and attach it to the rejection of sovereignty and the forthright acceptance of Canada.

What I am advancing here is far from being an argument for the status quo, although the status quo has its merits. It is rather an argument against trying to do what you cannot do, and in favour of applying your creative and transformative energies to those areas of our common life where they can really make a difference.

What of the other catalytic agent? Here I am speaking even more speculatively, but I am thinking of the political impact a new and younger generation may have on Quebec politics as its leaders assume positions of power. I am thinking of those who may not have fully absorbed the world view and traditional nationalist ideology from their elders, of the people whose future will be unequivocally shaped by globalization, the new communications technologies and the post industrial economy. Which way will these people jump, on the national question?

What will the new Quebec politics look like as the Lucien Bouchards and the Bernard Landrys and the Jacques Parizeaus pass from the scene?

If the rising generation responds positively to the style of politics and the re-orientation of public policies that Jean Charest and a remodelled Liberal Party might put on offer, there could be the catalytic force required to bring forth the new era I am talking about.

Thinking about Things Differently

Let me turn now to the fourth and final stage in my presentation, namely, a few concluding reflections on the possibility that our earnest efforts to address the national question over the last three decades is part of what has kept the problem in existence.

A great deal of our collective energies in the last few decades has been devoted to activities and initiatives that have their roots in one of two assumptions:

- that there is a problem, and intelligent efforts at reform may fix it
- that there is a problem, but reform may not fix it, and Quebec may depart

Is this the most helpful way of framing the matter that confronts Canada? There is, after all, a third possible assumption – namely, that there is a "problem," that it cannot be fixed, and that Quebec will not depart.

We are all of us embedded in a deeply liberal, progressive civilization in which it seems that everything we find amiss is a problem, and every problem must have a solution. For more than 30 years we have sought to define the problem, to make it explicit, to frame as precisely as possible what the issue of contention is, and then to make policies, take initiatives, and amend the constitution to resolve the matter. A problem solved is a problem gone away, a problem gotten rid of, and we have cried out for finality, for an end to the crisis.

Perhaps one of the reasons we have been unable to obtain satisfaction in this matter lies in the activist, rationalistic methodology we have implicitly utilized in seeking to address it. Maybe we have unwittingly paid too little heed to the merits of prudence, restraint, circumspection and, yes, avoidance. What if it is the case that what we are confronting is not a problem to be solved but a tension to be accommodated, an arrangement to be lived with, a practical situation which is not perfect, but eminently tolerable? Thinking about our national-unity problem in this way points us in an unconventional direction.

It alerts us to the possibility that in every decently functioning constitutional order, as in other human relationships, there may be no-go zones, radically divisive areas of political life which contain issues that cannot be resolved but only avoided. Indeed, it appears that many successful constitutional regimes manage their affairs, in part, by burying or covering over these vertiginous cleavages.

As it happens, there is a constitutional scholar who speaks directly to this point. Michael Foley, in *The Silence of Constitutions*[1] writes, not about Canada, but about two of the most successful and sophisticated constitutional regimes in the world – the United Kingdom and the United States. He refers to these dangerously unmanageable elements buried in the foundations of these and many other societies as "abeyances," and contends that a mature and prudent political order will implicitly attend to them by indirection, by encouraging the potentially warring parties to engage in mutually complicit acts of restraint and avoidance – a kind of whistling past the graveyard.[2] A failure to do so, a willingness to uncover and expose these abeyances, will often be the prelude to acute civil upheaval, and, once unburied, it will be very difficult to get them back under ground again.

In Canada, the noxious dialectic played out in recent years between the principle of the equality of provinces and the principle of Quebec as a distinct society points to just such an elemental force. It can be argued that during the last three decades we Canadians – true children of the age of reason, believing that every problem has a solution – have been busily digging up and exposing this constitutional abeyance. Having got it up and out in the open, we don't know what to do with it.

Conclusion

Perhaps we are at a moment in our national development when an abeyance-burying strategy, very different from what we have been doing, is feasible. Is it not possible to believe that there is the potential in Quebec and Canada for a profound shift in the manner in which we address the national question?

The historical role I have assigned to the unwitting Mr. Charest in these remarks is to help us all begin to get this unruly force safely buried under ground again. His assignment, should he choose to accept it, is to become Canada's Supreme Abeyance Interment Officer. I say, let the (re)burial begin.

Let us suppose that the future is indeed as murky and as unfathomable as I have described it. In that case, it would, at the very least, be unwise to rule this kind of paradigm shift out as a possibility. After more than 30 years of storm and ferment – who knows? – Canada and Quebec may want some quiet. It looks as if it is there for the taking.

NOTES

1 Michael Foley, *The Silence of Constitutions: Gaps, "Abeyances" and Political Temperament in the Maintenance of Government.* (London: Routledge, 1989). Foley speaks of "the continuing flaws, half-answers and partial truths that are endemic in the

sub-structure of constitutional forms. Abeyances refer to those parts of the constitution that remain unwritten and even unspoken not only by convention, but also of necessity. More precisely, abeyances represent a way of accommodating the absence of a definitive constitutional settlement and of providing the means of adjusting to the issues left unresolved in the fabric of the constitution. Sometimes ... the issues can be crucial; the only satisfactory way of defining them is to inhibit their development and to place them in abeyance as a condoned anomaly..." (10).

2 This phrase is the title of David Thomas's book, which applies the abeyance theory to Canada: *Whistling Past the Graveyard: Constitutional Abeyances, Quebec, and the Future of Canada* (Toronto: Oxford University Press, 1997).

INTERLUDE	Current Reflections on the Past: David Cameron in Conversation with Robert Vipond

2020

Rob Vipond, the editor of this volume, identified a period of about ten years during which I was not publishing on the topics discussed in this collection. He suggested that we engage in a retrospective conversation about the neglected period. This chapter, which admittedly ranges more broadly than the decade we identified, is the result of that suggestion.

RV: I wanted to speak with you about that crucial part of the national unity crisis that is bounded, roughly speaking, by the first Quebec referendum on "sovereignty-association" in 1980 at one end and the second referendum in 1995 at the other. To set the scene: The Parti Québécois under the leadership of René Lévesque won a stunning electoral victory in the Quebec provincial election, held on November 15, 1976. The PQ had promised that, if elected, it would hold a referendum on sovereignty, and the prospect that Quebec might seek to secede from the Canadian federation produced a frenzy of soul-searching in the rest of the country. The federal government responded in a number of ways, one of which was to create a Task Force on Canadian Unity (of which you were the Director of Research). After extensive consultations across the country, the Task Force produced a report – *A Future Together* – (of which you were the co-author with Ron Watts).

The report[1] – published in February 1979 – is such an interesting document because, right from the outset, you suggest that the goal was to explore political and constitutional reforms – "a third option," you called it – between Quebec sovereignty and the status quo. To call it interesting is maybe too bland. Perhaps a better descriptor would be "bold" because, at least implicitly, it seems as if the third option was something of an alternative to the anti-nationalist individualism that guided Pierre Trudeau throughout the period. Would you agree with that characterization?

Yet some observers have suggested that this third option was pretty much dead on arrival – both in Ottawa and Quebec City – because as the referendum campaign heated up, the debate quickly became both polarized and personalized in a way that didn't leave much space for reforms in the muddy middle. Is that fair?

DC: "Bold" is, I think, the right word. In two ways. First of all, as I point out in chapter 5 (*Not Spicer and Not the B & B: Reflections of an Insider on the Workings of the Pepin-Robarts Task Force on Canadian Unity*), Prime Minister Pierre Trudeau set up the Task Force simply to give Canadians a forum for expression and to report neutrally on what they were thinking and saying, not to advise on policy or strategy. He knew perfectly well what policies he wanted to pursue – the antinationalist individualism you allude to. Despite that, the Task Force commissioners decided early on that they wanted to offer their substantive ideas about how the crisis could be addressed, even though they recognized that their offering would not be warmly received by the government that brought the Task Force into being. Secondly, when they prepared their ideas, after intensive consultation with the public and discussion with policy experts, they came forward with a third option – a set of policy proposals that were thought to fall somewhere between the PQ's sovereignty-association, on the one hand, and Pierre Trudeau's anti-nationalist individualism on the other. This was not welcomed by the government of Canada, nor by Pierre Trudeau. Indeed, I think you could say that the Task Force's report was a declaration of intellectual independence on the part of the co-chair, Jean-Luc Pepin, and at least two of his commissioners, Solange Chaput-Rolland and Gérald Beaudoin.

For Trudeau, the issue was always about the patriation of the constitution with a domestic amending formula, the constitutional protection of French and English language rights, and the introduction of a charter of rights and freedoms into our basic law. It was never about the decentralization of federal power to Quebec or the provinces or about the constitutional recognition of Quebec's distinctive role as the "*foyer principal*" of the French community in North America.

Many within and outside Quebec were surprised to discover that the Task Force was prepared to break new intellectual and policy ground. At the First Ministers Conference, which met in Vancouver two weeks after the Task Force released *A Future Together* (25 January 1979), Claude Morin, a senior Parti Québécois strategist and then minister responsible for intergovernmental affairs in the PQ government, is reported to have said of the report: "We're not in the same boat, but we're sailing down the same river."

So when I say the adjective "bold" is well chosen, it's not only because the Task Force expanded the consultation mandate it had been given into the policy realm, but also because the policy ideas it advanced were definitively not wanted by the federal government. Jean-Luc Pepin paid a price for that. When he ran successfully in the February 1980 federal election that brought Trudeau and the Liberals back to power after the Joe Clark interregnum, Pepin, given his stature, was a shoe-in for a cabinet post of some kind. But Trudeau put him in the Transport portfolio, far, far away from the national-unity file with which Pepin had so much expertise and experience. He had no voice or role in the constitutional talks that led ultimately to the 1982 Constitution.

Dead on arrival. Well, in one sense that sums it up pretty well. As an approach and a set of ideas that were meant to contribute to the intergovernmental discussions and negotiations then going on, the Task Force report went nowhere. Trudeau and the federal government wouldn't touch it with a barge pole, and the provincial governments did little to give it life, even though the report contained thinking and ideas congenial to many. There was some interest in the report in the short-lived Joe Clark Conservative government (June 1979–March 1980), but it was defeated before it had a chance to affect the course of events. The report was also a significant influence on the *Beige Paper*, the set of constitutional and policy proposals that the Liberal Party of Quebec under Claude Ryan released in 1980, but since the Quebec Liberals never achieved power under Ryan, these ideas came to naught.

More generally, and over the longer term, the report carved out a political space that came to be shared by others. The 1982 Constitution carries the imprint of Pierre Trudeau and the federal government of the day, with its protection of Canadian minority language rights, the Charter of Rights and Freedoms, and the provisions for constitutional amendment. The fact, however, that its passage was roundly opposed by the members of the National Assembly in Quebec suggests that there was something missing in the 1982 arrangements so far as many in Quebec were concerned. The Meech Lake Accord, initially agreed to by all governments in 1987, was meant to repair that deficiency. Its understanding of what needed to be fixed rests on a view of the country that has much in common with that of the Task Force. So, not quite dead on arrival, even if the conceptualization of the country has not yet been fully incorporated into the constitutional framework of Canada.

RV: I want to ask you to elaborate a bit on 1982. I think there's a tendency to look back at the combination of patriation and the enactment of the Constitution Act, 1982, as an almost magical moment of constitution-making when a "new"

Canada was created. Yet that's not how many people interpreted it at the time. As you say, the Constitution Act was repudiated not just by the government of Quebec but overwhelmingly by the Quebec National Assembly as well. Hopes that federalism would be renewed following the 1980 referendum were largely disappointed. The Charter of Rights worried those, like Premier Sterling Lyon of Manitoba and Premier Allan Blakeney of Saskatchewan, who believed that it would undermine representative government and usher in what we might now call "juristocracy" – the rule of courts. Many of those on the other side who supported the robust protection of rights thought that the Charter had been fatally wounded by the inclusion of section 33 and the notwithstanding clause. And just about everyone criticized the process that produced the constitutional settlement as opaque and undemocratic.

So my recollection is that many people were less than happy with the constitutional deal of 1982. Indeed, there was a collection of essays that many of us used in Canadian politics courses at the time that bore the title *And No One Cheered* – which pretty much sums it up.

You were in Ottawa at the time. What was your – and the federal government's – perspective on the Constitution Act, 1982?

DC: Let me start with the charge of opacity first. If you consider the domestic constitutional process from the spring of 1980 to the Supreme Court Reference decision on 28 September 1981, I believe that what began as a closed intergovernmental process from which the public was largely excluded (June to September 1980) morphed into a public, federal Parliamentary process from which the provinces were largely excluded (October 1980 to the summer of 1981). I believe there was a procedural and a strategic dimension to this.

On the procedural side, the federal government led an intensive round of negotiations with the provinces that started shortly after the Quebec referendum on 20 May 1980 and ran into the early autumn. Members of the federal team strongly believed that the Government of Canada had to strike while the iron was hot – while the euphoria in English-speaking Canada unleashed by the referendum results was still palpable. They said: "We have to get this done before the snow flies." Jean Chrétien, the federal minister of Justice and Ottawa's point man on the constitutional file, boarded a government aircraft with a few advisers and visited every provincial capital in the hours following the referendum vote. Only Premier Lévesque, obviously bruised and hurting from the defeat, refused to see him. It was in these meetings, confirmed in a gathering of first ministers at 24 Sussex Drive, on June 9, 1980, that Chrétien got the agreement of provincial leaders that a hyper-intensive round of constitutional discussions should be launched immediately and completed as rapidly as humanly possible. That summer, meetings of the Continuing Committee of Ministers on the Constitution, co-chaired by Jean Chrétien and Roy Romanow, the attorney general of Saskatchewan, followed one after another at what was a scalding pace compared to normal intergovernmental processes. The committee meetings were held at various provincial capitals across the country; federal and provincial officials worked intensively on drafts in between.

All this effort led to the critical First Ministers' Conference (FMC) in Ottawa which ran from September 8–12, 1980. The intensive summer's negotiations had produced a set of 'best efforts' drafts, but no agreements, and the FMC did no better. Canadians got to watch much of it on national television, with rising anxiety as the unpleasant, discordant days dragged on. I was participating in the conference as a federal official, and just how bad things had become came home to me when a colleague and I took a break from the proceedings and went to the Byward Market to get some fresh air. We were wearing our conference tags. When we passed a parked police car with a couple of burly Ottawa cops sitting inside, one of them leaned out of the open window and said: "So how's it going?" We said: "Not so well," to which he replied: "You should send us in there. We're good at dealing with domestics."

Viewing the limited prospects of ever reaching agreement with the provinces on terms to which the federal government could agree, the prime minister decided to go it alone and bring a set of constitutional amendments through Parliament. He announced this in a national television address on October 2nd. This opened the door to all party and public participation in the constitutional process, much of it mediated through the special, joint parliamentary committee on the constitution whose hearings were televised; the second stage – the public, federal Parliamentary process – began, and the provinces, relatively speaking, faded into the background.

With respect to strategic factors, the second dimension of this story, let's begin with the fact that, although the first stage (June to September 1980) was clearly an intergovernmental, not a public process, all governments were acting very much with one eye on public opinion. The Trudeau government had in fact developed a strategy designed to align its aspirations as closely as possible with what it believed to be those of the Canadian public. In its public communications approach, it broke the constitutional proposals arising from the federal and provincial governments into two packages. It dubbed *its* proposals (patriation and amendment, a statement of constitutional principles, and a charter of rights, including language rights) the "people's package," contending that none of these proposals had anything to do with improving the position of the federal government, but rather with advancing the aspirations of citizens and strengthening the country. The other items on the list for negotiation (including the Senate and the Supreme Court, resource ownership, offshore resources, fisheries and communications) were designated by Ottawa as the "powers and institutions package." These were items that related to the power balance between the government of Canada and the provincial governments, or the key institutions about which governments were particularly concerned. Having made that distinction the prime minister then made it clear that he would not bargain the people's items against the items of interest to governments. He "would not trade rights for fish," as I recall one of the phrases at the time.

During the summer of constitutional negotiations, this proved to be an effective rhetorical tool, and successfully placed the provinces on the defensive. As I have said, after the failure of the September First Ministers Conference, the federal government decided to proceed unilaterally. When the televised legislative process began in the fall and civil-society organizations began to make their submissions, federal politicians and officials realized that the strategy they had developed in the summer for communications purposes actually had substantive reality in the minds of the populace. Groups and citizens who appeared before the Special Parliamentary Committee wanted the federal proposals, especially the Charter of Rights and Freedoms, to be made stronger. This meant that the Government was able to accept proposals for improving the draft constitutional provisions with the confidence that what they were doing had resonance with the public. As Peter Russell points out,[2] these proposals – improved as a result of public participation – "did more than expand the base of political support for the Trudeau government's unilateral initiative. The process itself created a new public expectation about popular participation in constitution making...."

The story through the fall and winter of 1980–81 to the completion of the Canadian process and the forwarding of the initiative to the British Parliament for action in early December 1981 confirms this shift in public expectation. The process was made up of an interplay between federal and provincial governments, Parliament, plus the new constitutional actor, the public.

Now, on to your main question, namely, how did I assess the achievement of the Constitution Act, 1982, at the time, and how did I understand the federal government's perspective? Let me start with my understanding of the perspective of the federal government. In a matter such as this, it is hard to separate the government from the senior people in Ottawa who were running the show at that time: Trudeau, Chrétien, and the balance of the Liberal cabinet and caucus, Michael Pitfield, Clerk of the Privy Council, Michael Kirby, the top official in the Federal-Provincial Relations Office, and others. The constitution and national unity had been central preoccupations of the prime minister since the 1960s, and he must have been relieved to have succeeded after so many years of failure, particularly when his defeat at the hands of Joe Clark in 1979 made it look as if his political career was over. The resounding defeat of the PQ in the Quebec referendum in the spring of 1980 boosted the morale and confidence of the federal leadership. Given the controversial undertaking that Prime Minister Trudeau gave Quebecers in the final days of the referendum campaign, namely, that voting no would not be interpreted as a vote against change and that Quebec's federal MPs would put their seats on the line to ensure that this time reform was achieved, there was both the confidence and the determination to see the constitutional reform process through to completion. Thus there was simple relief that this milestone had been achieved, however much blood may have been left on the floor. Not only that: the debates had been heavily informed by the bitter conflict between Quebecers in the sovereignist camp and Quebecers in the federalist camp. You were either on our team or the other team. The passage of the Constitution Act, 1982, meant that the federalist side had won, conclusively. First, the referendum win, then the Constitution. The wind was in their sails, and Pierre Trudeau's claim – confirmed by the 74 out of 75 seats in Quebec the federal Liberals held – that he represented Quebec as authentically as René Lévesque seemed persuasive to many.

There were several large, celebratory banquets held across Ottawa to celebrate this constitutional accomplishment. The dinner halls were filled with federal cabinet ministers, other senior members of the government, federal officials who had worked on the constitutional file, provincial leaders and their officials, and others. Jean Chrétien chaired the dinner I attended, and I recall feeling estranged from the mood of giddy celebration. I had worked closely and intensively with many of the people in the room, and I had no doubt that pushing the constitutional file to a conclusion had been the right thing to do in the circumstances. Yet to my mind the patriation of the Constitution was not the equivalent of winning a battle, but the partial achievement of a reform that the country needed. Much had been accomplished, undoubtedly, but much remained undone. It seemed passing strange that Quebec, the jurisdiction that had driven the constitutional process from the beginning, was the only jurisdiction to be left out at the end. Clearly, given Trudeau's dominance of the Quebec political scene, people contested the adequacy of that view at the time, and they still do, but my sentiments that evening could be characterized more as feelings of rueful satisfaction and concern than as full-throated celebration.

Like all such documents arrived at consensually (setting aside Quebec, of course), the Constitution Act, 1982 was the product of debate and compromise, and constitutional actors were understandably inclined to evaluate the achievement according to the extent to which their aspirations were realized within it. Trudeau and the federal government had to put some water in their wine to attract the support necessary for the passage of the Constitution Act, 1982; Trudeau was, I think, particularly unhappy with the inclusion of Section 33, the notwithstanding provision. Those in the provincial capitals and in opposition in the federal Parliament did not get all that they sought either. It is equally true that the Indigenous leadership, while it made major progress, had aimed for more, and organized interest groups and others experienced varying degrees of success. Nationalists – even moderate nationalists – in Quebec, though, could find little in the constitutional settlement that responded to the concerns they had been voicing for years.

What we can see today, with the benefit of almost 40 years of experience since the establishment of the Constitution Act in 1982, and what we could not see at the time, is the extent to which the real meaning of those reforms is found in the inferences that subsequent constitutional actors drew from them. The ongoing micro-constitutional processes, the day-to-day political activity of succeeding generations, and most particularly judicial interpretation have shaped the contemporary meaning of the earlier document. Much of it was potential at the time; its potential has been actualized as the years have passed. For example, juristocracy sounds like a bad thing – a system in which judges take power better exercised by legislatures unto themselves. Yet it is possible to have a form of juristocracy in which an evolving balance is struck, in dialogue with legislatures, the politicians, and the public between the provisions of the Constitution as they were written in 1982, and the everchanging realities of Canadian life. So much of our contemporary public life is embedded in the evolving understanding of the 1982 settlement that it is virtually impossible to imagine what our life today would have been like without it.

RV: I'm intrigued by your conclusion that the Constitution Act, 1982 was "the partial achievement of a reform that the country needed" and that while "much had been accomplished, undoubtedly, but much remained undone." I wanted to ask you about the "much remained undone" part. In hindsight, one can see that Quebec's unwillingness to agree to the CA '82 was a deep and open wound that needed to be healed. And one can connect the dots easily enough from the CA '82 through the election of Brian Mulroney (Canada – 1984) to the election of Robert Bourassa (Quebec – 1985) to the Meech Lake Accord (1987). But I wonder if the constitutional agenda was quite so clear and concise in the mid-1980s as that summary suggests. After all, the CA '82 explicitly required that there be a follow-up conference to consider "matters that directly affect the aboriginal peoples of Canada" (Section 37:2) – which did not go well. One might have thought more attention was due Indigenous issues to honour that constitutional commitment. By the mid-1980s, the idea of a Triple E Senate (equal, effective, and elected) was very much in the air as part of a larger set of proposals to reform national institutions in a way that would make them more responsive to regional concerns. Others were talking about democratizing the constitution in various ways. And there were some who predicted that the Mulroney government would leave well enough alone and consign constitutional reform to "the back burner" (as Donald Smiley put it) in order to pursue other big ticket items – like a free trade agreement with the United States.

So there were lots of agenda options on the table. Instead, we got intense, laser-focused constitutional discussions between Ottawa and Quebec – and, ultimately, a set of proposed constitutional amendments in what became known as the Quebec Round. Can you talk a bit about the dynamics of that period between the promulgation of the CA '82 and the Meech Lake Accord to help me understand how we got to Meech?

DC: I suppose it would be possible to argue that there was nothing inevitable about the emergence of the Quebec Round after 1982. The national-unity temperature cooled down after the patriation of the Constitution despite not having Quebec's consent, when one might have assumed instead that it would heat up. If the country had been able to leave well enough alone, it is possible that we might have entered into an extended period of constitutional peace. Certainly Pierre Trudeau thought so, with his bizarre, but possibly ironic assertion that with patriation the federation "was set to last a thousand years!"[3]

Several factors, though, militated against this. One is in fact the range of constitutional items people were seeking to address. You mention, for example, indigenous issues, the Triple E Senate, the more general reform of national institutions. These would be difficult to tackle with no participation from Quebec, and their active consideration would be a continuing reminder of what had not been achieved in 1982.

A second and related point is that there was a fairly widely shared view among many of the constitutional veterans across the country that the absence of Quebec's signature in 1982 was a major flaw in the agreement. Even, I suspect, many of those who held the Quebec government responsible for painting itself into a corner during the patriation negotiations nevertheless experienced some discomfort in encountering the vigorous opposition of the Quebec government and National Assembly. That many vigorously rejected this view, Trudeau first among them, there is no doubt. But the "unfinished business" argument had logical force and enjoyed fairly wide currency at the time, as Patrick Monahan ably demonstrates in the second chapter of his book, *Meech Lake: The Inside Story.*[4] Thus there was a degree of willingness to try to make amends, which was not a sentiment applicable at that time to the Indigenous file, which was treated more as an obligation to hold a meeting rather than to produce results.

Third, there was the play of party politics, which you mention. The Conservatives, heavily supported in Quebec, came to power in Ottawa in 1984, consigning the Liberals to the opposition benches. And the PQ was defeated by the Quebec Liberal Party in 1985. If it was indeed the case that a sovereignist party could never have reached any constitutional agreement with the rest of the country, that contention was now moot, given that the PQ had been replaced by a formally federalist party with an interest in advancing a modest constitutional package that had some chance of acceptance in the rest of the country. The political world had changed.

Fourth, there was the question of leadership. Like Pierre Trudeau, Brian Mulroney's power base was in Quebec, but with a very different constituency in the province – the conservative nationalists for whom the patriation exercise must have been a searing experience. In his Sept-Iles speech on 6 August, during the election, Mulroney made it clear he was committed to gaining the consent of the National Assembly of Quebec to the 1982 Constitution "with honour and enthusiasm." You can argue that his reasons for doing this were venal (to beat Trudeau at his own game) or honourable (to repair a breach in national unity), but there is no question that he acknowledged the breach and that this was an important commitment for him. And for his part, the highly experienced Robert Bourassa was back in the premier's chair in Quebec, determined to assess whether he could find a way for the constitution to be addressed without risking further fracturing of the country.

So I think these four factors – the range of constitutional issues on the table; attitudes at the time, particularly among those most engaged; party politics; and leadership – go some way towards explaining how Meech was the natural successor of 1982.

RV: Let's linger for a moment on the Meech Lake Accord. I have to say that, even after thirty years, I'm still not sure I understand the political and constitutional dynamics of those years, between 1987 and 1990, when Meech dominated the constitutional agenda. It all started in a way that seemed fairly simple and contained: Have the government of Quebec define the terms under which it could join "the constitutional family." Quebec focused on five areas of constitutional concern: recognition of the unique character of Quebec society; greater control over immigration to Quebec; greater say in nominating justices to the Supreme Court; constitutional recognition of the rules regarding opting-out of national programs, with financial compensation; and greater leverage over the constitutional amending procedure. Because these conditions were framed in constitutional terms and presented as constitutional amendments, the participation and consent of other provincial governments was necessary. The other nine provincial governments were willing to go along – as long as the constitutional changes applied equally to them (except, of course, for the distinct-society provision). But the provincial legislatures were less sure, and ultimately the Accord foundered in mid-1990 when two legislatures – Manitoba and Newfoundland – failed to ratify the pact within three years of its creation.

That's the skeleton in the closet, as it were. By the time of Meech, you were working for the government of Ontario – which was one of the more enthusiastic boosters of the Accord (if memory serves). And since then, you've had an opportunity to think about Meech as a scholar of Canadian politics. So the big question for me is: What went wrong?

Of course, there have been plenty of post mortems over the years, so let me sketch a few possible explanations and have you assess them. One explanation is essentially tactical in nature. The various governments made a huge error when they presented the Accord as an "all or nothing" package that required the unanimous consent of all the provincial legislatures even though not all of the proposed amendments required unanimity. This was compounded by allowing the process to drag on over three years, which inevitably meant that some of the premiers who supported Meech in 1987 were no longer in office to shepherd the Accord through their legislatures.

A second explanation is that the content or substance of the Accord was flawed. Some objected to the distinct society clause. Others thought that the provisions with respect to the federal spending power and opting out with compensation would eviscerate national programs and a shared sense of national identity. One way or another, Meech encountered strong headwinds when it went out for discussion.

A third set of criticisms centres less on what was in the Accord than on what was left out. This was personified most powerfully by the example of Elijah Harper, the only Indigenous representative in the Manitoba legislature, who used the legislature's procedural rules to scupper final consideration.

A fourth possibility, articulated most forcefully by Alan Cairns, is that neither the federal nor the provincial governments understood just how powerfully the spirit and logic of the Charter of Rights had already transformed the democratic expectations of citizens. Meech was a creation of governments, not citizens, and it was unacceptable to "Charter Canadians" who tend to think of themselves as the foundation of legitimate constitutional authority.

And fifth, maybe Meech was simply too complicated an exercise in legislative log-rolling. As Peter Russell has argued forcefully over the years, the comparative evidence is that such comprehensive, mega-constitutional initiatives are really, really difficult to pull off. This one arguably just collapsed of its own weight.

So there are five possible explanations for the demise of Meech. Maybe there are more, and surely no one explanation is sufficient by itself. Still, I'm curious to know. As someone who was both inside the process as a deputy minister and outside as a scholar, how do you weigh up these various explanations? And after all this negativity, is there something positive to take from the Meech experience?

DC: There's a sixth: Pierre Elliott Trudeau. Do a thought experiment. How would the Meech Lake process have unfolded if Trudeau's voice had been absent? First ministers agreed to the Accord on 30 April 1987; less than a month later, on 27 May 1987, before the formal legal text of the constitutional agreement had received intergovernmental support, Trudeau released his savage critique in the Toronto *Star* and the Montreal newspaper *La Presse*. To have a former prime minister and the father of the Canadian Charter of Rights and Freedoms attacking Meech root and branch surely galvanized those opposed and crystallized the negative opinion of many who were uneasy about the deal and worried about its possible implications. At the very least, it must have raised questions in the minds of the great many Canadians who were initially favourably disposed to the Accord and the reconciliation with Quebec. The very intemperateness of Trudeau's language served for many to underline just how radically bad the Meech Lake Accord must be. Describing the Meech Lake Accord as a "total bungle," Trudeau derided Prime Minister Brian Mulroney as "a weakling" and the nationalists of Quebec as "perpetual losers" and a "bunch of snivellers" who should "stop having tantrums like spoiled adolescents." The acceptance of Meech Lake would "render the Canadian state totally impotent," to be ruled eventually by "eunuchs." Whatever your opinion of Trudeau might have been, on the constitutional and national-unity front he was widely acknowledged to be a straight shooter, so his words hurt, and gave powerful encouragement to the dissident forces in the country.

I would add yet another factor. On 15 December 1988, the Supreme Court of Canada struck down the French-only provisions of Quebec's language law, Bill 101, on the grounds that they violated both the Canadian Charter of Rights and Freedoms and Quebec's own Charter of Rights. When Quebec Premier Robert Bourassa announced on 18 December 1988 that his government would employ Section 33, the notwithstanding clause of the 1982 Constitution, to reinstate the sections of the language law the Court had found to be in violation of the Charter, many of us at the time could sense a nail being driven into the coffin of the Meech Lake Accord. For many in English-speaking Canada, this decision showed the kind of Charter-flouting behaviour you would get if the Accord's distinct-society provisions became part of the Canadian Constitution. This was ironic, given that Premier Bourassa did not and could not appeal to a non-existent distinct-society provision, but rather to Section 33 of the 1982 Constitution, which Pierre Trudeau himself had reluctantly accepted and supported. Three of Premier Bourassa's anglophone cabinet members resigned as a result of this decision, and for the same reason Premier Gary Filmon withdrew the Meech resolution from the Manitoba legislature.

"If it were done when 'tis done, then 'twere well it were done quickly."[5] Macbeth was speaking of murder and mayhem, but there is a message about Meech here, too. The issue of time, which you mention above, played a role in the Meech Lake debacle, and touches on a number of the other explanations you enumerate. The Meech Lake Accord was a classical product of executive federalism – an agreement among first ministers reached behind closed doors. That did not make it a bad agreement in my opinion, but it made it acutely vulnerable to public scrutiny. And as you point out, with the passage of time some of the political leaders who negotiated the deal were replaced by others who did not have a vested interest in the passage of the Accord. I remember Diane Wilhelmy, the Quebec deputy minister responsible, visiting officials at Queen's Park soon after the Meech agreement had been reached, imploring us to ratify the Accord quickly. She argued – correctly, in the event – that, while Quebec had no doubt about Ontario's intention to follow through, Ontario's ratification would encourage others to follow suit more quickly than would otherwise be the case. We mistakenly believed that we could and should proceed at our own pace, not accepting the exemplary role we would play vis-à-vis other provinces.

The proverb has it that success has many fathers, but failure is an orphan. Meech seems to disprove that contention. Responsibility for its failure can be attributed to many different quarters. I believe the factors you mention each played a role, as did the additional considerations I have offered. And there are no doubt others. It is not to be expected that the fate of a complex, highly sensitive constitutional issue, which played itself out over three years, could be explained simply. Many actors and forces had a hand in putting the Accord together; many were implicated in taking it apart.

Is there anything positive to take from the Meech experience? That, I think, is hard to say. For those who opposed Meech Lake, I imagine they would say the positive thing is that the country dodged a bullet; thanks to its defeat, the Canadian government is not today a totally impotent thing run by eunuchs. For Indigenous people, Elijah Harper's quiet, eagle-feathered firmness sent a message to other Canadians, that they were no longer marginal players in the life of the country. They were gaining power, and they were going to use it. Elijah Harper refused to grant unanimous consent in the Manitoba Legislature in June 1990, ending all efforts to ratify the Accord. The Oka Crisis, involving Mohawk resistance to a proposal to build a golf course and condominiums on Native burial grounds, broke out that summer. Indigenous representatives were full participants in the next constitutional round, the Charlottetown process, which began shortly thereafter. Elijah Harper contributed to the growing presence of matters Indigenous in Canadian public life.

For supporters of the Meech Lake Constitutional Accord, it is difficult to discern much that is positive in its collapse. It looked and looks like a colossal missed opportunity. It left a bitter taste in the mouths of almost everyone, and ignited a surge of anger in Quebec that took a long time to dissipate. For there is no doubt that Meech was highly popular in Quebec. I was going back and forth from Queen's Park to Quebec City frequently during those three years, and I remember once taking a taxi into Quebec City from the airport and seeing a billboard by the highway selling the Honda Accord. There was a picture of the car with the simple caption: "*L'Accord du Lac Meech!*" Never before or after have I heard of a car company trying to sell its automobiles by appealing to a constitutional agreement. The effort to repair the breach led to the negotiation of the equally ill-fated Charlottetown Accord, and all the wasted energy associated with that. The failure of Meech lengthened the period of our constitutional agony, and delayed the shift of focus to other pressing concerns, such as getting the national budget back under control. The echoes of Meech can still be heard; Canada's current Parliament has 32 Bloc Québécois MPS, representing a party whose creation was the direct result of the failure of Meech. What is positive about all this is not the failure of Meech, but the country's underlying strength through this and other setbacks, its capacity to overcome these moments of crisis without ultimately doing violence to the capacity on all sides to adjust, to accommodate and to find workable middle ground on which life in Canada can continue.

RV: You mentioned the Charlottetown Accord of 1992 and the energy wasted on it. Wasted, I presume you mean, because the Accord was decisively rejected in a national referendum in October of that year. I wanted to ask you about this final attempt at mega-constitutional reform because a lot was going on. Once again, one can argue that the package collapsed under its own weight, and that the attempt to be inclusive and comprehensive backfired in the sense that the more inclusive the Accord became, the more critics found wrong with it. Once again, the intervention of Pierre Trudeau was decisive in turning opinion against the Accord – your trenchant critique of his critique notwithstanding! (See chapter 4.) And once again the rules established for success – approval, through a referendum, by every provincial electorate as well as Indigenous peoples – were impossibly high. I'd be eager to get your own take on what went wrong – especially since the government of Ontario (which you were advising) was one of the Accord's principal architects.

But I also wanted you to comment on my own somewhat eccentric analysis of the problem with Charlottetown, which is that the Accord exposed a crisis in the definition, meaning, and usefulness of the idea of sovereignty.

Here's what I mean. The idea of sovereignty has been one of the central ideas of modern political science, at least since the time of Hobbes and Bodin. The thing is, though, that sovereignty is actually two ideas that adhere to each other, and much of the history of modern liberal democracy has involved an attempt to soften and even walk back the implications of both sides of the sovereignty coin.

On the one hand, sovereignty, in Hobbes's view, had to be a singular power. One of the causes of civil strife, in his view, was the possibility that individuals would take the law into their own hands, as it were, to preserve themselves. That was what he called the problem of "private judgment," and the obvious problem was that if everyone did that, no one would be secure. The nub of this side of Hobbes has come down to us in the form of Weber's famous – and still standard – definition of the state as that entity that possesses a legitimate monopoly of coercive power. For those who care about individual liberty, however, the obvious problem with endowing any political institution with a monopoly of power is that it is terribly risky to concentrate power in one set of hands. As a result, much of the work of liberal democracy over the past couple of centuries has been to develop various ways to soften, limit, and diffuse the state's awesome monopoly on coercive power by creating institutions and processes of mutually limiting power. That's what checks and balances and the Bill of Rights were meant to do in the United States. That is what federalism, the Senate, parliamentary norms, and the party system were meant to accomplish in Canada. None of this threatened the state as such, but these institutions were designed to constrain the bluntest exercise of state power by creating a system of countervailing and mutually limiting powers. And the fact is that Canadians have had an ongoing conversation about the balance between concentrating power in government so as to give it capacity and energy on the one hand and building in more impediments to state power so as to reduce the risk of the arbitrary and heavy-handed use of state power. My point is that, throughout the 1970s and 1980s – that is, in the midst of the national unity debate and connected to it – Canadians were involved in a pretty serious re-evaluation of sovereign power in this sense. That is what the debate over the Charter (and it was a vigorous debate) was about – at least in part.

But Hobbes meant something else by sovereignty as well. Sovereign power was not just singular (as in Weber's definition); it was also accountable to no other authority. Hobbes argued that there had to be some power that was legally autonomous or supreme in the sense that its decisions were final and definitive. If not, there would be no end of appeals to, and claims of, superiority. But this characteristic, too, is risky because if a sovereign power can act in a way that is really unanswerable, whoever or whatever that power is may be tempted to act in a way that is absolute, arbitrary, and untrammeled, knowing that there is no other power to contradict or countermand it.

Here, too, however, there was pushback from the defenders of liberal democracy, John Locke first among them. To get round the implications of Hobbes's invitation to unaccountable power, Locke famously turned to "the people," gathered together in the form of civil society, as a "constituent" sovereign, as the *source* of all legitimate power but not actually constituted in such a way as to wield political power on a regular basis. The idea that the people – this abstract, pre-political assemblage – could make, re-make, and unmake a constitution provided an enormously powerful alternative to Hobbes's absolutism because it gave the people control over the basic rules of the game while maintaining critical distance from the cut and thrust of political contestation on the ground. The people are the fountain, the source, of legitimate power, but they do not actually rule. They have the power to establish and dis-establish, to create and re-create a regime, but they do not participate in direct ruling as a Hobbesian sovereign would directly rule. Instead, rule consists of a complex set of rules, norms, and procedures, more often than not nowadays embedded in a written constitution and subject to judicial review. I think it was A.V. Dicey who captured Locke's meaning when, in describing the constitution of the United States, he commented that "We, the people" are sovereign – but generally they slumber.

So here's the thing. As I said a minute ago, Canadians had a pretty thorough conversation about Hobbesian sovereignty in the first "constituted" sense – about how to soften the authoritarian implications of the monopoly of coercive authority without undermining the insight about sovereignty that everyone from Hobbes to Weber thought was crucial to the success of the modern state. But about the second part of Hobbes's definition of sovereignty and Locke's attempt to de-claw it, we had almost no conversation at all. In 1867, the Fathers of Confederation managed to create a new political community without having to think much at all about the ultimate source of political authority because they mostly assumed that the ultimate source was the Queen in the Imperial Parliament. Even after that answer was increasingly implausible – say, from the 1930s onward – the question "who is the constituent authority?" of the Canadian political community was almost never asked. If pressed, the default (and obviously unsatisfactory) answer was that Parliament is sovereign. But very few people dug deeper than that.

Until the rise of Quebec nationalism that is. Why? Because Quebec nationalists had a clear and attractive answer to that question: The constituent sovereign, the source of legitimate political authority, is the people of the Quebec nation. And that assertion – which is the assertion that lies behind the idea of national self-determination – changed the conversation. Federalists (especially outside of Quebec) could continue to talk about how to limit or direct state power – and many did. But now, facing this new claim about the constituent sovereignty of the Quebec nation, federalists had to provide an alternative theory of sovereignty to challenge that of the PQ. And that is how we ended up with a Charter of Rights that was part of something explicitly called a "people's package" and repeated assertions by people like Clyde Wells, premier of Newfoundland, that "it is the people's constitution." That is how Canadians became Lockeans.

But who, exactly, is this Canadian people? Undifferentiated, rights-bearing individual citizens from coast to coast? Members of a linguistically defined national community? The sum of all provincial societies? Indigenous peoples? Three founding peoples? That is where Charlottetown, like Meech before it, ran aground because it raised, but could not answer, this fundamental question of sovereignty. And it especially couldn't answer the sovereignty question if we thought we were following the Lockean playbook. For Locke, the definition of who comprised "the people" was settled; it was the inhabitants of a certain, geographically defined area. The constitution produced by this people became the expression of their commitments and aspirations. So, in the US it was "we, the people," already self-identified as such, who went on to define what their political community stood for and how it would work. We Canadians tried to go at it the other way round, backwards if you will. We thought that if only we could agree on our basic normative commitments, we could define who we were are as a people. And that just didn't – and probably couldn't – work.

This is one of the reasons I come back again and again to the so-called Canada Clause – the list of "fundamental Canadian values" with which the Charlottetown Accord begins. Some commentators, like Peter Russell, essentially dismiss the Canada Clause as a form of "symbolic gratification of the groups who contested the nature of Canada as a political community."[6] But I think this underestimates its importance. The Canada Clause was not just about symbolic gratification. It was a deeply serious and contested attempt to infuse the constituent sovereign, "the people of Canada," with substantive meaning. On the surface, the Canada Clause may have appeared as little more than a laundry list of more or less (in)compatible claims and aspirations that had little substantive meaning. I see it a bit differently. To me the Canada Clause in the Charlottetown Accord exposed the enduring depth and potential corrosiveness of the divisions in the country by asking explicitly a question about constituent sovereignty that Canadians had little experience and even less vocabulary to work with. Or to put it another way: The mega-constitutional era let the genie of popular sovereignty out of the bottle – and no one has found a way to coax it back in. And lest you think these are inconsequential debates that we should tune out, just take a look at Britain today. The Brexit debate in Britain has done basically the same thing for Britain that the mega-constitutional era did for Canada, raising fundamental questions about (popular) sovereignty with what appears to be little thought, strategic or otherwise, about the consequences. So while most people have long since forgotten about the Charlottetown Accord, I continue to think it important for an understanding of where we stand as a political community.

DC: Well, as my sainted grandmother would say: "You slobbered a bibful." How to respond? I am going to start by disagreeing, but, as I think my way through this, who knows where I might end up? Let's set aside the emerging role of the "people" for a moment, because there I think you have a point, which I'll return to later.

But look at the starting point of your argument. You assert that sovereignty, in its Hobbesian style, is a concept composed of two related ideas: singularity and legal autonomy –the notion that sovereignty must be held by a single, determinate entity of some kind; and the notion that it is the ultimate power that is accountable to no other power beyond it. Let's make sure first that I understand the distinction correctly. Take an example: the police in a well-ordered society are typically regarded as enjoying a monopoly on the legitimate use of violence. Militias, bands of citizens and the like, cannot legitimately "take the law into their own hands." There is, typically, a highly circumscribed right held by individuals to use violence in self-defence, which is to be employed only in extremis, when there is a pressing emergency and no reasonable recourse to the civil authorities, the police. This is singularity. Yet in every well-ordered society the police are held accountable for their actions; they must act within the law and their exercise of discretion is subject to review and sanction. This is accountability. The power of the police is assigned to them by the state. But who holds the state accountable? That is the issue of legal autonomy.

All right, let's look at singularity first. You say that because of the widely recognized dangers of concentrating power in the hands of a sovereign entity, liberal democrats have fashioned "various ways to soften, limit, and diffuse the state's awesome monopoly on coercive power," and as examples you mention checks and balances and the Bills of Rights in the United States, and federalism, the Senate, parliamentary norms, and the party system in Canada. First, let me say that I perceive a qualitative difference between "soften" and "limit" on the one hand, and "diffuse" on the other. The first two terms fit readily with the notion of concentrated power; attempts are made to moderate or put the brakes on the exercise of that concentrated power. But the third term, "diffuse," suggests to me an alteration in the degree of concentration itself. Concentrated light casts a focused, intense beam on a small space; diffused light scatters its beams across a wide area. On this understanding, diffused sovereignty risks failing the first test of singularity, and – at least, by that definition – risks ceasing to be sovereignty as such.   .

This discussion is not meant to be a kind of word game, but to set the stage for a consideration of sovereignty in the context of federalism. Was federalism an institutional effort to soften and limit sovereign power? Or to diffuse it? Disperse it? During the nineteenth century in Canada, sovereignty was assumed, as you say, to rest in the Queen in the Imperial Parliament, at first as an active, executive sovereign authority, later as a residual notion. Elements of the active executive understanding persisted in fragmentary form until the full patriation of the Constitution in 1982. The passage of the British North America Act in 1867 not only drew distinct British North American colonies together, but created a novel political regime with a new system for specifying and allocating authority within it, namely, federalism. For the first time, parliamentary government was combined with federalism, creating a parliamentary federation. This new arrangement involved the creation of a new political authority, and the association of the heretofore autonomous colonial units, all of them under a constitution. Is Confederation to be understood as an instrument for softening or limiting sovereign authority, or as an act of diffusion?

It seems to me that federalism can be understood as a radical rebuttal of the principle of sovereignty as it was classically understood. From the point of view of classical sovereignty, federalism was a bastard form of government. You can look for the locus of sovereignty, but you will be hard put to find it, and surely a sovereign authority that cannot readily be identified is a curious kind of thing. The sovereign Queen has faded like the Cheshire cat; that office continues to have an honourable role as a useful fiction, as can be seen when there are desultory attempts to begin a discussion about turning Canada into a republic. Why would one bother doing this? It would raise questions it would be difficult for us to answer. The notion of the sovereignty of Parliament doesn't really work, given that we have multiple parliamentary systems. And there was never a moment – at least, not until Charlottetown – when the Canadian people were explicitly invited to constitute the government of their shared political community, and Charlottetown, with its two simultaneous referendums asking the same question did not compellingly suggest a single people capable of constituent action.

Thus there are at least three ways in which the Canadian experience strayed from the classic conception of Thomas Hobbes, the second two linked closely together. First, there is Canada's experience as a colony, moving quietly over half a century towards national independence, the last step in the process being completed only in 1982. Sovereignty in Canada was in some significant measure held by the British Parliament or by the Queen in the Imperial Parliament, which gradually divested itself of that responsibility. Second, Canada is a federation, and under a federal constitution it is often argued that sovereignty is dispersed among the national and sub-national governments. While it is true that there are provisions in the Constitution Act, 1867 that suggest the pre-eminent status of the central government, our history has demonstrated conclusively that we live under a genuinely federal regime. Where is sovereignty to be looked for in such circumstances as these? One plausible answer is that it is dispersed among the federal units; a much less plausible contention, it seems to me, is that it is located in the federal parliament. This brings me to my third point. Some have argued that sovereignty in a federation may be found in the written constitution, but that seems unpersuasive unless you bring in the courts. In the absence of a supreme court, there would be no active agency giving effect to the will of the sovereign (the constitution). But does that then make the courts sovereign? Both before and after 1982, the courts have authoritatively interpreted the constitution and have struck down legislation of national and sub-national actors found to be incompatible with the country's basic law. Constitutional jurisprudence chiefly regulated matters related to the division of powers between the two orders of government prior to 1982, citizens' rights after. Parliament was not sovereign before or after in the Hobbesian sense, any more than the provincial legislatures were. However unsatisfactory the answer to the question of the location of what one might call federal sovereignty may be, I don't think the argument of parliamentary sovereignty is much stronger. Indeed, I think you could almost argue that the Canadian system is designed to obscure, not answer the question of the locus of sovereignty, and I have the sense that Canadians were quite comfortable with this messy non-Hobbesian system prior to 1982.

You argue that the debate and ultimate introduction of a Charter of Rights and Freedoms into the 1982 Constitution was at least in part a debate about the limiting of state power. Clearly, the functional rationale for a charter is to confine the scope of state power and to protect the liberty of citizens. So perhaps it *was* such a debate, but if so, it was federal sovereignty – state power in a federation – that was being discussed. The desire was to control the multiple governments that possess coercive authority over their citizens, not the singular power of the central government.

However, in all candour, I do not recall a popular outcry from citizens demanding the introduction of a charter of rights, and arguing that the tried-and-true common law system for guarding the rights of citizens had failed them. In some ways, it *was* failing them, no doubt; the codification of rights in a highly pluralistic society has some readily apparent advantages. But here, as elsewhere in our political life, I think the Charter of Rights and Freedoms was, at least in its origins, an elite gift to the Canadian public, not the outcome of popular mobilization. John Diefenbaker's Bill of Rights (1960) was a pallid imitation of the United States' Bill of Rights, never gaining much traction either in the courts or in public opinion. Pierre Trudeau's charter was a different animal, both in aspiration and in achievement. He sought and got an entrenched charter with teeth. Once the idea of an American-style bill of rights was on the table as a possibility, Canadians reacted favourably to it, but it was Trudeau who pushed the notion forward, partially as a cover for getting language rights approved at the same time. So if Canadians were re-evaluating sovereign power in their country in the '70s and '80s, they were doing so in a peculiarly Canadian way.

Now, let's turn to accountability. Who holds the sovereign to account? Hobbes's answer was: no one. Apart from anything else, it is a logical impossibility; the very definition of sovereignty excludes accountability. You note Locke's innovation, which was to make "the people" the constituent authority with ultimate control over the effective sovereign, the government, and you argue that the emergence of the notion of "the people" in Canadian political debate created a puzzle that couldn't be solved. The Canada Clause was the country's unsuccessful attempt to solve it. I do think you are on to something here, and I'd like to offer some further thoughts on the subject. What I think is new, and here is where we come into agreement, is the emergence of "the people" as a constitutional actor, and in some ways the conclusive constitutional actor. I believe that the 1982 process and the establishment of the Charter of Rights and Freedoms led Canadians to think somewhat differently about the constitution and whom it belonged to. They had already had, as you say, the experience of the Quebec referendum engaging the people of Quebec as the ultimate decision-maker on sovereignty and secession in that part of the country. After the bruising experience of Meech, politicians displayed no interest in going down the road of executive federalism again, and began madly to engage the public, with the promise of a formal referendum vote at the end on whatever had been negotiated. People came to believe that collectively they had the right

to decide. In this context I find your argument persuasive that the effort to negotiate the Canada Clause can be understood as a vain attempt to discover who
'the Canadian people' are. I will revisit this topic in the conclusion.

Oh, and Charlottetown. Ironically, despite all the effort to engage Canadians in the putting together of the Accord, I would say that it collapsed in part
because of the gulf that opened between those who negotiated the agreement
and the citizenry who were asked to approve it. Citizens were engaged at the
beginning and at the end of the process. In between, elite accommodation,
broadened this time to include representatives of Indigenous people, led to the
consensus package which grew like Topsy, it being the product of a thousand
compromises. The goal of Meech Lake was tolerably clear: to obtain Quebec's
agreement to the Constitution Act, 1982, by addressing five fairly specific
concerns. What was the goal of Charlottetown? It seemed as if it was to satisfy pretty much everybody. So extensive and unfocussed were the proposed
amendments that the best that the drafters could say of them was that they
had actually reached agreement and that it was a delicate balance. There was
thus relatively little capacity to respond effectively to specific critiques of the
substance, such as the strong opposition in English-speaking Canada to the
guarantee to Quebec of 25 per cent of the seats in the House of Commons in
perpetuity. Just achieving consensus, to the exhausted constitutional negotiators, seemed to be the great accomplishment. Small wonder that Canadians
found that line of reasoning unworthy of support.

RV: They found it not just unworthy of support, I think, but they were also
utterly worn out by the whole constitutional saga. At least in English Canada.
Yet in Quebec, the failure of the Charlottetown referendum – including in
Quebec – seems to have energized nationalist forces. First you had the 1993
federal election – the "earthquake" – in which the Bloc Québécois, led by Lucien Bouchard, won 54 seats and became the official Opposition. Then, in 1994,
the PQ was reelected in Quebec under the leadership of Jacques Parizeau. All
of which led, not surprisingly, to the 1995 referendum. You were advising the
government of Ontario at the time. How did you assess the situation leading up
to the referendum? And what did you take from what seemed like a near-death
experience for the Canadian federation?

DC: What I recall in the years after the collapse of Charlottetown is that most
of English-speaking Canada – barring the *vieux routiers* – turned away from
constitutional and national-unity/sovereignty matters, but Quebec did not.
There were thus two clearly separate spheres of experience and discourse, each
turning according to its own logic. Canada outside of Quebec had had it with
constitutional discussion and wanted nothing so much as to be able to stop
talking and thinking about it. Quebec, as you point out, was in an elevated state,

although initially I don't believe there was a strong public desire to see another referendum on independence held. However, when the government of Quebec under Premier Parizeau announced its plan to hold a referendum in October 30, 1995, the issue was engaged once again. I believe the rest of Canada was initially content to leave the management of the referendum to the federalist forces in Quebec and to the federal government. As the campaign proceeded, it became evident to more and more people in English-speaking Canada that Ottawa's leadership of the federalist forces was ineffective and over-confident. Relying on favourable opinion polls in the early going, Ottawa focused on underlining the negative economic consequences of a Yes vote. However, when Lucien Bouchard took over effective leadership of the Yes forces part way through the campaign, making a strong emotional appeal to the hearts of Quebecers, opinion in Quebec began to shift in favour of the sovereignists. Something approaching panic set in in the federal camp, which is why you had a shaken Prime Minister Chrétien, in a speech in Verdun on October 24th and a televised address to the nation on October 25th, promising recognition of Quebec as a distinct society, a veto for Quebec over certain constitutional amendments, and some decentralization of power to the province. And it is why a massive public demonstration in Montreal was organized on October 27th, involving tens of thousands of committed Canadians, many bused in from outside the province.

The vote on October 30th could not have been closer, with the federal side winning by a nose. But what if the sovereignists had won? Some have argued that in the confusion that would have followed a Yes victory, there would have been ample opportunity to get things back on track. My view is different. Lucien Bouchard brought poetry and moderation to the Yes side campaign when he was made the effective leader of the sovereignist forces after Jacques Parizeau stepped back. Bouchard was highly effective in reassuring Quebecers and increasing the sovereignist vote. But he was not the premier of Quebec: Jacques Parizeau was. Had the Yes side won, the power to act would have rested with the premier of the province, not with Bouchard, the Bloc Québécois leader in the federal Parliament. And Parizeau never hid his intentions; given the opportunity, he would move hard and fast to turn sovereignty from an aspiration to a fact on the ground, and he would have done so in the face of a demoralized and unprepared federal government. Hence I believe there would have been fateful consequences if the almost 54,000 vote advantage had fallen the other way.

In the event, there were two consequences of the actual referendum result that I would like to highlight: the first, not perhaps surprising and certainly long overdue; and the second, not really predicted by anyone.

The first was the determination of the federal government not to be caught with its pants down again. What was expected to be a relatively easy win for the No side turned into a nail-biting squeaker. It was reasonable to expect, with a result so close, that the sovereignists would gather their forces for a final push over the top. The prime minister had blocked out the main elements of Plan A in his Verdun speech; several initiatives meant to accommodate the nationalist forces in Quebec, and respond to the desire for reform. The non-constitutional implementation of these measures after the referendum vote made relatively little impact on Quebec opinion. But in any case, given the close result, it was time for Plan B – a hard-headed resistance to separation and a sketching out of how the Government of Canada would handle a vote for secession, should that occur. Chrétien brought Stéphane Dion, a Université de Montréal political scientist who had offered a tough-minded critique of the sovereignty move-ment, into the government. Dion proceeded to write a series of letters severely criticizing the rhetorical claims of leading Quebec sovereignists, much to their irritation. The federal government also joined the court case initiated by Guy Bertrand challenging the legality of the PQ's strategy for secession. The Su-preme Court, in its 1998 Reference decision, found that the unilateral secession of Quebec was illegal under both domestic and international law. With that court judgment in hand, the government of Canada introduced and passed the Clarity Act through Parliament, which set out in advance the principles that would guide the federal government in response to a Quebec referendum vote in favour of secession. These initiatives injected a healthy dose of realism into what had been a vague and misleading discussion of the consequences of a Yes vote and put the lie to the dubious contention that Quebec's march to independence would be relatively untroubled. Though we have not had to face such an unhappy eventuality, the country is in a much stronger position to deal with it, should it occur, as a result of these initiatives.

The second consequence, if consequence it be, is very different. Indeed, its relationship to the 1995 referendum is challenging to specify. It's the fact that the stuffing came out of the sovereignty movement. Ironically, getting closer than ever before to a positive vote on sovereignty turned out to be the prelude to the gradual demobilization of the sovereignty movement itself. I do not pro-fess to quite know how or why it happened, although one can identify many factors contributing to that outcome, but happen it unquestionably did. After 1995, Quebecers joined other Canadians in turning away from the passions and turmoil of the previous 35 years. Neither the Supreme Court Reference nor the federal Clarity Act could disturb the steady tranquility of their ways.

In the event, the 1995 referendum closed a parenthesis that had been opened some 35 years before, back in 1960 when the election of the Liberals under Jean Lesage launched the Quiet Revolution in Quebec. The intervening decades had seen the country put under severe stress, as both Quebec and the rest of Canada went through processes of rapid change. Existential questions relating to the viability of the country and the destiny of Quebec were the order of the day. Like a peat fire, they burned constantly beneath the surface of our political life, periodically flaring up and creating national-unity crises. For those like myself who had been firefighting that whole time, it still seems difficult to believe that it is quite over. And yet it is. The years 1960 to 1995 are now chiefly of historical interest. They do not cage a dangerous creature with the brooding potential to rise up and strike again. If we find ourselves in turbulent circumstances in the future, it will be a fresh new national crisis, not a continuation of the old one.

NOTES

1 The Task Force on Canadian Unity, *A Future Together* (1979).
2 Peter Russell, *Constitutional Odyssey: Can Canadians Become a Sovereign People?*, 3rd ed. (Toronto: University of Toronto Press, 2004) 115.
3 Pierre Elliot Trudeau, "'Say Goodbye to the Dream' of One Canada," Toronto *Star*, May 27, 1987. Also published in *La Presse*.
4 Patrick J. Monahan, *Meech Lake: The Inside Story*, (Toronto: University of Toronto Press, 1991) 14–37.
5 William Shakespeare, *The Tragedy of Macbeth*, 1.7.1–2.
6 Peter Russell, *Constitutional Odyssey*, 2nd ed. (University of Toronto Press, 1993), 203.

PART II Canadian Federalism and Beyond: Policies, Practices, and Values

RICHARD SIMEON AND DAVID CAMERON

12 Intergovernmental Relations and Democracy: An Oxymoron if There Ever Was One?

In Bakvis and Skogstad, eds., *Canadian Federalism:*
Performance, Effectiveness, and Legitimacy **2001**

*At the start of the new century, there was a good deal of discussion in Canada
about the relationship between federalism and good democratic practice. This
article assessed the current state of play and explored the obstacles to achieving a
more democratic, federal Canada. My co-author of this and the next contribution
was Richard Simeon, a close friend and colleague, and a wise and humane student of comparative politics and Canadian government. As it happens, the title of
this piece came from a casual comment by the editor of this volume, Rob Vipond.*

Donald Smiley, a distinguished student of Canadian federalism, coined the
term *executive federalism* to describe the central characteristic of Canadian
intergovernmental relations. In Canada's parliamentary system, the executive
arm of government (the prime minister, premiers, ministers, and their officials) dominates the legislatures (Parliament and the provincial assemblies).
The executive dominance characteristic of Westminster systems plays out in
the practices of Canadian federalism. When Canadian governments relate to
one another, it is almost exclusively via the instruments of their executives –
hence "executive federalism." This pattern is the essence of Canadian intergovernmental relations.

Smiley not only identified the phenomenon more clearly than anyone else;
he also launched a fierce critique of its democratic deficiencies.[1] In 1979 he
wrote:

> My charges against executive federalism are these:
>   First, it contributes to undue secrecy in the conduct of the public's business.

Second, it contributes to an unduly low level of citizen participation in public affairs.

Third, it weakens and dilutes the accountability of governments to their legislatures and to the wider public.

A large number of Canadian citizens appeared to make a similar judgment when they rose up to challenge the constitutional agreement known as the Meech Lake Accord, signed in 1987. What right, what mandate, did eleven "men in suits" meeting behind closed doors have to make fundamental changes in Canada's Constitution? In a new era of participatory politics, Charter-based rights discourse, and citizen distrust of elites of all kinds, the basic legitimacy of the Canadian pattern of intergovernmental relations was called into question (Cairns 1991; Citizens' Forum 1991; Nevitte 1996).

Subsequent developments in intergovernmental relations attempted to respond to the perceived democratic deficit. The Charlottetown round of constitutional discussion was preceded by much more open consultation, involved more participants at the bargaining table, and was eventually submitted to a nationwide referendum (Brock 1993). The Calgary Declaration of 1997, a provincial initiative to provide some recognition of Quebec's uniqueness along with other constitutional values, was submitted to citizen consultation before being passed in provincial legislatures.

Following the failure of successive attempts at constitutional reform, governments' attention shifted in the 1990s to the search for non-constitutional ways to renew the federation and demonstrate its "workability." Governments would now collaborate as equal partners in the development of national norms, standards, and policies. The most important and broadly based example of the new collaborative approach was the Social Union Framework Agreement (SUFA) signed by all governments except Quebec in February 1999. Given the experiences of Meech and Charlottetown, what was most striking about this and other agreements, such as the Agreement on Internal Trade (AIT), was that they were negotiated almost entirely in the classic arena of executive federalism, with minimal public involvement. Unlike Meech Lake and Charlottetown constitutional agreements, there was very little public reaction to them. As Bruce Porter of the Charter Committee on Poverty issues put it: "There has been no public participation in the development of this framework … no information provided to the public, no transparency and no public accountability" (Porter 1999).

What, then, is the relation between intergovernmental relations and democratic politics? How persuasive is the democratic critique of intergovernmentalism? Is it possible to imagine reforms to the process that might reduce, if not eliminate, the democratic deficit? These are the questions we address in this chapter, with particular, but not exclusive, reference to the implications of the new movement toward collaborative federalism best exemplified by the SUFA. We begin with a brief review of these recent developments, and then apply some democratic criteria to them.

Collaborative Federalism and the Social Union Framework Agreement

It is difficult to know whether collaborative federalism represents a distinctly different, or lasting, model for the conduct of intergovernmental relations. Its key elements are the sense that governance in Canada is to be conducted as a partnership between equal orders of government. Neither is to be subordinate to the other. National standards and norms are not the responsibility of Ottawa acting alone, but of governments acting collectively. The premises of the New Public Management are to be reflected in intergovernmental relations, with an emphasis on transparency, seamlessness in the delivery of services, and customer needs rather than legal or jurisdictional niceties. Federal-provincial accommodations would now be made through intergovernmental accords or agreements that would set out common goals and principles, clarify roles and responsibilities, co-ordinate delivery and enforcement, and, in some cases, establish mechanisms for the settlement of disputes. The collaborative model remains very much a work in progress, a project in the making, more advanced in some policy areas than others.

Several factors drove the emphasis on increased collaboration. The first was the failure of successive attempts at renewal of the federation through constitutional amendment (Russell 1993). Following the defeats of Meech and Charlottetown, there was a strong sense among both governments and citizens that the constitutional strategy had failed; now there should be a concentration on finding informal ways to demonstrate the workability of federalism and address it to emerging needs (Lazar 1998). These failures also led governments to respond to citizen pressures for a less adversarial intergovernmental relationship. The preoccupation with debts and deficits throughout the 1990s also had important effects. It produced the drastic cuts in federal social policy transfers to the provinces in the 1995 budget and the amalgamation of these transfers into the Canada Health and Social Transfer (CHST). If the federal government is no longer paying the piper, the provinces asked, what right does it have to call the tune? More broadly, writers like Tom Courchene (1997) and André Burelle (1995) argued that broad social and economic forces were fundamentally eroding Ottawa's political and fiscal capacity to set national standards. If the Canadian social and economic unions were to be sustained, then that could be achieved only in a more confederal model of collective government action.

The first major result of this new approach was negotiation of the Agreement on Internal Trade (1995). Other examples were agreements on enforcement of environmental regulations, labour force training, and benefits for children. The centrepiece, however, is the SUFA, which is focused on the central elements of social policy: health, education, and social welfare. As Alain Noël (2000) points out, "for the first time broad agreement codified the new rules that would govern intergovernmental relations in all areas of social policy, but also, by extension, in a number of sectors not considered in the document."

The social union initiative came from the provinces. In 1996, reeling from federal cuts, the Annual Premiers' Conference mandated the Provincial-Territorial Council on Social Policy Renewal to develop a new set of ground rules for the management of social policy in the federation. By 1998, provincial and territorial governments had a fully developed set of proposals that reflected a strongly provincialist model. These proposals included rules preventing Ottawa from initiating new social programs in areas of provincial responsibility without majority provincial consent, joint management of shared programs, with an independent tribunal to settle disputes, and the ability of provinces to opt out (with compensation) from federally initiated programs. However, by the time the federal government joined the talks, its willingness to defer to the provinces had eroded. Having slain the deficit, Ottawa was ready once again to assert its influence through the spending power and had new funds available to entice provincial agreement. Hence the SUFA signed in February 1999 is by no means the provincialist document once envisioned. Opting out with compensation was, compared with the earlier interprovincial agreement, now significantly qualified. Joint management of shared programs was replaced with the vaguer commitment to "collaborative identification of national objectives," with provinces determining the details of program design. The independent dispute settlement tribunal was replaced with a commitment to "collaborative" dispute avoidance and resolution, with the possibility of third-party mediation. Prior provincial consent (from six of the 10 provinces potentially representing a small minority of the population) was only necessary for new shared-cost programs, and not for new federal initiatives, involving direct federal payments to individuals or institutions. And the proposed limits on the federal ability unilaterally to alter funding arrangements were replaced with a simpler commitment to prior notification and consultation.

The Quebec government did not sign the SUFA. The intense intergovernmental discussions, both in the Annual Premiers' Conference (APC) and the ministerial council had taken place with remarkably little public awareness or discussion, and virtually no involvement of the groups and movements associated with social policy.

According to federal Intergovernmental Affairs Minister Stéphane Dion (1999), the SUFA demonstrates that the Canadian federation "is evolving towards greater cooperation and consensus building, while still respecting the constitutional jurisdiction of each order of government." In the end, though, the SUFA represented not so much a principled rethinking of the role of social policy in the Canadian federal system as it did an intergovernmental bargain shaped by the exigencies of the political moment. Hence, its long-term influence on the development of the federal system remains unclear. As a Saskatchewan deputy minister involved in the process argues, "It is only the first step ... an enormous amount of work remains to be done in order to breathe life into SUFA" (Marchildon 1999).

The SUFA includes a number of elements, including a broad set of general principles to guide governments in social policy, a commitment to joint planning and implementation, a reaffirmation, with some limits, of the federal spending power, and commitments to work collaboratively to "avoid and resolve disputes." How this agreement, and the collaborative model it appears to represent, serves democratic values is now addressed.

Thinking about Federalism and Democracy

Federalism and democracy exist in a complex relationship. At one level, federalism is linked to the idea of liberal constitutionalism, emphasizing limits on majority rule through the separation of powers, and the constraints on both local and national majorities imposed by the constitutional division of powers. Indeed, much of the development of intergovernmental relations in this century has been driven by the need to find ways around such constraints. At another level, federalism is more closely linked to participatory models of democracy, with an emphasis on governments competing for the loyalty of citizens by offering desirable packages of policies, on strengthening units of government closer to the people and more attuned to local needs, and on multiplying the arenas in which citizens can participate. Federalism also complicates thinking about democracy as majority rule by raising the question of which majorities, national or provincial, should rule in particular policy areas. This is especially problematic in deeply divided or multinational federal societies where regionally distinct interests and identities are strong. Moreover, federalism, like all other systems of multi-level governance, is inherently complex, placing high demands on the expertise and resources of citizens wishing to influence the system. Indeed, our focus is less on the democratic virtues or vices of federalism in the abstract, and more on democratic concerns that arise out of the inevitable interdependence of governments and the resulting necessity for extensive processes of intergovernmental relations. Our focus is less on federalism per se than on intergovernmentalism.

Three caveats need to be made at the outset. First, the democratic deficits associated with intergovernmental relations in Canada are not unique to

Canada. They are common to all multi-level systems, and the term itself was first used with respect to the European Union. Second, while we focus on the deficits associated with executive federalism, the discussion must be set in the context of other elements of democratic deficit in Canada's institutional structure. Among these are the costs of the electoral system in consistently producing highly unequal representation; the costs of the concentration of power in cabinets and first ministers, extreme even by the standards of other Westminster-type parliamentary systems (Savoie 1999); the associated weakness of legislatures and their members; and the failure of the Senate to provide effective regional representation at the centre. It is important to realize that these characteristics of the broader institutional structure have powerful effects on the character of the intergovernmental relations and help account for many of the problems we associate with them. Thus the electoral system exacerbates regional differences and makes more difficult the emergence of a nationally integrative party system. The weak Senate contributes to the inability of Ottawa fully to reflect the interests of all regions, and leads regional interests to turn to strong provincial governments. And the concentration of power in executive federalism is made possible by, and is simply one manifestation of, the pervasive executive control of Canadian political life – "court government." A regionally fragmented party system, the weak Senate, strict party discipline, and strong cabinets greatly diminish Ottawa's ability to act as an arena of integration and accommodation. The consequence is to place a particularly heavy burden on intergovernmental relations to act not only as mechanism for policy co-ordination, but also as much broader actor in Canadian government. To the extent this is the case, then it becomes more important to inquire into the democratic character of the processes of intergovernmental relations.

A third caveat is that intergovernmental relations in Canada are highly variable. Harmonious relations at one moment in time may become highly conflictual at another. Sometimes there is a focus on federal leadership and initiative; at other times there is a focus on the provinces and their initiatives. Moreover, the "high politics" of intergovernmental relations, debating constitutional change or national energy policy, differs greatly from the "low politics" of day-to-day co-operation among functionally similar ministries in a host of policy areas. And even in these functional areas, the level of co-operation among governments and the degree to which citizens and groups are able to become involved in intergovernmental processes may vary greatly. Students of federalism know far too little about these variations within the field (Simmons 2000). The point here is that we might assess the issue of democracy and its deficits differently depending on the policy areas and governmental agencies we are looking at. We need a much stronger test of democracy with respect to constitutional change, for example, than we do with respect to labour force training. This is because alterations to our basic constitutional arrangements are, practically speaking, forever; and they typically relate basic values to the distribution of authority. Labour force training, by contrast, is a specific policy field, managed through legislation, regulation, and service provision, all of which can be adjusted through normal political action, in light of changing economic and social circumstances.

Some Democratic Criteria for Assessment

If federalism is complex and multi-faceted, so too, of course, is democracy. What does it mean to say there is a democratic deficit, or to call for more democratic procedures in intergovernmental relations? We do not want to enter into an extended discussion of democratic theory here. A good survey is found in Whitaker (1983). But it is useful to distinguish a variety of conceptions or dimensions of democratic practice, in order to develop a set of criteria that we can then apply to our assessment of the practice of intergovernmental relations in Canada.

Democracy as Effective Governance

Perhaps the first and most basic expectation that citizens have in a democracy is that government policy and the delivery of services be effective, timely, and economical. Intergovernmental relations thus need to be assessed in terms of the extent to which they facilitate the management of interdependence and are able to achieve effective co-operation and co-ordination; reduce overlap, duplication, and contradiction in the work of different governments; and allow for coherent, consistent policy in areas where jurisdictional and fiscal responsibilities are shared, such as health care or the environment.

There is an important debate in the literature between those who stress the need for co-operation, joint decision-making, and collaboration as essential elements in policy development and delivery and those who stress the transaction costs associated with such processes – delay, lowest common denominator solutions, and the like. A system that relies too heavily on securing intergovernmental agreement can lead to "the joint decision trap." This concept was developed by Fritz Scharpf (1988) in the context of Germany and the European Union. In Canada, Albert Breton (1985) has powerfully argued for the virtues of "competitive" over "collaborative" federalism in a similar vein. More recently, Steven Kennett (1998) has argued that the "collective action problem" associated with intergovernmental bargaining is a strong barrier to securing the Canadian social union. However, as Patrick Fafard and Kathryn Harrison (2000: 207) argue, there are remarkably few academic studies of the policy consequences of federalism and intergovernmental

relations in specific policy fields. Governments in Canada have been experimenting with a wide variety of relationships: collaboration, unilateralism,
disentanglement, rationalization, joint delivery, delegated enforcement,
"one-stop shopping," and the like. Assessment of these alternatives across
policy fields, and distinguishing between general norms or standard setting,
policy development, and implementation and delivery, is an important part
of any democratic assessment of intergovernmental relations, but the surface
has hardly been scratched.

Democracy as Responsive Government

Democracy also requires that governments be responsive to citizens' concerns
and priorities. However efficient, a government that did not meet the basic expectations of its citizens would not be regarded as deeply democratic.

A democratic assessment must also ask, among other things, which interests are promoted or undermined by the practices of federalism. Perhaps the
dominant theme in the literature here – drawing from Harold Laski (1939)
and John Porter (1965) – is that federalism is fundamentally conservative. This
view has contemporary support in the thesis that decentralization necessarily
entails a "rush to the bottom." Many progressive groups in Canada continue
to look to the federal government as the source of innovation and see provincial governments as inherently likely to be more conservative. They are among
the chief critics of the movement toward more decentralization and collaborative models of federalism. Thus, environmentalists have been highly critical of
federal-provincial "harmonization" of environmental enforcement; and many
social-policy-oriented groups have been critical of the SUFA, seeing it as serving the interests of governments rather than citizens. This association between
federalism and conservatism, however, has little empirical support (Noël 1999;
see also Brooks 1999) and requires further investigation.

It is difficult to know whether the SUFA will enhance the quality of policy making in Canadian social policy. The principles it sets out are broad
and vague. Governments commit themselves to treating "all Canadians with
fairness and equity," promoting "equality of opportunity," and respecting the
"equality, rights and dignity of women and men." All Canadians are to have
"access to essential programs and services of reasonably comparable quality";
there is to be "appropriate assistance" to those in need. Funding for social programs is to be "adequate, affordable, stable and sustainable." All these terms
are open to wide variations in interpretation; they hardly constitute a template
against which governments can be judged. The only specific program commitments contained in the SUFA are the pre-existing conditions governing
the Canada Health Act. This ambiguity does not necessarily mean the commitments are meaningless. The fact that they have been articulated, however

broadly, in a quasi-constitutional document means that citizen groups of all kinds may be able to invoke them to lend strength in their battles against individual governments.

Perhaps more important is whether the SUFA itself will have the effect of increasing "mutual respect between orders of government and a willingness to work more closely together to meet the needs of Canadians." Governments have agreed to "undertake joint planning and share information," and "to collaborate on implementation of joint priorities." They are to give each other advance notice of policy changes that will affect other governments and to consult each other about them. Again, it is unclear whether such phrases are simply rhetoric, with little substance, or whether instead the values of consultation and the like have been, or will come to be, internalized in the minds of the ministers and officials who run the system. There is some anecdotal evidence that officials are now sometimes referring to these principles as a guide to action. However, at the larger political level, there is little evidence of major change. On politically salient issues like health care, the old dynamic of blame shifting and blame avoidance, turf protection and advancement seem to remain well entrenched. The level of distrust, especially among officials within central intergovernmental agencies, seems to contradict the rhetoric about trust and "mutual help." As John Ibbitson (2000) observes, "Policy is the first victim in the turf wars between Queen's Park and Parliament Hill."

Democracy as Representative Government: Transparency and Accountability

The logic of Canadian representative democracy is that executives and bureaucracies generate policy, for which they are then accountable to legislatures, and to citizens through regular elections. The key requirements from this perspective on democracy are first, transparency, and second, accountability. Transparency suggests that the decision-making process should be open and visible, not hidden behind a veil of secrecy. Accountability requires that citizens be able to hold governments responsible for their successes and failures, ultimately at the ballot box.

Federalism and intergovernmental relations pose several challenges for both transparency and accountability. With respect to transparency, most intergovernmental relations continue to take place behind closed doors. Along with national security, intergovernmental relationships are protected from scrutiny under freedom of information legislation. More generally, transparency suggests that citizens should be able to identify who is responsible for what governments do. On whose door should the citizen be knocking? Fiscal federalism in particular tends to draw a veil between action and consequence. For example, when in the 1995 budget the federal government converted a variety of social programs into the single block grant, the Canada Health and

Social Transfer (CHST), and reduced total funding substantially, it exacerbated a problem intrinsic to federal-provincial transfer arrangements. That is, how was a student to know what explained the rise in her university fees? How was an elderly person to know why the local recreation centre had been closed? Was it a result of a federal decision or a provincial decision; and if it was a combination of both, then what to do? A more recent example is the controversy over what proportion of the costs of health care are borne by each level of government. A recent authoritative study of health care funding concluded that we just do not know. This situation makes it easy for governments to blame each other for shortfalls in funding, but leaves citizens entirely in the dark. Nor is it clear that either order of government really has an interest in clarifying the matter. Transparency thus requires a knowledge about who does what. It also requires that the processes in which governments interact are visible and open.

Transparency also requires that the language in which intergovernmental relations is conducted be accessible and understandable. In 1979, Smiley argued that the arcane terminology of fiscal federalism would baffle all but a few dedicated experts, thus effectively freezing citizens out of the discourse. He would be no more pleased today. The acronymic shorthand that intergovernmental professionals employ in their day-to-day relations is obscure to all but a few.

Transparency is thus a prerequisite for accountability. But accountability in a system of multi-level government is highly complex and can have several different meanings. There is, first, the traditional accountability of executives to their legislatures and, indirectly, their citizens. To the extent that governments spend the money that they collect through transfers, rather than from their own taxpayers, accountability to citizens is blurred. So is the accountability of the federal government to its legislature when it transfers funds to the provinces with few conditions (as in the CHST) or none (as in equalization). However, for Ottawa to demand and secure the kind of information about the use of federal funds by the provinces that would satisfy the requirements of accountability to Parliament could imply a level of federal monitoring and control of provincial activities that would rightly be considered an entirely unacceptable intrusion into provincial autonomy. There is no easy solution to this dilemma.

A second dimension of accountability that arises in collaborative federalism is the accountability of governments to each other in the fulfillment of agreements and accords. This "horizontal accountability" across governments – and the procedures necessary to make it happen – can conflict with the traditional "vertical accountability" to legislatures. And to the extent that basic policy is shaped by intergovernmental accords or agreements, then a third level of accountability arises: that of the governments collectively to the citizens collectively for what they accomplish in the intergovernmental arena. Certainly, citizens can hold their particular governments to account for their conduct in intergovernmental affairs (assuming they know what is being done) through the normal processes of the ballot box. But the citizen has no way to hold the intergovernmental system itself to account, except indirectly. To the extent that such agreements become an increasingly important element in Canadian governance, then this question becomes more pressing. Whether or not citizens should have access to the courts to ensure enforcement of intergovernmental commitments becomes an increasingly relevant question.

Transparency and accountability have become important mantras of the "new public management" and of recent developments in intergovernmental relations. Making them effective remains a large challenge. The SUFA embodies a variety of commitments to enhance "each government's transparency and accountability." They agree to monitor and measure policy outcomes and report their performance to constituents, to share information and best practices, to work to develop comparable performance indicators, and so on. Fleshing out these commitments is one of the continuing tasks of the ministerial council. There is, however, no commitment to making intergovernmental meetings themselves more open and transparent. The emphasis is on "each government's" accountability to its own constituents rather than the collective accountability of governments to Canadians generally. As Canada's Auditor General points out, "accountability in collaborative arrangements involves shared accountability for overall results. The partners are collectively responsible for the success and operation of the collaborative arrangement" (Desautels 1999, 26). The mechanisms to achieve this are not in place. Without this, the sharing of responsibility embodied in intergovernmental agreements makes accountability more difficult rather than less (Delacourt and Lenihan 1999, 3).

Democracy as Public Deliberation: Citizen Engagement and Consultation

This is a conception that sees democracy as a "conversation" exploring goals and options not only among governments, but also between citizens and associations in civil society and their governments. It focuses on "engagement" of citizens and interest groups in the relevant policy communities.

The aspirations of deliberative democracy are seldom achieved in complex modern societies; in general, it remains an ideal to be sought, rather than an empirical reality. But does the process of executive federalism place particular hurdles in the way of a deliberative approach to policy, or make it more difficult for interest groups to participate in the process? Perhaps it does, to the extent that intergovernmental relations tend to be preoccupied with the institutional interests of governmental bureaucracies and executives. These are interests related not to substantive policy content, but rather to issues such as how is political credit to be won and blame to be avoided; how is turf to be invaded or protected, and so on. While such questions may be of little concern to citizens, they are meat and drink to intergovernmental professionals, especially those in central agencies who tend to be focused on overall political and strategic objectives, and who are likely to view substantive issues through this lens. To the extent that such strategic concerns – "intergovernmental gaming," as Greg Marchildon (1999) puts it – predominate, there is little room for participation of groups in particular policy areas.

There may be greater room for deliberation and consultation when responsibility for policy development is more concentrated in the hands of line ministries. In this case, officials are more likely to share common policy interests and professional backgrounds and to have common constituencies – and hence to have greater grounds on which to build consensus. Indeed, it appears that at this level of working relationships, interaction with affected interested groups is common, and some ministerial councils have also developed strong links to interest groups.

It is useful in this context to think of debates within the federal system in terms of two axes. The one is the federalism axis, built around the distribution of power, influence, and status, and based on broad images of the appropriate design of the federal system, whether province-centred or Ottawa-centred. The other is the policy axis, where the focus is on options and outcomes in specific policy areas, in which theories of federalism itself are of secondary concern. With respect to the first axis, federalism is an end in itself; with respect to the second it is a means to other, more substantive ends. These two axes interact in the real world of intergovernmental relations in complex ways and are often in tension with each other.

The SUFA includes a commitment "to ensure effective mechanisms for Canadians to participate in developing social priorities and reviewing outcomes." But again, there is no mention of whether and how citizens and groups will be incorporated into intergovernmental mechanisms and processes. The logic of the agreement is governments "working in partnership for Canadians," rather than in partnership with Canadians. Indeed, there appears to be a fundamental difference between the role of citizens in domestic politics, whether at the federal or provincial level, and their role when an issue becomes embroiled in intergovernmental relations. For example, in current debates over changes to the health care system, the citizens of Alberta are direct players in the internal debate over the provincial government's plan to introduce a larger role for the private sector. But when the battle is between Edmonton and Ottawa, citizens are largely outside the game, more bystanders or cannon fodder than participants. As Roger Gibbins observes, collaborative models, "at least at the margins [would] reduce the role and effectiveness of legislatures, of political parties, interest groups and the public. They would promote government that is less accountable, and in that sense, less democratic" (1997, 43–4).

Direct Democracy: Citizens as Decision-Makers

If deliberative and consultative democracy argues for greater citizen access to and participation in intergovernmental discussion, then the perspective of direct democracy argues that in intergovernmental disputes the ultimate arbiters and decision-makers should be citizens. We have appropriately reached this point with respect to constitutional amendment. Following successive referenda in Quebec, legislation in several other provinces, and the national referendum on the Charlottetown Accord, it is now arguably a constitutional convention that no major constitutional change will be made without popular ratification.

Direct democracy is unlikely to play a major role in the more mundane activities in intergovernmental relations. Nevertheless, it is useful to recall that there is a genuine tension, in a deeply divided society, between the simple majoritarianism of direct democracy and the idea that conflict and instability can best be handled by the carefully crafted bargains made among political elites.

Democracy as Recognition of Distinct Communities

As we noted at the outset, democracy as majority rule must have a different meaning in a federal or culturally divided society such as Canada than in a unitary or homogeneous society. Federalism, in principle, says "there are some questions that should be decided on a national level, and hence should be assigned to central power; and there are other questions upon which local priorities should prevail, and which should therefore be assigned to the provincial level." In practice, there is no coherent relationship between this principle of subsidiarity and the actual division of powers in the Constitution Act, 1867, drafted more than a century ago. The contemporary debates about national standards are precisely about what the balance between national norms and provincial variations should be, and about who – the federal government, the federal and provincial governments acting collectively, provincial governments acting together, or provincial governments acting on their own – should define and enforce these standards. These questions remain unresolved.

More fundamentally, if we think of Canada as a multi- or binational society, in which both Quebec and Aboriginal peoples have powerful claims to distinct status, then majoritarian views, whether imposed by the national government or by intergovernmental agreement, become highly problematic. If respect for difference, rather than simple majority rule, is the hallmark of contemporary democracy, then democratic federalism must entail substantial degrees of asymmetry.

Quebec has historically resisted federal intrusions into social policy through use of the spending power, and a consistent goal has been the freedom to opt out of joint programs. It participated in the provincial-territorial discussion on the social union, though it was worried that national standards developed collaboratively were potentially as great a threat to its autonomy as those developed centrally. When the final agreement was negotiated, with its reaffirmation of the federal spending power and its opting-out provision requiring governments to meet national objectives and respect the new accountability framework, the government of Quebec refused to sign. There is no reference to Quebec's distinctiveness in the agreement, or any response to its traditional demands. Quebec commentators have interpreted the agreement less as an example of genuine collaboration than as an example of "unitary federalism" (Burelle 1999). Far from an equal partnership, Alain Noël (2000, 44–5) sees the SUFA as an example of "hegemonic co-operation," based on hierarchical leadership from the top down: "It is not faithful to the federal principle or to Canadian tradition."

How the SUFA will work out in practice with respect to Quebec is unclear. It seems highly unlikely that it will provide the blueprint for imposition of nationally defined standards on Quebec. Perhaps more likely is that it will come to represent the de facto asymmetry of Canadian federalism that has not been achieved through constitutional recognition of the province's distinctiveness. Noël remains skeptical even of this: the fact is, he argues, that a "new pan-Canadian social framework is emerging, and it is unlikely Quebec can remain unaffected by its norms and constraints.... The only autonomy that is enhanced is the autonomy of the footnote, the negative autonomy of the non-participant" (Noël 2000, 46). To the extent that the agreement fails to recognize the multinational character of Canada, or the broad consensus of Quebecers that it is the National Assembly that should determine the character of the province's social policy, it undermines the democratic claims of the agreement.

With respect to the other dimension of fundamental cultural difference in Canada, the presence of Aboriginal peoples, the agreement is somewhat more forthcoming. It commits governments to "work with the Aboriginal peoples of Canada to find practical solutions to address their pressing needs." In December 1999, the Federal-Provincial-Territorial Ministerial Council met with ministers responsible for Aboriginal matters and leaders of national Aboriginal groups to explore ways to involve Aboriginal organizations in the social union process.

This analysis of the links between collaborative federalism, as exemplified by the SUFA, and a number of democratic values suggests that the governments that operate Canada's executive federalism are indeed sensitive to the need to respond to citizen concerns. Increased openness, transparency, and accountability do constitute a basic element of the agreement. But several caveats must be noted. First, the agreement itself is a purely intergovernmental document: there was little, if any, legislative, group, or individual participation in its formulation. Second, the image of the citizen that is embedded in the agreement is primarily that of the customer, or client, entitled to effective public services, seamlessly and efficiently delivered, but not that of an active participant and contributor. Third, the agreement includes no suggestions or guidelines with respect to citizen or legislative participation in future intergovernmental institutions. It is at best only a partial blueprint for the democratization of intergovernmental relations. And finally, whatever the failures of "court government" in developing and sustaining citizen participation in national or provincial legislatures, the fact remains that Question Period, legislative debates, and committee hearings provide far more structured access to decision-making within governments than do any of the existing or proposed mechanisms of executive federalism. To the extent that executive federalism is simply about achieving administrative co-ordination, this is not a serious problem: it is no more or less closed than other bureaucratic machinery. But to the extent that collaborative federalism becomes the forum for deliberation on fundamental social and political values, then the accountability framework spelled out in the SUFA is insufficient.

Prospects for the Future

We have argued that the commitment to a more collaborative form of federalism offers considerable prospects for enhanced co-ordination and policy agreement among the interdependent governments of Canadian federalism. It is a desirable response to the need to balance common standards and norms with the need for variety and responsiveness to local needs inherent in a diverse federation. And it reflects the Canadian reality of two politically, bureaucratically, and fiscally powerful orders of government, which must co-operate as equal partners. We have argued that in the SUFA and related agreements, governments have recognized that they are no longer operating a closed shop: their interactions must be more open, transparent, and accountable. Yet this recognition cuts across the grain of many of the dynamics and incentives that have characterized executive government and its attendant executive federalism in Canada. The democratization agenda remains. Thus, we conclude with some observations about possible ways in which intergovernmentalism might become more democratic.

Clarifying Who Does What

Collaborative federalism arose not out of principle, but out of necessity. It is not an ideal model of governance, but a practical one. It remains the case that democracy is best served by governments exercising clear authority in ways that render them accountable to their legislatures and citizens. Thus, more attention must be paid in collaborative discussion to clarifying roles and responsibilities as much as possible, and in such a way that citizens understand whom they can hold accountable about what. As John Richards suggests, "Accountability matters. One – and only one level of government should be responsible for any particular domain of social policy" (Lazar 1998, 83).

Opening Up the Process

In an interdependent world, there is no escaping the need for co-operation. Hence the continuing need to enhance the transparency of the intergovernmental process. The SUFA helpfully points the way. But much more needs to be done, through the internet and other devices, to bring the intergovernmental processes themselves under closer scrutiny. This can include, first, more meetings of ministerial councils open to the public and advance publication of the schedules of meetings and their agendas. Ministerial councils now routinely issue press releases following their meetings. Ministers should also make it routine practice to make statements to their respective legislatures or their relevant committees after all such meetings.

Second, it is desirable to involve citizen groups more fully in intergovernmental discussions. The extent to which this is the case now varies widely across different policy areas. There are many reasons for doing this, but one of them is that the presence of third parties, with policy goals, not governmental interests, at the centre of their concerns helps to ensure that the intergovernmental politics of turf and blame avoidance does not dominate substantive policy discussion. We need to find ways to integrate the intergovernmental axis of policy discussion with the public-private axis.

Enhancing Legislative Federalism

Reflecting the larger Canadian political system, the central characteristic of intergovernmental relations in Canada is its executive-dominated character. Democratic federalism would be much enhanced by bringing Parliament and provincial legislatures much more fully into the process: we need to counterbalance executive federalism with a larger measure of "legislative federalism."

Every legislature in Canada should have a standing committee on intergovernmental relations. All intergovernmental agreements should be discussed in committee, and major initiatives, such as the SUFA, should be subject to ratification by legislatures. More valuable, perhaps, would be the development of forums in which rank-and-file legislators from all parties in all jurisdictions could have the opportunity to exchange views on a regular basis. This might help counteract one of the ways in which Westminster-based parliamentary federalism, combined with a single-member-based electoral system, distorts representation. Governments, typically elected with less than a majority of the vote, then speak for their jurisdiction: we talk of Harris's Ontario, Klein's

Alberta, or Chrétien's Ottawa, when we know that rather than being unified, homogeneous units, there is a wide diversity of opinion in each of these. The result is not only a distortion of democratic representation, but also an exaggeration of regional differences that fosters conflict. We need to find ways to counterbalance the competition between rival executives as the predominant mode of intergovernmental relations. As this last suggestion implies, it is clear that the democratization of intergovernmental relations is only one element of a much broader democratization agenda in Canada's parliamentary federalism.

Conclusion

The foregoing analysis suggests that the Social Union Framework Agreement at present provides thin gruel for those concerned with enhancing democratic practices in Canadian federalism. Such a conclusion may be premature. It is important to recognize that multi-level government, whether in Canada, the European Union, or elsewhere, poses immense challenges to democratic participation and accountability. Governments have not responded to them completely, nor have independent scholars. The reality of the modern world is interdependence, from the local to the international levels. We have yet to find the language or the concepts to think about democracy in such a world.

The ministers and officials who negotiated the SUFA did recognize the need to respond to citizen concerns for greater transparency, accountability, and participation. All of these values are highlighted in the document itself. In this sense, the agreement provides an essential starting point for a deeper discussion of the prospects for democracy in modern politics. It suggests considerable potential for the future. Whether this potential is realized and further developed depends on two sets of factors. The first is the extent to which the norms and values embedded in the document become internalized in the minds of the officials and ministers who participate in the process. The second is the extent to which citizens and groups themselves embrace these values and pressure their governments to honor them. Is the association of collaborative federalism and democracy an oxymoron? Perhaps. But the challenge to citizens and governments is to disprove this proposition.

NOTE

1 Hence our title, which we owe to our colleague Robert Vipond. On hearing the subject of this chapter, his instant response was: "Democracy and intergovernmental relations? An oxymoron if I ever heard one."

REFERENCES

Breton, A. 1985. "Supplementary Statement." In *Royal Commission on the Economic Union and Canada's Development Prospects, Report,* vol. 3. Ottawa: Supply and Services.

Brock, K. 1993. "Learning from Failure: Lessons from Charlottetown," *Constitutional Forum* 4, no. 1–4: 29–33.

Brooks, S. 1999. "Comment." In *Stretching the Federation,* edited by R. Young. Kingston: Institute of Intergovernmental Relations, Queen's University.

Burelle, A. 1995. *Le mal canadien.* Montreal: Fides.

–. 1999. "Social Union: Placing the Provinces under Federal Tutelage," *Le Devoir,* 15 February 1999.

Cairns, A. 1991. *Disruptions: Constitutional Struggles from the Charter to Meech Lake.* Toronto: McClelland & Stewart.

Cameron, D., and R. Simeon. 2000. "Intergovernmental Relations and Democratic Citizenship." In *Governance in the XXIst Century: Revitalizing the Public Service,* edited by B.G. Peters and D. Savoie. Montreal: McGill-Queen's University Press.

Citizens' Forum on Canada's Future (The Spicer Commission) Report. 1991. Ottawa: Supply and Services.

Courchene, T.J. 1997. "ACCESS: A Convention on the Canadian Economic and Social Systems." In Institute of Intergovernmental Relations, *Assessing ACCESS: Towards a New Social Union.* Kingston: Institute of Intergovernmental Relations, Queen's University.

Delacourt, S., and D.B. Lenihan. 1999. *Collaborative Government: Is There a Canadian Way?* Toronto: Institute of Public Administration of Canada.

Desautels, L.D. 1999. "Accountability for Alternative Service-Delivery Arrangements in the Federal Government: Some Consequences for Sharing the Business of Government." In *Collaborative Government: Is There a Canadian Way?,* edited by S. Delacourt and D.G. Lenihan. Toronto: Institute of Public Administration of Canada.

Dion, S, 1999. "Collaborative Federalism in an Era of Globalization." In *Collaborative Government: Is There a Canadian Way?,* edited by S. Delacourt and D.B. Lenihan. Toronto: Institute of Public Administration of Canada.

Fafard, P., and K. Harrison. 2000. *Managing the Environmental Union: Intergovernmental Relations and Environmental Policy in Canada.* Kingston: Institute of Intergovernmental Relations, Queen's University.

Gibbins, R. 1997. "Democratic Reservations about the ACCESS Models." In Institute of Intergovernmental Relations, *Assessing ACCESS: Towards a New Social Union.* Kingston: Institute of Intergovernmental Relations, Queen's University.

Ibbitson, J. 2000. "Abortive Climate Talks Produce Little but Hot Air," *Globe and Mail,* 2 May 2000.

Kennett, S. 1998. *Securing the Social Union: A Commentary on the Decentralized Approach.* Kingston: Institute of Intergovernmental Relations, Queen's University.

Laski, H. 1939. "The Obsolescence of Federalism." In *The People, Politics, and the Politician,* edited by A.N. Christensen and E.M. Kirkpatrick. New York: Holt, Rinehart and Winston.

Lazar, H., ed. 1998. *Canada: The State of the Federation. Non-Constitutional Renewal.* Kingston: Institute of Intergovernmental Relations, Queen's University.

Marchildon, G.P. 1999. "Constructive Entanglement: Intergovernmental Collaboration in Canadian Social Policy." In *Collaborative Government: Is There a Canadian Way?*, edited by S. Delacourt and D.G. Lenihan. Toronto: Institute of Public Administration of Canada.

Nevitte, N. 1996. *The Decline of Deference.* Peterborough, Ont.: Broadview Press.

Noël, Alain. 1999. "Is Decentralization Conservative?" In *Stretching the Federation,* edited by R. Young. Kingston: Institute of Intergovernmental Relations, Queen's University.

–. 2000. "Collaborative Federalism with a Footnote." *Policy Options* 21 (May).

Porter, B. 1999. "Social Union Agreement Heartless Say Social Justice Groups," *Povnet* (www.povnet.web.net/socialunion). 4 February 1999.

Porter, J. 1965. *The Vertical Mosaic.* Toronto: University of Toronto Press.

Richards, J. 1998. "Reducing the Muddle in the Middle: Three Propositions for Running the Welfare State." In *Canada: The State of the Federation 1997, Non-Constitutional Renewal,* edited by H. Lazar. Kingston: Institute of Intergovernmental Relations, Queen's University.

Russell, P. 1993. *Constitutional Odyssey,* 2nd ed. Toronto: University of Toronto Press.

Savoie, D. 1999. *Governing from the Centre: The Concentration of Power in Canadian Politics.* Toronto: University of Toronto Press.

Scharpf, F. 1988. "The Joint Decision Trap: Lessons from German Federalism and European Integration," *Public Administration* 6, no. 3 (September): 239–278.

Simmons, J. "Approaches to Democratic Innovation in Ministerial Council Decision-Making." Paper presented at conference on The Changing Nature of Democracy and Federalism in Canada, University of Manitoba, April 2000.

Smiley, D.V. 1979. "An Outsider's Observations of Intergovernmental Relations Among Consenting Adults." In *Consultation or Collaboration: Intergovernmental Relations in Canada Today,* edited by R. Simeon. Toronto: Institute of Public Administration of Canada.

Whitaker, R. 1983. *Federalism and Democratic Theory.* Kingston: Institute of Intergovernmental Relations, Queen's University.

DAVID CAMERON AND RICHARD SIMEON

13 Intergovernmental Relations in Canada: The Emergence of Collaborative Federalism

Publius 2002

The ways and means of managing the business of the Canadian federation evolve over time as political parties and leaders change, as the socio-economic and ideological circumstances alter, and as the particular problems or issues facing the federation come and go. This article in Publius *explored a shift in the style of intergovernmental relations in Canada towards greater collaboration between and among governments.*

The central objective of this article is to describe and explain recent changes in federalism and intergovernmental relations in Canada at the beginning of the twenty-first century. "Executive federalism" or "federal-provincial diplomacy" has long been considered the defining characteristic of Canadian intergovernmental relations, with its combination of federalism and Westminster-style cabinet government.

In recent years, there have been some important changes in the conduct of federalism and intergovernmental relations in Canada. Executive federalism has been increasingly informed by a set of practices that we call "collaborative federalism," characterized more by the principle of co-determination of broad national policies than by either the Ottawa-led cooperative federalism of the post-World War II period or the more competitive federalism of later periods. While co-determination in the Canadian context generally involves the two orders of government working together as equals, it can also entail provincial and territorial governments taking the initiative on their own – acting collectively in the absence of the federal government – to formulate national policy. Adherents of collaborative federalism (mostly provincial governments and their supporters) view the governance of Canada as a partnership between two equal, autonomous, and interdependent orders of government that jointly decide national policy. Although Ottawa does not generally share this view of the nature of the national policymaking process, in several of the cases cited below, the federal government has been drawn into a process that is premised on this assumption.[1]

After summarizing developments within Canadian federalism since the Second World War, we describe the emergent pattern and explain its origins, functions, and practices. We conclude with an assessment and evaluation. How does this pattern differ from past practice of intergovernmental relations; how robust is it; is it likely to be extended to additional policy areas; and what are its consequences for effective and democratic policy-making?

Trends in Intergovernmental Relations

Several caveats should be made clear at the outset. We are not positing a dramatic break with the past; the distinctive pattern that we describe has its roots in what preceded it. There is much continuity in the evolving patterns of intergovernmental relations. The subject does not lend itself to analytically distinct ideal types, nor is there a single pattern of intergovernmental relations. It varies according to level (with first ministers' relationships most dominated by strategic and status concerns) and according to issue area. In some areas, a tradition of cooperation has developed; in others, mistrust dominates the relationship. The rhetoric of trust and cooperation, found in modern intergovernmental agreements often reflects aspirations rather than reality. Furthermore, despite the growth of collaboration, the institutions of intergovernmental relations in Canada remain, compared with some other federations, relatively ad hoc and under institutionalized.

The Evolution of Intergovernmental Relations Since World War II

As Canada has evolved, so have intergovernmental relations.[2] In the two decades after the end of World War II, the intergovernmental agenda was focused on the construction of the Canadian welfare state. This project deeply engaged federal institutions because, while most of its major elements lay within provincial jurisdiction, much of the policy design and funding came from Ottawa. Nevertheless, the system adapted to these new roles for government with few changes in the formal distribution of power. The key policy instrument was the federal spending power, exemplified by the proliferation of shared-cost programs. Governments were relatively decentralized, and close professional relationships developed among provincial and federal officials and ministers within specific policy areas. "Cooperative federalism" made the Canadian welfare state possible, while considerably influencing its timing and its design.[3]

During the 1960s, the country moved into a different phase. Quebec's Quiet Revolution unleashed a progressive nationalism that transformed Quebec and challenged traditional assumptions about Canadian federalism. This profoundly altered the intergovernmental agenda, placing the Constitution at its heart. The growth of the public sector at both levels meant that governments were increasingly likely to bump into one another in the execution of their mandates and in the pursuit of their political ambitions. Each order of government moved into new areas of public concern, with few constitutional constraints to hold them back. Moreover, by the 1970s, a growing regionalism, particularly in the West, and an increasing assertiveness in the English-speaking provinces as their budgets and bureaucracies grew relative to those of the federal government, added to the pressure. Pierre Trudeau's assumption of the prime ministership in 1968 sharpened the ideological conflict between Quebec City and Ottawa, and between Ottawa and several western capitals. Provinces were less and less prepared to defer to federal leadership. The cooperative federalism of the 1950s was supplanted by a more competitive dynamic.

Federal-provincial conflict came to a head in the early 1980s. On two key issues – the Constitution and energy policy – the federal government, led by Pierre Trudeau, challenged both Quebec nationalism and western regionalism. The federal government's National Energy Program (NEP) and its determination to patriate the Constitution with or without provincial consent had an explosive effect on intergovernmental relations.

These two initiatives forced fundamentally different visions of the country – Ottawa-centered, province-centered, and Quebec-centered – into painful public debate; they divided the country regionally, and posed difficult questions about the character of Canada's political communities and the role of governments in defining and shaping them. Moreover, these conflicts challenged the status and self-image of governments and political leaders, framing the issues in zero-sum terms in circumstances in which none of the participants could afford to lose. The public was drawn into these battles, at the beginning as a resource for the battling government actors and, later, as a participant in its own right.

By the mid-eighties, the intergovernmental agenda had changed once again. Building an electoral coalition that included all sections of the country, the Progressive Conservative government of Brian Mulroney promised a new era of federal-provincial harmony and cooperation. The NEP was dismantled; provinces were closely consulted in the government's major policy initiative, the negotiation of a free-trade agreement with the United States; and provincial governments were at first insulated from federal efforts at cutting national spending. Mulroney's major achievement was to secure the agreement of all Canadian governments to the Meech Lake Constitutional Accord (1987), designed to bring Quebec back into the "constitutional family" by according recognition of its distinct status within Canada.

Toward the end of this period, however, the Mulroney government made a series of decisions that contradicted its emphasis on regional equity and its commitment to intergovernmental collaboration, thus undermining federal-provincial harmony and accentuating inter-regional rivalries.[4]

Citizen opposition to executive federalism grew during this period. The passionate debates surrounding patriation and the adoption of a Charter of Rights and Freedoms in 1981–2 had fundamentally changed attitudes toward the Constitution; no longer was it a matter of governments sorting out jurisdiction; now it was about citizens and their rights. If this was so, then what right did "eleven men in suits" have to shape the Canadian Constitution? However, the negotiation of the Meech Lake Accord exemplified the old pattern of executive federalism. It was developed in secret, among heads of government, with the public deliberately excluded. Only Robert Bourassa's federalist Quebec government referred the draft agreement to the legislature before it was signed in final form. Despite the support of virtually all Canadian elites, a ground swell of public opposition paved the way for its defeat in 1990.[5] Two years later, after a process that did attempt to engage citizens more directly, another intergovernmental agreement, the Charlottetown Constitutional Accord, was defeated in a national referendum.[6] Governments came under intense pressure to make their relationships more open, transparent, and participatory. Several provinces passed legislation to require popular approval of future constitutional changes. Citizen mobilization on day-to-day intergovernmental relations since then has been much more muted, but governments have had to take account of the demand for transparency and accountability as they have moved toward the more collaborative model.

A second consequence of the constitutional failures of this period was the realization that fundamental constitutional change was probably beyond reach. With the fatigue and frustration that followed yet another failure, political leaders and citizens turned away from such inherently divisive exercises to focus on "making the federation work," finding solutions through the informal adaptation of what had already proved a highly flexible regime, rather than through constitutional change.[7] This was a major impetus for the move toward a more collaborative model.

Intergovernmental Relations after Charlottetown

Changes in governments and political leadership along with fiscal pressures also contributed to the shift. In 1993, Jean Chrétien and the Liberals took office in Ottawa. Chrétien is a pragmatic politician who had been burned by the

Constitution in the past and whose every instinct was to govern in a low-key, practical, step-by-step fashion, eschewing ideology or dramatic gestures. In 1994, the Parti Québécois (PQ) under Jacques Parizeau took power in Quebec City, displacing the federalist Liberals. This set the stage for the drama of the 1995 referendum on sovereignty and soured intergovernmental relations. The PQ had little interest in working with other governments. It would take whatever was available, and complain about the alleged injustices visited upon Quebec, but would decline to participate in the management of the affairs of the federation While Lucien Bouchard, Parizeau's successor as Quebec premier, showed greater interest in working with his provincial colleagues, the basic posture of minimal participation was sustained, as it has been with the resignation of Bouchard and the accession to the Quebec premiership of Bernard Landry in 2000.

Change was also occurring in the other provinces. Alberta Premier Ralph Klein, elected in 1992, initiated the war against big government with his social democratic New Democratic Party peers in neighbouring Saskatchewan not far behind. In 1995, a Conservative government, led by Mike Harris, took power in Ontario, committed to a "Common Sense Revolution"[8] with dramatic cutbacks, deregulation, and restructuring of government. Both Harris and Klein initially focused on a provincial agenda; they had little interest in developments elsewhere in Canada. Both soon discovered that no first minister can ignore intergovernmental concerns, and that citizens angered by policy change within the province could and would turn to Ottawa to protect their interests.[9] Success on their domestic agendas demanded some basic changes in how the federal system operated.

By the 1990s, the politics of fiscal deficits was also driving the shift to a new model of intergovernmental relations. There was now a broad public and governmental consensus that public sector debt was too high, that deficits had to be eliminated, and that the pain associated with bringing federal and provincial finances under control would have to be borne. All governments began to address these fiscal concerns, with some mix of costcutting, revenue generation, privatization, efficiency measures, and downloading.[10]

Central to Ottawa's deficit-reduction strategy was what might be called the exercise of the federal spending power in reverse. Utilizing this "disspending power," the federal government in 1995 substantially reduced its transfers to the provinces for social programs (a reduction from $18 billion to a floor of $11 billion, later adjusted to $12.5 billion, in federal support for health care, social assistance, and higher education). Federal transfers under these programs were rolled into the new Canada Health and Social Transfer (CHST), which promised greater freedom from federal conditions (though those under the Canada Health Act remained, as did the prohibition against restricting social assistance on the basis of residency).

The broad national consensus on the magnitude of the fiscal crisis meant that these actions did not occasion the intense intergovernmental conflict that might have been expected in other circumstances. The criticism was muted relative to the damage being inflicted on provincial budgets, though as deficit pressures eased in the late 1990s, demands intensified for a restoration of earlier funding levels. Second, Ottawa's power over the provinces, and certainly its legitimacy, were reduced along with the reduction in fiscal transfers. If Ottawa was no longer paying the piper, what right did it have to call the tune? Third, the federal cuts fostered a wave of "secondary downloading" – reductions in the transfers from provinces to their agencies (i.e., hospitals, municipalities, universities, colleges, social agencies, schools, and the like), and ultimately to citizens. The effects of federal-provincial relations thus reverberate throughout Canadian society. The net effect of this experience (i.e., federal cuts, downsizing the country's social, health, and educational systems, and coping with the full brunt of the public anxiety and opposition that this entailed) was to invest the provincial governments with a stronger sense of their autonomy, their responsibility, and their right to judge, within their spheres of jurisdiction, what the national as well as the provincial interest requires.[11]

The Emergence of Collaborative Federalism

These developments set the stage for the strengthening of "collaborative federalism," the process by which national goals are achieved, not by the federal government acting alone or by the federal government shaping provincial behavior through the exercise of its spending power, but by some or all of the 11 governments and the territories acting collectively.

It can take two forms. The first is collaboration among federal, provincial, and territorial governments (FPT in the current Canadian intergovernmental jargon), seeking an appropriate balance between federal, provincial, and territorial roles and responsibilities. FPT is based on the premise that all these governments possess strong fiscal and jurisdictional tools and that as a result of this interdependence, effective policy depends on coordination among them. The second is collaboration among provincial and territorial governments (PT), with Ottawa on the sidelines. This is based on the view that under the constitution, health, welfare, and education are provincial jurisdictions. "National" policies and standards in these areas, therefore, are matters for provinces to decide together; the central government does not have to do it. This development of some aspects of national policy through agreements reached among autonomous but associated actors (provinces and territories) introduced an element of "confederalism" into the Canadian system.

The collaborative model is also an alternative to constitutional change. Many of the issues unresolved in the failures of Meech Lake and Charlottetown have re-emerged in the intergovernmental arena – the economic union, the social union, "who does what" jurisdictionally, and the spending power. Now, rather than being expressed in the uncompromising language of constitutional clauses, and enforced by the courts, they are to be expressed as intergovernmental "Accords," "Declarations," and "Framework Agreements."

The first concrete example of this was the Agreement on Internal Trade (AIT).[12] When Charlottetown was defeated, Ottawa's hopes to clarify and extend its powers with respect to the economic union went down with it. The federal government therefore initiated multilateral negotiations with the provincial governments designed to reduce internal barriers to the mobility of goods, capital, people, and services in Canada. First ministers signed the AIT in 1994, and it was implemented in July 1995. Although its structure and content mirror the approach of international agreements such as the North American Free Trade Agreement (NAFTA), it is a nonbinding political arrangement; it contains, for example, a formal dispute-settlement mechanism, but its rulings do not have legal effect. A new Internal Trade Secretariat was established, but it has no significant authority, and citizens do not have direct access to it. Many restrictive practices were grandfathered. Yet, considering the difficulty the country has had in achieving a more fully integrated economic union, and provincial resistance to any increase in federal power over the economy, the AIT is a notable intergovernmental accomplishment; while its substantive provisions are weak, it is a useful first step.[13] It was developed with virtually no public involvement. Few Canadians realized the agreement was being negotiated; few realize it is now in operation.

The AIT reflects some important dimensions of collaborative federalism. It demonstrates that despite its constitutional responsibility for interprovincial and international trade, Ottawa has neither the power nor the legitimacy to define and enforce the Canadian economic union on its own. An alternative approach – to define the rules in the constitution and make them judicially enforceable – is also impossible. Hence, negotiated intergovernmental collaboration became the only way to make progress.

Identical forces are at work with respect to the "social union," which also figured in the agenda of Charlottetown. The social union, like the economic union, is predicated on the idea that a defining characteristic of a unified country is a shared and common set of aspirations, standards, and norms with respect to the basic elements of social citizenship. As with the economic union, two questions arise: How will common national standards be balanced against the variations that federalism encourages? And who is going to define and police the standards? In the case of the social union, a third question arises: How is the federal spending power – which lies at the base of Ottawa's fiscal transfers to the provinces and which was a crucial instrument in constructing the welfare state – to be exercised and how is it to be controlled? In the face of federal retreat, the provincial governments and territories took the initiative. First ministers commissioned their ministers responsible for social affairs to develop proposals, and an intensive period of ministerial and official meetings followed. Thus, as they came to terms with the new fiscal and policy realities, provinces began to work collaboratively to fashion common policy approaches and undertake joint initiatives, and to present coherent proposals to the federal government. Their evolving consensus, even when confronted with the indifference or opposition of the federal government, proved to be remarkably strong, considering the diversity of interests and circumstances represented around the table.

The intergovernmental discussions culminated in February 1999 when Ottawa and all the provinces except Quebec signed the Social Union Framework Agreement (SUFA). This agreement explicitly endorses Ottawa's power to spend in areas of provincial jurisdiction. But this power can no longer be exercised unilaterally. New joint programs will not be introduced, or existing ones changed, without due notice and substantial provincial consent. Provincial responsibility for program design and delivery is affirmed. SUFA contains the following elements: a statement of general principles; a mobility provision applying to the social policy field; commitments respecting public accountability and transparency; notice provisions; rules governing the exercise of the federal government's spending power; and procedures for dispute avoidance and dispute resolution. The agreement is to be reviewed within the first three years. While this framework agreement is a considerable achievement of collaborative federalism, it should be noted that the document remains loose and general in character, and that the proof of the agreement will be found in the commitment and follow-through the participating governments bring to its implementation. The early indications are not encouraging. Intensive discussion on a wide variety of policy files continues, but there is little sense of a commitment to joint problem solving.

The sovereignist government of Quebec joined the social union negotiations in the summer of 1998, recognizing that in the pending provincial election campaign, it would have some political difficulty justifying its non-participation in the intergovernmental process. It declined, however, to sign the February 1999 agreement on the grounds that after heavy federal pressure, the final compromise failed to protect Quebec's right to opt out of new shared programs without financial penalty, as had been agreed in earlier provincial drafts. Quebec's absence means that it continues to march to a different drummer, de facto if not constitutionally.[14]

The Social Union Framework Agreement is purely the product of participating governments; it was negotiated at meetings held behind closed doors, and had a very low public profile.[15] It was not until the February 1999 meeting of first ministers, which concluded the agreement, that the matter was brought seriously to the attention of Canadians. The agreement is a classic example of elite accommodation. The massive public mobilization, so evident in Meech Lake and Charlottetown, had not been repeated. This suggests that the stakes are lower, and public engagement is less, when governments seek accommodation outside the constitutional arena.

Despite the elitist process, the agreement does seek to respond to democratic concerns by placing considerable emphasis on accountability, transparency, the need to report back to Canadians about the performance of their social programs, and the necessity of securing ongoing input and feedback from citizens and interested parties. Some observers regard the citizen dimension as one of the central pillars of the agreement.[16]

The AIT and the SUFA are the clearest examples of the collaborative approach. They constitute, in the words of one senior provincial official, "a work plan for cooperation and a rulebook for competition."[17] But it has been manifest in a wide variety of other areas as well...

The Institutions of Collaborative Federalism

The collaborative model has had an important impact on the institutions of intergovernmental relations. Perhaps the most obvious is in the role and position of the Annual Premiers Conference (APC). Initiated at the instigation of Quebec in the 1960s as little more than a summer retreat for premiers and their families, the APC has evolved into a significant intergovernmental institution. Long overshadowed by the federal-provincial First Ministers' Conference (FMC), it has become more prominent as the frequency and significance of the FMCs have declined. Held every August under a rotating chairmanship, this association of provinces has become a full-fledged intergovernmental institution, professionally supported by provincial civil servants. The APC prepares and receives position papers, issues communiqués, and launches projects to be undertaken by the relevant ministers; it also has an on-going agenda of work that connects one meeting to another. The chair has assumed a substantive role as the spokesperson for the premiers between meetings. It was at one of these meetings that the social union initiative was begun.

In striking contrast to the growth of the APC is the declining importance of the FMC. The set-piece FMC, held in the National Conference Centre, with first ministers surrounded by phalanxes of ministers and officials, and with a combination of public and private meetings that were so prominent from the 1960s to the 1980s, has recently been absent, replaced by short working sessions.

Advocates of collaborative federalism have often seen the FMC as the pinnacle of the intergovernmental system, resolving conflicts at the highest level and providing direction to the network of lower level meetings, much like the

Council of Ministers in the European Union. Numerous commentators have suggested that FMCs be made at least annual events, and perhaps even given constitutional status. However, few have been called since the election of the Liberal federal government in 1993. This reflects the federal government's suspicion that a fully developed collaborative model will undermine its "senior" status, that FMCs provide a platform for political attacks on Ottawa, and that they elevate premiers from provincial politicians to national decision-makers. The weak presence of the FMC is one reason why the APC has taken on such an important role.

Another institutional forum that is assuming much greater importance is the ministerial council, sometimes federal-provincial, sometimes purely provincial. Such councils have existed for many years. Recently, however, their numbers have increased, they have become more institutionalized, and have played a more formal role in carrying out mandates assigned by first ministers. They have become the workhorses of the system, assuming a central role in the policy process, including, in some cases, developing close relationships with related interest groups. Councils now exist for ministries concerned with social policy renewal, forestry, transportation, education, and the environment. Other groupings of ministers go by names such as forums, committees, and meetings of "Ministers Responsible." Some meet regularly, others on an ad hoc basis.

The Provincial/Territorial Council on Social Policy Renewal has been particularly active. Acting under the instructions of the premiers, sectoral ministers and officials developed position papers and fashioned strategies for the consideration of the premiers and in preparation for federal-provincial discussion. The council was instrumental in developing SUFA, and it will play an important role in helping to make it work.

A key question in this process is the legal and political status of intergovernmental agreements. Many of the most important federal-provincial arrangements are not in fact formal contracts, though they may later be enshrined in federal and provincial legislation. The intergovernmental agreements themselves, however, are not legally binding or enforceable. This was made clear in a recent Supreme Court judgment that rejected a provincial appeal against a change in federal policy by asserting the supremacy of the government's accountability to Parliament. Taken to its limit, the logic of collaboration implies that governments should be legally bound by intergovernmental accords and that they should be accountable to each other. However, this is a major challenge in the Canadian constitutional system, which requires that each government be responsible to its own legislature and that governments cannot bind future legislatures. Thus, there is a deep tension between the logic of collaborative intergovernmentalism and the logic of responsible parliamentary government.

Assessing the Pattern of Collaborative Federalism

Although the content and specificity of intergovernmental processes and agreements vary widely, our review of several recent examples displays some common threads.

- The equality between provinces and Ottawa is underlined by the fact that most councils and meetings are co-chaired by a federal and a provincial minister.
- The northern territories of Canada – Yukon, the North West Territories, and the newly established Nunavut – are now integrated with the provinces. Meetings are federal/provincial/territorial or provincial/territorial despite the fact that the territories remain constitutional offspring of the federal government. This evolution toward provincial status has evoked remarkably little comment, even though it has some potential for changing the dynamic of intergovernmental relations because three more voices are added to the six smaller and poorer provinces.
- Quebec is relatively absent. Usually its representatives participate in meetings, but the Quebec government has disassociated itself from some of the agreements. Quebec's position is that fields like education, welfare, and health are exclusive areas of provincial jurisdiction, and that the ability of the federal government to spend money in such areas is illegitimate. For Quebec, national standards and norms emerging from intergovernmental consensus are little better in principle than federal unilateralism. It is remarkable, however, that successive *indépendantiste* premiers of Quebec have been able to develop effective working relationships with their fellow premiers despite the fundamental difference over Canada's future.
- Most agreements stress that the formal constitutional powers assigned to governments remain unchanged; the goal is to exercise these powers "in a coordinated manner."
- Minimizing duplication and overlapping in order to achieve greater efficiency and cost saving are universal themes.
- Consistent with the doctrine of the "New Public Management," agreements emphasize the need to share best practices, to develop performance indicators, and to monitor results. This is most evident in the text of SUFA.
- Framework agreements reached among all governments are often followed by individually negotiated bilateral agreements or by additional sub-agreements.
- All agreements pay lip service to the need for greater transparency and for clearer lines of citizen accountability in intergovernmental relations, but citizen access to the dispute settlement mechanisms of the AIT and SUFA remains very limited.
- An increasing number of agreements explicitly acknowledge the need to "engage stake holders" and to "build linkages to other structures in the broad social and economic environment."[18]

While these developments reflect a greater degree of institutionalization in Canadian intergovernmental relations, it is important not to exaggerate the change. Compared to Germany or the European Union, for example, Canadian intergovernmental relations remain highly fluid and ad hoc. The process has no constitutional or legislative base, little backup by bureaucrats linked to the success of the process rather than to individual governments, no formal decision-rules, and no capacity for authoritative decision-making. This means that the scope or extent of intergovernmental relations remains heavily dependent on whether the first ministers, especially the prime minister, find it advantageous or not. The system in this sense is fragile.[19]

It is far too early to judge the success of this new model. Indeed, different actors may define "success" very differently. For some, the process itself might constitute success if it leads to more cooperation and less intergovernmental conflict. There is strong public opinion evidence that suggests citizens want not more or less powers for any order of government, but an end to the wrangling between them.

For provinces, especially the more assertive ones, such as Ontario, Alberta, and British Columbia, success will be measured chiefly by their ability to wrestle the initiative from Ottawa, limit Ottawa's ability to intrude on their programs and priorities, and increase their autonomy in shared jurisdictions. For smaller, poorer provinces, autonomy will be less important than ensuring the continued flow of federal dollars. Quebec, on the evidence, approaches the emerging pattern with deep reservations, seeing advantages to the extent that it provides allies in their bid to constrain the government of Canada, but fearful that the extension of collaborative federalism might simply replace Ottawa's oversight and direction with the collective oversight and direction of the English-speaking provinces. The SUFA is seen less as a provincial constraint on the federal spending power than as a re-affirmation of it.

Success for Ottawa lies in its ability to retain its influence and visibility, particularly in an era of budget surpluses. It seeks to maintain links to citizens by providing benefits directly to them rather than indirectly through the provinces. Indeed, some of the factors that initially led Ottawa to accept collaborative federalism have now changed. In the 1990s, Ottawa was faced with a fiscal crisis that forced it, like it or not, to withdraw massively from many policy areas, including the devolution of both costs and responsibility to the provinces. At the same time, in the aftermath of the "near-death" experience of the 1995 Quebec referendum, Ottawa was anxious to demonstrate its commitment to cooperation. By the new century, with large fiscal surpluses (at least for the moment), with successive election victories, with no viable opposition on the horizon, and with a slow but steady decline in support for Quebec sovereignty, Ottawa appears less prepared to take a back seat to the provinces and more concerned to reassert its presence in the lives of Canadians. Clearly, this activist impulse will be shaped by the fall out from the tragedy of 11 September 2001. On one hand, a slowing economy may be pushed farther toward recession, thus reducing Ottawa's scope for action; on the other hand, the rise of security issues to the top of the national agenda puts the focus squarely on matters falling clearly within federal jurisdiction.

In general, most governments take a pragmatic approach to collaboration. Most seek to maximize their freedom of action and to minimize external constraints, fiscal or regulatory; some – especially the fiscally weaker jurisdictions – will be prepared to trade off some autonomy in return for adequate and stable financial assistance. Both Ottawa and the provinces will continue to guard their turf and to exploit every opportunity to win credit and avoid blame. This historic dynamic of executive federalism has not changed, and it is a major reason why the collaborative model is so fluid and ad hoc. Successful collaboration depends on high levels of mutual trust among the participants and on their internalization of its implicit norms. Instead, there is some indication of considerable cynicism among officials at both levels with respect to the rhetorical promises of collaboration.

Success will be defined very differently by those groups and by citizens not concerned with federalism or the relative status of governments, but rather with substantive policy and its outcomes. They will ask: Does this process enhance or impede the achievement of the policy objectives we are interested in? Answers will vary, of course, depending on the group in question. To the extent that governments can achieve together what none could do separately, to the extent that they can coordinate into a single whole policies and programs at all levels, and to the extent that the costs and frustrations of overlap and duplication can be reduced, then collaborative federalism serves all Canadians. Moreover, it suggests a reasonable way to balance the inevitable tension between national norms and standards on the one hand, and the desire to respond to the specific needs, circumstances, and preferences of different provincial communities on the other.

However, there are many potential costs to the collaborative model that have been well described in the literature on the European Union. The "joint decision trap" emerges when autonomous, interdependent actors committed to consensus decision-making seek to make decisions. The time and cost of coordination can escalate; solutions may be avoided or simply express the lowest common denominator.[20] The political and institutional concerns of the actors – for status and recognition, to win credit and avoid blame – can dominate the substantive issues themselves. None of these dilemmas is resolved easily.[21]

Perhaps the most acute challenge confronting collaborative federalism, as with executive federalism in general,[22] is the need to meet the democratic expectations of citizens. These expectations appear to outpace the very limited advances that have been made to democratize the process, and there is nothing in the process of collaborative federalism that will make this task any easier. Keith Banting, noting that federalism values and democratic values are often in tension, claims that Canadian social policy discussion since the Second World War is marked by "the strongest form of intergovernmentalism – the co-determination model." He warns that it is "worth remembering the democratic critique of such potent intergovernmentalism."[23] Another observer, Roger Gibbins, argues that collaborative models would, "at least at the margins, reduce the role and effectiveness of legislatures, of political parties, elections, interest groups and the public. They would promote government that is less accountable, and in that sense, less democratic." The combination of decentralization and intergovernmentalism "moves decisions out of legislatures and into fora relatively insulated from public pressure, partisan debate and electoral combat."[24] Many others, in Canada and elsewhere, express similar views.[25]

Many Canadian interest groups and movements – notably those associated with social policy and the environment[26] – have historically looked to federal leadership, believing the provinces lack either the resources or the political will to take a leading role. They worry about a possible "rush to the bottom." Hence, they tend to be skeptical of the collaborative model, seeing it as inherently decentralizing. In a carefully argued rebuttal, Alain Noël disagrees. He notes that there are "conservative and progressive arguments on both sides of the centralization/decentralization debate" and that "the Canadian welfare state became better anchored than the American one, largely *because* Canada was a more decentralized federation." He concludes: "Betting everything on elites and on central intervention is not only poor theory; it is also bad politics for the left."[27]

A final line of criticism sees collaborative federalism as little more than a "cartel of elites," in which federal and provincial governments manage the system in order to serve their own interests, while freezing out citizen and group interests. In this view, the danger is that some of the primary virtues of a federal system – innovation, experimentation, variety, and competition – will be lost in an over-zealous search for harmonization, consistency, and agreement.[28]

Collaborative Federalism: How Durable?

Is the pattern of collaborative federalism likely to be a durable feature of the Canadian federation? Some observers believe that it was at root simply a response to the growing fiscal incapacity of the federal government and that it will rapidly disappear with Ottawa's return to financial health. Certainly, the Government of Canada's budgets of 1999 and 2000 – flush with new revenues – seemed to suggest a return to an earlier period in which Ottawa used its resources to impose conditions on transfers to the provinces and to bolster its public visibility by transferring funds directly to citizens (as in its Millennium Scholarship program) rather than through provincial governments. Past experience has shown that the federalism of public affluence can be at least as conflictual as the federalism of fiscal restraint.

Moreover, there is some evidence that the emphasis on cooperation and collaboration may often be little more than rhetoric. It has not yet become fully internalized in the way federal and provincial politicians and officials think about each other. Indeed, even though the SUFA and other agreements are full of commitments to consultation, collaboration, trust, and other such sentiments, the reality often seems to be high levels of mutual distrust and deep unwillingness to accept constraints on one's freedom of action. This is much more evident at the level of first ministers and their central agencies than it is among line ministers and officials, who are more likely to share policy goals and political constituencies. Intergovernmental relations have many of the characteristics of two-level games, in which the participants must respond to two audiences. Yes, there are often strong incentives to collaborate, but equally often, these are trumped by the more immediate incentives of winning support on one's home turf. The final barrier to a deeper institutionalization of collaborative federalism remains the logic of responsible government in a Westminster system. Governments must remain accountable to their legislatures; they cannot be accountable to others. Hence, governments may exchange information, bargain, cajole, persuade, threaten, and even agree at an intergovernmental conference, but they cannot bind each other.

Yet there are reasons to believe that collaborative federalism will remain a feature of the scene in the future. One is that Canadians consistently rate cooperation among their governments as an important objective; collaborative federalism in Canada emerged in part in response to that demand. Another is that earlier approaches based on federal leadership and its use of the spending power are no longer as feasible as they once were. Indeed, Ottawa, recognizing that the game has changed, has made commitments sharply limiting its freedom to act in the old ways. A third is that the achievements of collaborative federalism – the AIT and the Social Union Framework Agreement chief among them – make it more likely that the procedure will be followed in the future. There is now some momentum behind the approach. Federal and provincial officials report that SUFA is increasingly being factored into the calculations of public administrators and interest groups. A fourth reason is that the provinces and territories have learned that they can make significant progress by setting their own agenda and working among themselves. The inter-provincial dynamic is a counterpoint to the federal-provincial relationship that classically defined intergovernmentalism in Canada. The institutionalization of the Annual Premiers Conference and ministerial councils adds administrative muscle to this development. A fifth reason is that governments have found that they can achieve accommodations through collaboration on substantive policy that are impossible to achieve in the constitutional forum.

More generally, the evolution of the Canadian federation over the last four decades has been substantially defined by two powerful forces: nation-building in Quebec and province-building elsewhere. Both forces have had a major impact on the government of Canada and its ability to call the intergovernmental shots. Although it has by no means been a zero-sum game, the maturing of provincial governments has altered the balance of power within Confederation and has redefined the manner in which Ottawa can seek to achieve its objectives. Collaborative federalism fits logically into the broad development of Confederation during the last four decades.

To say that collaborative federalism is likely to be a feature of intergovernmental relations in the future is not to say that it will be the only game in town. Many of the things that matter most to Canadians – and therefore to the federal government – fall broadly within provincial jurisdiction. Provinces often act quite independently of each other, and when there is coordination or parallel policy development, it may be a result of the need to respond to similar problems or pressures, or simply emulation of others' examples, rather than the result of explicit discussion and agreement. To the extent that Ottawa's freedom of action is constrained when it enters into collaboration with provinces, it will seek other approaches where its ability to act will be unimpeded. For example, in the future, Ottawa might exploit every opportunity to take initiatives in the social policy field via the tax system or by means of direct grants to individuals and organizations. An example of the first, using the tax system, is the Child Tax Credit, although this initiative was the product of federal-provincial cooperation; an example of the direct grant approach is Ottawa's Millennium Scholarship Fund, a controversial undertaking, particularly in Quebec. While the pursuit of these alternatives does not, of course, permit Ottawa to avoid all political controversy, it puts it in a freer position in which its capacity to act is not subject to the will of the provinces. Ottawa will collaborate when it feels it has to; so will the provinces.

Conclusion

Collaborative federalism also needs to be set in the larger context of multilevel governance in Canada. It will become increasingly necessary to look to the role of local, territorial, and Aboriginal governments and their interface with provincial, national, and international institutions. This article has followed a standard Canadian pattern; municipalities have not figured greatly in our analysis. This is so not only because municipalities have no independent constitutional status, but also because provinces tend to control the structure and powers of local governments tightly, robbing the very governments that are closest to the citizen and the most involved with the quality of their daily lives of much of their potential dynamism and vitality. This has occurred at a time when cities and city regions are the centers of economic and cultural innovation, are increasingly multicultural, and, in many cases, are increasingly linked to national and international networks rather than to their provincial hinterlands. Enriching democratic multigovernance must involve them.

In addition, Canada is experimenting with yet other institutional forms outside the traditional federal-provincial-municipal framework. Canada's northern territories are acting more and more like provinces than federal protectorates. The creation of the new territory of Nunavut, its population made up largely of Inuit people, is Canada's first full de facto experiment with Aboriginal self-government. Aboriginal peoples elsewhere in Canada are also seeking to define their own models of self-government. They too will become players in a multigovernance world.

Finally, Quebec has been a relatively minor character in the development of collaborative federalism. With the sovereignist Parti Québécois in office for much of the period under review (from 1994 to the present), it has been a limited and reluctant participant. There are signs, however, of a transformation in politics and attitudes in Quebec. The sovereignty movement is currently in retreat. There appears to be a deep public fatigue with the perpetual debate on the national question, dominated by hard-line sovereignists on one hand and by hard-line federalists on the other. This is encouraging an as yet inchoate search in the province for a fresh political discourse.[29] Many thought that the federal government's 1996 reference of the question of Quebec secession to the Supreme Court of Canada[30] and the passage in 1999 of the federal Clarity Act outlining the federal government's approach to a possible secession bid would arouse nationalist sentiment, but this did not occur. Finally, in the federal election on 27 November 2000, the sovereignist Bloc Québécois (BQ) won fewer seats than it had in either of the other two previous electoral contests it had participated in (38 seats in 2000, as compared to 44 seats in 1997 and 54 seats in 1993). More significant, perhaps, was the fact that the federal Liberals in 2000 received a higher proportion of the popular vote in Quebec than did the BQ (44.2 per cent as compared to 39.9 per cent).

This raises the possibility that Quebec may re-engage in a federalist rather than a sovereignist discourse, particularly if the federalist Liberal Party of Quebec under Jean Charest wins the next provincial election, and if the federal Liberals can overcome their deep distrust of their provincial counterparts. If Quebecers do opt for the *beau risque* of full participation in the collaborative system, and if its provincial partners are prepared to accept that this may result in a substantial element of asymmetry or "variable geometry," then the collaborative model will take on added impulse.

Strong forces push for a further elaboration of the collaborative model – the relatively even balance of federal and provincial power and status, the high degree of interdependence among governments, the desire for administrative efficiency and clarity, and the interests of citizens in the collective ability of governments to meet their needs. Yet much of the logic of Canadian federalism stands in the way. The lack of a unifying national party system, the lack of mobility of officials and politicians between the two levels, the competition to gain credit and avoid blame, the importance of regional and ideological divisions among governments, and the inequality in wealth distribution among the provinces – all these push toward an adversarial relationship. As Canada enters the new millennium, these opposing forces remain in contention. Collaborative federalism does not have its own internal dynamic. It will grow, or not, only insofar as it meets the needs of federal and provincial elites, and their constituents, as they face the challenges of the new millennium. It is now part of what Donald Smiley described as the federal "condition" in Canada.[31]

NOTES

1 This was clearly the case, for example, with the Social Union Framework Agreement.
2 See, for example, Stefan Dupré, "Reflections on the Workability of Executive Federalism," *Intergovernmental Relations*, ed. Richard Simeon (Toronto: University of Toronto Press, 1985), 1–32; Donald V. Smiley, *Canada in Question: Federalism in the Eighties*, 3rd ed. (Toronto: McGraw-Hill Ryerson, 1980); Richard Simeon and Ian Robinson, *State, Society, and the Development of Canadian Federalism* (Toronto: University of Toronto Press, 1990).
3 Keith Banting, *Federalism and the Welfare State in Canada*, 2nd ed. (Montreal: McGill-Queen's University Press, 1987).
4 Among the many examples we note just a few: a decision to award the maintenance contract for the Canada CF-18 military fighter to Montreal instead of Winnipeg; a cap placed on the growth of federal payments to the wealthier provinces under the Canada Assistance Plan, which entailed sharing of the costs of welfare; immigration, where Quebec reached an unusually advantageous agreement with Ottawa and where provinces and municipalities were left to deal with the economic and social challenges of integrating new immigrants.
5 See Ronald L. Watts's discussion: "Canadian Federalism in the 1990s: Once More in Question," *Publius: The Journal of Federalism* 21 (Summer 1991): 169–190.
6 Robert C. Vipond, "Seeing Canada Through the Referendum: Still a House Divided," *Publius: The Journal of Federalism* 23 (Summer 1993): 39–55.
7 See the essays in Harvey Lazar, ed., *Canada: The State of the Federation, 1997: Non-Constitutional Renewal* (Kingston: McGill Queen's University Press, 1998).
8 Modeled in large part on the United States Republican's "Contract with America."
9 This, despite Ottawa's own aggressive deficit cutting that severely affected the provinces. It was most evident in the health care field.

10 See Casey Vander Ploeg, *Red Ink IV: Back from the Brink?* (Calgary: Canada West Foundation January 1998). This is the fourth in a series, which commenced in 1993.

11 Thomas Courchene, "ACCESS: A Convention on the Canadian Economic and Social Systems," *Assessing ACCESS: Towards a New Social Union,* ed. Institute of Intergovernmental Relations (Kingston, Ontario: Institute of Intergovernmental Relations, 1996), 77–112, and André Burelle, *Le mal canadien* (Montreal: Fides, 1995), among others, added a powerful intellectual stimulus. Globalization and fiscal crisis, Courchene argued, were draining power from Ottawa downward to the provinces and upward to supranational institutions. Ottawa had neither the fiscal ability nor the political legitimacy to set and enforce national standards. If the Canadian "social union" was to be preserved, it could only be done through the provinces acting together. Provinces must be brought "more fully and formally into the key societal goal of preserving and promoting social Canada." André Burelle proposed a partnership based on interdependence and "non-subordination."

12 Plans to implement a functional consolidation of Canadian stock exchanges, announced in the spring of 1999, offer an example of the extent to which transnational economic integration is imposing a discipline on domestic, non-governmental regulators, whether the governments will it or not. The consolidation planning was undertaken by the exchanges themselves, in recognition of the imperatives of world financial markets, and in several cases against the first preferences of the relevant Canadian governments themselves. See William D. Coleman, "Federalism and Financial Services," *Canadian Federalism,* eds. Herman Bakvis and Grace Skogstad (Toronto: Oxford University Press, 2001), 179–196.

13 Such critics as Daniel Schwanen and Robert Howse, while applauding the AIT as a useful first step, argue that it needs to be strengthened. See Daniel Schwanen, *Drawing on Our Inner Strength* (C.D. Howe Institute Commentary, June 1996), and Robert Howse, *Securing the Canadian Economic Union* (C.D. Howe Commentary, June 1996). They recommend, for example, that the Secretariat should be empowered to analyze obstacles to implementation and to recommend solutions, that the member governments should vote by qualified majority rather than by the consensus system currently in place, that access to the dispute settlement mechanism should be extended to private parties, and that public education on the existence and purposes of the AIT should be undertaken. See also Mark R. MacDonald, "The Agreement on Internal Trade: Trade-offs for Economic Union and Federalism." *Canadian Federalism,* eds. Bakvis and Skogstad, 138–58.

14 Opinion on the French-speaking scholarly community in Quebec is arrayed strongly against the Social Union Framework Agreement. The Government of Quebec commissioned a number of academics to offer their assessments of the agreement; they were consistently negative. Alain Noël, a political scientist at the Université de Montréal, makes the critical argument very well in "Without Quebec: Collaborative Federalism with a Footnote?" Paper presented at the Saskatchewan

Institute of Public Policy Conference, *Perspectives and Directions: The Social Union Framework Agreement*, Regina, 3–4 February 2000.

15   There is no question but that the social union *process* was a provincially driven initiative until the last stage. There is debate, however, about whether the social union *agreement* works more to the advantage of Ottawa or the provinces. The variety of ways in which it has been interpreted is one of its more striking features. See, for example, the debate between David Cameron, who argues that the federal spending power is subjected to regulation and control under SUFA and constitutes a good arrangement for Quebec, and Claude Ryan, who contends that SUFA sharply increases federal scope for action under the spending power and is unacceptable for Quebec. David Cameron, "The Social Union Agreement: A Backward Step for Quebec?" *Globe and Mail*, 9 February 1999; Claude Ryan, "The Agreement on the Canadian Social Union as Seen by a Quebec Federalist," *Inroads* 8 (1999): 25–41.

16   Matthew Mendelson and John McLean, "Getting Engaged: Strengthening SUFA Through Citizen Engagement." Paper presented at the Saskatchewan Institute of Public Policy Conference, *Perspectives and Directions: The Social Union Framework Agreement*, Regina, 3–4 February 2000.

17   Quoted in Bakvis and Skogstad, eds., *Canadian Federalism*, 11.

18   See discussion in F. Leslie Seidle, "Executive Federalism and Public Involvement: Integrating Citizen's Voices." Paper presented to the Conference on *The Changing Nature of Democracy and Federalism in Canada*, Winnipeg, 14 April 2000.

19   This is also the case in another parliamentary federation, Australia. There a highly promising exercise in intergovernmental collaboration, the COAG process, effectively came to a halt when the national government was changed in 1996.

20   See Fritz Scharpf, "The Joint Decision Trap: Lessons from German Federalism and European Integration," *Public Administration* 66 (Summer 1988): 236–278.

21   For discussion of this in the Canadian context, see Albert Breton, "Supplementary Statement," *Royal Commission on the Economic Union and Canada's Development Prospects, Report*, Vol. III (Ottawa: Supply and Services, 1985); Steven Kennett, *Securing the Social Union: A Commentary on the Decentralized Approach* (Kingston: Institute of Intergovernmental Relations, 1998).

22   In 1979, Donald Smiley, the dean of Canadian students of federalism, opened his critique of executive federalism this way: "My charges against executive federalism are these. First, it contributes to undue secrecy in the conduct of the public's business. Second, it contributes to an unduly low level of citizen participation in public affairs. Third, it weakens and dilutes the accountability of government to their legislatures and to the wider public." "An Outsider's Observations of Intergovernmental Relations Among Consenting Adults," *Confrontation or Collaboration: Intergovernmental Relations in Canada Today*, ed. Richard Simeon (Toronto: Institute of Public Administration of Canada, 1979).

23   Keith Banting, "The Past Speaks to the Future: Lessons from the Postwar Social Union," *Canada: The State of the Federation, 1997*, ed. Harvey Lazar, 39–69, 64.

24 "Democratic Reservations about the ACCESS Models," *Assessing ACCESS: Towards a New Social Union* (Kingston: Institute of Intergovernmental Relations, 1997), 43–44. See also Susan Phillips, "The Canada Health and Social Transfer," *Canada: The State of the Federation, 1995,* eds. Douglas Brown and Jonathan Rose (Kingston: Institute of Intergovernmental Relations, 1996), 65–96; and Margaret Biggs, *Building Blocks for the New Social Union* (Ottawa: Canadian Policy Research Network, 1996).

25 In the European context, see Marcus Horeth, "The Trilemma of Legitimacy-Multi-level Governance in the EU and the Problem of Legitimacy," (Discussion paper C 11, Center for European Integration Studies, Rheinische Friedrich-Wilhelms-Universitat Bonn, 1998), 6–7.

26 See, for example, Patrick Fafard, "Groups, Government, and the Environment," *Managing the Environmental Union: Intergovernmental Relations and Environmental Policy in Canada,* eds. Patrick Fafard and Kathryn Harrison (Kingston: Institute of Intergovernmental Relations and Saskatchewan Institute of Public Policy, 2000), 81–104; and Robert Howse, "Federalism, Democracy and Regulatory Reform: A Skeptical View of the Case for Decentralization," *Rethinking Federalism: Citizens, Markets and Governments in a Changing World,* eds. Karen Knop et al. (Vancouver: University of British Columbia Press, 1995), 273–293.

27 Alain Noël, "Is Decentralization Conservative?" *Stretching the Federation,* ed. Robert Young (Kingston: Institute of Intergovernmental Relations, 1999), 195–218.

28 This view is expressed most forcefully by Albert Breton. See his Supplementary Statement, *Royal Commission on the Economic Union and Canada's Development Prospects, Report,* volume III (Ottawa: Supply and Services Canada, 1985).

29 Alain Dubuc, a senior editorial writer for Montreal's largest daily newspaper, *La Presse,* wrote a series of eight editorials exploring this issue entitled "Réinventer notre avenir: Des idées pour sortir du cul-de-sac" ("Re-inventing our Future; Ideas for Getting Out of the Dead End"). Reprinted as "We Must Break This Vicious Circle," *Policy Options,* June 2000, 8–28. See also Gilles Paquet, *Oublier la Révolution tranquille: Pour une Nouvelle Socialité* (Montreal: Liber, 1999); Jean-Luc Migué, *Étatisme et déclin du Québec: Bilan de la révolution tranquille* (Montreal: Editions Varia, 1999); Michel Venne, ed., *Penser la Nation québécoise* (Montreal: Editions Quebec-Amérique, 2000).

30 *Reference Re Secession of Quebec,* [1998] 2 S.C.R. 217. See also, Peter Leslie, "Canada: The Supreme Court Sets Rules for the Secession of Quebec," *Publius: The Journal of Federalism* 29 (Spring 1999): 135–151.

31 Donald Smiley, *The Federal Condition in Canada.* Toronto: McGraw-Hill Ryerson, 1987.

14 Inter-Legislative Federalism

In J. Peter Meekison, Hamish Telford, and Harvey Lazar, eds.,
Canada: The State of the Federation 2002   2004

I explain the origins of this article in the opening paragraphs below. It is an attempt to contribute an additional element to the general discussion of parliamentary reform, and, more specifically, to address the question of strengthening the role of legislatures in our executive-dominated federation. Specifically, it suggested a number of initiatives that might be undertaken that would foster productive relations among Canada's legislatures, federal and provincial, related to the management of the federation.

This chapter has its origins in an article Richard Simeon and I wrote for the Canadian Centre for Management Development a couple of years ago on intergovernmental relations and democratic citizenship.[1] While struggling with ways in which the Canadian intergovernmental system might be reconciled a bit better with democracy, open government, and public accountability, we wrote a couple of paragraphs on enhancing legislative federalism. Noting that powerful institutional forces – in particular, the tyranny of party discipline and the failure of the Canadian Senate – sharply limited the capacity of legislatures to play a role of any consequence in monitoring intergovernmental relations, or to act as arenas of public debate about federal issues, we proposed several modest reforms aimed at strengthening the role of legislatures in intergovernmental relations.[2]

It was some time after that that I came across C.E.S. (Ned) Franks's excellent paper, "Parliament, Intergovernmental Relations and National Unity." Originally prepared in 1997 for the Privy Council Office, it appeared in amended form as a Queen's Institute of Intergovernmental Relations Working Paper in 1999.[3] Happily, a revised version appears in this volume as "A Continuing

Canadian Constitutional Conundrum: The Role of Parliament in Questions of National Unity and the Processes of Amending the Constitution." Franks's work is a thorough and creative consideration of what might be done to strengthen Parliament's role in intergovernmental relations and its contribution to national unity. Recognizing the structural tensions between parliamentary government and federalism, it focuses on the weakness of Parliament and the consequent feebleness of Parliament's intergovernmental role, engendered by, among other things, the domination of the executive and party leaders; excessive partisanship; short-term amateur membership in the legislature; and the well-known problems associated with the Canadian Senate. Franks puts forward some proposals for reform, none of which require formal constitutional amendment. He divides his reform proposals into two categories: incremental improvements designed to make "the present structures of national decision-making work more effectively"; and a far-reaching set of revisions designed to shift the whole system in the direction of a more consensual form of government.[4]

Franks is far from naive; he is not inclined to concoct abstract schemes with little connection to real-life concerns. Writing originally in the aftermath of the Charlottetown debacle and the 1995 Quebec referendum, there was a sense of urgency in his analysis, and he made a convincing case that our institutional constraints shackle our capacity to cope effectively with many of the federal and national-unity challenges we face. As he says:

> Canada has made the least reforms to its machinery of parliamentary democracy
> of any of these countries [Britain, Australia and New Zealand], yet it also suffers
> from the worst stresses and risks of disintegration. These two phenomena are not
> unconnected.[5]

Nevertheless, he cites sympathetically Donald Smiley's pessimism about expanding the capacity of Canadian legislatures to influence the processes of executive federalism,[6] and his rejection of proposals that would require formal constitutional amendment is a sign of his effort to keep ideas for improvement in the realm of the possible. Franks's remark, however, that, in terms of institutional reform, "Canada has proven to be the most conservative of all parliamentary governments,"[7] is intriguingly ambiguous: it might be understood as an indicator of pessimism, or alternatively as a comparative indicator that Canada ought to regard itself as having a wide latitude for innovation should it develop a genuine taste for reform.

Proposal

It was clear to me upon reading "Parliament, Intergovernmental Relations and National Unity" that I had nothing useful to add to this sophisticated study. It had pretty systematically canvassed the ways in which our federal Parliament might be given an increased role in the practical management of the federation. But that study and my work with Richard Simeon got me thinking. What if it were possible for federal, provincial, and territorial legislatures to find a means of working in concert on certain common issues, thereby supplementing the dominant processes of executive federalism? What about what might be called "inter-legislative federalism"?

Let me explain. The business of the federation is currently carried out via the fluid processes and lightly institutionalized organizations of executive federalism in which first ministers, Cabinet ministers and public officials negotiate – or fail to negotiate – arrangements providing for the matters in which both orders of government have an interest and responsibility. Stéphane Dion, minister of intergovernmental affairs, makes the point well in a speech comparing the German and Canadian federal systems:

> In Canada, the absence of a parliamentary forum that would institutionalize the relations between the two orders of government means that federal-provincial co-operation is conducted almost exclusively by the executive branches: the first ministers and the federal and provincial ministers meet regularly to coordinate their actions. They consult and inform one another of legislative or other initiatives they intend to take.[8]

Much of what Canada's governments have achieved over the years has been accomplished through these mechanisms of executive federalism, but no student of the Canadian federation would fail to acknowledge their serious deficiencies. Donald Smiley's searing critique still rings true more than two decades after he wrote it:

My charges against executive federalism are these:

- First, it contributes to undue secrecy in the conduct of the public's business.
- Second, it contributes to an unduly low level of citizen participation in public affairs.
- Third, it weakens and dilutes the accountability of governments to their legislatures and to the wider public.[9]

Roger Gibbins is not alone in contending that the recent trend toward more collaborative forms of executive federalism – reflected, for example, in the negotiation of the Social Union Framework Agreement in 1999 – has, if anything, worsened the problem by obscuring yet further what is effectively one of the country's critical decision-making processes, and by removing it still more from effective popular and legislative control. Parliament is locked out; the provincial and territorial legislatures are locked out; and so are Canadian citizens.[10]

Inter-legislative federalism – that is to say, the development of relationships among Canadian legislatures, perhaps focused on key intergovernmental issues – might be of some assistance in opening up the enclosed world in which federal, provincial, and territorial politicians and officials conduct the business of the Canadian federation. By so doing, it might also in time contribute to shifting our executive-driven legislatures at least a short distance along the continuum toward a legislative-centred model of legislatures.

As Franks points out, a central problem with our system of intergovernmental relations, and one that many believe is getting worse,[11] is the degree to which the processes of executive federalism escape the legislative accountability which lies at the heart of our system of responsible government. This is related to the strength and autonomy of the executive branch in our system – at both levels. And a central problem with our legislatures – federal, provincial, and territorial – is their general weakness and their incapacity to impose accountability on governments and leaders. This too is related to the strength and autonomy of the executive branch in our system. Given the high importance of intergovernmental relations in Canada, then, the search for stronger lines of accountability linking intergovernmental processes back to legislatures is a top agenda item for reform. In addition, there exists the problem of the accountability of both executives and legislatures to citizens and to the public – accountability in another form. This tangle of accountabilities, then, is at the core of the issues I am seeking to address in this chapter. Inter-legislative federalism could open up both the intergovernmental relations system and the legislative processes to some extent, making executives more accountable to the people's representatives in their respective legislatures, and making the political system itself more open and accountable to the public.

What are the prospects for this reform idea? Prima facie, there is little reason to believe that its fate will be any different than that of a dozen other reform proposals in the general area that have fallen victim to Canada's institutional conservatism and the natural preference of its political leaders to retain a system of which they are the prime beneficiaries.

- There have been impressive analyses of our electoral system and our party system, and their deleterious impact on responsive government and national unity, but the old ways live on in splendid contempt for the vain attempts to make some positive change.[12]
- I read my first proposal on Senate reform when I was a callow undergraduate at the University of British Columbia; I cannot count the number of proposals for Senate reform that have passed before my glazed eyes since then. Yet the Senate endures, untainted by renovation.
- There have been frequent measures proposed for the improved operation of Parliament itself designed to invest it with more autonomy, and greater life

and purpose, but the changes actually effected in response to these propos-als have been modest, and laments about the irrelevance of Parliament have continued unabated.[13]

A reforming zeal appears for the most part to have passed our provincial assemblies by as well. Franks makes the following comment:

This paper has considered parliamentary government at the federal level, but much of what has been said also holds true, indeed is more true, for the provincial level. Executive domination, amateur short-term membership, weak opposition, ineffective committees, in many ways are exacerbated in provincial legislatures. This, when coupled with the importance of provincial premiers and a few key min-isters in executive federalism, gives rise to a federal-provincial dynamic that does not properly or truly reflect the complexity and divisions of opinion within the provinces.[14]

The partial exception to this rule seems to be the National Assembly of Que-bec. For many years, it has been my belief that Quebecers have operated the British parliamentary system – adapting it to their own unique needs while respecting its genius – better than any one else in the country. At moments of high importance the National Assembly has been the unquestioned, central institutional focus of the people of Quebec and the cockpit of democracy in that community.[15] The National Assembly has also, I think, exercised its duty of holding the executive to account better than have other legislatures in this country.[16] It has innovated in some of the institutions and processes it has established.[17]

As Peter Dobell points out, Quebec has adopted a number of practices that are "carefully designed to enhance the opportunities for deputies to play a meaningful role and to promote a more co-operative relationship between gov-ernment and opposition parties."[18] Contrasting the very limited contribution that Canadian legislatures make to institutional innovation with the more sub-stantial role played by legislatures in Great Britain and most European coun-tries, Dobell singles out Quebec as an exception. A reform package approved by the National Assembly in 1984 overhauled the committee system. Members of the opposition chair four of the National Assembly's ten committees. Chairs and vice-chairs are elected by a double majority, which is to say, by separate majorities of both government and opposition committee members. The plan for the committee's business, developed by the chair and co-chair, who are from opposite sides of the assembly, is again confirmed by a double majority vote. Committee membership is stable, usually lasting for the life of the assembly. Unlike Ottawa, the relevant minister usually joins the committee for its delib-erations when his or her legislation is being discussed. As Dobell remarks, these and other reforms have "generated a more co-operative relationship between the parties, more frequent amendment of legislation in committee, and greater 'job satisfaction' for deputies."[19]

Quebec aside, however, the prospects for reform *within* Canadian legislatures have, until recently, appeared to be dishearteningly poor; all the more difficult, then, is it to believe that the introduction of unfamiliar innovations *between and among* legislatures is possible to achieve. If Parliament and our provincial assemblies are unequivocally executive-dominated, rather than legislative-centred, and if, further, Canadians and their governments have consistently displayed a rock-ribbed resistance to innovation, then proposals for deepening and expanding relations between and among legislatures face forbidding odds. Indeed, given that the initiatives considered in this chapter would be more readily accomplished to the extent that the participating legislatures inclined more to the legislature-centred end of the continuum than to the executive-centred end, we seem to have multiplied the difficulty, rather than diminishing it.

Yet there are some signs of change. For starters, there appears to be a growing interest among our political and policy elites in democratic reform, including the reform of our central political institutions. Conferences, projects, and reports assessing the state of democracy in Canada and prescribing modest to far-reaching change are legion. Only a few can be cited here. The influential Institute for Research on Public Policy (IRPP) has devoted considerable resources to conferences and publications on the theme "Strengthening Canadian Democracy."[20] Under the auspices of the Canadian Studies Program at Mount Allison University, a large team of researchers is producing a multivolume series examining Canadian government and politics under the rubric of "The Canadian Democratic Audit."[21] The Law Commission of Canada has a major project underway on electoral reform,[22] while organizations as diverse as the Fraser Institute, Elections Canada, the Centre for Research and Information on Canada, the Canada West Foundation, and the Canadian Policy Research Networks have organized conferences or commissioned reports to assess Canadian democracy and attempt to improve it. Among the groups actively lobbying for democratic reform are Democracy Watch, Fair Vote Canada, and the Canadian Taxpayers Federation. A steady stream of books – including contributions from left- and right-wing writers, prominent journalists, academics, engaged citizens and others – address questions of democracy in Canada: Gordon Gibson's *Fixing Canadian Democracy,* Judy Rebick's *Imagine Democracy,* Jeffrey Simpson's *The Friendly Dictatorship,* Donald Savoie's *Governing from the Centre,* and several of the volumes in the "Underground Royal Commission" series, such as Patrick Boyer's *Just Trust Us* and Paul Kemp's *Does Your Vote Count?*[23]

Clearly, members of the policy community in Canada are concerned with the contemporary state of our political institutions and practices, but what of the public? Reforms that directly challenge the position and prerogatives of those holding political power are unlikely to progress far in the absence of citizen interest and solid popular support. Public opinion data suggest some grounds for hope on this score. In reviewing these data it is important to distinguish generalized ideas of democracy from attitudes about the actual practice and institutions of democracy. A national study conducted in 2000, for example, found 71 per cent of Canadians satisfied with "the way democracy works in Canada" but only 58 per cent similarly disposed to "government" and 53 per cent towards "politics."[24] According to the public, the most significant determinant of discontent with democracy in Canada is political inefficacy – i.e., the feeling that citizens have no real impact on decision-making in the polity. Fifty-five per cent of Canadians cite political inefficacy as the explanation for low voter turnout, as compared with 23 per cent who believe it is caused by lack of political education. In this same survey, 77 per cent of respondents agreed with allowing free votes in Parliament, up from 72 per cent a decade before while the percentage of Canadians who say that the first-past-the-post electoral system is "unacceptable" because of "wasted votes" has risen from 39 per cent in 1990 to 49 per cent in 2000. Between 1974 and 1996, confidence in the House of Commons fell from 49 to 21 per cent and the percentage of Canadians expressing "a great deal of confidence" in political parties dropped from 30 to 11 per cent.[25]

Certainly politicians – both in and out of office – believe Canadian democracy needs work, and hope to reap political benefits by putting forward proposals for democratic reform which will find favour with Canadians dissatisfied with their system. Both Canada's outgoing prime minister and the country's putative prime minister-in-waiting have stepped up to the plate. Prime Minister Jean Chrétien has made political party finance reform one of the signature pieces in his heritage agenda, facing down substantial opposition from within his own caucus. Paul Martin has made dealing with the "democratic deficit" a prominent plank in his policy platform.[26] The former Parti Québécois government created a Cabinet portfolio entitled "Minister Responsible for the Reform of Democratic Institutions" which, significantly, has been retained by the new Liberal government. Serious investigations into major electoral reform – possibly encompassing a shift to an electoral system based on proportional representation – are underway in Prince Edward Island and British Columbia. In British Columbia, the government has committed itself to hold a referendum on whatever proposal for reform of the province's electoral system a citizens' assembly recommends. Premier Gordon Campbell's government has also introduced fixed provincial election dates, and has been holding Cabinet meetings in public, with the information posted on the government's website. In Ontario, the three major political parties all featured democratic reform in their manifestoes in the 2003 general election.[27] The Ontario Liberal Party under Dalton McGuinty, for example, announced while in opposition a number of significant democratic reforms it said it would introduce if elected to office. These include fixed provincial election dates; spending limits for parties, elections, and leadership contests; "citizen juries" to examine policy ideas; more freedom for members of Provincial Parliament and more clout for legislative committees; and a referendum on the electoral system.

There are, then, some grounds for believing that a taste for democratic reform has been growing in this country, and that the reduction of the power of the first ministers together with an increase in the autonomy and responsibilities of the members of Canada's legislatures, is a significant part of most reform proposals. If that is so, a proposal to develop the idea of inter-legislative federalism fits well into the current policy environment.

Some Ideas for Putting Inter-Legislative Federalism into Practice

Before bringing forward some thoughts about how one might introduce elements of inter-legislative federalism, it is worth pausing to consider what kind of legislative work would be susceptible to this kind of process. The closer the work is to the formal law-approving functions of the chambers, the less likely that this kind of inter-legislative contact would be appropriate. It would seem that activity involving several legislatures would make the most sense at an early, general stage in the policy-making and legislative cycle, when governments have not yet committed themselves to a specific course of action, but are in a position to receive advice and guidance from members of the legislature. Indeed, at the start of any inter-legislative reform effort, there may be a real advantage in restricting the focus chiefly to information sharing and broad, general topics. It would surely make sense in the early going to stay clear of the more sensitive domains of public policy in which executives have an especially active interest. As we will see below, this appears to be the general practice of bodies that perform these sorts of functions in other parliamentary contexts.

Let me now list some ideas for consideration that would, if implemented, introduce an inter-legislative component into the operation of the Canadian federal system.

Periodic Meetings of Federal and Provincial Representatives within a Given Province

In every province there are two sets of representatives serving the same set of citizens – more than two, if you include the municipal realm. It would be useful for all the people's representatives of a given territory to meet periodically to exchange information and ideas. The socio-economic conditions and development opportunities specific to a given province would naturally offer a central focus for discussion, given that all elected officials in a province – federal, provincial, and municipal – have to confront these matters as part of their responsibilities.

As it happens, British Columbia has held a meeting of just this kind. Convened by the Gordon Campbell Liberal Government, the so-called Provincial Congress was held on 26 February 2002, the second of a series of four dialogues planned by the province. It brought together all members of the BC Legislature, all BC Members of Parliament (MPs) and Senators, mayors of the 15 largest cities in the province, the presidents of the five regional municipal associations in BC, the President of the Union of BC Municipalities, and Aboriginal leaders. It explored future directions for the province, and held sessions on the economy, the province's demographic prospects, health care and the environment, and Aboriginal issues. With representatives from all spheres of government, the Congress was, in Premier Campbell's words, designed to "discover what it is we share, and how we can work together to provide our citizens with the services they need in a thoughtful way."[28] Premier Campbell judged this to be a useful and positive event, and his government plans to hold others of the same sort in the future.

The Participation of Representatives from One Jurisdiction in the Processes of the Other

When a legislature is examining a topic with significant extra-jurisdictional impacts, it would be possible to invite the participation of representatives of other jurisdictions. At first blush, this sounds strange, but in fact we have a concrete example of this, with Quebec being, again, the innovator. The Commission on the Political and Constitutional Future of Quebec (the Bélanger-Campeau Commission) is known more for its proposals than its process, but in fact it was a highly unusual body that exemplifies the distinctive and often creative fashion in which Quebec has adapted the British parliamentary system to its own needs and preferences. Established in September 1990 in the wake of the demise of the Meech Lake Accord, its mandate was to examine the political and constitutional future of Quebec.

Its composition was remarkable. Half of the 36 members appointed by the National Assembly were members of the National Assembly; the other half were not. Both the premier of Quebec, Robert Bourassa, and the leader of the Opposition, Jacques Parizeau, were members. The co-chairs, Michel Bélanger and Jean Campeau, were prominent Quebec businessmen. There were representatives from the municipalities, from the business and trade union sectors, and from the co-operative, educational and cultural sectors.

In addition, and of particular relevance to the topic of this chapter, three federal MPs were named as members.[29] They were Lucien Bouchard, then leader of the Bloc Québécois; Jean-Pierre Hogue, a Conservative backbencher representing Outremont; and André Ouellet, Liberal MP for Papineau-Saint-Michel.[30] Neither the Liberal nor the Conservative representative signed the final report, which is not surprising, given its contents.

The commission offers an intriguing example of the way in which political leaders from both federal and provincial jurisdictions, in conjunction with citizens from many walks of life, can lead a broadly based process of public discussion engaging significant sectors of the larger political community – and do so with respect to an acutely divisive issue.

The Creation of a Federal-Provincial-Territorial Parliamentary Association

The Parliament of Canada is engaged in a fairly wide range of international relationships with foreign legislatures. Given that a federation is a system with multiple legislatures, it would be possible to establish a similar domestic inter-parliamentary association, and, in developing it, draw on the extensive international experience that decades of federal parliamentary participation provides.

The Parliament of Canada has membership in 10 official parliamentary associations – five bilateral and five multilateral.[31] The bilateral associations are with the United States, France, Japan, the United Kingdom, and China. The multilateral associations are the following: the Commonwealth Parliamentary Association; *Assemblée parlementaire de la francophonie*; the Inter-Parliamentary Union; the Canadian NATO Parliamentary Association; and the Canada-Europe Parliamentary Association.

Members of the Senate and the House of Commons are involved in all of these. For each, members elect an executive committee to plan and coordinate activities with their bilateral counterparts or with the international secretariat of the multilateral organizations. Each executive committee is supported by an executive secretary who is responsible for the day-to-day operations of the organization. Additional support staff from the Senate and the Commons assist as necessary. A Joint Inter-Parliamentary Council, functioning under the authority of the two Speakers, oversees general budget and administrative matters. Financial allotments are approved by the Senate Standing Committee on Internal Economy, Budgets and Administration, and by the House of Commons Board of Internal Economy. Association budgets are about 90 per cent for travel; there is relatively little money available for staff support and research.

The only international inter-parliamentary association to have assumed an "executive oversight" role is the *Assemblée parlementaire de la Francophonie* (APF). Section 2.1.5 of the APF constitution establishes a formal link with the *Conférence des Chefs d'État et des gouvernements ayant le français en partage*. The APF has given itself the mandate to oversee plans and decisions made by the annual summit of the heads of state and governments of the Francophonie.[32]

The bilateral inter-parliamentary associations of which Canada is a member typically have the general and anodyne goal of exchanging information and promoting better understanding. They normally meet once a year, but sometimes organize special working sessions on specific or urgent issues. The multilateral associations tend to pursue more specific objectives linked to the character of the relationship, such as the promotion of peace and co-operation through the United Nations, the increase in knowledge of the concern of the North Atlantic Alliance, or the promotion of the French language and cooperation among francophone countries.

There is a Canadian branch of the Commonwealth Parliamentary Association (CPA). Its annual meetings, rotating among the various capitals, bring together legislative representatives from Ottawa, the provinces and the territories, but the focus is on how the legislatures work, not on policy substance. Regional parliamentary seminars are also held, but again, the focus is on process. The Canadian branch of the CPA also supports the Centre for Legislative Exchange, established in 1971 and closely associated with the Parliamentary Centre. It serves all Canadian legislatures, and arranges annual visits to Washington or to a US state capital, sponsoring discussion of such issues as border problems, transportation, and the like. Separate from the CPA, speakers of Canadian legislatures meet annually in January, as do house table officers, who meet normally in the summer.[33] In addition, the Public Accounts Committees of the Canadian legislatures meet annually, and these meetings with federal, provincial, and territorial participation, might serve as an example to build on.[34]

A Canadian version of an inter-parliamentary association would be quite different from the international versions, given that all participating legislatures would be members of the same country, but models and guidance could nevertheless be drawn down from Canada's extensive international experience. The budgetary, administrative, and management arrangements used currently by the two houses of Parliament could provide a point of reference for an all-Canadian initiative, but a more substantial business agenda could surely be developed, given that the time spent in international associations simply familiarizing oneself with the other's political system would not be required, and participants could therefore concentrate more directly on substantive matters of common interest. In the early 1980s, there was an initiative of this kind. The Parliamentary Centre obtained funding to organize some meetings of federal and provincial legislators. There were several such meetings, each lasting three to five days, involving ten to 12 participants, and discussing matters of substance. Legislators with expertise in the given area were invited to attend. Each meeting involved sessions in Ottawa and events outside of Ottawa. The first was held on rail abandonment, and the group travelled by rail to some of the sites being considered. The second was on fisheries, and the group went to St. John's.[35]

The Establishment of a National Conference of Canadian Legislatures

The United States, with its congressional dispersal of power at both the national and state levels, has generated a rich array of highly sophisticated organizations to express the diverse relations among the federated units, both interstate and state-federal. The National Governors' Association and the National Republican Legislators Association are just two examples of the many that exist. Many of these are peculiar to the American system, and would have little applicability elsewhere.[36]

Nevertheless, one such organization is worth mentioning here as one thinks about how inter-legislative federalism might be developed in Canada. The National Conference of State Legislatures (NCSL) is "a bipartisan organization dedicated to serving lawmakers and staffs of the nation's 50 states, its commonwealths and territories."[37] Founded in 1975, with offices in Denver and Washington, the NCSL is a substantial and sophisticated organization, holding meetings and seminars, providing consulting services, undertaking research and publications in areas of concern to state legislatures, and facilitating the exchange of information on a wide array of issues of concern to American state legislators.

There is no reason why many of the functions it performs would not be of equal benefit to Canadian provincial legislators and staffs. Canada is endowed with 13 provincial and territorial legislatures. A fuller appreciation of how these democratic systems are evolving could only help to improve the vigour and level of democratic discourse in this country. A Canadian legislative website could support the exchange of ideas and the circulation of information about best practices. An association of Canadian legislatures might start modestly, and concentrate initially on institutional and procedural matters, but, as confidence and mutual knowledge among the participants grew, and common staff resources were established, it would become possible for the association to move into more substantive areas. Such an organization could be established as an intergovernmental body only involving the provinces and territories. However, given Canada's specific circumstances, the arrangement should also be extended to include the federal Parliament as well.

Conclusion

The introduction of a degree of inter-legislative federalism could make a modest contribution to the strengthening of Canadian democracy by expanding the role, perspectives, and the effectiveness of the country's legislators; to the functioning of federalism, by supplementing the dominant practices of executive federalism with the addition of a legislative dimension; to governmental performance, through greater information exchange among jurisdictions on innovations, experiments and best practices; and to Canadian unity, by offering an additional integrative bridge across regions and provinces – one, moreover, which is not focused on turf or status, as executive intergovernmental institutions tend to be.

Were some or all of these proposals judged to be desirable, they could be implemented at the will of Canadian legislatures and political leaders. None of them, of course, requires constitutional change, and, in fact, a single legislature could get the process started by taking an initiative on its own. But these ideas run up against the same obstacles that Ned Franks identified in his paper on parliamentary reform in Ottawa – namely, the institutional conservatism of Canadians and the self-interest of first ministers and executive bodies in the federation. It can be argued that the need to get a multiplicity of federal actors on board for much of what is proposed here further complicates the situation.

Yet, despite the historical dominance of parliamentary traditionalism, there are, as we have seen, hopeful signs in the public and in a number of jurisdictions of a growing taste for reform. There are several promising initiatives that seek to improve democratic government in Canada, and inter-legislative federalism fits in well with some of the ideas for institutional innovation. There are a number of possibilities to get the ball rolling. One jurisdiction could commit itself to an initiative, and invite the others to come. It all could start with an invitation and a first meeting. British Columbia's Premier Gordon Campbell has already done this in a small way. As well, the long experience in Canada's Parliament with various inter-parliamentary associations, and the degree to which the organizational and budgetary arrangements for these bodies have been institutionalized within the structure of Parliament, may give federal parliamentarians some capacity for autonomous action, if they choose to exercise it in this way.

In addition, if these ideas, and others like them, are deemed to be of some potential utility, civil-society institutions might take the first step in organizing some critical review and further development of them. Reform proposals could be further refined and more carefully explored, as could the means of bringing them into being. As I have said, the Institute for Research on Public Policy has been running a very useful series of meetings and publications on strengthening Canadian democracy and parliamentary institutions;[38] a think tank such as the IRPP, or the Parliamentary Centre, or a university with strength in legislative studies, might convene a conference or a series of working sessions, involving legislators, to test these ideas further.

I would not wish to be misunderstood. I do not believe that such initiatives as these, even if they were fully implemented, would radically alter our executive-dominated parliamentary democracy or transform the pattern of executive federalism. Regard them, rather, as sites of modest legislative self-assertion with some potential, in time, to enliven and reinvigorate our desiccated system of responsible government – not to mention the arcane pathways of Canadian intergovernmental relations.

NOTES

1 "Intergovernmental Relations and Democratic Citizenship," in *Governance in the Twenty-First Century,* eds. B. Guy Peters and Donald Savoie (Montreal: McGill-Queen's University Press, 2000), 30–58.

2 Ibid., p. 95: The establishment of standing committees on intergovernmental relations; the holding of debates or committee hearings on intergovernmental issues before First Ministers Conferences; legislative ratification of all major intergovernmental agreements; and the participation of Opposition members on governmental negotiating teams.

3 C.E.S. Franks, "Parliament, Intergovernmental Relations and National Unity," Working Paper 1992 (2) (Kingston: Institute of Intergovernmental Relations, Queen's University, 1999). For convenience, I will quote from this version of the paper.

4 Ibid., p. 31.

5 Ibid., p. 36.

6 Ibid., p. 27.

7 Ibid., p. 34. Clearly, the introduction of the *Charter of Rights and Freedoms* in 1982 was a very substantial reform of our institutional arrangements and has profoundly affected Canadian government, but I presume that Franks is referring specifically to the operational machinery of Parliament itself.

8 "Germany and Canada: Federal Loyalty in the Era of Globalization." Notes for an address to members of the Atlantik-Brücke, Feldafing, Germany, October 28, 2001.

9 "An Outsider's Observations of Intergovernmental Relations Among Consenting Adults," in *Confrontation or Collaboration: Intergovernmental Relations in Canada Today,* ed. Richard Simeon (Toronto: Institute of Public Administration of Canada, 1979).

10 Roger Gibbins, "Shifting Sands: Exploring the Political Foundations of SUFA," in *Policy Matters/Enjeux publics,* 2, 3 (Montreal: Institute for Research in Public Policy, July 2001).

11 Keith Banting, "The Past Speaks to the Future," in *Canada: The State of the Federation, 1997,* ed. Harvey Lazar (Kingston: Institute of Intergovernmental Relations, Queen's University, 1998); Roger Gibbins, "Democratic Reservations About the ACCESS Models," *Assessing ACCESS: Towards a New Social Union* (Kingston: Institute of Intergovernmental Relations, Queen's University, 1995); Ghislain Otis, "Informing Canadians – Public Accountability and Transparency," in *The Canadian Social Union Without Quebec. Eight Critical Analyses,* ed. Alain-G. Gagnon and Hugh Segal (Montreal: Institute for Research on Public Policy, 2000). Writing

in the mid-1980s, Paul Pross argued differently. He contended that the diffusion of power within the executive branch and the increasing role of interest groups have led to the enhancement of Parliament's role in the policy process. "Parliamentary Influence and the Diffusion of Power," *Canadian Journal of Political Science* (June 1985): 235–66.

12 For example: Alan Cairns, "The Electoral System and the Party System, 1921–66," *Canadian Journal of Political Science*, 1 (March 1968): 55–80; *A Future Together: Observations and Recommendations,* The Task Force on Canadian Unity (Ottawa: Queen's Printer, 1979), 104–06; Michael Cassidy. "Fairness and Stability: How a New Electoral System Would Affect Canada," *Parliamentary Government,* 42 (August 1992).

13 In addition to Franks's work, see Canada, House of Commons, 1985. *Report of the Special Committee on Reform of the House of Commons* (The McGrath Report).

14 Franks, "Parliament, Intergovernmental Relations and National Unity," 31.

15 The National Assembly has performed this central role, for example, during the referendum processes, at moments during the patriation of the constitution in 1980–82, and on the occasion of the failure of Meech Lake. At critical moments in the life of Quebec society, Quebecers turn quite naturally to the National Assembly. whose televised proceedings are, at such times as these, among the most heavily watched television in the province.

16 Quebec, for example, was the only province to review and approve in its legislature the draft of the Meech Lake Accord before the agreement was accepted by all governments in its final form at the Langevin meetings in the spring of 1987.

17 Ironically, it is the government of Quebec that has recently raised the possibility of a complete overhaul of its legislative processes. On 21 March 2002, Jean-Pierre Charbonneau, the minister responsible for the reform of democratic institutions, announced the creation of a reform secretariat. Stating that *"nous sommes mûres pour une grande réflexion nationale,"* the minister raised the possibility of a substantial "congressionalization" of Quebec's parliamentary system: direct popular election of the head of government; separation of the legislature and the executive, giving MNAs greater freedom of action; the selection of ministers from outside the National Assembly; and fixed provincial election dates. He also floated the idea of introducing proportional representation. *(Communiqué* c3062, 23 March 2002.) Whether the minister's grandiose call for the creation of *"un grand et vaste chantier de réformes fondamentales"* was seriously intended or a desperate pre-election sally will, in the light of the Parti Québécois' electoral defeat, remain unknown. What is clear is that it responds to no passionately expressed desire on the part of Quebecers to change the system by which they are governed – certainly none that I am aware of.

18 Peter Dobell, "Reforming Parliamentary Practice: The Views of MPs," Institute for Research on Public Policy, *Policy Matters* 1, 9 (December 2000):12, 25–26.

19 Ibid., p. 12.

20 Much of this material is available on the Institute for Research on Public Policy website at <www.irpp.org>.

21 For an overview see <www.mta.ca/faculty/arts/canadian_studies/demaudit_overview_15aug.pdf>.

22 See <www.lcc.gc.ca/en/themes/gr/er/er_main.asp>.

23 Gordon Gibson, *Fixing Canadian Democracy* (Vancouver: The Fraser Institute, 2003); Judy Rebick, *Imagine Democracy* (Toronto: Stoddart, 2000); Jeffrey Simpson, *The Friendly Dictatorship* (Toronto: McClelland and Stewart, 2002); Donald Savoie, *Governing from the Centre: The Concentration of Power in Canadian Politics* (Toronto: University of Toronto Press, 1999); Patrick Boyer, *"Just Trust Us": The Erosion of Accountability in Canada* (Toronto: Breakwater Productions, 2003); and Paul Kemp. *Does Your Vote Count?* (Toronto: Breakwater Productions, 2003).

24 Paul Howe and David Northrup, "Strengthening Canadian Democracy: The Views of Canadians," *Policy Matters,* 1, 5 (July 2000): 7. Unless otherwise indicated, all data in the paragraph are taken from this survey.

25 Patrick Boyer, "Reconsidering the Role of Citizens – The Case of the *Underground Royal Commission*." Paper presented at the Annual Meeting of the Canadian Political Science Association, Halifax, 6 May 2003.

26 See his speech to the Osgoode Hall Law School, reported in *The Globe and Mail,* 22 October 2002; see also, Paul Martin, "The Democratic Deficit," *Policy Options* (December 2002–January 2003): 10–12. Martin's reforms are designed to give backbench MPs more freedom to amend or reject government bills and to review prime ministerial appointments.

27 See Ontario Progressive Conservative Party, "The Road Ahead: Premier Eves' Plan for Ontario's Future," 50–52 <www.ontariopc.com>; Liberal Party of Ontario, "Government that Works for You: The Ontario Liberal Plan for a More Democratic Ontario." <www.ontarioliberal.com/2000/PDF/democratic/democratic.pdf>; Ontario New Democratic Party, "Public power: Practical Solutions for Ontario," 67–72 <www.publicpower.ca/our_platform/publicpower_platform.pdf>. The previous three paragraphs are drawn in part from a report on democracy in Ontario prepared by David Cameron, Celine Mulhern, and Graham White for the province's Panel on the Role of Government.

28 Premier Gordon Campbell, Address to the Federation of Canadian Municipalities. Toronto, 18 October 2001.

29 "Three members of the House of Commons of Canada appointed on a proposal of the Prime Minister [Premier of Quebec] after consultation with the Leader of the Official Opposition, who were elected at the last general election to represent an electoral district in Québec, and who continue to do so." In *An Act to Establish the Commission on the Political and Constitutional Future of Quebec,* S.Q. 1990, ch. 34.

30 It is worth noting that the participation of the federal MPs was not sanctioned by the House of Commons. It was a political decision made by the party leaders at the time.

31 Information in these paragraphs is taken from the Parliament of Canada website at <www.parl.gc.ca>.

32 I am indebted to an anonymous reader for this information.

33 Interview with Peter Dobell, Parliamentary Centre, 20 December 2001.

34 I am indebted to an anonymous reader for this suggestion.

35 Interview with Peter Dobell, Parliamentary Centre, 20 December 2001. This initiative eventually petered out. Peter Dobell notes that these sorts of meetings need to be carefully designed, to ensure that they do not simply become a forum for intergovernmental or interjurisdictional squabbling. This touches on an important point made by Dr. Tsvi Kahana, executive director of the Centre for Constitutional Studies at the University of Alberta, in correspondence relating to an earlier draft of this paper. He argues that one of the reasons that Canadian legislatures have a bad name is their poor deliberative performance, and worries that a proposal that offers legislators the capacity to do more of that which gave them a bad name in the first place – namely, engage in debate – might exacerbate the problem in the public mind, rather than alleviate it (email to author, 23 January 2002).

36 To display how different the constitutional and political context is from that of Canada, one need only consult the National Governors Association website, at <www.nga.org>, where it is stated with pride that "*Fortune* Magazine recently named NGA as one of Washington's most powerful lobbying organizations." Canada's provincial premiers do not see themselves or their interprovincial organization, the Annual Premiers Conference, as Ottawa lobbyists, but as constitutionally grounded federal actors, in this sense equal to their federal counterpart, the Government of Canada.

37 The information for these paragraphs comes from the National Conference of State Legislatures website at <www.ncsl.org>. Interestingly, paralleling the observation of the National Governors association, NCSL asserts that it is "recognized as the states' most effective lobbying voice in Washington, DC."

38 The series is called "Policy Matters/Enjeux publics."

DAVID R. CAMERON AND JACQUELINE D. KRIKORIAN

15 Recognizing Quebec in the Constitution of Canada: Using the Bilateral Constitutional Amendment Process

University of Toronto Law Journal 2008

In a period when comprehensive constitutional reform was off the table, and rightly so, Jacqueline Krikorian and I explored whether there was a more targeted constitutional process that might secure the recognition of Quebec in the Canadian constitution. In this paper, we argued that the bilateral amending formula, requiring only the consent of Quebec and the federal government and Parliament, might be deployed to address this issue.

I. Introduction

For almost half a century, Canada has struggled to address the constitutional concerns of Quebec. Much of the debate, particularly in recent years, has focused on whether or not the country's Constitution should recognize the francophone population in Quebec as a nation or distinct society with characteristics and needs palpably different from those of other provincial communities in the Canadian federation. At issue is how to best acknowledge, support, and preserve the French language and culture that are, without doubt, the defining characteristics of the contemporary Québécois identity.[1]

This perennial Canadian issue could begin to be addressed by using a little-known constitutional provision referred to as the bilateral amendment. While the United States requires a kind of super-majority consensus among states to change its national constitution, Canada created a number of different procedures for amending its Constitution. One of these, the bilateral constitutional amendment process, permits a single province, in conjunction with the federal government, to adopt a constitutional amendment that pertains only to its residents.

To date, bilateral constitutional amendments have been adopted on only a handful of occasions; these have not proved controversial in the national context, although some have touched on potentially sensitive issues, such as language and religion. This bilateral procedure could be used to recognize and entrench French as the predominant language in the province of Quebec.

To discuss this proposal, the remainder of this article is divided into five parts. Part II briefly reviews the unsuccessful attempts by the country's political leadership to address Quebec's historical grievances by amending the Canadian Constitution. Part III considers Quebec's legislative attempts to ensure that its most distinctive feature – the French language – is both promoted and protected within the province. In Part IV our analysis turns to the rules and case law governing constitutional amendments, particularly as they pertain to bilateral amendments. Part V analyses some of the extra-legal factors that have been considered by the federal government to determine whether or not a proposed bilateral amendment is acceptable. In Part VI, we consider some of the options available to the governments of Canada and Quebec to recognize Quebec's specificity in the Constitution via the bilateral amendment process.

II. Canada's Constitutional Quagmire

Although there have been repeated attempts to amend Canada's Constitution since the 1960s, only one comprehensive constitutional amendment has ever been adopted.[2] In 1982, the national government in Ottawa and nine of the ten provincial governments agreed to make several significant changes to the Constitution, among them the following. First, a bill of rights, formally known as the Canadian Charter of Rights and Freedoms[3] (the Charter), was entrenched into the country's Constitution. Second, provisions were adopted to modify the country's constitutional amendment process, ensuring that Canadians, and not the British government, would have ultimate control over changes to Canada's Constitution in the future.

The 1982 amendments, however, were made without Quebec's consent. Major changes were made to the country's structures of governance without the approval of the province that housed close to a quarter of the country's population and that, moreover, had been the most ardent advocate of constitutional reform.[4] As Patrick Monahan has explained, such a situation is not sustainable:

> The 1982 constitution explicitly recognized the multicultural character of the country as well as the rights of the aboriginal peoples of Canada, but made no mention of the distinctive character of Quebec. After years of Quebec's seeking to have its aspirations accommodated, culminating in the emotional referendum campaign of 1980, the terms of the new constitution essentially ignored Quebec's agenda for change.

This is not to suggest that the decision to proceed in the absence of the province of Quebec in 1981 cannot be justified. It may well be that the separatist commitment of the Quebec government of the time provided a moral justification for proceeding without their consent. But the conclusion that the consent of Quebec's elected provincial representatives could be ignored forever is insupportable. At some point it would be necessary to make good on the promises and failed negotiations of the previous decade.[5]

Yet, while many have accepted that Quebec's constitutional needs must be addressed, there has been no consensus as to how to achieve this goal.

In the mid-1980s, Prime Minister Brian Mulroney, in conjunction with all of the provincial premiers, including Robert Bourassa of Quebec, proposed a constitutional amendment to remedy Quebec's concerns. Known as the Meech Lake Accord,[6] it provided that the Canadian Constitution would be interpreted in a manner consistent with "the recognition that Quebec constitutes within Canada a distinct society."[7] This clause was paired with a statement recognizing "that the existence of French-speaking Canadians, centred in Quebec but also present elsewhere in Canada, and English-speaking Canadians, concentrated outside Quebec but also present in Quebec, constitutes a fundamental characteristic of Canada."[8] The initiative received widespread support in Quebec for two reasons. First, it had considerable symbolic implications: it recognized the francophone community in Quebec as a permanent and distinctive feature of the Canadian identity. Second, many argued, the provision ensured that the courts would show deference to any challenged legislative measures designed to protect the French language and culture in Quebec. Judges, in other words, would more carefully consider the collective rights of what could now be referred to as the *Québécois nation* before striking down legislation because it infringed on individual rights such as equality and freedom of expression.[9]

The Meech Lake Accord, however, did not receive the necessary legislative support in Newfoundland and Manitoba. From the perspective of francophones in Quebec, the failure was simply another rejection of the French reality by English Canadians. And, in part, this was an accurate perception. Although there was considerable enthusiasm for the proposed measure in Quebec, Canadians outside the province resented its Quebec-centred focus; there was a sense that only the French benefited from the measure and that it did not adequately respond to other constitutional issues facing the country.

In 1992, the country's leaders tried to remedy the political fallout from the failure of Meech Lake by introducing another constitutional amendment. Known as the Charlottetown Accord, this initiative once again addressed the concerns of Quebec. The draft legal text proposed the insertion of a so-called Canada Clause into the text of the Constitution that would require that the Constitution, including the Charter, be interpreted in a manner consistent with specified fundamental characteristics. The Canada Clause, in effect, set out the make-up of the country by identifying its most significant demographic features. One aspect of this clause provided that "Quebec constitutes within Canada a distinct society, which includes a French-speaking majority, a unique culture and a civil law tradition,"[10] while others related to gender equality, racial and ethnic equality, and the right of Aboriginal Canadians to promote their languages. As one observer declared, this constitutional proposal "gave everything to everybody."[11]

But, as was true of the Meech Lake Accord, a great deal of public and expert debate revolved around the interrelationship between the various provisions. More specifically, there was considerable uncertainty about the various components of the Canada Clause and how they would interact with one another. There was considerable discussion of the relationship between the distinct society provision and two of the other fundamental characteristics in the list: the Canada Clause, clause 2(1)(h), which states that "Canadians confirm the principle of the equality of the provinces at the same time as recognizing their diverse characteristics," and clause 2(1)(d), which states that "Canadians and their governments are committed to the vitality and development of official language minority communities throughout Canada." Even legal experts were unable to explain convincingly how these provisions – with competing constitutional visions – were to be reconciled.

Like its predecessor, the Charlottetown Accord amendment failed – in this case, on the basis of a popular vote. Fifty-four per cent of Canadians opposed the initiative. In Quebec, opposition to the Charlottetown Accord was even greater: 57 per cent of its voters opposed the proposal.[12] Although many factors account for the accord's defeat in Quebec, one issue dominated all others: Quebecers believed that, unlike the Meech Lake Accord, which had focused exclusively on Quebec's concerns, the proposed constitutional amendment addressed too many issues and, in the process, watered down the value and significance of the distinct society clause.

The Meech and Charlottetown experiences left francophones in Quebec concerned that the rest of Canada was not sufficiently sensitive to their language and culture. In the 1995 sovereignty referendum in Quebec, in which approximately 94 per cent of Quebec's 5 million voters cast their ballots, only 50.58 per cent voted against a process that might have led to separation. Although the referendum question itself was far from clear,[13] the results sent a startling wake-up call to the rest of Canada.

One of the chief grounds for resisting further constitutional discussion – even for those who believed, in principle, in the need for some constitutional change – was the phenomenon of linkage. Practically and politically, it proved impossible to propose a single amendment to the Constitution to address Quebec's concerns without, at the same time, addressing an unmanageable range of demands from the country's other constitutional actors. One cannot offer to address Quebec's concerns without also confirming the equality of the provinces, tackling the reform of the Senate, responding to the constitutional aspirations of Canada's Aboriginal peoples, seeking to strengthen the Canadian economic union, and so on. Support for one constitutional priority is contingent on the acceptance of another, and so a large, unwieldy package of constitutional changes is rapidly constructed.

The lesson that most people took from the bruising encounters of the 1980s and 1990s, therefore, was that the country was playing with fire in attempting substantial constitutional reform and that we would all be better off if, for the foreseeable future, the country abstained from further constitutional adventures. In fact, the constitutionality of secession, rather than the substantive reform of the Constitution itself, became the focus in the years following the 1995 referendum.[14]

Canada has thus been trapped in an unsatisfactory state of irresolution with respect to national unity since 1982. Quebec – as reflected in its government, its legislature, and, arguably, its people – has not assented to the constitutional arrangements by which it is governed. While this appears at the moment to make little difference in the day-to-day lives of ordinary citizens, it is a state of affairs widely regarded as unsatisfactory for a constitutional democracy. Moreover, it is seen by many as exposing the country to an unacceptable risk of fracture should a crisis arise. Yet while many would acknowledge that there remains some unfinished business as far as Quebec is concerned, doing nothing seems to be the best option available to policy makers. There has been a sense that an impasse between Quebec and the rest of Canada is better than another round of failed constitutional talks.

Canadians were taken by surprise, therefore, when, in November 2006, their national government initiated a constitutional discussion by introducing a resolution in the House of Commons proclaiming that it "recognize[d] that the Québécois form a nation within a united Canada."[15] Although the minister for intergovernmental affairs resigned in protest,[16] legislative support for the initiative was overwhelming. Members of Parliament from all political parties, including the Bloc Québécois,[17] endorsed the resolution, and it was adopted in a vote of 265 to sixteen.[18]

As Prime Minister Stephen Harper explained, the rationale for the motion was simple: "Quebecers want recognition, respect, and reconciliation ... they do not want another referendum."[19] He noted that recognizing the Québécois as a nation was intimately "linked" to the province's French language, explaining that "if you're speaking of a Québécois nation you're speaking of French."[20] Stéphane Dion, now Liberal Opposition leader, effectively agreed. He said that he supported the motion because, in a "sociological sense, we, the Québécois, are a nation, because we form a large group within Canada – nearly a quarter of the population – and we have an awareness of our unity and a desire to live together."[21]

Three days later, in a 107 to 0 vote, Quebec's legislative body, the National Assembly, formally responded to Ottawa's initiative by "recogniz[ing] the positive nature of the motion."[22] The Harper resolution, however, was viewed as an "opening gesture" rather than as a full response to the historical grievances of the province. As former Bloc Québécois and later Liberal MP Jean Lapierre explained, although the motion is "symbolic," it is only a "small step." For him, "reconciliation with Quebecers and Quebec's acceptance of the Constitution will require a great deal more work."[23] Exactly what he thought needed to be done, however, was not explicitly set out.

It would seem, therefore, that there is now an opportunity to move forward to address the constitutional issue in a substantive manner. The broad political support for the Harper initiative indicates that there is considerable common ground between Quebec City and Ottawa. Arguably, the resolution could be built upon by incorporating its essential elements into the Constitution. Such an amendment could recognize the specificity of the province by effectively acknowledging the Québécois nation in Canada by entrenching its core characteristic, the French language (and possibly the French culture), into the Constitution via the bilateral amendment process.

III. Quebec and Bill 101

While efforts were being made at the federal level to address Quebec's historical grievances, francophones in Quebec turned to their local provincial government to deal with their concerns. In 1976, with the election of the first secessionist government, Quebec's quest for recognition of its distinctive language and culture entered a new phase. Under the leadership of Premier René Lévesque, the Parti Québécois demanded that a new relationship be forged between Canada and Quebec in the form of "sovereignty-association." Lévesque announced that he would hold a province-wide referendum on the initiative to demonstrate its public support.[24]

The new premier also made it clear that one of his government's most important priorities was to protect the French language. In fact, during his first press conference, Lévesque promised to strengthen existing provincial language legislation.[25] And he did just that. Less than a year after forming the government, the Parti Québécois introduced the Charter of the French language.[26] It is not an exaggeration to say that its provisions shocked the anglophone community in Quebec in their requirements to establish the primacy of French in the life and affairs of the province.[27]

This language legislation, commonly known as Bill 101, was designed to entrench the linguistic rights of the francophone community in Quebec. French was to be the only official language in the legislature, courts, and offices of government.[28] Residents were guaranteed the right to use French in labour and business relations, and in some commercial contexts English was restricted.[29] And, although there were some categories of exceptions, French became the required language of instruction for most students in both elementary and secondary school systems.[30] Bill 101, in other words, not only entrenched the status of the French language in Quebec but did so at the expense of its minority English population. George Springate, the Liberal Member of the National Assembly representing the predominantly anglophone riding of Westmount, argued that the adoption of Bill 101 was "undemocratic" and called on all Quebecers to remain in the province and "fight for their rights."[31]

[...]

IV. The Bilateral Constitutional Amendment Process

With the proclamation of the Constitution Act, 1982, the authority to amend the Constitution was transferred to Canada from Great Britain. Part V of the Constitution Act, 1982, is entitled "Procedure for Amending Constitution of Canada"; in fact, it contains five different amendment formulas. The first, set out under s. 41, provides for amendments that govern important issues applicable to the nation as a whole:

> 41. An amendment to the Constitution of Canada in relation to the following matters may be made by proclamation issued by the Governor General under the Great Seal of Canada only where authorized by resolutions of the Senate and House of Commons and of the legislative assembly of each province:
> (a) the office of the Queen, the Governor General and the Lieutenant Governor of a province;
> (b) the right of a province to a number of members in the House of Commons not less than the number of Senators by which the province is entitled to be represented at the time this Part comes into force;
> (c) subject to section 43, the use of the English or the French language;
> (d) the composition of the Supreme Court of Canada; and
> (e) an amendment to this Part.

Given the significance of the issues identified, all ten provincial legislatures as well as the Parliament of Canada need to approve any such changes.

The second amending formula, set out under s. 38, applies to other issues of a general nature. Unanimity among the provinces and the national government is not required, however; instead, these amendments need only the authorization of Parliament and the support of two-thirds of the provinces representing at least 50 per cent of the population. But in 1996, the required procedure under the s. 38 amendment process was, in effect, legislatively modified with Parliament's adoption of Bill C-110.[32] This law requires not only that s. 38 amendments introduced by ministers of the Crown have the support of seven provinces constituting at least half of the population but also that "the seven agreeing provinces must include the five 'regions' stipulated in the Act, namely, Ontario, Quebec, British Columbia, two Atlantic provinces and two Prairie provinces."[33] The measure, in other words, built in a kind of "regional veto" for constitutional amendments made pursuant to s. 38.[34] And, although it is only a statute of Canada, this arrangement may, over time, gather quasi-constitutional status, assuming that its repeal becomes increasingly difficult to contemplate.

The third and fourth amendment procedures pertain to matters affecting individual legislatures, both federal and provincial. Under s. 44, subject to ss. 41 and 42, Parliament may unilaterally amend any matter relating to its executive, the House of Commons, or the Senate. Similarly, the s. 45 amendment process, subject to s. 41, authorizes a provincial legislature to change the constitution of the province. Under the s. 41 proviso, however, some limits are placed on provincial governments: most notably, they cannot make any unilateral amendment regarding "the use of the English or French language" in the province.

The fifth approach to amending the Constitution is referred to as "the bilateral constitutional amendment process." Pursuant to s. 43 of the Constitution Act, 1982, either a provincial legislature or legislatures or the federal Parliament may initiate a constitutional provision that applies to one or more, but not all, provinces:

43. An amendment to the Constitution of Canada in relation to any provision that applies to one or more, but not all, provinces, including

(a) any alteration to boundaries between provinces, and

(b) any amendment to any provision that relates to the use of the English or French language within a province, may be made by proclamation issued by the Governor General under the Great Seal of Canada only where so authorized by resolutions of the Senate and House of Commons and of the legislative assembly of each province to which the amendment applies.

These bilateral constitutional amendments are, moreover, expressly exempted from the scope of the legislation that provides for the regional veto.[35]

Benoît Pelletier, a constitutional lawyer and the current minister of Canadian intergovernmental affairs for the government of Quebec, describes s. 43 in one of his scholarly works as one of the most difficult articles to interpret in Part V of the 1982 Constitution. It raises, he says, a host of questions. What is its real scope? Which provisions of the Constitution are applicable only to "one or more, but not all, provinces"? With respect to specific cases involving s. 43, which provinces are contemplated by the phrase "each province to which the amendment applies"? What is the substantive content of s. 43, paras. (a) and (b)? What other situations may be covered tacitly by s. 43?[36]

Although it is true that the rules governing the bilateral amendment process are relatively vague, we are learning something about the nature and scope of s. 43 by seeing how it is being used. The bilateral constitutional amendment process has been adopted on at least seven separate occasions – four times by Newfoundland[37] and once each by Quebec,[38] Prince Edward Island,[39] and New Brunswick.[40] The extensive use of this amendment process can be attributed, at least in part, to the relatively simple procedural rules governing this form of amendment. To be approved, a s. 43 bilateral constitutional amendment requires that a resolution be authorized by the Senate, the House of Commons, and the provincial legislature or legislatures affected by the amendment. Alternatively, a s. 43 amendment can be authorized without Senate approval if the House of Commons adopts the same resolution on two different occasions separated by a period of no fewer than 180 days.[41]

Moreover, there is no requirement to obtain the approval of other governments at the provincial level for a bilateral constitutional amendment:

> When a constitutional provision concerns only provinces and is limited in its application to them, when it is limited territorially and does not affect the federal government but only certain provinces, you still need the agreement of the federal Parliament, and it of course has a veto. But apart from that, all that is needed is the agreement of the province to which the amendment applies.[42]

Provinces not affected by a proposed bilateral amendment, therefore, are not formally involved in the process. These governments may be consulted during a bilateral amendment initiative, but their approval is not required.

In terms of their scope, bilateral amendments may be adopted on any constitutional matter that involves one or more – but not all – of the provinces. To date, provincial legislatures have always acted individually when initiating such a change, but in theory this type of constitutional amendment could be initiated and adopted by several provinces, so long as Parliament cooperated. This is a formula with relatively few constraints, and, arguably, its full potential is not yet known.

There are no specific limitations expressly built into the s. 43 bilateral constitutional amendment process. Section 43 does provide, however, that a constitutional change may *include* amendments involving the borders between provinces or "the *use* of the English or French language within a province."[43] In other words, proposed changes to the Constitution affecting the way in which French and English are used within a province are, at a minimum, permitted under the scope of a s. 43 amendment.

Section 43's specific reference to the use of French and English as a matter that is allowable under the rubric of a bilateral constitutional amendment is an exception carved out of the rigorous s. 41 amendment process, which requires unanimity. This provision expressly provides that s. 41 amendments can pertain to the use of the French and English languages *subject to s. 43*.[44] Exactly where the dividing line exists between a matter regarding the use of French and English within a province and the use of French and English in the national context is not clearly defined. This uncertainty stems, in part, from the fact that neither Parliament nor the provincial legislatures have exclusive jurisdiction to enact legislation pertaining to language. In the past, the courts have stated that each level of government has the legislative competence to pass language laws pertaining to matters that fall under its jurisdiction.[45]

What is clear, however, is that the s. 43 bilateral constitutional amendment process allows for a provision pertaining to the *status* of English and French linguistic communities within a province and not simply to the *use* of these languages within the provincial context. In 1993, New Brunswick, in conjunction with the federal government, adopted a bilateral constitutional amendment mandating that English and French were to "have equality of status and equal rights and privileges, including the right to distinct educational institutions."[46] In other words, New Brunswick's bilateral constitutional amendment did not simply affect the way in which the official languages are *used* but, more specifically, addressed their standing or position within the province. This constitutional amendment, therefore, effectively creates a precedent that allows for bilateral amendments to confer some kind of status on language within a province.

It is interesting to note, moreover, that the New Brunswick bilateral amendment was not expressly approved in a provincial referendum.[47] Nor did it receive the unanimous support of the legislature. Opposition critics such as Edwin Allen of the Confederation of Regions Party argued that the amendment was "the most serious divisive and ultimately destructive proposal that ha[d] ever come to the floor." He explained that it would create two separate communities in New Brunswick by effectively bestowing a "distinct status" on the francophone community in the province.[48] McKenna, however, justified the bilateral amendment on the basis that it was necessary to protect the French and English linguistic communities in the future:

> The purpose of the equality amendment we are debating today is to provide an expression in the Canadian Constitution of the equality of status of the English and French linguistic communities in the province. This constitutional guarantee will ensure a more secure future for all New Brunswickers and recognizes the diversity and the richness of our two linguistic communities.

Anthropologists tell us that language is culture; if a language disappears, so, too, does the culture. The dynamic society we have in this province is based on both the English and French cultures.[49]

McKenna emphasized that the bilateral amendment did not alter the fundamental nature of New Brunswick's linguistic communities, as it was "simply a recognition of what we have built and what exists today, [and it] does not really deliver any new goods." Rather, it acted as a way to secure the existence of the French and English communities in the future by ensuring "that all that is special about being a New Brunswicker will not just be here today but will be protected for tomorrow."[50]

McKenna was able to introduce this measure because there are no other constitutional checks or limitations on proposed bilateral amendments. Case law supports the principle that one constitutional provision is not required to conform to another. In *Reference Re Bill 30, An Act to Amend the Education Act (Ont.)*,[51] the Supreme Court of Canada addressed the relationship of the Charter to other constitutional provisions. More specifically, it examined the constitutional validity of an Ontario bill that provided for "a policy of full funding for Roman Catholic separate high schools in Ontario."[52] At issue was the extent to which the provincial government had jurisdiction to adopt such legislation pursuant to the education provision set out in s. 93 of the Constitution Act, 1867. Justice Wilson wrote the majority opinion on behalf of herself and three of her colleagues. She stated that legislation legally enacted under one part of the Constitution cannot be set aside by another part: "It was never intended, in my opinion, that the *Charter* could be used to invalidate other provisions of the Constitution."[53]

Similarly, in *Adler v. Ontario*,[54] the Supreme Court examined the constitutionality of Ontario legislation implemented pursuant to s. 93 of the Constitution Act, 1867. One of the matters analyzed in the Court's decision pertains to an apparent conflict between this 1867 constitutional provision governing education and ss. 2(a) and 15 of the Charter regarding religious freedom and equality rights. Justice Iacobucci, writing for the majority, applied the precedent established in *Reference Re Bill 30*, explaining that one constitutional provision cannot be used to render another invalid.[55] In other words, the Court held that legislation enacting the provisions of s. 93 of the Constitution Act, 1867, is immune from Charter scrutiny by virtue of the fact that s. 93 is itself immune from Charter scrutiny.[56]

Moreover, constitutional observers have repeatedly dismissed the idea that a proposed bilateral constitutional amendment needs to conform to existing constitutional measures.[57] During Senate hearings on a proposed bilateral amendment for Newfoundland, several noted experts repeatedly denied that the proposed amendment needed to comply with the Charter:

All parts of the Constitution have to be read together, no part of the Constitution can be used to trump, invalidate or nullify the effect of any other part of the
Constitution. That's a provision that goes back to 1867. It did not emerge with the
Charter.... I gather it was suggested to you yesterday that because the [C]harter is
earlier than the [proposed bilateral amendment], ... somehow the timing of these
provisions is important. This is not a principle that has ever been recognized in the
interpretation of the Constitution, and if it was, then the [C]harter would be read
down to give effect to the 1867 Constitution. The reality is that the Constitution is a
fundamental document and all parts will be read together irrespective of timing.[58]

If enacted, Term 17 [Newfoundland's proposed bilateral constitutional amend-
ment] will become part of the Constitution of Canada, thus it will be shielded
by the well-established principle that one part of the Constitution, let's say the
[C]harter, cannot be used to invalidate or repeal another part of the Constitution.
As a result, [its] provisions ... will enjoy a measure of Charter immunity.[59]

In other words, any proposed bilateral amendment need only conform to the
substantive legal and procedural requirements set out in the text of s. 43 of the
Constitution Act, 1982, not to those of other provisions adopted either before
or after the Charter became law.

V. The Practical Implementation of the Bilateral Amendment Process

Although the legal requirements for a bilateral constitutional amendment are
neither onerous nor complex, a number of considerations must be addressed.
Parliament will not automatically accede to a province's request for an amendment without a review of a number of constitutional, political, social, and economic concerns. An examination of the public discussion relating to previous
bilateral constitutional amendments suggests that, in the past, five factors have
dominated these debates.

First, in weighing the merits of a proposed bilateral amendment, the federal government has considered which level of government had jurisdiction
over the issue. In other words, was the proposed initiative one that fell under
the province's legislative competence? For example, when the government of
Quebec sought to change the foundation of its schoolboard system from a denominational to a linguistic basis, the relatively tolerant reaction of the federal
government was based, in part, on the fact that provincial governments have
exclusive jurisdiction over the field of education. It would seem, therefore, that
bilateral amendment proposals that deal with issues that fall clearly under the
provincial government's responsibility are more likely to receive approval from
the federal legislature.[60]

Second, during past bilateral constitutional amendment discussions, considerable emphasis has been placed on the nature and extent of the consultation

process. Observers have repeatedly commented on whether members of the public affected by a proposed amendment have been given a meaningful opportunity to participate in discussions surrounding any possible changes.[61] Although there are no specific constitutional requirements regarding nongovernmental participation in such bilateral changes,[62] earlier initiatives have involved extensive public hearings and, in the case of Newfoundland and Labrador, two province-wide referenda. Consequently, it would be unlikely for an amendment to proceed without some kind of public participation.

Popular support for constitutional change within a province is a third factor that has played a key role in the amendment process. To what extent does the public endorse the government's initiative? Federal political leaders have repeatedly stated that considerable backing for constitutional change must exist within the affected province before such change can proceed.[63] In other words, it would be highly unlikely that the federal government would support a bilateral amendment that did not have the popular support of a province's residents.

A fourth and related factor that has been considered during bilateral amendment debates pertains to the sentiments of the minorities affected by the change. David Schneiderman has argued that "where minority rights may be prejudicially affected, Parliament has a particular duty to strictly scrutinize the proposed amendment."[64] Patrick Monahan extends this point, suggesting that Parliament should not support proposals that do not have the support of these communities:[65]

> Does the proposed amendment enjoy support of the minority that is to be affected by the amendment? In effect, I would propose that a majority of the minority rule. Before you can remove these rights, there must be evidence to support the view that a majority of this class, when taken as a whole – recognizing that some members of the class will be opposed – approves that amendment.[66]

Similarly, Stéphane Dion, former minister of intergovernmental affairs, emphasized to a parliamentary committee looking into the issue that the Liberal government would not have adopted a bilateral constitutional amendment if "the minority does not lend you reasonable support."[67]

At the same time, however, it is important to recognize that receiving input and support from minorities affected by a proposed constitutional amendment is a political consideration, not a legal requirement. The fact that minority communities are consulted does not mean that they must approve or support such changes. For example, the Newfoundland Court of Appeal rejected a challenge to the validity of the s. 43 bilateral constitutional amendment on state-funded religious education on the basis that it affected and was opposed by a number of religious communities in the province.[68] In *Hogan v. Newfoundland (A.G.)*,[69] the Supreme Court of Newfoundland, citing constitutional expert Peter Hogg, explained that the amending provisions in Part V of the Constitution Act, 1982, constitute "a complete code of legal (as opposed to conventional) rules which enable all parts of the 'Constitution of Canada' to be amended."[70] The Court held that as long as the procedural requirements of s. 43 are met, a bilateral constitutional amendment is valid even if it affects the rights of minorities:

> Neither the rule of law nor respect for minorities prevents the application of s. 43 to the amendment of Term 17. The appellants' position ignores the inescapable fact that the Constitution entrusts minority rights to the majority. The structure is designed not to prevent constitutional amendment but to ensure, by making the process more difficult than the passage of an amendment to any other bill, that the rights are given "due regard and protection." The appropriate provision in Part V of the Constitution, having been complied with, the validity of the amendment to Term 17 cannot be questioned.[71]

In other words, while political considerations require that members of the public and of affected groups to be consulted when proposals for a bilateral constitutional amendment are being considered, there is no legal obligation that minority communities approve of the changes.

Lastly, the values reflected in a proposed bilateral amendment have also been the focus of attention. At issue is the extent to which the initiatives conflict with human-rights matters that have been endorsed by Canada in varying domestic and international arrangements. As constitutional scholar Anne Bayefsky explains, we "shouldn't be drafting constitutional amendments that we know full well bring conflict with the [C]harter into full view and risk":[72]

> What about the goals of the legislation? Are they consistent with the Canadian Charter of Rights and Freedoms, its spirit? Are they consistent with the goals of equality, multiculturalism, and freedom of conscience and religion, or as I say, potentially xenophobic?[73]

Similarly, in his presentation to the joint committee considering Newfoundland's bilateral initiative, Dion pointed out that although his government was *not required* to adopt constitutional amendments that adhere to the provisions of the Charter or of international human-rights law,[74] the proposed amendment under discussion was "not incompatible with the Canadian [C]harter or international charters."[75]

Discussion of the seven previous bilateral amendments has been relatively uncontroversial in the Canada-wide context, despite the fact that five of the seven have altered constitutional arrangements relating to language, religion, or both – historically, highly contentious and divisive issues in Canadian public life. Clearly, time, circumstance, and intent play a critical role in determining the extent to which specific constitutional proposals attract controversy.

VI. Quebec and the Bilateral Amendment Process

To date, Quebec's constitutional concerns have not been addressed in a manner that would make it acceptable for its residents, its government, or its legislature to formally consent to the 1982 Constitution. For reasons outlined above, events are at an impasse. The recent success of the initiative of the government of Canada, however, appears to suggest that there may be an opportunity for progress. Building on the resolution recognizing the Québécois as a nation within Canada, the House of Commons and the National Assembly could introduce a bilateral constitutional amendment that would give official status to the French language in the province of Quebec and possibly recognize the French culture in the province.

A bilateral constitutional amendment addressing language issues is expressly permitted under s. 43 of the Constitution Act, 1982.[76] New Brunswick, in conjunction with the federal government, adopted such an amendment for this very purpose when it bestowed a kind of enhanced status on the French and English languages. Moreover, the Supreme Court of Canada has already both accepted and endorsed the notion that French is the predominant language in Quebec. In *Ford*, it held that the National Assembly could adopt a law providing that French would have greater public visibility than English, expressly stating that the government of Quebec could require the French language to be given predominance on signage in order to reflect the "*visage linguistique*" of the province. In the process, the Court effectively acknowledged and endorsed the notion that the vitality of the French language and culture in Quebec is a valid public-policy goal.

In this context, it would be possible for the governments of Canada and Quebec to use New Brunswick's bilateral constitutional amendment as a precedent to introduce a measure that builds upon the essence of the November 2006 House of Commons resolution recognizing the Québécois nation in Canada. We are arguing, in other words, that a bilateral constitutional amendment is a potential *process* by which the long-standing concerns of Quebec could begin to be addressed in the Constitution. Our overall objective here is not to provide solutions to the constitutional impasse, or even the text of a possible provision; rather, our goal is to map out a process by which the real and valid concerns of the francophone community in Quebec might successfully be addressed and to indicate the issues that could be considered if and when such discussions should occur.

We envision that such an amendment would reaffirm Quebec's existing legislative authority and act as an interpretive provision that informs how the

Constitution is read and understood in Quebec. We are not advocating a measure that allocates new powers or redistributes existing heads of power; such a proposal would change the nature and balance of Canadian federalism and require the consent of all the provinces. Rather, we are arguing for consideration of a bilateral constitutional amendment that pertains only to Quebec. To this end, we believe there are at least two options worthy of consideration. The first is to introduce an amendment to s. 16 of the Charter dealing with official languages, while the second is to introduce a provision similar in nature to s. 27 of the Charter[77] that would apply exclusively to Quebec.

The first option for a bilateral constitutional amendment would be a variation of the existing constitutional provisions governing New Brunswick's language rights, as set out in ss. 16 and 16.1 of the Charter:

> 16. (2) English and French are the official languages of New Brunswick and have equality of status and equal rights and privileges as to their use in all institutions of the legislature and government of New Brunswick.
> ...
> 16.1. (1) The English linguistic community and the French linguistic community in New Brunswick have equality of status and equal rights and privileges, including the right to distinct educational institutions and such distinct cultural institutions as are necessary for the preservation and promotion of those communities.
> (2) The role of the legislature and government of New Brunswick to preserve and promote the status, rights and privileges referred to in subsection (1) is affirmed.

The focus of the proposed bilateral constitutional amendment would pertain to the French language, and possibly the French culture, in Quebec. It could entrench French as the official language of the province and acknowledge that the National Assembly has the authority to both preserve and protect Quebec's distinct cultural institutions. Such a provision would, in effect, simply reflect the existing status of the French language in Quebec by constitutionalizing the *raison d'être* of the provisions legally enacted in Bill 101. Although the government of Quebec already has the legislative capacity to adopt such measures and, in this sense, would not be gaining new powers or rights, a constitutional amendment of this nature would entrench the status of one of the core elements of the Québécois nation in the province, as well as beginning to address one of Quebec's legitimate core concerns – namely, the amendment of the Canadian Constitution in 1982 without Quebec's priorities being addressed and without Quebec's consent. In this sense, our proposal is positive in nature – to constitutionalize the rights of the French community, not to detract or take away from the existing rights of anglophones in the province. In fact, a provision in the proposed bilateral amendment expressly recognizing and protecting the existing rights of the English community in the province of Quebec[78] would be an essential part of any bilateral amendment, in order to reassure the anglophone community in the province that their status has not been altered.

A second option for a bilateral amendment recognizing the predominance of French in Quebec would be to adopt a provision akin to s. 27 of the Charter:

> 27. This Charter shall be interpreted in a manner consistent with the preservation and enhancement of the multicultural heritage of Canadians.

Section 27 is an interpretive provision in the Constitution that reflects how Canadians wish to have their constitutional statute read and understood. It provides a context and guide for legislatures and courts. It informs how the Constitution is to be interpreted, but it does not give special powers or legislative authority to one government or community over another; rather, it acknowledges the importance and value that Canadians accord to multiculturalism and provides an assurance that these considerations will give guidance to any court that must render a decision in a constitutional challenge to a government measure or action. We believe that a provision similar in nature to s. 27 could be introduced as a bilateral constitutional amendment, with the proviso that it applied to Quebec. Like s. 27, such a measure would act as an interpretive clause that would recognize the value and status of the French language and culture in the province. It is our position that the Québécois nation is no less deserving of recognition in the Constitution than is our multicultural heritage and that, in the context of Quebec, such recognition is extremely important both politically and symbolically.

Although the phrases "Québécois nation" and "distinct society" could be part of a bilateral amendment, and the issue should certainly be debated, we believe that they are probably best left out. If such a proposal introduced either of these expressions into the lexicon of Canadian constitutional debates, understandable concerns would be raised that the ambit and impact of this phraseology is unknown. Moreover, the use of "distinct society" language would evoke memories of earlier divisive and unsuccessful efforts at recognizing Quebec. Better, we think, to leave the parliamentary resolution as the background and context of a clear and more focused undertaking. Thus, we would suggest that the nature of the bilateral amendment should be focused on the use and status of the French language and, possibly, the French culture. The overwhelming success of the Canadian government's resolution recognizing the Québécois as a nation – which Harper explained was specifically linked to the French language – suggests that Parliament accepts that the specificity of Quebec and the French language is a distinctive feature of the Quebec reality, a position that is obviously accepted by the National Assembly of Quebec.

The governments of both Canada and Quebec would need to satisfy themselves that the criteria used in previous bilateral amendments had been met in this case, namely, that broad consultation had occurred, that there was a strong measure of public support in Quebec for the measure, that minority opinions had been taken into account, and that the proposed initiative was consistent with the spirit of the Charter.

We also think it is worth noting that one of the main reasons that the Meech Lake and Charlottetown Accords were so strongly contested was not simply the fact that the amendments required the consent of other provinces but also that each purported to declare something about the country as a whole.[79] Thus the notion of Quebec as a distinct society collided with that of Canada as a federal society characterized by equal provinces, cultural diversity, gender equality, and the presence of Aboriginal peoples. This is not the case with the suggestions we have put forward. The bilateral amendment process involves two government actors – the National Assembly and government of Quebec, on the one hand, and Parliament and the government of Canada, on the other – not all the provinces and territories. Furthermore, the amendment makes no attempt to capture a Canadian vision and situate Quebec within it; rather, it identifies one vital element in Quebec's existing laws and complex reality and offers that element a degree of constitutional recognition.

Such a bilateral amendment would serve two important public-policy objectives. First, the constitutional provision would have considerable symbolic importance for Canadians both inside and outside of Quebec. It would draw some of its symbolic power from the fact that the national status of the Québécois has been affirmed by the legislatures of Canada and Quebec. It would solidify the existing law and policy of Quebec as well as the jurisprudence of the Supreme Court of Canada. Moreover, it would provide a greater sense of security to francophones who, in the future, may be faced with challenges to their language rights that we cannot anticipate today.

A second rationale for this type of bilateral amendment is that it would be used as an interpretive aid in any future constitutional litigation challenging measures to promote or protect the French language in Quebec.[80] Like the New Brunswick bilateral constitutional amendment, it would not provide any new rights or "goods" but, rather, would ensure that the courts would recognize the constitutional value of the French language and culture when they render decisions involving constitutional challenges to measures enacted in Quebec. Although Quebec legislation entrenching French language rights might still be found to violate, for example, the Charter's freedom-of-expression or equality measures, a bilateral constitutional amendment of this nature would, in effect, mandate the courts to carefully balance the language rights of the Québécois community within the province and the rights of the individual before striking down a contested statute. In Canada, rights and freedoms are not absolute. When a court finds that a legislative measure violates the rights and freedoms set out in the Charter, the impugned provision does not automatically become null and void; rather, the court is mandated to take a second step and to consider whether the need to protect the rights of the individuals affected by the impugned provision outweighs society's interest in maintaining it.[81] In other words, judges balance the public interest in maintaining a law against the individual's interest in having his or her rights and freedoms unfettered by government regulation. A bilateral constitutional amendment that entrenched French as the official language of Quebec in the Constitution would ensure that judges carefully consider the needs of the Québécois as a community within the province of Quebec before striking down a language law that curtails the rights of an individual.

The proposed amendment, moreover, would not limit existing language rights for anglophones in Quebec. Section 133 of the Constitution Act, 1867, ensures that the English and French languages are used in both the National Assembly and the federal and provincial courts operating in the province. Similarly, the education provisions in the Constitution under s. 23 of the Charter, which provide for access to English-language education for some students, would remain in effect. And, to avoid any confusion or uncertainty among the population on this issue, the bilateral constitutional amendment could and should, as we have suggested, specifically provide that it does not abrogate existing constitutional rights set out in these sections.

We recognize that this proposal may provoke controversy because some may feel that it has the potential to affect the standing of the English minority in Quebec. In the years since the passage of Bill 101, however – through court cases, legislative adjustment, and social adaptation – Quebec has achieved a condition of 'linguistic peace,' in which the anglophone minority, by and large, has accepted the basic provisions of Bill 101, has learned French, and has accommodated itself to the position of English in the linguistic landscape of Quebec. The proposed amendment would recognize contemporary reality and give greater security to the French language and to francophones within the framework of the Constitution of Canada. We also believe that, in the "big picture," by assuring the Québécois nation that they have a secure future within the Canadian federation, we would be providing stability and security to the anglophone community in Quebec.

Our discussion of possible amendment strategies is by no means meant as the last word on the subject. In fact, our goal is simply to illustrate how the s. 43 *process* might be used to recognize Quebec's historic concerns in the Constitution. The exact wording of a possible amendment and the decision as to which of these (or other) approaches might be adopted should arise out of discussions among individuals and communities within Quebec and between the governments of Canada and Quebec. Our aim here is simply to indicate a viable process for constitutional change, set out some of the possible options, and invite further analysis and consideration.

From our perspective, the insertion of constitutional protection for the French language in Quebec into the Canadian Constitution would be a powerful declaration that the health and majority status of French in its *foyer principal* is a constitutive feature of Quebec and a legitimate object of Canadian public policy. Symbolically, Canada would be making a long-overdue peace with Québécois nationalism. Despite being an amendment not directly involving the nine other provinces, such a step, because of the necessary assenting role of Parliament, would be regarded as a direct and powerful recognition of the enduring importance and legitimacy of the French fact in Canada. While it may not fully address the Canadian constitutional impasse, it would be a step (and a long-overdue one at that) in remedying the country's incapacity to recognize the reality of Quebec in an idiom the Québécois themselves understand and accept.

NOTES

1 In 1968, René Lévesque, the founder of the province's first major secessionist party and later premier of Quebec, explained that the French language is the core feature of the Québécois: "We are *Québécois*. Being ourselves is essentially a matter of keeping and developing a personality that has survived for three and a half centuries. At the core of this personality is the fact that we speak French. Everything else depends on this one essential element and follows from it or leads us infallibly back to it." René Lévesque, *An Option for Quebec* (Toronto: McClelland & Stewart, 1968) at 14 [Lévesque, *Option*].

2 For an overview of the history of constitutional amendments see Anne F. Bayefsky, *Canada's Constitution Act 1982 and Amendments: A Documentary History* (Toronto: McGraw-Hill Ryerson, 1989); James Ross Hurley, *Amending Canada's Constitution: History, Processes, Problems and Prospects* (Ottawa: Communications Group, 1996); Peter Oliver, 'Canada, Quebec and Constitutional Amendments' (1999) 49 U.T.L.J. 519; Peter Russell, *Constitutional Odyssey: Can Canadians Become a Sovereign People?* 3d ed. (Toronto: University of Toronto Press, 2004).

3 *Canadian Charter of Rights and Freedoms*, Part I of the Constitution Act, 1982, being Schedule B to the *Canada Act, 1982* (U.K.), 1982, c. 11.

4 See, e.g., Alan C. Cairns, *Charter versus Federalism: The Dilemmas of Constitutional Reform* (Montreal and Kingston: McGill-Queen's University Press, 1992).

5 Patrick Monahan, *Meech Lake: The Inside Story* (Toronto: University of Toronto Press, 1991) at 20.

6 *Constitutional Accord 1987* (Ottawa: Queen's Printer, 1987).

7 Ibid. at s. 2(1)(b).

8 Ibid. at s. 2(1)(a).

9 The meaning and likely effects of the proposed amendment became highly contested in the political debate that ultimately led to its failure. One of the

controversies related directly to the relationship between the two clauses cited, and whether 2(1)(a) would undermine 2(1)(b).

10 Draft Legal Text (9 October 1992), based on the Charlottetown Accord of 28 August 1992, at s. 2(1)(c).

11 Max Nemni, "The Patriation of the Constitution and the Making of the Canadian Nation," in Bertus de Villiers and Jabu Sindane, eds., *Managing Constitutional Change* (Pretoria, South Africa: HSRC, 1996) 125 at 155.

12 Harold D. Clarke et al., *Absent Mandate: Canadian Electoral Results in an Era of Restructuring*, 3rd ed. (Vancouver: Gage, 1996) at 159.

13 The question was, "Do you agree that Quebec should become sovereign, after having made a formal offer to Canada for a new Economic and Political Partnership, within the scope of the Bill respecting the future of Quebec and of the agreement signed on June 12, 1995?"

14 See, e.g., the Supreme Court of Canada's opinion regarding the process of secession in Canada in *Reference re Secession of Quebec*, [1998] 2 S.C.R. 217, and, in response, the federal government's legislative measure on the "rules" governing secession in Canada: *Clarity Act*, S.C. 2000, c. 26. For varying analyses of the secession issue, see David R. Cameron, ed., *The Referendum Papers: Essays on Secession and National Unity* (Toronto: University of Toronto Press, 1999); Stéphane Dion, "The Dynamics of Secessions: Scenarios after a Pro-separatist Vote in a Quebec Referendum" (1995) 28 Can.J.Pol.Sci 533; Pierre Martin, "Association after Sovereignty? Canadian Views on Economic Association with a Sovereign Quebec" (1995) 21 Can.Pub.Pol'y 53; Dane Rowlands, "International Aspects of the Division of Debt Under Quebec Secession: The Case of Quebec and Canada" (1997) 23 Can. Pub.Pol'y 40; José Woehrling, "Les droits des minorités linguistiques et culturelles en cas d'éventuelle accession du Québec à la souveraineté" (1994) 28 R.J.T. 1035; Robert A. Young, "How Do Peaceful Secessions Happen?" (1994) 27 Can.J.Pol.Sci. 683; Robert A. Young, "Maybe Yes, Maybe No" in Douglas M. Brown and Jonathan W. Rose, eds., *Canada: The State of the Federation, 1995* (Kingston, ON: Institute of Intergovernmental Relations, 1995) 47.

15 *House of Commons Debates*, No. 087 (27 November 2006) at 1245 (Hon. Stéphane Dion).

16 "Tory cabinet minister quits post over motion" (27 November 2006), online: CBC, http://www.cbc.ca/canada/story/2006/11/27/chong-quit-061127.html

17 The Bloc Québécois is the secessionist political party based in Quebec that sees itself as representing Quebec's francophone interests in the House of Commons. It is separate and distinct from the Parti Québécois, whose *raison d'être* is similar but which operates as the secessionist party at the provincial level.

18 *House of Commons Debates*, No. 087 (27 November 2006) at 2035.

19 Ibid. at 1425.

20 "Who's a Québécois? Harper isn't sure" (19 December 2006), online: CBC News, http://www.cbc.ca/canada/story/2006/12/19/harper-motion.html

21 *House of Commons Debates*, No. 087 (27 November 2006) at 1245 (Hon. Stéphane Dion).

22 The full text of the motion reads:THAT the National Assembly: take note of the fact that the House of Commons approved, last 27 November, by a wide majority and with the support of the leaders of all the political parties represented in the Canadian Parliament, the motion moved by the Prime Minister of Canada, which reads as follows: "That this House recognize that the Québécois form a nation within a united Canada"; recognize the positive nature of the motion carried by the House of Commons and that it proclaim that this motion in no way diminishes the inalienable rights, constitutional powers and privileges of the National Assembly of the Québec nation.See Quebec, National Assembly, *Votes and Proceedings*, No. 065 (30 November 2006) at 697, 698.

23 *House of Commons Debates*, No. 087 (27 November 2006) at 1310.

24 Lévesque's scheme called for "sovereignty-association," meaning political sovereignty and an economic association with the rest of Canada. For a general overview of his vision see René Lévesque, "Lévesque offers 'total dedication' to separation" *The Globe and Mail* (17 November 1976), 7. For an earlier iteration of his views, see Lévesque, *Option*, supra note 1. A referendum on the issue was held in Quebec in May 1980; 59.6 per cent of those voting said No to the proposal, while 40.4 per cent supported it. This outcome triggered the patriation process that culminated in the passage of the Constitution Act, 1982.

25 See Don MacPherson, "PQ promises end to Bill 22 tests," *Montreal Gazette* (17 November 1976), 1.

26 *Charter of the French Language*, S.Q. 1977, c. 5 [Bill 101]. Until the 1960s, language was not the focal point of public policy in the French-Canadian struggle for *survivance*; private institutions, such as the Catholic Church, took primary responsibility for maintaining the French language. After the Quiet Revolution, however, a series of language laws passed by the National Assembly of Quebec sought to strengthen the status of French: Bill 63 (1969); Bill 22 (1974); Bill 101 (1977); and Bill 178 (1988). It was, in fact, Bill 22, passed under the first Bourassa administration, that made French the official language of Quebec. See Alain-G. Gagnon and Mary Beth Montcalm, *Quebec: Beyond the Quiet Revolution* (Scarborough, ON: Nelson Canada, 1990) at 175–96.

27 Bill 101, ibid. at s. 1.

28 Ibid. at ss. 2, 3, 7–40.

29 Ibid. at ss. 4, 5, 41–70.

30 Ibid. at ss. 6, 72–88.

31 Quoted in Hal Winter, "The talking's over – Bill 101 is now law" *Montreal Gazette* (27 August 1977), 1.

32 *An Act Respecting Constitutional Amendments*, S.C. 1996, c. 1 [*Constitutional Amendment Act*].

33 Peter W. Hogg, *Constitutional Law of Canada*, looseleaf (Toronto: Carswell, 1997) at 4–23.

34 Tim Swartz and Andrew Heard, "The Regional Veto Formula and Its Effects on Canada's Constitutional Amendment Process" (1997) 30 Can.J.Pol.Sci. 339.

35 *Constitutional Amendment Act,* supra note 32 at s. 1(1).

36 Benoît Pelletier, *La Modification constitutionelle au Canada* (Toronto: Carswell, 1996) at 227 [Pelletier, *Modification*].

37 *Constitution Amendment Proclamation, 1987* (Newfoundland Act), S.I./88-11, C.Gaz. 1988.II.887; *Constitution Amendment Proclamation, 1997* (Newfoundland Act), S.I./97-55, C.Gaz. 1997.II.1; *Constitution Amendment, 1998* (Newfoundland Act), S.I./98-25, C.Gaz. 1998.II.339; *Constitution Amendment, 2001* (Newfoundland and Labrador), S.I./2001-117, C.Gaz. 2001.II.2899. Three of these pertained to the relationship between education and religion in the school system: by 1998, Newfoundland had used the bilateral amendment process to create a secular school system that allowed for non-denominational religious instruction in the classroom. The fourth bilateral constitutional amendment adopted by Newfoundland formally changed the name of the province from "Newfoundland" to "Newfoundland and Labrador."

38 *Constitution Amendment, 1997* (Quebec), S.I./97-141, C.Gaz. 1997.II.1. Quebec effectively ended denominational school boards and replaced them with linguistic ones. With the exception of the French Protestant school boards, this measure was relatively non-controversial.

39 *Constitution Amendment Proclamation, 1993* (Prince Edward Island), S.I./94-50, C.Gaz. 1994.II.2021. Prince Edward Island adopted a constitutional bilateral amendment that allowed for a bridge – in lieu of a ferry – to link the island to the mainland.

40 *Constitution Amendment Proclamation, 1993* (New Brunswick), S.I./93-54, C. Gaz. 1993.II.1588, entrenching equal status for the French and English linguistic communities in the province.

41 Section 47(1) of the Constitution Act, 1982, provides that "[a]n amendment to the Constitution of Canada made by proclamation under section 38, 41, 42 or 43 may be made without a resolution of the Senate authorizing the issue of the proclamation if, within one hundred and eighty days after the adoption by the House of Commons of a resolution authorizing the issue, the Senate has not adopted such a resolution and if, at any time after the expiration of that period, the House of Commons again adopts the resolution."

42 Daniel Proulx, Faculty of Law, University of Ottawa, *Minutes of the Proceedings of the Special Joint Committee to amend Section 93 of the Constitution Act, 1867 concerning the Quebec School System* (21 October 1997) at 26 [*Proceedings of Section 93 Joint Committee*].

43 [emphasis added].

44 Section 41(c) of the Constitution Act, 1982, provides that "[a]n amendment to the Constitution of Canada in relation to the following matters may be made by proclamation issued by the Governor General under the Great Seal of Canada only

where authorized by resolutions of the Senate and House of Commons and of the legislative assembly of the province: ... (c) subject to section 43, the use of the English or French language."

45 *R. v. Beaulac*, [1997] 1 S.C.R. 768 ("The power to make laws with regard to the use of official languages has not been formally inscribed in sections 91 and 92 of the Constitution Act, 1867. It is an ancillary power to the exercise of legislative authority over a class of subjects assigned to Parliament or to provincial legislatures").

46 Constitution Act, 1982, s. 16(3).

47 On 26 October 1992, New Brunswick voted 61.3 per cent in favour of the Charlottetown Accord, which contained a provision pertaining to the equality of the two linguistic communities in New Brunswick. See New Brunswick, Legislative Assembly, *Journal of Debates (Hansard)*, No. 44 (4 December 1992) at 4712 (Hon. Frank McKenna). Thus New Brunswick's initial strategy was to subject the proposal to the general amendment procedure. It was only after Charlottetown failed that the province and the federal government reverted to the s. 43 bilateral amendment procedure.

48 Ibid. at 4721 (Edwin Allen).

49 Ibid. at 4708 (Hon. Frank McKenna).

50 Ibid. at 420 (Hon. Frank McKenna).

51 [1987] 1 S.C.R. 1148.

52 Ibid. at 1158.

53 Ibid. at 1197, 1198. Note that judges writing minority opinions in this case expressly agreed with Justice Wilson on this issue. See Justice Lamer's comments ("I also agree with Wilson J. as to the effect of the *Canadian Charter of Rights and Freedoms* on section 93 of the Constitution Act, 1867"; at 1209) and Justice Estey's comments, writing on behalf of himself and Justice Beetz ("[the Charter] cannot be interpreted as rendering unconstitutional distinctions that are expressly permitted by the Constitution Act, 1867"; at 1206–7).

54 [1996] 3 S.C.R. 609.

55 Ibid. at 643, 644.

56 Ibid. at 639.

57 That said, there is one exception to this interpretation. See comments made by Anne Bayefsky, *Minutes of Proceedings of the Special Joint Committee on the Amendment to Term 17 of the Terms of Union of Newfoundland* (20 November 1997) at 3 [*Proceedings of Term 17 Joint Committee*].

58 Ian Binnie, *Proceedings of the Term 17 Joint Committee* (21 November 1997) at 3, 4. Note that at the time Binnie made this statement he was advising the government of Newfoundland on the constitutionality of the Term 17 amendment.

59 Stéphane Dion, Minister of Intergovernmental Affairs, *Proceedings of Term 17 Joint Committee* (1 December 1997) at 8.

60 See comments made by David Schneiderman, *Proceedings of the Term 17 Joint Committee* (20 November 1997) at 4.

61 See ibid.; Dion, *Proceedings of the Term 17 Joint Committee* (18 November 1997) at 3, *Proceedings of the Term 17 Joint Committee* (1 December 1997) at 7, *Proceedings of Section 93 Joint Committee* (4 November 1997) at 9; Bayefsky, *Proceedings of the Term 17 Joint Committee* (20 November 1997) at 2.

62 Some provincial governments have adopted legislation requiring referenda for constitutional amendments.

63 Stéphane Dion, former minister of intergovernmental affairs, addressed the nature and extent of public support for bilateral amendments throughout his appearances before the joint House of Commons and Senate committees regarding the Newfoundland and Quebec education system proposals. With respect to the Newfoundland initiative, Dion noted that the amendment had substantial support from the majority of the province's population: "If support for the amendment had stood only at 52 or 53%, I would not have advised Premier Tobin to bring it before Parliament." *Proceedings of the Term 17 Joint Committee* (18 November 1987) at 3, 10. Similarly, speaking before the committee examining the Quebec proposal, Dion explained that "a reasonable consensus" existed for the measure. *Proceedings of Section 93 Joint Committee* (21 October 1997) at 1.

64 Schneiderman, *Proceedings of the Term 17 Joint Committee* (20 November 1997) at 5. Also see comments by Patrick Monahan, Faculty of Law, York University, *Proceedings of Section 93 Joint Committee* (29 October 1997) at 3.

65 Monahan, ibid.

66 Ibid.

67 Dion, *Proceedings of Section 93 Joint Committee* (21 October 1997) at 14.

68 The application for leave to appeal to the Supreme Court of Canada was dismissed by L'Heureux-Dubé, Bastarache, and LeBel JJ on 9 November 2000 (appeal no. 27865).

69 (2000), 183 D.L.R. (4th) 225, 2000 NFCA 12 (CanLII) [*Hogan* cited to CanLII].

70 Ibid. at para. 73, citing Peter W. Hogg, *Constitutional Law of Canada*, [4th ed. (Scarborough, ON: Carswell, 1997)] at 4–4.

71 Ibid. at para 125.

72 Bayefsky, *Proceedings of the Term 17 Joint Committee* (20 November 1997) at 15.

73 Ibid. at 11.

74 Dion, *Proceedings of the Term 17 Joint Committee* (1 December 1997) at 8.

75 Ibid. at 9, 12.

76 Peter W. Hogg, *Constitutional Law of Canada*, looseleaf (Scarborough, ON: Carswell, 2005) at 4–27, n. 103; Proulx, *Proceedings of Section 93 Joint Committee* (21 October) 1997 at 32; Pelletier, *Modification*, supra note 58 at 253.

77 Section 27 reads: "This Charter shall be interpreted in a manner consistent with the preservation and enhancement of the multicultural heritage of Canadians."

78 A possible model for this second provision might be s. 21 of the Charter, which reads: "Nothing in sections 16 to 20 abrogates or derogates from any right, privilege or obligation with respect to the English and French languages, or either

of them, that exists or is continued by virtue of any other provision of the Constitution of Canada." An additional option might be to detail the rights and privileges of English in Quebec, in a manner parallel to what is done for French and English in Canada and New Brunswick in ss. 17, 18, and 19. Section 23, which relates to minority-language educational rights, would of course continue to apply.

79   Meech Lake's proposed new s. 2 of the Constitution Act, 1867, recognized French- and English-speaking majorities and minorities across Canada, as well as Quebec as a distinct society, and spoke of the roles of the Parliament of Canada and the provincial legislatures, as well as specifically of the role of the legislature and government of Quebec. The proposed Canada Clause in the Charlottetown text referred to Canada's system of government; Aboriginal peoples; Quebec's distinct society; official language minority communities; cultural and racial diversity; individual and collective rights; gender equality; and the equality of the provinces, as well as the legislatures and governments of Canada and the provinces and the legislative bodies and government of the Aboriginal peoples.

80   What Peter Hogg said of the interpretive provision of Meech Lake (s. 2(1) of the legal text) is relevant here: "Subsection 1 is expressly an interpretive provision. It neither confers power nor denies power. It will be relevant only where other constitutional provisions are unclear or ambiguous, and where reference to the ideas of linguistic duality or distinct society would help to clarify the meaning." Peter W. Hogg, *Meech Lake Constitutional Accord Annotated* (Toronto: Carswell, 1988) at 12.

81   This second step of any Charter analysis is undertaken pursuant to s. 1, which provides that "[t]he *Canadian Charter of Rights and Freedoms* guarantees the rights and freedoms set out in it subject only to such reasonable limits prescribed by law as can be demonstrably justified in a free and democratic society." The leading case on the interpretation of s. 1 of the Charter is *R. v. Oakes*, [1986] 1 S.C.R. 103.

16 The Paradox of Federalism: Some Practical Reflections

Regional and Federal Studies 2009

Jan Erk, one of the guest editors of an issue of Regional and Federal Studies, *asked if I would contribute my thoughts. The central question for the issue was whether federalism fosters or inhibits secession. I had had a lively private correspondence with Ron Watts, perhaps the most distinguished student of federalism of his generation, and the exchanges had given me the occasion to set down some of my thinking on the matter. This material formed the basis of the practical reflections contained in this article. They were informed by the challenges of post-conflict constitutional development I had experienced in Sri Lanka, Iraq, and elsewhere, and by my membership on the Board of the Forum of Federations.*

Introduction

This collection of essays on the paradox of federalism tackles one of the central conundrums of federal theory, and one of the issues of greatest practical concern to those considering the federal option. Does federalism foster secession or inhibit it? Many of today's conflict-ridden political communities, considering the introduction of federal structures as a possible resolution of their problems, would dearly love to know the answer to the question.

The opening paper by Jan Erk and Lawrence Anderson sets out the issue very clearly and reviews the scholarly literature on the subject. Erk and Anderson explore the paradox in the light of three dimensions: the will and capacity of the sub-units (and presumably of the central government as well); institutional design (for example: the nature and number of subunits; the distribution of powers; representation in central institutions; the electoral and party systems;

the judiciary); and what they call uncodified factors, the extra-constitutional socio-economic factors that provide the context within which the formal structures and processes of government exist. What I propose to do here is offer some reflections about federalism and secession that have arisen out of practical experience working on federal issues in existing, emerging, and potential federations. For purposes of this discussion, I will concentrate primarily on three countries: Sri Lanka, Iraq, and Canada.

As I see it – at least in the short term – the institutional structure of federalism is a distinctly secondary matter when it comes to understanding why a country is or is not facing secession. It is not that it doesn't matter, but that it matters far less than a number of other forces and factors, which mostly fall into the Erk and Anderson uncodified category. This is not to deny that federalism gives subnational units political resources that can be deployed in the service of a secessionist movement. But it is to say that the active utilization of these institutional resources in the service of secession is unlikely in the absence of other more significant factors, such as a territorially concentrated minority's protracted experience of discrimination and exclusion.

That is the short term. In the longer term, I am not so sure. It is clear that, with the passage of time, the formative power of institutions is considerable, and the political identities that are often at the root of secessionist movements can be as much the product of institutional structures and processes as the reverse. Just as nation states may become more distinctive and differentiated as the years pass, so may subnational units, especially if they are the home of ethnocultural minority groups (Young 1995, 182–183). Differentiation does not always or necessarily happen, however, and even if it does, this does not automatically lead to increased tension and the risk of fracture. Indeed, as Quebec's experience shows, the reverse process can sometimes lead to increased tension. Historically, French Canada stood apart from the rest of North America, with a lifestyle and culture that were palpably different; the rise of the secessionist movement in Quebec in the 1960s was the product in part of a process of modernization, in which, according to several social indicators (urbanization, secularization, participation in the market economy), Quebecers became *more like* Canadians elsewhere in the country.

Nevertheless, one can get a glimpse of the constitutive power of federal structures by looking at what sometimes happens when new subnational units are created in federations. In Canada, Saskatchewan and Alberta, for example, were carved out of the North West Territories in 1905. That they are the willed creation of an actor at a defined historical moment can be seen in their shape – rectangular, with borders as straight as a surveyor's line, except for the south-western frontier of Alberta, which is defined by the Rocky Mountains, which the province shares with British Columbia. The north-south boundary between Alberta and Saskatchewan is simply a meridian of longitude.

Quite rapidly after their establishment as new provinces in the Canadian federation, Saskatchewan and Alberta began to develop their own distinctive character. Settlement patterns and the emerging political economy of the two communities led to a growing differentiation of one from the other. What had begun as little more than arbitrary lines drawn on a map by federal officials quickly became the borders of distinctive communities. Politically, both were populist, but Saskatchewan developed a left-wing political culture, while Alberta generated a right-of-centre politics. I am not saying that the creation of these provincial institutions produced a secessionist movement, although at times during the post-war period it would have been only a slight stretch to speak of Albertan nationalism, as the province's political leaders self-consciously went about constructing a provincial state and community defined by its oil and gas wealth, its integration into the mid-West North American oil and resource culture, and its commitment to an ideology of private enterprise and individualistic self-reliance – a far cry from the communitarian political culture of Saskatchewan next door, which proved to be the birthplace of Canadian socialism (and public healthcare in Canada). The observation of experiences such as these cannot but make one respectful of the creative power of institutions, operating over the long haul.

Nevertheless, I would contend that the role of political structures such as these is primarily, although not exclusively, instrumental. They provide significant resources to politicians and communities within larger political systems to do what it is they wish to do. But only to a limited extent do the structures themselves lead provincial or subnational actors to wish to do something they would not otherwise want to do. Primarily, they assist in the realization of needs and aspirations that are shaped by forces that transcend the simple realities of federalism. While it is true, for example, that the systematic oppression of a region by a federal government dominated by another community can foster secessionist sentiments, it is equally true that the same result can occur for the same reasons in a unitary state; it is the fact of oppression, more than the availability of subnational political authority, that makes the difference. Sri Lanka's experience illuminates this fact. The secessionist violence of the Liberation Tigers of Tamil Eelam (LTTE) broke out within a unitary state, and their *chateau fort* has always been the north, where the Indigenous Tamil population has traditionally been concentrated. Ironically, until recently, the long-running civil war produced a kind of unconstitutional caricature of federalism in Sri Lanka, in which the writ of the national government stopped in many parts of the north, and the LTTE independently operated schools, hospitals, the police force, and social services. (The territory which the LTTE controls is currently being significantly reduced as the military force of the Sri Lankan government pushes the Tigers back into smaller enclaves.)

Federalism Then and Now

In classical liberal theory,[1] individuals escape from the state of nature and enter civil society by agreeing to a social contract that establishes legitimate political power from which all will benefit and by which all will be bound. Similarly, in classical federal theory, autonomous political communities freely join together to form a new, complex polity from which all will benefit and by which all will be bound. The constitution is federalism's social contract.

Contemporary federal experience, however, is rather different. Instead of the image of free peoples coming together to build something better, the picture today is often of warring communities, locked in a political relationship from which they cannot escape. Federalism, in such melancholy situations as these, often presents itself as each community's reluctant second choice – a system designed to make an unsatisfactory situation habitable.

The challenges confronting the founders of contemporary federations of this sort are, therefore, rather different from what classical theory assumes. Instead of showing the federating communities the mutual benefits that justify coming together in a new federal union, federal lawgivers are often faced with the bleaker task of taking something apart, of replacing an existing political union, which has ceased to be just or viable, with a more complex political association constructed on the foundation of pluralism.

In the contemporary world, the federal moment seems as often as not to arrive toward the end of acute civil conflict, when a grudging realization emerges among the combatants that the old regime cannot stand, but that the utter collapse of the state is not tolerable either. Federalism, then, often appeals to countries and to an international order struggling with ethno-cultural conflict, separatist movements, and terrorism. It may be that the cradle of federalism in the twenty-first century will be found as much in countries such as Sudan, the Congo, Sri Lanka, Nepal, and Iraq as in, let us say, the United Kingdom or Italy.

What seems undeniable is that for the last decade or so, we have been living through an intense period of innovation and experimentation in federal and other forms of governance (Griffiths, 2005: xv, 3; Hueglin and Fenna, 2006: ch. 1; Watts, 1999: 4–6). At first blush, it seems equally undeniable that in many, if not most, of the cases confronting the contemporary world of federal innovation the relevance of earlier experience associated with the constitution of federations from previously autonomous units seems to be of relatively limited value. Historically, the central issue confronting federal countries, such as the USA, Switzerland, and Canada, at their founding seems to have been the costs and benefits of a new form of political association, rather than the political calculus of secession. Federalism by composition does not seem to raise the question of secession in as acute a way, as does federal creation by devolution.

Yet, closer scrutiny of these "classical" cases leads us to refine this observation. The federal union was adopted by the United States in 1789 on the ashes of the failed confederation which had been in existence since 1781. It took a brutal civil war in the 1860s to answer the question whether American states had a right to secede from the union. The Swiss federation was created in 1848 after the Sonderbund Civil War of the previous year. Through a series of referendums in the 1970s, the new canton of Jura was created out of part of the canton of Berne; the presence of the Swiss army was required at one point to keep the peace, so intense was the conflict over what might be termed a form of "internal secession." Two of the six British North American colonies that participated in the talks leading to the establishment of the Canadian federation in 1867 declined to join at the beginning, not being prepared to trust their community's welfare to this new, untried political organization. And Nova Scotia, one of the four founding members of the new federation, attempted unsuccessfully to secede the year after the federal bargain was struck. The contemporary Quebec sovereignist movement is, of course, well known internationally. The state of West Australia, too, tried unsuccessfully to secede from the Australian federation 32 years after it was formed in 1901.

So it would be a mistake to conclude that the challenges of integration and the question of secession are matters unknown to the classical, successful federations that blazed the trail for others. Each of them had to wrestle with the suspicion and fear that attends a new and untried political organization. All have known periods of significant tension and uncertainty; all, so far, have survived.

The central question posed for this issue of *Regional and Federal Studies* implies the prior existence of a federation or decentralized political system from which secession is a possibility. In seeking to understand whether federal and decentralized systems foster or inhibit secession, the natural approach is to examine the conditions or circumstances that appear to encourage or discourage fracture. The papers in this issue display the complexity of the question and the variety of real-life answers that may be offered in response, whether it be a question of Bosnia and Kosovo, Punjab, the UK, Spain, Italy, or Belgium.

In these concluding reflections, though, it may be of value to employ a somewhat different approach in tackling this question – namely, to reflect on the circumstances or conditions that permit a federal form of government to come into being in the first place. Certainly, this is an acute issue for many of the "federation-seeking" countries emerging out of circumstances of violent conflict. If we can understand the factors that support the emergence of a federal regime, we may be in a better position to appreciate the forces that may lead to its collapse. If it is possible to identify the conditions that appear to be necessary for a federation to establish itself in the first place, one can then speculate about what happens when some or all of these conditions cease to exist in functioning federations. Secession might be understood, from this point of view, as the withdrawal of the critical conditions needed for the continued existence of the federal system. What can one say, then, about the prerequisite conditions for the construction of a federal regime?

Prerequisites

There has been some significant discussion of this issue, although it would be wrong to conclude that a consensus or a satisfactory conclusion has been reached on the subject. I will refer to the writings of K.C. Wheare (1963) and Ronald L. Watts (2004) in this discussion.

One of the frustrating – but, from our point of view, potentially significant – characteristics of much of the consideration of federal prerequisites is the fact that it is very difficult to disentangle those features that are peculiarly related to the introduction and maintenance of a federal regime from those that underlie decent, constitutional, democratic systems of any kind, whether federal, unitary, consociational, parliamentary, or congressional. The difficulty is this: many of the things that might be identified as prerequisites of a federal system also look pretty much like prerequisites of a properly functioning liberal democratic state of whatever kind.

Let us take K.C. Wheare's list in chapter 3 of *Federal Government*, "Some Prerequisites of Federal Government." His analysis is based on the assumption that federalism emerges out of the common desire of previously more or less autonomous units to associate; it does not really deal with devolutionary federal processes, where the considerations look quite different. Wheare's starting out position – that federalism requires a desire to live under a single government, combined with a desire to live under regional governments and a capacity to work under this dual system – seems sound for any circumstances, but, as he acknowledges, it does not get you very far. It is little more than the attitudinal definition of the federal principle itself.

The factors expressing a desire for shared rule, according to Wheare (military insecurity/common defence, desire for independence from foreign powers, hope of economic advantage, some form of anterior political association, geographical neighbourhood, similarity of political institutions, political leadership) seem most easily related to integrative federalizing processes. They may have something to say about the globalizing and multigovernance dynamics at the international level, but less about many of the most acute domestic or within-state federal challenges facing communities in the twenty-first century.

In a presentation to a colloquium in Switzerland on the relevance of federalism as a tool of conflict management in the Near East, Ronald Watts (2004, 8) presented a list of the significant political processes and practices on which the effectiveness of different federations has depended:

1 disposition to democratic procedures
2 non-centralization as a principle
3 checks and balances to limit the concentration of political power
4 open political bargaining for making collective decisions
5 genuine group power-sharing within central institutions, often consociational
6 respect for constitutionalism and the rule of law

Clearly, the first and the sixth on this list sustain good government in general, whether federal or not. The practices identified in points 2–5 above are more obviously, although by no means exclusively, related to effective federal operations.

If, for example, one takes the fifth – power-sharing within central institutions – clearly, that can be a vital component in the effective operation of a culturally diverse unitary state and, indeed, an incapacity to share power in this way can be a spur to introduce federal elements into a pluralist political community under stress. Unalloyed majoritarian democracy in a unitary state can create injustices, driving a political community towards secession movements or pressures for federal reform, which is why, perhaps, Watts's statement concerning the first process above is qualified ("a strong disposition to democratic procedures *since they presume the voluntary consent of the different groups of citizens in the constituent units*"). A popular appreciation of the limits as well as the power of democracy, including a respect for minorities, seems essential in a federal regime, but it seems equally essential in a diverse community endowed with a unitary state, if it is to remain just and stable.

Later in the same paper (15–16), Watts speaks directly of five necessary preconditions for federal or confederal solutions to operate effectively in moderating multicultural conflict:

1 the will to federate
2 underlying shared values and objectives
3 trust
4 development of a political culture emphasizing sharing and co-operation and fostering respect for constitutional norms and structures and the rule of law
5 supportive economic conditions, including complementary economies, common economic interests, and the moderation of economic disparities

Again, what is striking about this list is the fact that all but the first (which is, in a sense, a formal requirement) apply as much to the workability of non-federal solutions as federal or confederal solutions. If preconditions 2–5 are sufficiently present in a society, it is perhaps a pardonable exaggeration to say that almost any political system can be made to work; if they are absent, then no constitutional or political regime is likely to work, or work very well.

If this line of reasoning is broadly correct, then the issue for those countries emerging from serious conflict is not so much "What are the preconditions necessary for a federal solution?" but "How does one cope with the absence of some or all of the preconditions necessary for a constitutional, broadly consensual, democratic solution of any kind?" That is an awesomely difficult question, and one to which I would be the first to admit I do not have the answer, but it does not seem to me to be a specifically federal challenge.

Sri Lanka and Iraq are two countries that have been actively discussing federal models in recent years. The Sri Lankan efforts during the 2002–05 peace negotiations under the auspices of the Cease Fire Agreement were shelved with little accomplished, and civil war has broken out again. Iraq proceeded further faster, at least in constitutional development, negotiating a federal constitution in the summer of 2005 that is now being fitfully implemented. How do they line up with the five preconditions outlined above? It seems to me that both are notably deficient in meeting preconditions 2–5. Iraq, at the moment, dramatically fails test 5 (supportive economic conditions); Sri Lanka, less so. But, on the question of shared values, trust, and a supportive political culture, both are in very bad shape, and this reality sets the terms that must be met in fashioning any workable political settlement, not just a possible federal arrangement.

If the terms thought necessary for the introduction of a federal political system are absent, why has federalism been so central to the political debate in these two cases? A theoretical alternative would be to tackle directly the issues of trust, shared values, and political culture, and leave the choice of constitutional arrangement for another day. I assume that the reason why factors such as these are not being focused on is because there is a recognition that trust cannot be established, shared values cannot be created, and political cultures cannot be changed directly and in the immediate term. These developments occur in the course of doing something else, as indirect by-products of other human activity. What other kind of human activity seems a plausible candidate here? In most cases, it is thought to be the peace process itself. It is the discussions, the negotiations, the trade-offs, and compromises – it is this testing crucible of finding accommodations under severe pressure that, if successful, turns enemies into associates in a common enterprise, transforms enmity and suspicion into trust, and begins to reveal the common interests and purposes that lie beneath entrenched conflict. South Africa, buttressed by extraordinary leadership, seems to be one of the few instances in which a generally successful transition has been made.

This offers an account of why we do not typically attempt to tackle these principled deficiencies head on, but it does not explain or justify the selection of federalism as the preferred institutional arrangement. Why federalism? As often as not, and certainly in the cases of Sri Lanka and Iraq, it is because there appears to be no other better alternative. It is not a first choice; it is everybody's second choice. The Sinhalese majority and the Government of Sri Lanka would prefer a unitary state; so would many of the Sunnis of Iraq. The Sri Lankan Tamils, at least as represented by the LTTE, and the Kurds of northern Iraq, would rather have an independent state. Neither of the parties to these conflicts can get what they want, if negotiation rather than force is to settle the issue. Federalism is what the parties fall back on. So the relevant question at this point is not, properly speaking: "Why federalism?" but rather "Is there any other alternative that is better?" If the answer to that question is no, one is left with the task of trying to work something out, despite the forbidding obstacles to its realization.

The factors that seem to lead to the selection of federalism as the best – or the least bad – arrangement in the circumstances, include the following:

- The parties to the conflict, or the participants in the process, begin from preferred positions that are mutually incompatible – secession and independence, on the one hand; and a centralized, unitary state, on the other.
- Neither side, through force or diplomacy, is capable of imposing its will on the other.
- International actors are flatly opposed to secession, but recognize the actual or potential injustice and discrimination embedded in the maintenance of the existing arrangements.
- The pressures to make peace, or to achieve a negotiated settlement, are greater than the incentives for going – or going back – to war.

These are hardly the preconditions for the establishment of a successful federation, but they are the brute pressures that lead the parties in conflict to this negotiating ground. It is clear that, in these circumstances, the prospect of a successful outcome is modest, but it seems to me that it would be equally modest if one had some other political and constitutional end in view. The difficulty lies not so much with the absence of the necessary preconditions for federalism, but with the absence of the necessary preconditions for successful peacemaking and constitution building of any kind.

Indeed, it is my view that consociational forms and practices would have sufficed to sustain a unitary Sri Lankan state if they had been conscientiously introduced four decades ago; it is, as much as anything, because of the utter failure to do so that the country finds itself faced with a starker, simpler choice today: to negotiate an end to the violence and civil conflict, or to carry on like two scorpions in a bottle. If a negotiated termination of the civil conflict is to be achieved, it will in the present unhappy circumstances necessarily entail some form of federalism. This analysis cannot leave one optimistic about the prospects for federalism in Sri Lanka, but neither can it leave one optimistic about the prospects for peace and reconstruction in Sri Lanka more generally. Yet, it would seem perverse to set aside all discussion of federalism in that country because it will be so very difficult to achieve. If there was a plausible, preferable alternative, so be it: but if there is none, then *faute de mieux* the effort to construct some form of federal system in the country seems a worthwhile enterprise.

A parallel, although not identical, stream of analysis seems to me to apply to Iraq as well. It possesses a federal constitution, although it is not by any means a fully federal country yet. If Iraq ceases to be a going concern at some point, it would seem obtuse to visit the blame on its federal structure. Surely, its failure to survive as a single political community, federal or not, will be the result of its sad history and toxic political culture, more than the product of its particular constitutional regime. As Ron Watts (1999, 110–11) said in a chapter on the pathology of federations, "it is not so much because they are federations that countries have been difficult to govern but that it is because they were difficult to govern in the first place that they adopted federation as a form of government."

Canada and Quebec

For many years, Canada has had one of the most powerful secessionist movements in the modern world, and some brief reflections on that experience may be of some use in considering the theme of this issue. The creation of Quebec as a subnational unit in 1867 permitted that predominantly francophone society to develop in substantial degree according to its own genius, first as a conservative, Catholic realm and, more recently, as a modern, urban, secular, French-speaking society. The Canadian federation has so far managed to accommodate these transformations, including the rise in the 1960s and 1970s of a very powerful secession movement. The sovereignty movement in Quebec displays a couple of distinctive features relevant to our story. First, it has been non-violent. Since the October Crisis of 1970, the Quebec sovereignists have been relentlessly democratic and peaceful in the pursuit of their ambitions. Secondly, it has been, paradoxically, an independence movement which has not really been in pursuit of full-scale independence. With the exception of a few hard-line separatists, the movement has consistently sought sovereignty *plus* continued, close association with the rest of Canada – sovereignty with a difference. As a Québécois wag put it: "What do Quebecers want? They want a free and independent Quebec within a strong and united Canada."

Why is this so? Why has the movement been peaceful, and why has it aimed as much at an altered relationship with the rest of Canada as at outright independence? My suspicion is that these two distinctive features are related to the country's standing as a constitutional, democratic – and deeply federal – state. It has never been plausible to argue that the Québécois are an oppressed people. And when advocates of the independence of Quebec emerged in the 1960s, there was never any inclination to brand them as traitors. Secession was seen to be within the ambit of free and legitimate expression and, implicitly, I think, other Canadians reacted to the challenge within the frame of reference of what might be called the double-consent theory – namely, that it was not just Canadians as individuals, but the two main linguistic communities of Canada that need to consent to the state for it to retain its authority.

Not only that; political power in Canada, since the rise of the sovereignist movement in the 1960s has been flowing to the provincial governments, in part because of the demands of Quebec nationalists for greater autonomy. Both the demand for self-rule and the demand for shared rule – in this case, equitable francophone participation in the affairs of the Canadian government – have been addressed, at least in significant degree. And, just as Quebec has been transforming its society, so too has the rest of Canada been changing – especially in the cities – moving from a traditional, British view of itself, to a multi-racial, highly pluralistic society, powerfully shaped by waves of post-war immigration. If the country is free, democratic, prosperous and – however untidily and imperfectly – flexible in accommodating the evolving requirements of the national minority, how seriously will its members feel the need to leave? These features of Canadian society have sustained the country during its worst moments, which have been when questions of national identity have been allowed to rise to the symbolic and constitutional level.

The last four decades of national-unity debate have engendered another characteristic of Canadian society, and it too has shaped the country's approach to secession.[2] The Quebec sovereignty movement's sustained and powerful challenge to the very existence of the country has fostered an uneasy realization among many Canadians that their hold on Canada is a matter of *contingent possession*. It has not been possible during these years to assume that the country in which Canadians live is effectively eternal, that it will always be there for its citizens. Canadians have had to recognize that it may not. With the assistance of the Supreme Court of Canada, Canadians have learned that even the possible dismantling of one of the most successful countries in the world could be justified by the values they hold dear, and could be executed by democratic means. In its decision in the *Quebec Secession Reference*, the Supreme Court of Canada identified four fundamental, unstated principles that support Canada's constitutional order: federalism; democracy; constitutionalism and the rule of law; and respect for minority rights. It discovered a constitutional duty to negotiate with Quebec in the event that a clear majority of the citizens of Quebec in response to a clear question favoured the secession of the province. In doing so, it established in constitutional law the contingent nature of Canadian political affiliation.

Not for Canada the ringing declarations of France, *une république indivisible*, or Italy, *La Repubblica, una e indivisibile*, or Brazil, *formada pela união indissolúvel dos Estados e Municípios e do Distrito Federal*, or Australia, one indissoluble Federal Commonwealth under the Crown of the United Kingdom of Great Britain and Ireland; Canada, for its part, will exist as long as Canadians will it. As Ernest Renan said, a nation is a "plébiscite de tous les jours." There are worse foundations on which to construct a political community. Canadians are learning that the values for which the country stands can and should obtain even during its possible break-up. This lesson deprives the country of national glory, but it speaks to the practical functions the state is expected to perform – in Canada, to provide the blessings of peace, order, and good government. It reminds Canadians that the state itself is a human artefact, reared up to serve the interests and needs of the people for whom it is responsible, not an entity endowed with intrinsic moral or spiritual value. What Canada asks of its citizens is adherence to the constitution and the values underlying the constitutional order, not doctrinal acceptance of a universal patriotic creed. It is within the framework of these values that the accommodation of diversity – even, possibly, the accommodation of secession – is to be found. Canadian experience encourages the "desacralization" of the public realm. What Canadian today believes that it is the sacred duty of citizens to preserve the state and the national community and that, to seek the opposite, is treason? Canadians cannot afford that view. How, with that view, would the country do business with the substantial minority of the population who hold democratically to the conviction that the Canadian experiment has more or less failed and should be wound up? How would they treat with what is often a sovereignist Government of Quebec, or with a sovereignist political party in the federal Parliament?

Here, it seems, is a case in which the accommodation of a national minority appears to have blunted the force of secession. In fact, the apparent willingness to accommodate the actual secession of Quebec, should that be necessary, appears to have been part of the context in which the power of the secessionist movement in Canada has, at least for the time being, waned. The situation is reminiscent of the paradoxical comment that was sometimes made by Quebec nationalists: "Recognize our right to national self-determination so that we won't use it." The daily plebiscite has so far been favourable to Canada.

Conclusion

This leads us back to where we began. Does federalism foster or inhibit secession? As with so many good questions in social science, the answer seems to be yes. It offers institutional resources to actors to help them achieve what they want to accomplish, but what they want to accomplish is only to a relatively limited extent shaped by the institutions of federalism. Federalism is unlikely to hold an unjust regime together; but, equally, it is unlikely to pull a just regime apart. Justice – rather than a glorified governing instrument – is surely closer to the heart of the matter than federalism.

To the extent that, in a liberal democratic regime, the crude proxy of justice is consent, federalism introduces the communitarian dimension of justice often missing in unitary states. If, for example, there are national communities within the boundaries of a political regime, if there are territorially concentrated linguistic or ethnic groups, or regional religious communities, then there is a need to justify the political order, whether federal or not, on communitarian principles as well as individualistic ones. It seems reasonable to conclude that the likelihood of there being a secession movement in a given polity turns more on how people are treated than on whether or not they are federally governed.

NOTES

1 These three paragraphs are drawn from Cameron, 2007a.
2 The next two paragraphs are drawn from Cameron, 2007b, 82–83.

REFERENCES

Cameron, D. 2007a. "Making Federalism Work." In *Iraq: Preventing a New Generation of Conflict*, edited by M.E. Bouillon, D. Malone, and B. Rowswell, 153–167. Boulder and London: Lynne Rienner.

Cameron, D. 2007b. "An Evolutionary Story." In *Uneasy Partners: Multiculturalism and Rights in Canada*, edited by J.G. Stein, D.R. Cameron, J. Ibbitson, W. Kymlicka, J. Meisel, H. Siddiqui, and M. Valpy, 71–94. Waterloo: Wilfrid Laurier University Press.

Griffiths, A.L., ed. 2005. *Handbook of Federal Countries, 2005*. Montreal: McGill-Queen's University Press.

Hueglin, T.O., and A. Fenna. 2006. *Comparative Federalism: A Systematic Inquiry*. Peterborough: Broadview Press.

Watts, R.L. 1999. *Comparing Federal Systems*, 2nd ed. Montreal: McGill-Queen's University Press.

Watts, R.L. 2004. "Federal Co-existence in the Near East: General Introduction." Paper presented at the Jean Nordmann Foundation Colloquium on "Federalism: A Tool for Conflict Management in Multicultural Societies with Regard to the Conflicts in the Near East," Fribourg.

Wheare, K.C. 1963. *Federal Government*, 4th ed. Oxford: Oxford University Press.

Young, R.A. 1995. *The Secession of Quebec and the Future of Canada*. Montreal: McGill-Queen's Press.

17 Church and State in a Binational Multicultural Society: The Case of Canada

In Anita Shapira, Yedida Stern, and Alexander Yakobson, eds.,
The Nation State and Religion: The Resurgence of Faith   2013

At the suggestion of Derek Penslar, the distinguished scholar of modern Jewish history, the Israel Democracy Institute invited me to an international workshop on religion and the nation-state. I was asked to present the paper on Canada. Having recently read Ahmet Kuru's stimulating book on secularism in the United States, France, and Turkey, I decided to look at secularism in Canada, and in particular to seek to understand why secularism presented itself so differently in Quebec and English-speaking Canada. Kuru's volume offered a helpful framework within which to think through this issue.

Religion and language were the two most problematic matters British authorities had to confront when New France passed into the hands of Britain in the latter part of the eighteenth century. British policy makers lived in a country with an established Protestant religion; they had now to cope in their new imperial possession with a coherent, 65,000-member strong community in British North America that was Roman Catholic and French. Forced to decide between expulsion, suppression, or accommodation, the British ultimately chose accommodation, though not without hesitation, and perhaps not always for the best of reasons.

The Quebec Act of 1774 has often been called the charter of French Canada. Passed in anticipation of the pending American Revolution of 1775–81, the Quebec Act offered French Canada, and especially its elites, much of what they sought: toleration of French Canada's way of life, the establishment of the Roman Catholic Church and its power to collect tithes, a special oath to permit Catholics to hold civil office, an acceptance of the seigneurial land holding system, and recognition of French civil law. All these provisions were made in the hope of securing the loyalty of the French-Canadian community in the face of the pending American rebellion. The Quebec Act placed political authority in the hands of the governor and an appointed council, again giving reassurance to the French-Canadian elites that their interests would not be trampled by an unruly English assembly.

The Constitutional Act, passed in 1791 after the American Revolution had successfully delivered independence to the United States, recognized the loss of territory to the United States, and attempted to cope with the heavy influx of Loyalist immigration to British North America by dividing Quebec into Upper and Lower Canada, implicitly acknowledging Lower Canada as the homeland of the French Canadians. It retained French civil law and the establishment of the Roman Catholic Church in Lower Canada, and supported the introduction of representative government in both Canadas, with French Canadians enjoying political rights to vote and run for office in the Lower Canada Assembly.[1]

Modern Canada's founding document, the Constitution Act, 1867, provides critical protection to the two religious communities, guaranteeing the right to denominational schools – in Quebec, for the Protestant minority, and in Ontario, for the Catholic minority. Issues of church and state, then, are embedded in the founding of Canada. But Catholic-Protestant relations, so central to Canada's history, have receded in importance in the last half-century; indeed, today, they have virtually disappeared as a public issue.

In recent years, however, Canada, like many other Western countries, has been learning to cope with the many other religions its immigrant populations have brought to its shores. For the most part, this has been unproblematic, but there have been challenges. Conflict within British Columbia's Sikh community has led to violence on several occasions, and Canadian Sikh militants were behind the biggest act of terrorism in Canadian history, the bombing of Air India Flight 182, which went down in the Atlantic in 1985, killing 329 people. But in general, in Canada, I think it is fair to say, the evolving relationship between religion and the state has not been nearly as fraught as it has been in many other countries. The growing presence and impact of Islam has occasioned discussion in Canada, as it has in other Western societies, particularly since 9/11. Nevertheless, while church-state relations are at times the subject of public debate in Canada, and occasionally legal dispute and political action, rarely do discussions reach the heated and passionate levels one witnesses in many other countries.

It is true, though, that our history of wrestling with the relationship between Roman Catholics and Protestants intersects in complex ways with the secular patterns within which Canadians lead their contemporary lives. In my consideration of church-state relations in Canada, I will examine two dimensions of Canadian social and public life: first, the fact that Canada is a country composed of two societies, today defined chiefly by language; and second, that it is a multicultural society, profoundly shaped by its cultural diversity, the product of waves of continuing, substantial immigration.

Matters of Religion in Canada Today

Canada is clearly a secular society, by which I mean a political community in which matters of religion are largely left to the private realm and in which religious forces have minimal effect on political matters.[2] There is today no established church in Canada. The Constitution Act, 1867, does not mention God or religion except, as I have said, to protect (in Section 93) the right of the Catholic minority in Ontario and the Protestant minority in Quebec to denominational schools. In contemporary Canadian civil society, both in English-speaking Canada and Quebec, religion is deemed to fall in the private sphere, religious pluralism is the order of the day, and there is a widely accepted attitude of live and let live.

Canada is also a binational society.[3] Perhaps the best way of understanding that is to look at its linguistic composition. While the country's 34 million people speak an impressive range of languages, there are only two linguistically complete societies. It is possible to live a full, modern life in French or in English in Canada. Francophones in Quebec can lead a complete life – educationally, socially, culturally, politically – in French, just as Anglophones elsewhere in Canada can in English. The existence of these two national communities, defined today chiefly by language, but embodying very different historical experiences, constitutes the defining fault line in Canada. Immigrants to Canada enter into one or other of these two national groups. The hypothesis of this essay is that the history, character, and political experience of these two communities have fostered somewhat different approaches within the two societies to the management of religion in the public sphere.

I am arguing that there are differences in the secular patterns and practices in Quebec, as compared to the rest of Canada. English-speaking Canada seems to be at ease with, and, at times, almost casual about the varieties of religious forms and practices in its midst, and the diverse ways in which religious belief and spiritual matters penetrate, or fail to penetrate the public realm. Quebec, less so; the Québécois commitment to secularism appears to be more vigorous than elsewhere in the country, and perceived challenges to the principles of secularism seem to occasion great anxiety and opposition. More seems to be riding on the matter in Quebec. Secularism appears to be something that has simply happened over time to English-speaking Canada; in Quebec, secularism – in recent years, sometimes described as *laïcité* there – seems in some measure to be willed.

This essay explores the different pattern of relationships between church and state in French Quebec and English-speaking Canada. It will provide an account of the somewhat distinctive approaches to secularism in the French-speaking and English-speaking societies of Canada, and argue that these can be explained chiefly by the different historical experiences of each, and the distinctive situation each finds itself in within North America.

Assertive Secularism versus Passive Secularism

A recently published book offers what I think is a very helpful framework for analyzing the Canadian experience. Ahmet Kuru's *Secularism and State Policies toward Religion: The United States, France, and Turkey* seeks to explain the differences in secularism in France, Turkey, and the United States. Kuru makes a distinction between assertive secularism *(laïcité de combat)* and passive secularism *(laïcité plurielle)*.[4] Assertive secularism, according to Kuru, "requires the state to play an 'assertive' role to exclude religion from the public sphere and confine it to the private domain."[5] Passive secularism, on the other hand, "demands that the state play a 'passive' role by allowing the public visibility of religion."[6] While not contending that these are ideal types to be seen in pure form in the real world, Kuru argues that France and Turkey exemplify assertive secularism, while the United States exhibits chiefly the passive version.[7]

Kuru seeks to explain the differences historically; he argues that in France and Turkey there was an *ancien régime* characterized by an alliance between the monarchy and a hegemonic religion, which at a critical historical juncture was successfully challenged by a republican movement. This, he argues, is the formula that led to anti-clericalism and assertive secularism. Kuru argues that in the United States there was no *ancien régime,* certainly no local monarchy, and there was a variety of Protestant denominations, rather than one dominant religious institution – thus setting the conditions for the emergence of passive secularism, and not fostering anti-clericalism.

As I understand Kuru, the key elements explaining the emergence of the assertive form of secularism are a hegemonic, undemocratic civil authority, plus a dominant religion, which together compose an *ancien régime*; a sudden upheaval or critical juncture in which the old order is challenged and overthrown; its replacement by what he calls a republican movement. The key elements explaining the appearance of passive secularism are the absence of an authoritarian political regime; a degree of religious pluralism and the incipient toleration often associated with it; incremental change, rather than an abrupt break with the past; and more pragmatic political opposition to traditional patterns of belief and conduct, rather than radical, system-breaking resistance.[8]

The Argument

Wrongly, I would argue, Kuru places Canada simply in the passive secular camp,[9] not recognizing that the French-speaking society in Canada has had a strikingly different historical experience, as compared with the English-speaking part of the country, and that that experience has shaped a somewhat divergent approach to contemporary church-state relations.

I propose to argue that Quebec inclines to assertive secularism as a result of the lengthy dominance of the Catholic Church and its often uneasy alliance with the ruling, alien imperial elite, which, in British North America, stood in for a politically authoritarian monarchy.[10] Thus, French Canada for much of its history experienced a kind of new-world *ancien régime*. During the first half of the twentieth century, efforts at reform were stifled, and the three principal provincial actors all thought it in their respective interest to preserve the old order as best they could. The provincial government, the Roman Catholic Church, and the English business community – each for its own reasons – largely believed that sustaining Quebec's traditional forms and practices was the best thing to do. Quebec's critical historical juncture, its "republican moment," was the Quiet Revolution at the beginning of the 1960s. Much of what had gone on before was rejected. While the material conditions of Quebec had been changing throughout the twentieth century, there was nevertheless a dramatic ideological shift during and after the Quiet Revolution – from the religious to the secular, from the rural to the urban, and from an agricultural to an industrial and commercial mentality. Both the old political order and the Roman Catholic Church were actively and explicitly rejected by the emerging secular elites and by much of the population during this period.

The Quiet Revolution was a secular, social and political challenge to the established order. The Church and its constitutive principles were rapidly abandoned; the privileged socio-economic position of the Anglo elite in Quebec was aggressively contested by the francophone majority; and the rise of the sovereignist movement under the leadership of René Lévesque constituted the rejection of the traditional federalist political order, along with its conventions and accommodations.

English-speaking Canada on the other hand displays passive secularism because it was never subject to a hegemonic religion – there were always English-speaking Catholics and a diversity of Protestant denominations – nor was it, seriously speaking, subject to an authoritarian governance structure. The circumstances of the new world made that impossible, and in any case English Canadians felt themselves to be part of the British Empire, and took pride in their country's status as a member of the British Empire and Commonwealth. While British authority in Canada could not be considered domestic, neither was it alien or foreign. The same could not be said for French Canadians. Moreover, the stream of immigrants to English Canada in the nineteenth and twentieth centuries, which historically had no parallel in French Canada, meant that there was a constant ethno-cultural leavening going on that sustained and extended religious pluralism and encouraged a more tolerant attitude to religious belief in the English-speaking provinces.[11]

It would be a mistake to over dramatize the difference. I suspect it is more a matter of nuance and degree than a full-scale qualitative differentiation. Canada, Quebec included, is one country, after all, and there is a range of highly significant common institutions that lend a degree of coherence to the country and its people. While Quebec uniquely has a civil code, which deals with matters of private law, otherwise, the common law prevails. There is an integrated court system, in which the Supreme Court of Canada is the ultimate arbiter of all legal disputes in the country. This means that, if appealed, disputes in any part of the country relating to religious beliefs and practices can find themselves being authoritatively settled by judgments of the Supreme Court, giving a national scope to the relevant jurisprudence. The Canadian Charter of Rights and Freedoms is valid throughout Canada and in all jurisdictions,[12] although many provinces have their own human rights codes, and Quebec has its own charter within this national framework. The Canadian Charter and Charter jurisprudence shape the country's response to religious diversity by promoting a rights-based approach to religious faith that focuses on preventing discrimination against minority groups, as distinct from France's emphasis on sustaining the state's autonomy from religion. In addition, the Québécois and English-speaking Canadians are profoundly North American peoples, having lived on this continent for centuries, and both have been subject to the pervasive influence of the United States. Finally, there is federalism; despite Canada being a highly decentralized federation, patterns of church-state relations are embedded in the common constitutional framework of the country. All of this limits the degree to which Canada's two societies – or its ten provinces – stray from the norm.

Faith and Politics in Canada's Two Societies

There is a factor in Quebec's history that helps to explain its secular differentiation, which Ahmet Kuru understandably does not include in his analysis. This is because he is dealing with states, not with national communities within states. Quebec was and is a minority nation in a larger political community – ethnically, religiously, culturally, and linguistically different from the larger Anglophone community, whose members have traditionally had more in common with their American cousins to the south than with French Canadians. After the British took over in 1759–60, the Catholic faith became the indispensable defining characteristic in the defense of a people who saw themselves as a threatened minority in a sea of Anglo-Saxon, English-speaking, Protestant North Americans.[13]

When that bulwark was dismantled in the 1960s, one of the pillars of French Canada's identity crumbled. It was rapidly replaced by another. *French Canada,* the concept of a community that spread into other provinces far beyond the borders of Quebec, was replaced by the notion of the *Québécois* (French-speaking Quebecers) and the idea of *Quebec* as the homeland of the French people in North America. The Québécois, located in a jurisdiction in which they were the majority, thought themselves to be the only French Canadians in North America with any realistic hope of long-term survival. The government of the province of Quebec replaced the Catholic Church as the institutional guardian of the French factor in North America, and it took over most of the social services and educational functions the Church had been providing up until then. In its efforts to build up and protect a modern French society, it put the rest of the country to the test, arguing for changes in language practices, changes in the ethno-linguistic structure of the Quebec economy, and changes in the constitutional order.

The Quiet Revolution narrowed and sharpened the distinctive features of this modernizing national community. Where once the dimensions of identity were understood to be multiple – Catholic, French, rural – they were reduced effectively to one; the Québécois were defined by language, by the singular fact that they spoke French. In his 1968 manifesto, *An Option for Quebec*, René Lévesque, who would become the first sovereignist premier of Quebec, wrote: "At the core of this [Québécois] personality is the fact that we speak French. Everything else depends on this one essential element and follows from it or leads us infallibly back to it."[14] This re-shaping of identity was inevitable, once Quebecers became more like the rest of North American society in their life-style and aspirations, and the markers of religion and rurality were discarded. Until the 1960s, no Quebec government had established a language policy; it was not seen to be necessary.[15] By the end of the decade, this had changed; a succession of governments passed language legislation, culminating in the Parti Québécois' Bill 101 in 1977. Language has been a central policy preoccupation ever since.

When Catholicism was abandoned in the 1960s the floodgates opened and the transformation was astonishingly speedy. Prior to 1960, every significant nationalist movement or political party in Quebec was Catholic; by 1972, not a single one was.[16] Perhaps the most eloquent social testimony of this change is found in the precipitous decline in Quebec's birthrate. Quebec's fertility rate dropped from close to four children per couple in 1956 to below 2.1 by 1972, less than what is needed simply to maintain population size.[17] In a few short years, Quebec's birthrate fell from the highest to the lowest in Canada. Jean Chrétien, prime minister of Canada from 1993 to 2003, reflects this transformation in his own life, with one foot in each of the two worlds. He was the eighteenth of nineteen children, nine of whom perished in infancy. He and Aline Chrétien have just three children, one of them adopted. Today, Quebecers are significantly less inclined than other Canadians to marry when they form families.

Along with these alterations in social practices, there came the realization that French Canada's traditional posture vis-à-vis immigrants to the province would have to change, too. Traditionally, immigration was seen as the domain of English Canada. French Canada, which was ethnically defined by descent from the original French explorers and settlers who came to New France in the sixteenth and seventeenth centuries, did not welcome immigrants and newcomers, except for the occasional Irish Catholic, and counted on its high birth rate to maintain its demographic strength in the federation – *la revanche des berceaux* (the revenge of the cradles). With the birth rate's rapid decline in the 1960s, that source of demographic security was disappearing. As long as Quebec-bound immigrants continued to learn English and assimilate into the Anglophone community, the position of French Canadians in Quebec, and in Canada as a whole, would continue to be weakened. Altering that pattern, and forcing immigrants to integrate into the French Quebec community, rather than the English, was a main reason for Bill 101.

Gradually, with the shift in Quebec's approach to immigration, the implicit assumption that Québécois were ethnic French Canadians living in Quebec was abandoned, in favor of the more inclusive notion that Québécois were all French-speaking people in Quebec, of whatever origin. With the security provided by Bill 101, immigrants gradually ceased to be perceived as a threat to the survival of the francophone community, and came to be understood instead as a strategic survival resource, compensating to some extent for the precipitous fall in the French Canadian birth rate.[18] Not surprisingly, this shift was not easy, nor was it made by everyone,[19] but over the last forty years or so, a remarkable reconceptualization of identity has occurred.

Multiculturalism and *Interculturalisme*

With the arrival of increasing numbers of immigrants from all over the world and the growing presence of cultural pluralism in the country, Canada developed a policy of multiculturalism in the early 1970s. The policy was institutionalized in 1985 with the passage of the Canadian Multiculturalism Act, which states in the preamble that "the Government of Canada recognizes the diversity of Canadians as regards race, national or ethnic origin, colour and religion as a fundamental characteristic of Canadian society and is committed to a policy of multiculturalism designed to preserve and enhance the multicultural heritage of Canadians while working to achieve the equality of all Canadians in the economic, social, cultural, and political life of Canada."[20] Quebec is the only province to have developed a formal policy on cultural pluralism and integration within its jurisdiction. Enunciated in a 1990 Policy Statement on Immigration and Integration (*Let's Build Quebec Together*), it sets out the "moral contract" shaping relations between Quebec society and newcomers.

It states that "French is the common language of public life;" that Quebec is "a democratic society that expects and encourages everyone to participate and contribute;" and that Quebec is "pluralistic and open to outside contributions, within the limitations imposed by respect for basic democratic values and the need for intercommunity exchange."[21]

The policy has come to be known as "interculturalisme." There has been a strong desire on the part of many Québécois to differentiate between the Canadian and the Quebec variety, arguing that the intercultural approach to the management and accommodation of cultural pluralism is quite different from that of multiculturalism. There is, however, a line of argument that is critical of this position, contending that there is very little difference between the two, either in spirit or substance.[22]

While room exists to debate whether there is a significant difference between these two approaches, there are two features relating to Quebec's policy on cultural pluralism that are clearly distinctive. The first arises out of the fact that Canada is a federation. Quebec's policy of interculturalism relates to those matters for which Quebec is responsible – education, health care, municipalities, and so forth; Canada's multicultural policy, on the other hand, quite appropriately concerns itself with those matters falling into the federal sphere of responsibility. Thus the matters to which the two policies apply are different. The second clear distinction lies in the matter of language. Both policies seek the fruitful integration of newcomers into the life of the country. For the Canadian government, with its two official languages, that can mean integration into either the French-speaking or the English-speaking Canadian community. Both are entirely acceptable. In the English-speaking provinces, English is so dominant that no language policy is necessary. Not so, in Quebec. A provincial policy on cultural pluralism, which would allow for the integration of immigrants to Quebec into the Canadian English-language community, would be utterly unacceptable and a direct challenge to Quebec's collective survival strategy. Recall our discussion of Bill 101; as much as anything, that language legislation was designed to ensure that immigrants to Quebec learn and use French, rather than English, and that they associate themselves with the French-language majority within Quebec, rather than with the English-language majority in all of Canada.

These two factors – constitutional jurisdiction and language use – are clear and significant differences that set the federal and provincial worlds apart from one another. But the first has little to do with a policy on cultural pluralism as such; it speaks rather to the sphere of responsibility in which the policy would apply. The second – the language of integration – is significant; it is at the centre of the broader set of social goals and interests within which the policy of interculturalism is set. As Pierre Anctil says, "the main difference between the two notions has been the necessity in Quebec society of integrating immigrants in the French language. From this perspective, interculturalism does not contradict the stated multicultural ideology used elsewhere in Canada."[23]

Rising Tension in Quebec

In recent years, fed by widespread media reporting, there were signs of significant public anxiety in Quebec about the extent to which cultural and religious pluralism was being satisfactorily reconciled with Québécois national identity. In the mid-2000s, a number of incidents, widely reported in the French-language press, occurred. These included: "the wearing of a hijab by a girl while playing soccer; requests for places of worship within certain public facilities, the wearing of a kirpan by a young Sikh in a public school, the separation of men and women in public swimming places, and whether a YMCA near Outremont should grant the request of a neighbouring Hasidic community to shield its windows from outside view because supposedly scantily clad women could be seen by the Hasidic boys next door."[24]

Things came to a head when the council of the small town of Herouxville, with a population of under 1,300 and no visible minorities, passed a code of conduct in January 2007 setting out the standards and practices immigrants to the community would be expected to live up to. The code noted, among other things, that stoning women or burning them alive was forbidden in the municipality. Herouxville attracted widespread international attention and derision, and helped to concentrate Quebecers' attention on the question of the accommodation of religious and cultural pluralism.[25]

In this atmosphere of rising tension, the premier of Quebec, Jean Charest, created a commission in February 2007 to look into the question of *accommodement raisonnable*. Entitled *La Commission de consultation sur les pratiques d'accommodement reliées aux différences culturelles* (Consultation Commission on Accommodation Practices Related to Cultural Differences), it soon became known as the Bouchard-Taylor Commission, after its co-chairs, the eminent sociologist, Gérard Bouchard and the internationally renowned political philosopher, Charles Taylor. As far as I am aware, no other Canadian province has been moved to establish a commission of this sort to look into the question of accommodating cultural and religious pluralism.

One of the things the commission did was to examine very carefully the environment and the series of controversies that led to its own establishment. Arguing that it was fundamentally a crisis of perception rather than of institutional or policy failure, the commission divided the relevant twenty-two years into four periods: *antecedents* (December 1985–April 2002); *the intensification of controversy* (May 2002–February 2006); *the time of turmoil* (March 2006–June 2007); and *a period of calm*, running from July 2007 to April 2008. The commission found that there had been seventy-three cases or incidents worthy of review over the twenty-two years examined, and that about forty of them (about 55 per cent) occurred during the sixteen-month period the commissioners identified as *the time of turmoil*.[26] It was toward the end of this tempestuous and troublesome period (February 2007) that Premier Charest established the commission.

Without doubt, one of the reasons why the premier created the commission when he did was the fact that he hoped to cool off a sensitive issue prior to the provincial election of March 2007. His Liberal Party was being pressed by the sudden rise to prominence of a new political formation, the Action Démocratique du Quebec (ADQ), a nationalist, right-of-centre party defending the autonomy of Quebec. Its young leader, Mario Dumont, made a number of speeches during 2005 and 2006, and early 2007, attacking the provincial Liberals for being too soft on immigrants and for not defending the mainstream values of French Quebec. The March 2007 provincial election saw the ADQ draining support away from both the Liberals and the PQ, winning 41 of 125 seats in the National Assembly, displacing the PQ to become for the first time the official opposition, and holding the Liberals to minority government status.[27]

The Bouchard-Taylor Commission embarked on an extensive and sometimes controversial process of consultation, and produced its report in May 2008, with thirty recommendations. It elaborated a distinction between "restrictive" and "open" secularism, broadly similar to Ahmet Kuru's assertive and passive forms, and recommended the latter.[28] It sought to foster a better understanding of interculturalism and secularism, and the relationship between the two. The widespread public consultations undertaken by Bouchard and Taylor seemed to have allowed the population to blow off steam, and, by the time the Commission reported, much of the anxiety and concern had dissipated.

The Government did little to implement the Commission's recommendations, although, interestingly, it rapidly and definitively rejected one of the suggestions that the co-chairs had made. Bouchard and Taylor had proposed, consistent with the need for the state to be neutral in a pluralist society, that the crucifix that hung in the National Assembly above the Speaker's chair be removed. Premier Charest instantly rejected this proposal and got all-party support for his position in the National Assembly with a motion that affirms Quebecers' "attachment to our religious and historic heritage represented by the crucifix." While this position seems inconsistent with the clear secular direction in which Quebec society has been moving since the Quiet Revolution, and certainly contrary to the principle of open secularism as Bouchard and Taylor understood it, the refusal by all political parties to remove the crucifix may tell us something about the type of secularism that prevails in the province.

My reading of the meaning of this act is suggested in the resolution itself. It speaks of "attachment to our religious ... heritage." It does not speak of the attachment of Québécois to the contemporary forms and practices of the Roman

Catholic Church. It does not claim that the Church matters today. What matters is the historic role that the Church played in the survival of the French Canadian community in North America. To remove the crucifix and thus seem to deny the critical role of the Church in the past is what attracted the opposition of the province's legislators. The Catholic Church is seen to have helped preserve the French-Canadian nation; no party wanted to be against that. If a proposed reform threatens identity and collective survival, even symbolically, you can expect that it will be opposed. That, I think, is what explains the superficially curious and contradictory behavior of the members of the National Assembly, and it takes us to the heart of Quebec's somewhat distinctive form of secularism. Should the two come in conflict, the perceived survival needs of a vulnerable national minority community will by and large trump its commitment to secular values; this, as much as anything, invests Quebec's approach to matters of church and state with its distinctive flavor.[29]

As Pierre Anctil has written:

Perhaps, because of its unique culture and history, Québécois society seemed to be out of tempo with the more sedate approach to pluralism found in Anglophone Canada; Québec directly confronted the major fundamental issues that were also evident elsewhere in the country. Could it be that Québec offered a markedly different type of answer to the emergence of religious pluralism, one that was more decidedly interventionist on the part of public authorities, while relying at the same time on a more radical separation of church and state? Was Quebec proposing an avenue which, although based on the same general notions of human rights and freedoms, reflected its own distinctiveness within the Canadian ensemble?[30]

Conclusion

Ahmet Kuru's account of the differences in the patterns of secularism in the United States, France, and Turkey is helpful, I think, in framing a discussion of what seem to be two somewhat different styles of secularism in Quebec and the rest of Canada. What Kuru's typology does not take into account, however, is the binational reality of Canada – understandably so, since he was comparing the secular patterns of states, not the secular patterns of national communities *within* states. In binational Canada, there is a vital, additional factor to be considered – namely, that Quebec is best understood as a vulnerable, French-speaking minority nation within a larger political community, the majority of whose members speak English. This is a fairly powerful lens through which to view the somewhat different relations between church and state within each of the two language communities. Yet Kuru's approach is useful, I think, in placing Quebec's political experience since the 1960s in a broader and deeper historical context, and in helping us to assess the impact of the critical historical juncture of the Quiet Revolution on the character of secularism in Quebec.

NOTES

1 The two previous paragraphs are drawn from a chapter I wrote, entitled "Quebec and the Canadian Federation," appearing in *Canadian Federalism: Performance, Effectiveness, and Legitimacy*, eds. Herman Bakvis and Grace Skogstad, 3rd ed. (Toronto: Oxford University Press, 2012).

2 Ahmet Kuru identifies two main characteristics of secular states: "(1) their legislative and judicial processes are secular in the sense of being out of institutional religious control, and (2) they constitutionally declare neutrality toward religions; they establish neither an official religion nor atheism" (*Secularism and State Policies Toward Religion: The United States, France, and Turkey* [Cambridge: Cambridge University Press, 2009], 7).

3 I do not propose to study the relationship between Aboriginal forms of spirituality and the style of civic participation of Native people, but perhaps a brief word is in order here. When Aboriginal people lost power vis-à-vis the Europeans during the first half of the 19th century, they and their cultures were pushed to the margins of Canadian consciousness and life. In the Constitution Act, 1867, the only reference to Aboriginal people (Section 91[24]) simply placed them in federal jurisdiction. At this point, the cross-cultural impact became a one-way street, with Canadians and their political institutions imposing, often coercively, European practices, languages and religions on Native people and their children. Native people ceased to be active agents in the historical evolution of the country. In the 1960s, what we used to call Canada's "two founding peoples" – by which we meant the French and the English, not the Aboriginal people and the Inuit – began a radical debate about the character and very existence of Canada; this opened up political space for Aboriginal people to insert themselves back into Canadian history as active participants. Buttressed by a degree of constitutional recognition in the Constitution Act, 1982, a series of successful court cases and land claims, together with a number of high impact acts of civil disobedience, Aboriginal people began to shape public discourse, academic study, and, to some extent, civic forms and practices, and radically altered European Canadians' perception of them and their place in Canada. One of the consequences of this was that Native spirituality and the distinctive Aboriginal relationship with Mother Earth began to penetrate public consciousness and practices. For example, when Aboriginal organizations secured a place at the table during the Canadian constitutional round of negotiations in the early 1990s, some of the talks opened with Native ceremonies, such as drumming, and the sweetgrass ritual.

4 Ahmet T. Kuru, *Secularism and State Policies toward Religion: The United States, France, and Turkey* (New York: Cambridge University Press, 2009).

5 Ibid., 11.

6 Ibid.

7 Scholars have identified the different types of secularism in many different ways. However, Kuru's typology seems particularly apt, given that it is systematically articulated and offers an organized way in which to approach the issue in the

Canadian context. The Quebec Bouchard-Taylor Commission, discussed later in this essay, makes a distinction between "restrictive" and "open secularism," which bears some similarity to Kuru's approach.

8 In the American case, resistance developed to what came to be perceived as an external authoritarian regime, the British monarchy. The American Revolution, therefore, did not involve an overturning of the political order in the Thirteen Colonies, but the expulsion of Britain. That, plus the acceptance in America of a degree of religious pluralism, set the stage for passive secularism.

9 Kuru, *Secularism and State Policies toward Religion* (above n. 4), 27. Because the issue I am dealing with in this essay is whether it is appropriate simply to place Quebec in the passive secularism camp, I will focus on religion and the state in Quebec, and not in the rest of Canada.

10 Perhaps not surprisingly, the Church played something of a dual role. It was an institution that facilitated the accommodation of French Canada to the new imperial authorities, but it did so by delivering some recognition and protections for French Canada within British North America. For many years, the Church presented itself as having a grander mission as well, namely, as the bulwark of Catholicism in North America.

11 Robert T. Handy, *A History of the Churches in the United States and Canada* (Oxford: Clarendon Press, 1976), 345.

12 The Charter's preamble speaks of Canada being "founded upon principles that recognize the supremacy of God and the rule of law." Article 2(a) guarantees freedom of conscience and religion, and Article 15(1) outlaws discrimination on the basis of religion.

13 Gregory Baum writes: "This profound loyalty to the Church may seem like an anomaly in the middle of the twentieth century. Yet whenever a people has been conquered by empire and must struggle for its collective survival, the Church easily becomes a symbol of identity and resistance. This happened in Poland, Ireland, and Quebec." "Catholicism and Secularism in Quebec," in *Rethinking Church, State and Modernity: Canada between Europe and America*, ed. David Lyon and Marguerite Van Die (Toronto: University of Toronto Press, 2000), 150. See Kuru's rather different point (*Secularism and State Policies toward Religion* [above, n. 4], 26).

14 René Lévesque, *An Option for Quebec* (Toronto: McClelland and Stewart, 1968), 4.

15 Alain Gagnon and Beth Montcalm, *Quebec: Beyond the Quiet Revolution* (Scarborough: Nelson Canada, 1990).

16 David Seljak, "Resisting the 'No Man's Land' of Private Religion: The Catholic Church and Public Politics in Quebec," in *Rethinking Church, State, and Modernity* (above n. 13), 133.

17 Kenneth McRoberts, *Quebec: Social Change and Political Crisis*, 3rd ed. (Toronto: McClelland and Stewart, 1993), 139.

18 See Gérard Bouchard and Charles Taylor, *Building the Future: A Time for Reconciliation. Abridged Report* (Quebec: Government of Quebec, 2008), 40. Popularly known as the *Bouchard-Taylor Report* and cited hereafter as such.

19 Atavistic notions of community are more likely to emerge in moments of stress. Bitterly disappointed by the outcome of the 1995 Quebec referendum on sovereignty, then Premier Jacques Parizeau blamed the loss on "money and the ethnic vote."

20 *Canadian Multiculturalism Act*, R.S. 1985, c.24 (4th Supp.), preamble.

21 Cited in the *Bouchard-Taylor Report* (above n. 18), 38.

22 For example, Daniel Baril, "L'interculturalisme n'est que le multiculturalisme à la québécoise," *Tribune libre de Vigile*, 15 January 2011.

23 Pierre Anctil, "Introduction" in *Religion, Culture, and the State: Reflections on the Bouchard-Taylor Report*, ed. Howard Adelman and Pierre Anctil (Toronto: University of Toronto Press, 2011), 4. Bouchard and Taylor distinguish Quebec interculturalism in four ways: "a) anxiety over language is not an important factor in English Canada; b) minority insecurity is not found there; c) there is no longer a majority ethnic group in Canada (citizens of British origin account for 34% of the population, while citizens of French-Canadian origin make up a strong majority of the population in Quebec, i.e., roughly 77%); d) it follows that in English Canada, there is less concern for the preservation of a founding cultural tradition than for national cohesion" (*Bouchard-Taylor Report* [above n. 18], 39.).

24 Anctil, "Introduction" (above n. 23), 7.

25 Alain Dubuc, in a column for *La Presse,* makes an interesting point, however. He writes that "Although Herouxville's reaction was xenophobic, immigrants may not be the main target of this revolt.... There is something else at work here, and it's the revolt against the big city, its ideas, its lifestyle, its influence. What happened in Herouxville is the ultimate expression of the fracture between the metropolis and the regions.... Herouxville was angered by the tolerance of Montrealers, by their passivity towards the changes brought out by immigration, by their multi-ethnic culture, their rejection of religion, their 'gay village' and their arrogant elites. For small towns such as Herouxville, the real threat to their identity has little to do with veil-clad Muslim women, it is the urban world that is gradually drifting away from the traditional model." Quoted in a *Globe and Mail* column by Lysiane Gagnon, 26 February 2007.

26 *Bouchard-Taylor Report* (above n. 18), 13–16.

27 The ADQ experienced only brief success. In the snap election Premier Jean Charest called in 2008, the Party was soundly defeated, and lapsed into relative obscurity. Mario Dumont stepped down as leader of the Party.

28 See the discussion in Jose Woehrling, "The B-T Report 'Open Secularism' Model and the Supreme Court of Canada Decisions on Freedom of Religion and Religious Accommodation," in *Religion, Culture and the State,* (above n. 23), 86–93.

29 To indicate the degree to which context matters, consider the fact that the National Assembly of Quebec, with the support of the Parliament of Canada, passed a bilateral constitutional amendment in 1997 of Article 93 of the *Constitution Act, 1867,* which offered constitutional protection to the denominational schools of the religious minorities in Ontario and Quebec – a deal-breaking requirement of

Confederation in 1867. With virtually no controversy, the federal and provincial governments were able to pilot an amendment through the two legislatures which permitted Quebec to abandon the system of Catholic and Protestant school boards and replace them with linguistically based, French- and English-language school boards.

30 Anctil, "Introduction," (above n. 23), 4–5.

18 Canada's Constitutional Legitimacy Deficit: Learning to Live with It

In Keith Banting, Richard P. Chaykowski, and Steven F. Lehrer, eds., *Thinking Outside the Box: Innovation in Policy Ideas* **2015**

The paper that is included as chapter 15 was based on the fact that significant constitutional reform to "bring Quebec into the Constitution" was not deemed to be feasible. This paper, too, is grounded in that perception, but it takes a different approach, exploring the multiple streams of affiliation and recognition that together constitute legitimacy in a state. While the fact that Quebec has not assented to the 1982 Constitution is an undeniable breach in our arrangements, there are a number of other legitimacy supports – practical, day-to-day recognition, traditional loyalty, and acceptance based on output or performance – that help to explain why Québécois generally acknowledge the appropriateness of membership in the Canadian state.

The Breach in Canadian Constitutionalism

The 1982 patriation of the Canadian Constitution is a highly contested moment in the country's history. It divided Canadians at the time, and – witness the 2013 controversy over Chief Justice Bora Laskin's alleged conduct during the Supreme Court's consideration of the Patriation Reference – it divides us still.[1]

Although I was working for the government of Canada on the federal side during the 1982 constitutional round, I believed the patriation of the Constitution without Quebec's consent created a serious legitimacy deficit, given that that province, home to one of the country's two linguistic communities, had originated postwar constitutional discussion and needed, on any principled view, to be a consenting part of any new constitutional settlement. It is problematic in a federation to think of democratic legitimacy deriving simply from popular sovereignty, from "the will of the people" at the level of the country as a whole. Federalism, with its constitutionally defined federal and constituent units, pluralizes the notion of "the people," and it disperses sovereignty. Implicitly, then, it disperses the sources of legitimacy. Thus the vast majority of federal constitutions require the consent of some or all of the federal units to amend the country's basic law. Equally, in a binational or bicommunal polity, it is difficult to understand how a constitutional settlement that is rejected and opposed by one of these communities can be regarded as legitimate. That is why Pierre Elliott Trudeau's argument that the patriation of the Constitution was legitimate because he had 74 out of the 75 federal seats from Quebec was rhetorically clever, but specious. The formal opposition of the National Assembly of Quebec to patriation confirmed the existence of a breach in the Canadian constitutional order that has not been repaired to this day.

Not everyone accepts this view, but it is the dominant opinion in Quebec, and it is held by many in the rest of Canada: the Meech Lake and Charlottetown Accords were abortive attempts to mend that rent in Canada's constitutional fabric. I was a strong supporter of Meech Lake, and lamented its collapse. I have long believed that, until the people of Quebec through their National Assembly give their consent to the constitutional arrangements under which they are ruled, the country will remain fragile and vulnerable to fragmentation during periods of crisis.[2]

I still believe that there was a breach in legitimacy in 1982, but I am now not so sure that as a result the country will remain fragile and vulnerable. In this chapter, I intend to explore the proposition that Canada is less fragile and vulnerable than some of us have thought – less fragile, because, I will argue, a country rests on multiple sources of legitimacy, not just one, which means that a gap in one of the sources does not comprehensively deprive the state of all political legitimacy. Risks to the country's stability in the future will derive, not from the historical breach in legitimacy, but from systematic mismanagement or from a crisis that shakes the federation to its foundations.

If this is so, then the standing challenge of finding a way to get Quebec to sign on to the Constitution when the time is right should perhaps be set aside in favour of the more prosaic need to run the country well. What might plausibly be done constitutionally at some point will not mend the breach, and what might mend the breach cannot plausibly be done. Let us consider, for example, the 2006 parliamentary resolution recognizing the Québécois as a nation within Canada. This initiative was supported by the government and the National Assembly of Quebec, and opinion polls suggest, not surprisingly, that it was well received by Québécois, although less well in the rest of Canada.[3] But there was no suggestion at the time that this gesture might lead Quebec to reconsider its refusal to sign on to the 1982 Constitution.

Would a constitutional amendment, recognizing the existence of the Québécois as a people, do the trick? Several years ago, a colleague and I developed the idea that the recognition of Quebec's status within Canada could be constitutionalized via a bilateral constitutional amendment, explicitly recognizing its French language and culture, rather in the way that Quebec replaced denominational with linguistically based schools in 1997 (Cameron and Krikorian 2008).[4] We argued that there are good reasons to believe that this could be done, given the right alignment of political forces in Ottawa and Quebec City, since it would involve only the federal government and Quebec, but not the other provinces. This might deliver the constitutional recognition long sought by many in Quebec.

However, I have come to believe that it is unlikely that even this would induce Quebec to sign on to the 1982 Constitution and repair the breach in legitimacy. There are two reasons why this is so. The first is that, to accept that a constitutional amendment in itself is sufficient to repair the breach would appear to many Quebecers to definitively set aside all prospect of any future substantive constitutional change in Quebec's favour; even if only theoretical, it would seem like a loss of leverage. The second reason turns on the idea of recognition. Meech Lake's strong appeal rested in part on the fact that the rest of the country was formally recognizing Quebec for what it was in its own eyes; the shock and anger in Quebec at the rejection of Meech arose out of the realization that it did not. The bilateral constitutional amendment does not perform this broad recognition function. In fact, the reason why it is practicable is because the rest of the country is not given a voice in the proceedings.

If it is correct that low-key, bilateral initiatives that do not draw in the rest of the country are not sufficient, I would argue that what then seems to be necessary – some more broadly based, countrywide redrawing of the Canadian social contract on terms that Quebec would accept – is not possible. Meech Lake was the instrument that would have accomplished this, but it was not accepted in English-speaking Canada, and in my view, given the evolution of the country, it is even less likely that its equivalent would be accepted today.

I think here we are in fact entering "abeyance country." Many will be familiar with Michael Foley's book, *The Silence of Constitutions: Gaps, "Abeyances" and Political Temperament in the Maintenance of Government* (1989), which argues that sophisticated constitutional societies cope with conflicts too deep to resolve by avoiding them, burying them beneath the surface of political and constitutional life. The parties to the conflict become mutually complicit in working to ensure that these unresolved, unresolvable issues do not boil up unexpectedly and put the whole constitutional order at risk. The significant but flawed achievement of 1982 sits atop just such an unbridgeable gulf.

If you follow the logic of this analysis, the task of politics in the Canadian context is not to look for an opportunity to formally resolve the conflict, but rather to seek to maintain the circumstances in which the two incompatible and mutually contradictory visions of the country never move to centre stage in our constitutional and political discourse. For an abeyance strategy to be successful, each vision of the country needs to have adequate space within which it can be expressed in practice and in daily life, even while any frontal effort to reconcile the two, especially at the symbolic level, is avoided.

It appears that considerations other than high constitutional politics – like living without fuss, and without serious inter-community tensions, and enjoying the practical capacity to develop your society as you choose – are more important in shaping the acceptability of Canada in the eyes of Quebecers at this stage of their existence. Interest in reopening the constitutional debate is low in Quebec, as is the desire to hold another referendum on sovereignty.[5] It hasn't hurt, either, that in recent years Canada has been doing relatively well economically while the rest of the western world has been going through terrible economic turmoil. Maybe it is time to recognize that *not* addressing the issue – not trying to redraw the Canadian social contract – will lead to the strengthening of the country, rather than to its demise. Arguably, that is the lesson of our recent past.

The Quebec Elections of 4 September 2012, and 7 April 2014

There is another thing needed if abeyances are to be kept below ground, namely, the shared desire that this be so on the part of the actors on each side of the divide. If one of the major actors wishes to force a confrontation over these profoundly unresolved matters, it will be difficult to avoid. This brings us to the two most recent Quebec elections. The Parti Québécois won the election of 4 September 2012, and reigned until its defeat at the polls in April 2014. Clearly, during its 18 months in power, the PQ had no wish, implicit or otherwise, to avoid or skirt the irreconcilable differences that lie between English-speaking and French-speaking Canada. Quite the reverse; they wish to exploit those differences to unsettle the Canadian state. In Foleyesque terms, the PQ believes that the abeyances between French and English are so deep and unbridgeable, the schism so radical, that no overarching just and consensual political and constitutional order can be sustained. They have never given up on this conviction; their primary task, as they see it, is to persuade the Québécois of the validity of this view.

Given their modest electoral victory in September 2012, the PQ could not interpret the result as a mandate to pursue sovereignty in any serious way. The Quebec electorate found a way to give political power to the sovereignist party without licensing the aggressive pursuit of sovereignty itself. With the Coalition Avenir du Québec not ready for prime time, the Liberals overdue for a period in the penalty box, and the PQ committed to pursue sovereignty or create the conditions necessary to make that pursuit possible, Quebec voters granted the Parti Québécois the most tentative of mandates. The PQ won a minority government with a lower popular vote than they had received in the previous election, coming in just four seats ahead of the discredited Liberals.[6] Quebecers thus kept their options for the future open, and pretty much ensured that the sovereignty and referendum questions would be placed firmly on the back burner. This outcome was well attuned to an electorate with little interest in pursuing sovereignty.

Not being able to address the sovereignty question directly, the PQ government instead sought to pump up the nationalist volume by manufacturing a divisive crisis where there was none. Their Charter of Values articulated an understanding of *laïcité*, or secularism, in Quebec and, if implemented, would have forbidden public-sector employees from wearing or displaying "conspicuous" religious symbols. It also would have made it mandatory to uncover one's face when delivering or securing public services in the province. The Charter appealed to elements of the PQ's hard nationalist base, but at the expense of deeply unsettling many members of Quebec's minority communities. Party strategists calculated that an early election call could return them to power, possibly with a majority government, and that the election itself would help to awaken the nationalist feelings of the French-Canadian majority in the province.

The April 2014 election results told a very different story. With the help of the sovereignist fist pump of their star recruit, Pierre Karl Péladeau, the PQ went down to a humiliating defeat, losing 24 seats, receiving the lowest popular vote in two and a half decades, and becoming the first government since Jean-Jacques Bertrand's Union Nationale administration in 1970 to be booted out after a single term in office. Philippe Couillard's Liberals gained 21 seats and formed the government with a comfortable majority.[7] The outcome was a clear rejection of what the Parti Québécois had on offer. If the PQ elites wanted to regenerate conflict and division within Quebec and Canada, it was apparent that the voters of Quebec did not.

Why is there little current interest in sovereignty in Quebec? One might have thought that the resurgence of Catalan nationalism in Spain and the prospect of a 2014 referendum on independence in Scotland might reawaken interest in the national question in Quebec. What is more, to the extent that interest in sovereignty is linked to the state of social and political relations with the rest of Canada, and in particular intergovernmental relations between the government of Quebec and the federal government, it could be argued that there are lots of reasons for Quebecers to feel discontented. The country is led, after all, by a staunchly conservative Albertan who, having tried without success to make yards in Quebec, has learned that he can govern without it. Prime Minister Stephen Harper demonstrated during the prorogation contretemps in 2008–09 that he was prepared to throw the national-unity baby under the bus in order to stay in power, offending many Québécois with his corrosive assault on the Bloc as a bunch of separatists. He paid a stiff electoral price in Quebec for doing this, dropping 5 per cent in popular vote and losing half of his 10 seats there in the May 2011 election, despite gaining 23 seats nationally and securing his first majority government.

In addition, the federal government's celebration of the monarchy, its aggressive support of Israel, the abolition of the gun registry, its criminal-justice position, its effort to create a national securities regulator, its recalcitrance on the environment – all of these policy positions are antithetic to mainstream opinion in Quebec. One might have thought that there was plenty to work with if a Quebec government wanted to pick a nationalist fight with Ottawa, and stir up feelings of anger and alienation in Quebec.

Yet it didn't happen. The Parti Québécois seemed to be pretty much alone in the boxing ring, and at serious risk of injuring itself. Part of this is the result of an Ottawa-Quebec City dynamic that is very different from that which prevailed when the Liberals were in power in Ottawa. During that time, there was a "within-the-family" quality to the relationship, with federal ministers representing Quebec more than willing to go head-to-head with their Quebec counterparts, challenging their arguments and criticizing their policies (Hébert 2013b). It is very different today. The Conservatives, governing in Ottawa, do not have a strong political base in Quebec. Prime Minister Harper's approach has been very different from that of, say, former Prime Minister Chrétien. Harper displayed little interest in doing battle with the PQ and Premier Marois, which meant that their sallies, meant to provoke, tended to fall to the ground. Where once there was a fear on the federal side that, if left uncontested, the arguments of the sovereignists would carry the day, the effect of the Harper strategy of non-engagement is to deprive the sovereignty issue of oxygen, particularly given the fact that the Québécois are not currently preoccupied with the matter. But there is more than simply the tactic of not rising to the bait in play here. There are deeper philosophical convictions about how to understand and operate Canada's federation; these have considerably altered the country's intergovernmental reality. To understand what has happened, we need to move back in time.

The Reappearance of the Theory of Classical Federalism

There is a tradition of thinking in French-speaking Canada that goes back to the founding of the country in 1867. The notion that Confederation was as much about separation (of Upper and Lower Canada) as it was about union (of the four original British North American colonies) played an important role in the discussions of the day, and fostered a powerful interpretation of the real meaning of the new federal association. By entering into Confederation, French Canada was gaining a significant measure of self-government, and the space to manage its own affairs within Quebec separately from the English-speaking Canadian majority. This idea lay behind the emergence of the theory of classical federalism, which generations of French-speaking Canadian thinkers in the twentieth century contended was the proper way of understanding the Canadian federal association: watertight compartments of federal and provincial authority, with each jurisdiction tending to its own responsibilities and staying out of the sphere of the other.[8] Maurice Duplessis lived by that credo, playing what was generally a defensive game vis-à-vis the federal government throughout much of his career as premier; believing in limited government, he was faced, especially after the Second World War, with an activist government in Ottawa, flush with public resources and bursting with ideas about how to spend them. To back up his resistance to Ottawa's activism, Duplessis established the Tremblay Commission, which developed what was perhaps French-Canada's fullest philosophical justification of the classical view of federalism.[9] French-speaking Canadian intellectuals of the day espoused this federal theory. It remained a significant current in the debate in the decades after the Quiet Revolution, although not in the traditionalist form articulated by the Tremblay Commission (see the discussion in Coleman 1984; see also Rocher 2009). The effort to confine the federal spending power, limiting or ending its use in areas of provincial jurisdiction, rested on the belief that even if the spending power were not subject to effective legal limitations, a broader federal ethic would acknowledge the justice of constraining it in the context of a federal association involving, not simply ten provinces, but two national communities.

Largely satisfied with the expanding role of Ottawa during the Second World War and thereafter, English-speaking Canadians in the postwar years generally tended to be much less scrupulous about patrolling the frontier between federal and provincial jurisdiction. Successive federal governments evinced no great desire to see their freedom of action constrained, particularly when the use of the spending power in postwar Canada had played such a significant role in building up the Canadian welfare state and connecting Ottawa to citizens in the areas that mattered most to them. The perennial debates on federal fiscal transfers are saturated with conflicting arguments about the extent to which Ottawa has the right to intervene in the provincial domain. The Canada Health Act's prohibition of extra billing is emblematic of the federal government's traditional desire to influence provincial behaviour in fields clearly within the jurisdiction of the provinces.

Enter Stephen Harper and his theory of "open federalism." Perhaps somewhat surprisingly at this late stage in our country's history, we have a prime minister who seems to believe in a more classical view of federalism and the division of powers, and who is to a substantial degree prepared to live by its canons. Stephen Harper's political formation in Calgary no doubt contributed to the emergence of this view of the country; "building firewalls" is simply a particularly aggressive way of articulating the necessity of protecting provincial jurisdiction and provincial resources from the incursions of the federal government.[10] His strongly conservative ideology aligns neatly not only with small government in general but with decentralized government, and with clearer, simpler lines of accountability. In addition, the political weakness of the Conservative Party in Quebec on his watch makes careful respect for Quebec's constitutional autonomy a prudent and sensible strategy. Finally, I think, there is federal theory. As we shall see below, Stephen Harper simply appears to believe in classical federalism, and is severely critical of the traditional interventionism of the Liberal Party. It is not, I think, an approach designed exclusively with Quebec in mind, but is meant to be a federal theory of general application. However, there is no doubt that its relevance to Quebec is meant to be one of its virtues.

As Adam Harmes (2007) has shown, Stephen Harper began outlining his approach to the management of the federation some time ago, starting with an article in the *National Post* in October 2004.[11] There, he called for renewed respect for the constitutional division of powers, vigorous federal government leadership in areas of clear federal responsibility (defence, maintenance of the economic union), and the need for a more principled and orderly approach to federal-provincial-territorial relations, in contrast to then Prime Minister Paul Martin's let's-make-a-deal ad hocery. The Policy Declaration, approved at the March 2005 Conservative National Policy Convention, promised the restoration of "the constitutional balance between the federal and provincial and territorial governments," noting the need to "ensure that the federal spending power in provincial jurisdictions is limited," and accepting the existence of a fiscal imbalance.

The Conservative election platform for the 2006 federal election promised "a charter of open federalism" and explained the fiscal imbalance as the result of large federal surpluses combined with provincial deficits arising out of high social service costs. The Conservative's Quebec campaign document recognized the importance of provincial autonomy for Quebec and "the special cultural and institutional responsibilities of the Quebec government." In a speech to the Quebec Chamber of Commerce in December 2005, Harper said he would "monitor" the use of the federal spending power, which in his view was "outrageous" and which, echoing Premier Robert Bourassa's vocabulary, had given rise to "domineering and paternalistic federalism."

After the Conservative minority government was elected in early 2006, Prime Minister Harper said in an interview that the federal government "has gotten into everything in recent years, not just provincial jurisdiction but now municipal jurisdiction," and that he would rather "see Ottawa do what the federal government is supposed to do."[12] In a 2006 speech to the Board of Trade of Metropolitan Montreal, he said that open federalism "means respecting areas of provincial jurisdiction. Open federalism means limiting the use of the federal spending power.... Open federalism represents an opportunity to free Quebec from the trap of polarization."[13]

The fullest statement of the open federalism approach is found in a discussion paper annexed to the 2006 federal budget, which was entitled *Focusing on Priorities: Restoring Fiscal Balance in Canada*. It speaks of how unplanned federal surpluses have led the federal government to introduce significant new spending initiatives in areas of provincial jurisdiction, while neglecting its own responsibilities, thus blurring accountability; how fiscal transfers need to be put on a principle-based, long-term track; and how it is important for both orders of government to work together to increase the efficiency and competitiveness of the economic union (Canada. Department of Finance 2006).[14]

This articulation of open federalism constitutes a highly significant shift in Ottawa's traditional conception of its role in the federation, as one can see if one thinks of the string of Liberal governments from Pearson to Martin. With the emergence of neo-nationalism and the sovereignty movement in Quebec in the 1960s, the country embarked on an extended period of what might be called competitive nation-building in Quebec City and in Ottawa. Faced with a feeling of primary loyalty to Quebec among French-speaking Canadians in that province, and the gradual emergence of province-building strategies in several other provinces, successive federal governments, certainly those of Trudeau and Chrétien, were deeply concerned to deliver what they believed would be loyalty-generating programs and services to Canadian citizens, and many of these fell within provincial jurisdiction. There was a lengthy period of jockeying for constitutional position and competing for the loyalty of Canadians. With the decline in the strength of Quebec nationalism and the election of the Conservatives to office in 2006, there has been a marked shift in approach.

Prime Minister Harper clearly recognizes that, on prudential political grounds if nothing else, the federal government will have to continue to support the major transfer programs to the provinces,[15] but his effort to set out early his government's level of commitment suggests a desire to settle this issue, not by exhaustive quid pro quo negotiations in which the federal government potentially gains some oversight or shaping role in return for granting the money, but by making it clear that Ottawa will provide what it sees as a reasonable level of resources without expecting much in the way of return (Canada. Department of Finance 2011).[16] His approach suggests, as well, his desire to de-dramatize intergovernmental relations, and to reduce the profile of federal-provincial-territorial summit meetings in the management of the federation. He is not strongly attracted to the holding of first ministers conferences as a means of managing the federation, and has called very few during his tenure of office.[17]

Stephen Harper's hands-off approach denied the Parti Québécois government an easy target. The traditional critique of the interventionist use of the federal spending power is harder to sustain, as is the more general contention that the default inclination in Ottawa is to interfere in provincial affairs. If a credible claim could have been mounted that the federal government was undermining Quebec's identity and obstructing the legitimate pursuit of what it sees as its distinctive socio-political model, that would have resonated widely in Quebec, but such an argument cannot seriously hold water in the present circumstances. And it is a good deal more difficult to make nationalist headway by attacking the conduct of the federal government in its *own* sphere of jurisdiction.

More difficult, certainly, but perhaps not impossible, at least in the longer term. For the Harper government has – again consistent with its open federalism approach – been aggressively pursuing its ambitions within the policy domains for which it is responsible: lowering taxes and offering steady management of the national economy, including the effort to establish a national securities regulator; tilting Canada's Middle East policy in favour of Israel; giving vigorous support to the military; following the United States in environmental policy; abolishing the long gun registry; getting tough on criminals; celebrating the Conservatives' preferred national symbols (the Queen and the War of 1812, rather than the Charter of Rights); and making the melting North a high priority.

Some of these national policy initiatives are unobjectionable, and are likely to attract support in the province, but several appear to be antithetic to majority thinking in Quebec.[18] The recent tightening of conditions for the receipt of Employment Insurance payments is causing concern as well. So far, though, critical opinion about the overall direction of federal policy does not seem to have crystallized in Quebec, but it may at some point, and it is hard to imagine that, at least in this respect, the federal Conservatives will have a good story to tell to Quebecers in the next federal election. The broadly neoliberal agenda of the Harper Conservatives holds little appeal in Quebec, where the centre of political gravity is a good deal to the left of the current orientation of the federal Conservative Party. Nevertheless, public opinion surveys on the low level of support for sovereignty or for reopening the constitutional file, the PQ's performance in the 2012 and 2014 Quebec elections, and the general difficulty the PQ government has had in advancing its sovereignty agenda – all seem to suggest that at the moment Quebecers would prefer to live in the country rather than try to dismantle it, and a good case can be made that the federal government's management of the federation, if not its political ideology, has had something to do with it.

What image of the country is implied by the present federal government's implementation of the theory of open federalism? It seems to me it bears some resemblance to a two-nations conception of Canada, without the name. The sense of shared identity is strong enough in the English-speaking provinces to prevail even if the English-speaking provinces increasingly exercise their responsibilities with reduced federal leadership and a diminished national policy context. In Quebec, the vigorous sense of a distinct Québécois identity will be sustained and may even be deepened, as the government and National Assembly fashion policies autonomously and with limited intergovernmental discussion. Each linguistic community will fashion arrangements best suited to its understanding of its distinctive needs and aspirations, though English-speaking Canada's will be mediated largely through the provinces.

The maintenance and possible deepening of Canada's binational reality will be troubling for those who believe that the fragility of the country will be increased as a result. But there may not be cause for concern on these grounds. Canada, properly speaking, is not, and never has been a nation-state. It has always contained more than one national community. What we may be returning to is a modern version of the *status quo ante*. Until the Quiet Revolution, the French and English in Canada understood themselves to be living in clearly different communities – during much of our history, defined not just by language and geography, but by religion, culture, and the character of each community's relationship to emerging industrial society. The sovereignty movement and the 1982 amendments to the Constitution, particularly the introduction of the Charter of Rights and Freedoms, forced Canadians to reflect on what they had in common and on what the grounds of Canadian citizenship were. It would be difficult to argue that any serious degree of consensus emerged. The re-emergence of greater distance between these two communities is not without historical precedent, and may actually foster more public contentment with the country's state of affairs than did the "in-your-face federalism," which in some measure prevailed between the 1960s and the 1990s.

This may be fair enough as far as it goes, but a federation, however one understands the distribution of powers or the degree of autonomy of its component units, must make provision for a set of common institutions and processes to take care of those issues that fall to the central authority. Here, as we have seen, there are grounds for concern. Quebec's demographic weight in the federation is in steady decline, and its representation in the councils of the current federal government is minimal. If national governments are regularly formed without significant political representation from Quebec, and govern in a manner that is largely antithetic to Quebec's interests or the preferences of Québécois, the sense of being an indispensable player in the ongoing practice of federal democracy is reduced, as is the feeling that the system is addressing one's interests. In these circumstances, national unity – or should we say "binational unity"? – could be threatened. System maintenance has always been an elite project in Canada, but no less worthwhile for all that; however, that process relied on organized networks and venues – including political parties, party caucuses, cabinets – where representatives of the communities could address conflicts and negotiate national policies.[19] If these are attenuated, the capacity for mutual accommodation and the timely resolution of conflict between the two national communities decreases as well.

The Question of Legitimacy

Let us, in the light of this discussion, return to the matter of legitimacy. As children of the Enlightenment, many of us have some version of the social-contract model in our heads, in which a political order is constituted by the will of the people, ostensibly at a particular historical moment – namely, at the founding of the regime, in the form of an agreement on a constitution. This is a compelling understanding of the source of legitimacy, and many democratic states have come into being in part as a result of a popular referendum, or – where political entities of some sort already exist – with the agreement of the people's representatives. This is legitimacy grounded in active consent. Once a state is up and running, constitutional amendments may be understood as a kind of alteration in the terms of the original social contract, often held to the same high standard of approval that governed the original act. It is, generally speaking, this understanding of political legitimacy that leads many people to view Quebec's refusal to accept the 1982 constitutional amendments as an indicator that there has been a breach in the legitimacy of Canada's constitutional foundations; Quebec and the Québécois did not agree to the rules – or the amendment of the rules – under which they are governed.

If there is truth in the contention that the breach is unlikely to be repaired in the foreseeable future, how is one to understand the present situation? Are the Québécois simply living under an illegitimate Constitution? Does the refusal to recognize the legitimacy of the 1982 patriation of the Constitution deprive the Canadian political system of its authority?[20] In some way, clearly it does, but I want to argue that the notion of legitimacy is a good deal more complicated than the Enlightenment model, taken on its own, suggests.[21]

The authority of a political system in reality rests on multiple threads of recognition and acceptance that lead citizens to willingly obey the agents of the state. Among them, I would identify four that can be understood to play a role in the Canadian case. First, there is what I have called social-contract legitimacy, which is the formal, consent-based, system-level recognition of authority that I have discussed above. Then there are what might be termed "quotidian" legitimacy, traditional legitimacy, and output legitimacy. Each of these, I would argue, plays a role in the support of the authority of the Canadian state, and although they tend to hang together, the absence of one does not mean the absence of all the others, nor are they experienced by the members of a political community in exactly the same way.

Quotidian legitimacy refers to the acceptance of the system of rules and regulation within which one lives – not the coercive submission to the will of a sovereign, but the recognition that the rules are generally appropriate and that obedience to them is generally rational. The patriation of the Constitution was regarded as illegitimate by many Québécois. Yet, once patriated, its authority was accepted; that is to say, its provisions, and the judicial process for inter-preting the provisions, were recognized by Quebecers to be binding on them as they are on other Canadians. Beneath the Constitution, as well, the panoply of legislation, regulations, and policies continued to be accepted by the citizens of Quebec, as they were before the patriation of the Constitution. This practical, day-to-day form of acquiescence to the civil order is similar to the form of le-gitimacy associated with the acceptance of the rationality of the rule of law in Max Weber's work (Weber 1946).[22]

Traditional legitimacy refers to the acceptance that often comes with long-established custom and practice.[23] The experience of what is familiar can grow over time into an acceptance of what is appropriate. Québécois have lived within the Canadian regime for almost 150 years, and in close association with British North Americans for generations before that. Even practices you might not in the abstract independently select for yourself can become habit-forming if engaged in long enough, at which point the natural human affection for what is familiar competes with the value you would place on the activity if you sub-jected it to rational consideration. I suspect the loyalty that even a sovereignist feels toward Canada is in part a product of this historical experience.

Finally, there is what we might call output or performance legitimacy. An entity that consistently delivers the goods is often granted a form of recognition by the recipients of these benefits that goes beyond the limited acknowledgement of the specific goods received. The European Union is thought to have derived much of its acceptance among European peoples from their perception that it brought them concrete benefits – peace and prosperity. So successful has the European association been that the EU and its predecessor organizations have made the notion of war among the peoples of Europe virtually unthinkable. What is more, until recently, the growing strength of the European economic union appeared to bring remarkable material benefits to all its members. With the recent euro crisis, the calculus of material benefits and burdens for many Europeans has shifted; you will find, for example, few Greeks applauding the virtues of the EU and the European idea, and the number of Eurosceptics across the EU has considerably increased. It is apparent that output legitimacy on its own is insufficient as the ba-sis of a political order; when the benefits turn into burdens, there need to be other rational supports for the political system. But part of the loyalty Canadians feel for their country clearly arises out of its success. Canada has provided to Québécois and other Canadians material bounty, political freedom, and a high degree of se-curity. The enjoyment of these gifts over generations secures popular recognition, and is a buttress to the other forms of political legitimacy on which the state relies.

This brief discussion of the complex webs of sentiment and recognition that contribute to the landscape of political legitimacy places the breach of 1982 in a different light. Legitimacy does not involve one narrow answer to one narrow question – namely, was the Constitution patriated without the consent of the people of Quebec? – but a broadly grounded assessment of both the benefits and the values associated with membership in the Canadian civil order. For most Canadians, that assessment is highly favourable. For Quebecers, the assessment is more mixed, but I suspect it is favourable nonetheless. The breach is real, and unresolved; the social contract was fractured by the experience of 1982. Yet when one brings the other forms of legitimacy into the equation – quotidian, traditional, and output legitimacy – it seems clear that on balance most Quebecers find membership in the Canadian federation, broadly speaking, a just and beneficial experience, worthy of their recognition and acceptance. That this is so can perhaps be seen in the gradual subsidence of sovereignty sentiment and the continued affection so many Québécois express for Canada. That this is so can perhaps be seen as well in the hundreds of Québécois soldiers who have fought in Afghanistan and served their country elsewhere in the world.

NOTES

1   A recent book alleged that Chief Justice Bora Laskin improperly kept Canadian and British officials informed about the progress of the patriation discussion within the Supreme Court (Bastien 2013). The Supreme Court undertook an internal investigation and found no evidence of impropriety.
2   An alternative view would contend that on two occasions since 1982, Quebecers made mega-constitutional choices through referendums. The first time, they rejected the Charlottetown Accord, and in 1995 they rejected the sovereignist option, albeit by the thinnest of margins. While this is true, very few francophone Québécois would accept that these acts of constitutional choice-making have displaced or dissolved the breach of 1982.
3   The resolution has a very low public profile. For a time the PQ sought to use the resolution as a stick to beat the federal government with, arguing that there must be policy consequences to such a declaration. This drew fleeting attention to the resolution, although not in a way that increased its legitimacy value.
4   Interestingly, it was former PQ premier Pauline Marois who presided over the constitutional establishment of linguistically based schools when she was Quebec's minister of education.
5   "Sondage Léger Marketing – Constitution: vive le statu quo!" Le Devoir, 20 March 2013. It is ironic that the controversy in the winter of 2013 about whether to amend the Clarity Act's provisions regarding a future sovereignty referendum took place chiefly in the House of Commons among the federal opposition parties, with little resonance in Quebec (Hébert 2013a).
6   The results were: PQ 54 seats and 32 per cent of the popular vote; Liberals, 50 seats and 31 per cent of the popular vote; CAQ, 19 seats and 27 per cent of the popular vote. In the previous election, the PQ won 35 per cent of the popular vote.

7 The results were as follows: PQ 30 seats and 25 per cent of the popular vote; Liberals, 70 seats and 41.5 per cent of the popular vote; CAQ, 22 seats and 23 per cent of the popular vote.

8 While this view became important in Quebec in the twentieth century, it did not originate there. It is Oliver Mowat, premier of Ontario from 1872 to 1896, who was the first champion of provincial rights. Indeed, the provincial rights movement in Ontario might also be understood in part as a claim relating to autonomy in a binational community – in this case, autonomy vis-à-vis Catholic, French-speaking Quebec.

9 Royal Commission of Inquiry on Constitutional Problems, established in 1953 and chaired by Justice Thomas Tremblay.

10 As a founding member of the Reform Party, Stephen Harper believes not only in provincial autonomy, but in the vigorous participation of Canada's regions in the affairs of the national government. His longstanding desire to reform the Senate is evidence of this.

11 I rely on Harmes's excellent article for the substance of the next three paragraphs.

12 Interview with L. Ian Macdonald in *Policy Options*, March 2006.

13 Address to the Board of Trade of Metropolitan Montreal, http://www.conservative.ca/.

14 Harmes explicates clearly how this federal theory aligns with Stephen Harper's neoliberal economic philosophy.

15 Canada Health Transfer, Canada Social Transfer Equalization, and Territorial Formula Financing.

16 The 2011 announcement was made in anticipation of the expiration of the current arrangements in 2013–14.

17 At the July 2012 meeting of the Council of the Federation, the premiers called for "meaningful consultation" and "formal discussions" between Ottawa, the provinces and the territories "before modifications are made to any of the major federal transfer programs, as these constitute the pillars of Canadian fiscal federalism" (Council of the Federation 2012). The sensitivity of the process of renegotiating the federal transfers is shown by the fact that the Quebec government pulled out of a Council of the Federation working group on health-care innovation on the grounds that the other provinces and the territories were steering toward co-management and the acceptance of federal intrusion into provincial jurisdiction (Seguin 2013).

18 Particularly troublesome would be the emergence of a pattern of neglect with respect to the representativeness of the country's common institutions, extending for example, to the error in appointing a unilingual auditor general (Taber 2011).

19 David Cameron and Richard Simeon (2009) found that civil society's leaders had a special role in managing the French-English reality in the voluntary sector.

20 Pierre Trudeau had achieved a decisive victory in the 1980 federal election, with the Liberal Party winning 74 of the 75 seats in the province. Seventy-one of the 75 members of Parliament elected from Quebec supported patriation. It is also

true that the proposed amendments had clearly attracted sufficient provincial support to meet the criterion set out by the Supreme Court in its reference opinion; the support of nine provinces out of ten more than addressed the Court's view that "a substantial degree" of provincial consent was needed to take a legitimate proposal to London. One can make a vigorous case, and Prime Minister Trudeau did exactly that, that there is no spot or blemish on the patriation process. For reasons outlined in the chapter, this does not seem to me to be persuasive.

21 *The Stanford Encyclopedia of Philosophy* contains a thorough discussion of the rich array of meanings associated with the notion of political legitimacy under the heading by that name. http://plato.stanford.edu/entries/legitimacy/.

22 See also Weber's ([1947] 1964) *Theory of Social and Economic Organization*. In "Politics as a Vocation" Weber (n.d.) speaks of one form of legitimacy as "domination by virtue of 'legality,' by virtue of the belief in the validity of legal statute and functional 'competence' based on rationally created *rules*" (2).

23 Weber's (n.d.) second type of legitimacy is traditional: "the authority of the 'eternal yesterday,' i.e., of the mores sanctified through the unimaginably ancient recognition and habitual orientation to conform" (2). Weber's third type, charismatic, we do not discuss here.

DAVID R. CAMERON

Conclusion

What Was Present Becomes Past

Rob Vipond, with great kindness and generosity, has put together this collection of my writings on nationalism, federalism, and the Constitution. It has afforded me an opportunity I otherwise would probably have missed, namely, to reflect on 40 or so years of my career, and – in parallel and more importantly – to review four critical decades in the life of our country. I was an undergraduate student at the University of British Columbia in the early 1960s when the Quiet Revolution commenced in Quebec. My first direct encounter with what would become the greatest existential crisis post-war Canada has faced was as a junior researcher in Ottawa with the Royal Commission on Bilingualism and Biculturalism in the summer of 1964. That would begin a personal and professional engagement with Canada's national unity issue, reflected in the pages of this volume, that lasted until the latter part of the 1990s when the country was finally able to move beyond this preoccupation.

Someone entering university at 18 years old today would have been born well after the national-unity crisis had passed. I appreciate that what was for me a defining period and focus of my career is for them little more than an historical memory. For them, the country's national-unity crisis must parallel in some ways my experience of the Depression of the 1930s; I was born in 1941, after the Depression was over. Although I had no direct encounter with the Depression, I experienced an echo effect from that searing economic collapse, given that my Mother had suffered through it. Born into a large Manitoba farm family in 1903, she was in her late twenties when the Depression began, and was marked for life by her encounter with radical economic pain and uncertainty. I scraped every last bit of butter off the butter wrapper until I was in my twenties, solely because I saw my Depression-formed Mother doing it all the time when I was a kid.

As I write this, the sovereignist war horses of the era are dead or in their 80s and 90s: René Lévesque, Camille Laurin, Jacques Parizeau, Bernard Landry – all dead; Claude Morin, 90 years old, Lucien Bouchard, 81. Robert Bourassa, the uneasy federalist who twice served as premier of Quebec (1970–76 and 1985–94), passed away in 1996. On the federal side in Ottawa, Pierre Trudeau is gone. Indeed, none of the so-called Three Wise Men whom Lester Pearson brought into his cabinet from Quebec in the sixties – Trudeau, Jean Marchand, and Gérard Pelletier – is still alive. Jean Chrétien, who began as a junior minister in Pearson's government, and played a key role in both the 1980 and the 1995 referendums and the patriation process in between, is 86. Key provincial premiers of the era, Allan Blakeney of Saskatchewan and Peter Lougheed of Alberta, died in 2011 and 2012. Clyde Wells, the scourge of the Meech Lake Accord as premier of Newfoundland and Labrador, is now 82 years old. It's all getting to be a long time ago.

That this difficult period of our history is fading into the past is something to be thankful for. What is more, that it is fading offers a chance for the beginnings of historical perspective and the opportunity to start to think about, not just what happened, but what it meant and what we might learn from it.

The accommodation of more than one national community within the bounds of a single state is a challenge that many countries face in the modern era. In that sense, Canada's situation is far from unique. Looking only at Europe, Switzerland, Belgium, the former Czechoslovakia, the former Yugoslavia, Spain and the United Kingdom all have a place in this global story. Outside of Europe, similar challenges abound. Taking just two examples, India is a subcontinent of nationalities as much as it is a country, and China's limited tolerance for ethno-cultural diversity within its borders is on painful display in its treatment of the Uighur minority. International experience demonstrates that societies find the accommodation of these forces of diversity very difficult. Indeed, it is one of the enduring challenges of modern times.

Canada is no stranger to the impact of these forces, but how the country and its citizens and political leaders have managed these acute stresses is very much a Canadian story, with distinctive failures and achievements. Part of the Canadian story is tragedy. Without question, the darkest stain in our history has been our treatment of the country's Indigenous people. It has been a black and dirty business by any measure, and the fact that other settler societies have done the equivalent in no way lets Canada off the hook. Given this history, our contemporary efforts to redress the situation are without doubt laudable, although they have come too late and have been woefully slow to bear fruit. Undoing the damage of the ages, we are finding, is not easy or quick. Unhappily, but appropriately, Canada is known internationally for its lamentable treatment of Indigenous people.

However, at the same time, Canada is positively recognized internationally for certain capabilities and qualities in short supply elsewhere. Since the deracialization of our immigration laws in the 1960s, the country has welcomed a continuous stream of immigrants and refugees from the four corners of the globe. The result is what you see around you, especially in our larger cities: quite remarkable levels of ethno-cultural diversity with what in international terms are high rates of public acceptance. The world has noticed – witness the pieces on this subject in newspapers such as *The Economist*.[1] Almost a fifth of the country's population is foreign born, a substantially higher share than in the United States, and yet its social mobility is higher. More than half of the population of Toronto has been born outside the country. Yet support for immigration remains high.

Our Charter of Rights and Freedoms, and the jurisprudence that has interpreted it since 1982, are widely admired and referred to as a source of guidance in many other countries.[2] We are a constitutional people with a high regard for the rule of law, whatever place on the ideological or nationalist spectrum you inhabit. This has been of central importance in making our remarkably successful, highly decentralized system of federalism function effectively.

What is more – and more central to our purpose here – Canada has successfully navigated one of the most powerful secession movements any modern democratic state has had to encounter, and it is to this matter that I would like now to turn.

Starting Positions

When a popular secession movement arises in a democratic state, I believe that there are two interrelated choices, more important than almost any of the others that follow, that are made, typically right at the outset of the process. One is made by the secessionist forces; the other, by the forces supporting union. The steps that are taken at this point will typically set out the broad path the country will follow for the rest of its journey. Once committed, it is highly difficult to reverse or alter course. For the secessionist movement, the choice relates to the following question: Will we pursue our goal by constitutional, democratic means, or will we step outside the constitutional order and employ extraconstitutional, potentially violent means to achieve our goal of secession? For those opposing secession, the question is: Do we rule secession out as an unlawful and unconstitutional act, treating the secessionists in consequence as law breakers? Or do we acknowledge the inherently political character of the issue and address the challenges politically?

I would argue that the opening moves in the national-unity struggle are of crucial importance in shaping everything that follows. In Canada, that was certainly the case. In the 1960s, there were admittedly small, separatist groups that avowed or condoned violence; indeed, the Front de Libération du Québec (FLQ) engaged in a series of significant acts of violence during that decade, which came to an end with the October Crisis in 1970.[3] Although the *felquistes* (FLQ members) occasionally articulated the aspirations of many Quebecers, if not the methods Quebecers would condone, they were never able to move beyond their status as a tiny dissident group in the province. As soon as separatism went mainstream with the Parti Québécois, any appeal to violence was categorically ruled out. René Lévesque, the founding leader of the PQ, was unequivocal on that point and never wavered; he was instrumental in defining the sovereignty project in Quebec as non-violent and political. Sovereignty would be achieved democratically and peacefully, or not at all. This was a principled position of first-order significance and a contribution to the public life of Quebec and Canada for which the founder of the PQ gets less credit than he deserves.

If mainline sovereignists in Quebec pursued independence by non-violent, political means, the federalists, under the leadership of Pierre Trudeau, reciprocated: they never asserted that those who were peacefully advocating sovereignty were traitors to their country, subject to police action and legal prosecution. The federalists treated secession as a political matter as well, implicitly accepting the proposition that a referendum could play a critical role in determining popular preferences on such a key issue as the separation of Quebec.

When you look at the highly different approach adopted by the Spanish state, faced with Catalan separatism, you can see what a fateful decision this is, and just how much it defines everything that follows. Consistent with Article 2 of the Constitution of Spain, which forbids secession, the government of Spain tried to block and disrupt the 2017 effort of Catalonia to hold a referendum on independence, sending thousands of police to the region. It suspended the regional government, replacing it with direct Spanish rule. It prosecuted a dozen leaders of the movement, and sought to extradite Carles Puigdemont, a Catalan leader who fled the country rather than remain and face prosecution and jail time. Systematic suppression of a broad, popular desire to secede runs the risk of channeling the opposition forces into non-constitutional pathways. On the other hand, seeking to address the matter politically opens the country to the possibility of geographical fragmentation, an issue I will discuss further below.

Employing a very different approach from that of Spain, the United Kingdom government worked with the government of Scotland to set the rules of the first referendum on Scottish independence, held in 2014. The 55 per cent vote to stay within the UK was thought at the time to settle the matter for a generation, but the subsequent 2016 UK referendum on Brexit and the decision of the UK Parliament to take the United Kingdom out of the European Union, have brought the matter of Scottish independence to the fore again, given that a strong majority (62 per cent) of Scots voted against leaving the EU. The current position of the British Government under the premiership of Boris Johnson, however, is that there shall be no second Scottish referendum, despite the declared intention of the Scottish first minister, Nicola Sturgeon, to hold one and despite the formal request the Scottish government has submitted to the UK government. If Scots demonstrate a strong and consistent desire to hold another referendum on independence ("indyref2," in popular parlance) – for example, by supporting the SNP in the next election, expected in 2021 – it will be very difficult to hold the line. The UK government in that situation would face a fateful choice, determining whether or not to stick to its policy and in effect follow the path of the Spanish government. It is hard to see how that would turn out well, but to do otherwise would be to genuinely contemplate the break-up of Britain in the wake of a Yes vote for independence in Scotland.

A Contingent Country

None of the major players in the Canadian struggle over Quebec sovereignty ever took the position that the secession of Quebec from the rest of Canada was categorically impossible. Those fighting for and against the secession of Quebec in both the 1980 and the 1995 referendums made it clear in their actions and rhetoric that they believed Quebecers were making a real decision with real consequences. Towards the end of the process, the Supreme Court in the 1998 Secession Reference case made it plain that, while Quebec did not enjoy a right of self-determination under either domestic or international law, it was still clearly possible for Quebec to secede, and to secede within the terms of the Constitution of Canada. The Court's focus was on the process, on how that question could be determined, paying due respect to the constitutional principles underlying the federal association and the interests and requirements of all the parties. The federal legislation that followed on the release of the Court's opinion, the Clarity Act, similarly concentrated on the how, not on the why or whether.

Lying behind that position was an understanding of the country that became clearer and clearer over the decades of struggle. Canadians gradually came to appreciate that their country was not sacred and eternal; as I said in chapter 18, we have no equivalent to Section 2 of the Spanish constitutional provision – "The Constitution is based on the indissoluble unity of the Spanish nation, the common and indivisible country of all Spaniards." Or of France's *une république indivisible*. Or Italy's *la Repubblica, una e indivisibile*. Or indeed of Australia's "one indissoluble Federal Commonwealth under the Crown of the United Kingdom of Great Britain and Ireland." Our implicit working assumption has been that Canada is indeed in principle divisible, and that its continued unity rests finally on a shared commitment of its citizens to keep it together. Its continued existence is contingent on the will of its population, on *un plébiscite de tous les jours*, a daily plebiscite.

The Purpose of the State

And I would argue that lying behind *that* position is a view that internationally is less acknowledged and even less discussed. In a world of aggressive nationalism and a pronounced bias in international law and relations in favour of protecting the sovereignty of those states which exist, there is a simple, but radical counter-proposition – namely, that states are meant to serve the citizens, not citizens the state, and that therefore states cannot ultimately escape accountability, any more than can any other political institution. Here it is worth quoting at length the words of the American Declaration of Independence:

> We hold these truths to be self-evident, that all men are created equal, that they are endowed by their Creator with certain unalienable Rights, that among these are Life, Liberty and the pursuit of Happiness. That to secure these rights, Governments are instituted among Men, deriving their just powers from the consent of the governed. That whenever any Form of Government becomes destructive to these ends, it is the Right of the People to alter or to abolish it, and to institute new Government, laying its foundation on such principles and organizing its powers in such form, as to them shall seem most likely to effect their Safety and Happiness. Prudence, indeed, will dictate that Governments long established should not be changed for light and transient causes; and accordingly all experience hath shewn that mankind are more disposed to suffer, while evils are sufferable, than to right themselves by abolishing the forms to which they are accustomed. But when a long train of abuses and usurpations, pursuing invariably the same Object evinces a design to reduce them under absolute Despotism, it is their right, it is their duty, to throw off such Government, and to provide new Guards for their future security.

This is classic John Locke. The argument justified the break of the Thirteen Colonies from Britain; its logic was *not* accepted to accommodate the South's desire to secede from the United States republic. However, its logic ultimately lay behind the manner in which Canadians grappled with the question of the secession of Quebec. That the sovereignty of Quebec was not achieved – despite the backing of a large and popular political party which for many years controlled the government of a powerful province in a highly decentralized federation – is possibly owing to what is referred to in the latter part of the quotation cited above. Canada was not in fact engaged in a long train of abuses and usurpations designed to bring Quebecers under absolute despotism. No one, not even a hard-core separatist, could argue this. That being so, the dictate of prudence prevailed: "Governments long established should not be changed for light and transient causes." Given that the benefits of Canadian association were considerable, and such evils as there were, were eminently sufferable, Quebecers were reluctant to abolish the forms to which they were accustomed. Not to mention that other Canadians and the Canadian government itself had shown themselves capable of listening to the grievances and concerns of Quebec, and willing to change, if not in all matters, at least in many.

There is at least one way in which the situation of the American colonists and the plight of Canadians differs. The Declaration speaks of "the people" having the right to alter or abolish a despotic regime. The Colonists, physically separated from their government by the Atlantic Ocean, experiencing a common sense of political oppression, all holding the same status as members of a British colony, most sharing British origin and culture, found it fairly easy to speak of themselves as a single people (so long as they excluded slaves). It was only afterwards, once the United States was up and running, that the gulf in identity and the absence of key shared values, especially between the North and South, made their presence felt.

Sovereignty and "the People"

But in the Canadian context, who are "the people?" Earlier in this volume Rob Vipond and I began a discussion of this matter, and I would like to pick up on that conversation and extend it here.

Canada, like other federations, had a founding moment. It did not simply emerge imperceptibly from the past as a long-existing historical reality. It was willed into existence by the founders in 1867. Sir John A. Macdonald is well known for having wanted to create a unitary state, but that was not in the cards for two reasons. There were pre-existing colonial societies with local institutions and governance structures that enjoyed the loyalty of the given population. They were not prepared to give up these familiar realities for a new and untried political structure. Then there was Quebec, which was the *foyer* of a national community, distinct in language, religion and culture, and origin. All had been British colonies and all had had the experience of living under the umbrella of the British empire. At the time of Confederation, there was no question of setting up the new regime in the name of a Lockean "Canadian people" who understood themselves to be in some sense a coherent community. Rather, it was a gathering together of distinct British North American peoples and institutions into a new political association designed to bring benefits to each associated member. All would be better off together than apart; they would not cease to be themselves in doing so.

I think Rob Vipond is right in claiming that Canadians found themselves during the Charlottetown negotiations in the early 1990s trying to work backwards from shared civic values to a national identity sufficient to support a Lockean theory of the people as the constituent authority. And the emphasis Rob placed on the seriousness and importance of the Canada Clause casts it, appropriately, in my opinion, in a new light. It also helps us to see what a fruitless quest this was. Deeply federal societies are not to be found in John Locke territory. They support a form of political association that is meant not to have to rely on an assumption of singular, popular constituent authority. In a deeply diverse federal country, it is the very association, the agreement itself, that lies at the foundation of the state. The state is meant to draw together in a new, mutually beneficial association diverse communities or "peoples." It is then sustained, not by national identity, but by delivering the benefits for which the association was created. Over time, and with accumulating historical experience, an overlay of national identification and loyalty can be expected to emerge, as it has in Canada, but at its origin a federation is more like what Allan Blakeney, the former premier of Saskatchewan, called it, a giant mutual insurance company.

Hobbes posited a state of nature as the condition in which atomized individuals lived lives of radical insecurity – solitary, poor, nasty, brutish and short. The social contract to which each such individual notionally agreed took them out of that condition by subjecting them all to a sovereign. Locke's argument blurred the breathtaking clarity of Hobbes's account by contending that the state of nature was a kind of civil society; individuals in this much less precarious condition agreed to form a state to improve their individual positions and to better enjoy the fruits of collective action. If the state turned against them, they retained the right of rebellion and the capacity to return to a "government-less" state of nature or to rear up an alternative political authority in its place. Although different, the social contracts of Hobbes and Locke were both conceptual theories designed to uncover the legitimate foundations of the state, based on individualistic assumptions.

In the case of federations, there is a literal social contract – namely, the constitutional agreement that establishes the federation. The difference from traditional social contract theory, though, is that the associated members are communities, not individuals. Locke's political theory focuses primarily on the legitimate authority that can be fashioned by individuals living in a stateless civil society. Federal theory posits multiple civil/political societies joining together in a new pluralist association. It is rather as if there are multiple civil societies of the sort Locke posits as the foundation of states; they come together in a larger political association of civil societies, from which the members of each of the participating civil orders are deemed to benefit. In such an arrangement, there can be no single Lockean constituent authority; the foundations of that meta-association must be different from the Lockean version.

This is my effort to explain why the attempt to fashion a Canada Clause, to the extent that it was meant to depict the identity of the sovereign people underlying the Canadian state, was destined to fail. It misunderstood the nature of the people and communities composing the country, and it misunderstood the nature of the political association upon which Canada was founded.

But does the absence of a shared identity mean that there is no foundation of popular legitimacy on which to found a state such as Canada? Peter Russell puts the question straight in *Constitutional Odyssey*, which is organized around the question: "Can Canadians Become a Sovereign People?" He writes: "If a constitution derives its legitimacy from the consent of the people, then those who share a constitution must first agree to be a people."[4]

At this point we need to introduce a distinction between identity and action. A sovereign people could be defined by certain characteristics they share – by their identity (per the Canada Clause). Or they could potentially be understood in function of their capacity for collective action. It is not clear to me which Peter Russell has in mind when he speaks of the people in constitutional government. He writes that the Charlottetown experience may have taught Canadians

> something useful about their capacity to act as a constitutional sovereign people. As constitutional sovereign the Canadian people could say "no" to all manner of constitutional proposals, but they could not say "yes" to anything that touched those matters of national identity and constitutional vision on which they were so profoundly divided. Canadians were now a sovereign people in only a negative sense. They could and would insist on direct approval of constitutional proposals that changed the fundamentals of their constitution. But they can use their constitutional power only to reject, not to approve, changes in anything fundamental.[5]

Here I think we have ideas of both identity and action in play. First of all, with respect to identity, Canadians have not been able to agree on "those matters of national identity and constitutional vision on which they were so profoundly divided." They have been unable to agree on a shared sense of themselves as a people, on their identity. However, with respect to the notion of a constituent people displayed through collective action, Russell says Canadians are now in fact a sovereign people, but only in a negative sense, only in their capacity to reject proposed changes in their basic constitutional arrangements.

What about their capacity to say yes? Russell claims correctly that so far Canadians have proven themselves unable to positively agree on anything which touches on something as fundamental as identity or vision. What this leaves out, I think, is the possibility that Canadians might agree, not on a shared vision or identity, but on the terms of their association under the constitution. A constitution, after all, is not only about vision and identity. Indeed, I would argue it doesn't even have to be centrally about these matters. It can concern itself primarily with matters of power and institutions and jurisdictions. It needs to establish the state and its status both internally and externally; it needs to address the question of political power – who has it, how it is distributed and controlled; it needs to provide for the rule of law and the protection of the liberty of its citizens; it needs to indicate the place of civil society and the private sphere and the relationship between these and the state; and it needs to create or recognize the key public institutions of the political community. Does it need to define or conceptualize the sovereign people? Or imply it? The British North America Act, now the Constitution Act, 1867, is a pretty prosaic document laying out most of the matters listed above, but saying the minimum necessary about the people whom Confederation is expected to benefit. It served the country well for over a century. When it did speak about aspects of the political community, it was not primarily to identify what members held in common, but to cope with the lines of differentiation that kept them apart – language, religion, geography, historical experience.

The 1982 Constitution, at least in this respect, carried on that tradition. There is no preamble to the Constitution Act, 1982; it begins directly with Part I, the Canadian Charter of Rights and Freedoms. Part I itself, however, has an extraordinarily brief preamble, not even titled as such; it refers to the principles upon which Canada is founded: "the supremacy of God and the rule of law." No reference to the citizens or the people who compose the country. And when sociological characteristics of the Canadian population figure in the Constitution Act, 1982, it is to single out portions of the Canadian people for specific recognition, not to speak of what Canadians hold in common. There is detailed provision for Canada's two official languages (Articles 16–23), recognition of the Aboriginal and treaty rights of the Aboriginal peoples of Canada (Articles 25 and 35), and an interpretive provision relating to "the preservation and enhancement of the multicultural heritage of Canadians" (Article 27). Significantly, from this perspective, the 1982 Constitution was agreed to by the prime minister and the premiers (except for the premier of Quebec) and approved by Parliament and the provincial legislatures (except Quebec's), albeit after substantial televised public consultation by the Special Joint Committee on the Constitution, 1980–81.[6] But the Canadian people played no formal constitutive role.

So Peter Russell is correct in saying that Canadians so far have expressed themselves as constitutional actors only in the negative sense of rejecting proposals that have been put before them. But the fact that they haven't said yes yet does not mean that they may not say yes at some point in the future. The Swiss experience suggests that this is perfectly possible.

The Swiss Federal Constitution also focuses on the terms by which the units composing the Swiss federation have come together, not on the identity or cultural unity of the Swiss people. Although it does posit the existence of the Swiss people, it does not seek to describe their identity. The preamble begins: "The Swiss People and the Cantons ... adopt the following Constitution."[7] Note that it is the cantons, the regional units, as well as the people of Switzerland, that are the constitutional actors in establishing the constitution. The cantons are the Swiss equivalent of the Canadian provinces, but it is worth noting that "the

People" – the other constitutional actor in the Swiss Confederation – is missing in the Canadian case, and is replaced by the federal Parliament.

The preamble of the Swiss Constitution speaks of a determination "to live our diversity in unity respecting one another," and Article 2 sets as one of the purposes of the Swiss Confederation the promotion of "the inner cohesion, and the cultural diversity of the country." Similar to Canada's Constitution, when the Swiss Federal Constitution discusses matters of culture and identity, it is as likely to address the significant identity diversity of the country and how it is to be handled as it is to express an underlying Swiss cultural unity. Article 4 recognizes four national languages: German, French, Italian, and Romansh. The field of culture is a cantonal matter (Article 69). Cantons designate their own official languages, respecting "the traditional territorial distribution of languages," and taking into account "the indigenous linguistic minorities" (Article 70). Regulating "the relationship between church and state is the responsibility of the Cantons" (Article 72).

It is worth highlighting at least one area of constitutional culture in which the Swiss differ decisively from Canadians (and from the inhabitants of most other countries, for that matter). They have proven themselves capable of deploying referendums, with positive and negative voting outcomes, as instruments of collective decision-making, both at the federal and at the cantonal level. One can clearly identify the Swiss people as a constitutional actor in their capacity to engage in collective action through referendums. The 1999 Federal Constitution was brought into being by two processes: a national referendum with a positive vote of 59 per cent; and the approval of 14 of the 26 cantons. I would argue, then, that the Swiss are a sovereign people, not only in their capacity for collective action, but also in their agreement on the terms by which they will live under the Constitution, if not in their commitment to cultural or social or linguistic unity. Perhaps the failure of the Canada Clause lies in its effort to specify the last factor, rather than focussing on the first two.

There is another dimension here worth mentioning. The notion of the sovereign people as constitutional actor most obviously suggests a capacity for collective action, typically via referendums, as in the Swiss case. This appears to be what Peter Russell has primarily in mind. It would seem that decision-making on the basis of majority votes is recognized as legitimate by the Swiss, even if votes relate to vital and sensitive matters, such as the approval of the Swiss Constitution. But note that it is a double majority – of the population and of the constituent federal units; it was ratified, as we saw, with a majority in favour on the part of both the population and the cantons. This process appears to work in Switzerland.

Yet the political culture of a country may make referendums as a decision-making device problematic. Arguably, that is the case in Canada. It is one thing to hold a referendum on secession within Quebec, the homeland of one of Canada's national communities (although the divisions within the Quebec population made for bitter conflict within the society); it is quite another to seek to hold a referendum on a critical matter within Canada. Consider the World War II referendum proposing to release the prime minister from his pledge not to impose military conscription for overseas military service; it, as we saw, succeeded in dividing the country along English-French lines. Then there is the Charlottetown vote. In one sense this was not even a national referendum. Though there was a single question, the federal government oversaw the vote in nine provinces and the territories, while the Quebec government oversaw the vote in Quebec, and almost as much attention was paid to the results in Quebec vis-à-vis the rest of Canada as was paid to the overall national outcome. One is tempted to say that we Canadians are not good at using the referendum instrument, but I think a deeper and truer assessment would recognize that, especially on sensitive constitutional matters, it is difficult to think of Canadians as a single, undifferentiated people and treat a national majority outcome for or against as authoritative. Was Mackenzie King released from his pledge not to introduce conscription for overseas military service in the Second World War? Yes, if you count the total votes for and against, which delivered a strong positive majority of 66 per cent. But no, if you acknowledge that the initial pledge was chiefly directed at reassuring the French Canadians as Canada went to war, and they voted massively (72 per cent)) against the proposition in the referendum. This is the sign of a deeply diverse federal people. With a population of this kind, referendums are as likely to uncover and deepen social cleavages as they are to do anything positive. Does that mean that Canadians can never become a sovereign people? Yes, perhaps, if the successful use of the referendum is the only basis on which to ground a claim of popular sovereignty. But that surely cannot be the end of the matter.

There is perhaps something worth examining about the way the problem is being framed. It would be almost universally recognized that Canada is a legitimate democratic state; legitimacy in a democracy is grounded in popular consent. If Canadians have not endowed their political system with legitimacy through a formal collective act, such as a referendum, then how have they done so? I would argue, and have argued elsewhere,[8] that there are a number of streams of popular legitimacy that support the Canadian state, and that, in fact, undergird most legitimate political orders.

I will mention four: social contract; "quotidian"; traditional; and performance legitimacy. What I am calling social-contract legitimacy I have already discussed above, reflected in the contention that Canadians can become a sovereign people through an act of collective will, usually expressed in a popular referendum. This source of legitimacy Canada lacks. The second source of legitimacy – quotidian – is the day-to-day acceptance of the propriety of the rules by which you and your fellow citizens live, and the consequent rationality of abiding by them. This entails a form of recognition, not of the coercive side of the law and the civil order, but of the rational or reasonable character of that law and that order. The third source of legitimacy is traditional, and speaks to the acknowledgment people often make to the legacy of the past, to the practices, norms, and customs that have come down to them from previous generations. Edmund Burke speaks eloquently of the allegiance many people feel towards the long-established and the familiar. The fourth source of legitimacy is performance based. If a political regime consistently serves the interests of citizens, if it delivers peace and stability, assistance in times of need, economic opportunity, freedom to fashion one's life as one wishes, the protections of the law, it will attract support and recognition.

A state would be a fragile thing if it rested on only one source of legitimacy rather than on a confluence of multiple streams of allegiance and recognition, and it would be a mistake to privilege one at the expense of all the others. That is what is risked by placing too much emphasis on a single collective act to determine the presence or absence of a sovereign democratic people, if by sovereign democratic people we mean the organized political community that legitimizes a constitutional polity. We have seen in many other countries the consequences of doing so, often in moments of constitutional transition. Frequently, in countries seeking to move beyond acute civil conflict, a popular referendum will be held to approve a new constitution. However, the new regime is faced with trying to survive without the supports of any of the other streams of legitimacy: the laws and rules are perceived to be unfair and skewed in their application; the historical experience of citizens is one of discrimination, exploitation and conflict; and the goods of government are inadequate or selectively distributed, and do not serve the interests of the broad population. One might argue that a government, democratically installed by referendum, but lacking in the other sources of recognition and support, has at best a modest chance of success, whereas a government, endowed with the popular allegiance derived from quotidian, traditional and performance legitimacy may get along quite well without the approval of a popular referendum. I would argue that the latter condition describes Canada's status not too badly, and that Canadians are as sovereign a people as one is likely to find in the contemporary democratic universe.

There is an important distinction to draw between the social-contract model of legitimacy and all the others I have mentioned. The former, certainly to the extent that it relies on the referendum instrument to express it, suggests a specific act at a specific moment in time, undertaken once, and over and done with. The other three which I have briefly discussed – quotidian, traditional and performance legitimacy – are nurtured by a thousand daily acts of commission or restraint. They are streams fed by the culture, attitude and conduct of millions of citizens, day in and day out. They both renew themselves and evolve imperceptibly, shaped by the myriad choices citizens make in their everyday lives. And as Canadians move through time, adapting as they must to changing pressures and circumstances, so too do their governments, seeking to preserve and renew the lines of trust and obligation which tether them to the citizens they serve.

Canada is in many ways a fractured and incomplete country. It contains instances of flagrant injustice. There have been good reasons over the years for people and communities to contemplate withdrawing their consent from Canada in the hope of finding something better suited to their needs and better aligned with the requirements of justice. Indigenous peoples in Canada have suffered under a systematically unjust regime – "a long train of abuses and usurpations," evincing "a design to reduce them under absolute despotism," in the words of the Declaration of Independence. However, the country has proven itself – often obstinately and reluctantly – capable of listening and capable of change. It is that greenness, that absence of ossification, that willingness of the country finally to listen to the calls of justice that have so far sustained the winning conditions for the plebiscite that constitutes the ever-renewing daily life of Canada.

NOTES

1 "Canada's Immigration Policy: No Country for Old Men," *The Economist*, 10 January 2015. "Canada: The Last Liberals," *The Economist*, 29 October 2016. "Migrating Nerds: Indian Technology Talent Is Flocking to Canada," *The Economist*, 22 December 2018.

2 David S. Law and Mila Versteeg, "The Evolution and Ideology of Global Constitutionalism," *California Law Review*, 99, no. 5 (October 2011): 1163–1257.

3 The propriety of the Trudeau Government's declaration of the War Measures Act in response has been the subject of spirited debate in the years since.

4 Peter Russell, *Constitutional Odyssey: Can Canadians Become a Sovereign People?* 3rd ed. (Toronto: University of Toronto Press, 2004), 6.

5 Ibid., 228.

6 Peter W. Hogg and Annika Wang, "The Special Joint Committee on the Constitution of Canada, 1980–81." *The Supreme Court Law Review: Osgoode's Annual Constitutional Cases Conference* 81. (2017). https://digitalcommons.osgoode.yorku.ca/sclr/vol81/iss1/2

7 *The Federal Constitution of the Swiss Confederation*, April 18, 1999. https://www.fedlex.admin.ch/eli/cc/1999/404/en

8 David Cameron, "Canada's Constitutional Legitimacy Deficit: Learning to Live with It," in *Thinking Outside the Box: Innovation in Policy Ideas*, eds. Keith Banting et al. (Montreal and Kingston: McGill-Queens University Press), 277–294.

Copyrights and Permissions

Index